WHAT IS TRUTH?

A Comparative Study of the Positions of
CORNELIUS VAN TIL
FRANCIS SCHAEFFER
CARL F. H. HENRY
DONALD BLOESCH
MILLARD ERICKSON

James Emery White

BROADMAN
& HOLMAN
PUBLISHERS

Nashville, Tennessee

White, James Emery, 1961–
    What is truth? ; a comparative study of the positions of Cornelius
Van Til, Francis Schaeffer, Carl F. H. Henry, Donald Bloesch, Millard
Erickson / James Emery White.
        p.   cm.
    Includes bibliographical references.
    ISBN 0-8054-1156-9
    1. Truth (Christian theology)—History of doctrines—20th century.
2. Evangelicalism—United States—History—20th century. I. Title.

BT50.W355 1994   92-388299
201—dc20   CIP

CONTENTS

━━━━━◆━━━━━

FOREWORD

By Colin Brown

"If Christ has not been raised," wrote the apostle Paul to the church at Corinth, "your faith is futile" (1 Cor. 15:17, NIV). In his letter to the infant church in Rome, Paul declared that what may be known about God is plain to all humankind, and therefore all are held responsible before God. "For since the creation of the world God's invisible qualities—his eternal power and divine nature—have been clearly seen, being understood from what has been made, so that men are without excuse" (Rom. 1:20). These two statements are examples of biblical truth-claims. Such claims are fundamental to historic, biblical Christianity. But what is truth? How do we know it? How do we establish truth-claims? How do we think of evidence, presuppositions, and world views? What part should philosophical discussion play in the presentation of the gospel today and in the life of faith?

James Emery White's study of *The Concept of Truth in Contemporary American Evangelical Theology* is an in-depth analysis of the way five leading evangelical thinkers have handled such questions. Three of those thinkers—Cornelius Van Til, Francis Schaeffer, and Carl F. H. Henry—helped to shape the way an entire generation of evangelicals thought in the era following the Second World War. The other two—Millard Erickson and Donald G. Gloesch—are in the vanguard of shaping the way that evangelicals think today.

White's study exhibits a comprehensive knowledge of these writers and their background. Its originality lies in the way that the five thinkers are brought together and subjected to minute inspection. As a secondary theme White shows how their approaches to the question of truth relate to the question of the inspiration and authority of Scripture. White's work had its origin in a dissertation presented to the Southern Baptist Theological Seminary for the degree of doctor of philosophy. I was privileged to be invited to serve as the external examiner of the dissertation. I warmly recommended the award of the degree, and I am delighted that this important study is now made available to a wider public.

Colin Brown
Professor of Systematic Theology and Associate Dean
Center for Advanced Theological Studies
Fuller Theological Seminary
Pasadena, California
December 1992

PREFACE

The author would like to express his appreciation to the following individuals who engaged various segments of this study and offered insightful criticism which assisted the overall quality of the final product: Lewis V. Baldwin, Donald A. Carson, Timothy George, and Stanley S. Gundry. Particular gratitude is expressed to David S. Dockery, friend and brother, who has time and again extended the gift of supportive friendship and who contributed to this study in countless ways. A special word of thanks is also extended to Colin Brown who graciously read the entire manuscript.

I want to acknowledge the kind cooperation of Carl F. H. Henry and Donald G. Bloesch. Gratitude is also expressed to the many willing and able staff persons of the James P. Boyce Centennial Library of the Southern Baptist Theological Seminary and the Divinity Library of the Jean and Alexander Heard Library of Vanderbilt University who were indispensable in regard to the immense amount of research a product of this nature demands.

This study began as a doctoral dissertation at the Southern Baptist Theological Seminary in Louisville, Kentucky, so I want to express a word of appreciation to my doctoral supervisory committee, consisting of William L. Hendricks (supervisor), Bill J. Leonard, and Wayne E. Ward, all of whom provided trenchant criticism in the context of supportive friendship. A special word of appreciation must go to Dr. Hendricks—mentor and friend—for affording me the privilege of such a rewarding and stimulating relationship throughout my many years of graduate education.

Finally, to my wife Susan go unspeakable words of love and appreciation for providing a context in home and heart which allowed this to be initiated, pursued, and realized; she made every page possible.

James Emery White

INTRODUCTION

An analysis of the concept of truth in contemporary American Evangelical theology is most timely, for although the correspondence theory of truth has predominated in Evangelical conceptions of truth, it is now being tested by many Evangelicals who have differing conceptualizations of truth.[1] As a result, fundamental discussions are taking place in a dominant American religious movement that hold the possibility for a major reshaping of that movement's theology.

This study attempts to answer several questions, such as the following: Is the correspondence theory the dominant concept of truth in contemporary Evangelical theology? If it is not the predominant theory, what is? To what degree has the correspondence theory been modified by Evangelicals through contemporary insights into the nature of truth? Is there a trend toward a concept of truth which is new to the history and tradition of American Evangelical theology, and if so, what is this new understanding of truth? Finally, how can this study serve to offer a concept of truth that is both conducive to theological construction and faithful to Evangelical distinctives?

---

1. Evidence of tension within the Evangelical camp regarding the correspondence theory of truth can be found in Norman Geisler's "The Concept of Truth in the Inerrancy Debate," *Bibliotheca Sacra*, vol. 137, no. 548 (October-December 1980), 327-339, where he argues that those Evangelicals who are beginning to reject biblical inerrancy do so on the grounds that they no longer hold to a correspondence theory of truth, but embrace an "intentionality" view of truth (a statement is true if it accomplishes what an author intended it to accomplish, and false if it does not), which is based on a pragmatic theory of truth; an example of this "intentionality" view among Evangelicals would be G.C. Berkouwer, *Holy Scripture: Studies in Dogmatics* (Grand Rapids: Eerdmans, 1975), 182-184.

The thesis to be explored is that the concept of truth in contemporary American Evangelical theology is largely the correspondence theory of truth, which understands truth to be that which corresponds with fact and is both objective and absolute. Perhaps evangelical Edward John Carnell has expressed this concept most succinctly: truth is "that which corresponds to things as they actually are."[2]

Two important delimitations for this study are as follows: first, although epistemology, apologetics, and hermeneutics are often linked with the subject of truth for Evangelical theologians, this analysis only enters into an examination of these areas to the degree that they relate to the concept of truth. The issue to be examined throughout this study is specifically "what is the operative concept of truth?" Second, though the issue of truth is pertinent to efforts in every branch of study throughout history, delimitations of this study warrant that this analysis only be concerned with selected American Evangelical theologians of the last three decades (1960-1989). The reason for this methodological stance flows from the very nature of Evangelicalism itself. Since Evangelicalism is a mosaic of individuals and denominations, parachurch groups, and institutions, the concept of truth must be explored through a survey of the writings of selected contemporary American Evangelical theologians. Those examined are Cornelius Van Til,[3] Francis A. Schaeffer,[4] Carl F. H. Henry, Millard Erickson, and Donald Bloesch.

My selection of these particular Evangelicals will be seen by some as appropriate but by others as a rather misguided and perhaps truncated perusal of Evangelical scholarship. A defense of my selection would therefore seem to be in order. Each of these contemporary American Evangelical theologians has written extensively and has had a wide influence on both the academic and popular level. Schaeffer's popularity and influence among Evangelicals is widely recognized. Van Til, and especially Henry, Erickson, and Bloesch, have enjoyed both academic and popular favor. Henry, Erickson, and Bloesch have produced widely referenced systematic theologies. Also, each of these figures has been more than attentive to the concept of truth in his theological reflection.

---

2. Edward John Carnell, *An Introduction to Christian Apologetics* (Grand Rapids: Eerdmans, 1950), 46; a view that was held with tension later in his life, see Rudolph Nelson, *The Making and Unmaking of an Evangelical Mind: The Case of Edward Carnell* (Cambridge: Cambridge University, 1987).

3. Although Van Til was born in Grootegast, the Netherlands, he can still be classified as an American Evangelical. His family immigrated to America in 1905 when Van Til was ten years old, and Van Til then resided in the United States as an American citizen until his death in 1975.

4. Although Schaeffer's home for many years was the study center of L'Abri Fellowship in Switzerland, he can still be classified as an American Evangelical. He was born in 1912 in Philadelphia, Pennsylvania, and lived in the United States from 1978 until his death in 1984.

Even further, and to my thinking most important, I am convinced that these five thinkers have impacted the thought of mainstream Evangelicalism more than any other assembled grouping. Many Evangelical thinkers could easily have been included, and if the selection had been on content and quality of thought alone, quite arguably should have been included. To examine the concept of truth in contemporary American Evangelicalism, it seemed best, however, to examine the most *influential* thinkers and writers within contemporary American Evangelicalism. On that basis, I am convinced that one would be hard pressed to find five more influential persons than those selected by this study. You could quite possibly discount the quality of their thought in relation to other Evangelical thinkers, but it would be difficult to discount their influence compared to other Evangelical thinkers.

A series of questions is put to each individual and his work, including but not limited to the following: (1) What is their concept of truth?; (2) Where does this concept stand in relation to the correspondence theory of truth?; (3) Is the idea of truth as objective and absolute appropriate in each man's theology, and what is meant by the use of those terms; (4) At what points does the theory of truth reflect the insights of conceptualizations that differ from the correspondence theory of truth?; (5) What are these new concepts or categories of truth that are being employed?; (6) What understanding of revelation is presupposed by each concept of truth?; (7) What do the various authors perceive is gained by the use of these concepts?

These chapters concern themselves almost exclusively with the concept of truth presented by the particular Evangelical theologian under examination. At the end of each of these chapters a critique is offered which presents how fellow Evangelicals have assessed that particular theologian's concept of truth.

The final section examines more fully the overall concept of truth in contemporary American Evangelical theology in terms of the questions raised by those outside of the Evangelical community. An introduction to those questions is suggested in the summary sections following each chapter of the second section. The final section offers a summary of the concept of truth in contemporary American Evangelical theology as evidenced by the Evangelical theologians surveyed in this work and puts forth two suggestions for the direction and shape the Evangelical conceptualization of truth that might be considered for future theological construction.

Chapter One

THE QUESTION
OF TRUTH

What is truth? This has been the ultimate question for philosophers and theologians since the dawn of civilization, captivating human thought throughout the course of intellectual history.[1] It is not surprising that the study of truth has always dominated theological reflection, for "truth is at the center of religious faith, for religion is concerned with ultimate reality."[2]

---

1. Perhaps the best introduction to the conversation on *truth* as it has been carried on throughout western civilization is found in "Truth," *The Great Ideas: A Syntopicon of Great Books of the Western World*, vol. 2, ed. Mortimer J. Adler and William Gorman (Chicago: Encyclopaedia Britannica, 1952), 915-938; see also the many philosophical discussions on "truth" throughout Frederick Copleston's nine-volume *A History of Philosophy* (New York: Doubleday, 1946-); for a focus on philosophy and western thought (including the concept of *truth*) as it relates to religion and specifically Christianity, see Colin Brown, *Christianity and Western Thought: A History of Philosophers, Ideas and Movements*, vol. 1 (Downers Grove: InterVarsity, 1990); from this point forward the word *truth* will not be set in italics, although the author wishes to acknowledge that the meaning and definition of truth is far from uniformly established.

2. Constance J. Tarasar, "The Minority Problem: Educating for Identity and Openness," *Religious Pluralism and Religious Education*, ed. Norma H. Thompson (Birmingham, Ala.: Religious Education Press, 1988), 198.

The Correspondence Theory of Truth

The dominant theory of truth in Western thought has been the correspondence theory of truth.[3] The correspondence theory of truth usually understands truth to be that which corresponds with fact and is both objective and absolute. If I make the statement "It is raining," it is true only insofar as it is indeed actually raining. The truth of the statement is demonstrated by its correspondence with reality. The strength of such an approach is that it operates on a level of certainty that cuts through subjective opinion. It is also the most common-sensical view of truth, for the average person would clearly affirm that what is true is that which actually "is." The dilemma with such an approach is that not all statements have a ready reference that is quickly demonstrable, such as "There is a God."

The Coherence Theory of Truth

The correspondence theory of truth is usually understood to be in classic opposition to the absolute idealists who understand truth as coherence, meaning that the more systematically coherent our beliefs are, the truer they are.[4] If a system of thought does not contradict itself, then it is a mark of truth. The obvious strength of such a view is that a system of thought that contradicts itself at key points is highly problematic. The difficulty with a coherence view of truth is that it is hard-pressed to make ultimate statements regarding truth, for it is conceivable to have two coherent systems that are in direct contradiction with each other.

---

3. For an overview of the correspondence theory of truth, see A. N. Prior, "Correspondence Theory of Truth," *The Encyclopedia of Philosophy*, ed. Paul Edwards, 8 vols. (New York: Macmillan and The Free Press, 1967), 2:223-232; Anthony C. Thiselton, "Truth," *The New International Dictionary of New Testament Theology*, vol. 3, ed. Colin Brown (Grand Rapids: Regency/Zondervan, 1986), 874-902; Bertrand Russell, *The Problems of Philosophy* (London: Oxford University Press, 1959), 119-130; the classical understanding of the correspondence theory of truth can be found in the writings of Aristotle, such as the following works in *The Great Books of the Western World*, ed. Robert Maynard Hutchins, vol. 8 (Chicago: Encyclopaedia Britannica, Inc., 1952): "Metaphysica," trans. W. D. Ross, 1D11.b.26ff; "Categoriae," trans. E. M. Edgehill, 4.a.10-4.b.19; and "Deinterpretatione," trans. E. M. Edgehill, 16.a.10-19.

4. For an overview of the coherence theory of truth, see Alan R. White, "Coherence Theory of Truth," *The Encyclopedia of Philosophy* 2:130-33; see also Francis Herbert Bradley, "On Truth and Coherence," *Essays on Truth and Reality* (Oxford: Clarendon Press, 1914), 202-218.

The Pragmatic Theory of Truth

Another established theory of truth opposed to the correspondence theory is the pragmatic theory. This argues that what is "true" is that which "works."[5] This perspective offers a functional attraction for effectiveness that is highly valued in the modern world. The difficulty with a pragmatic view of truth is that it leaves out the question of morals. The end seldom, if ever, justify the means. Hitler's campaign of hate against the Jews may have been effective in terms of genocide, but few would compliment it with the status of ultimate truth in terms of morality.

Many other theories of truth litter the landscape of ancient and contemporary thought; still the correspondence, coherence, and pragmatic theories of truth are dominant.[6] Each theory attempts to offer the means by which we can determine what constitutes reality. The appearance and lively discussion of so many theories helps demonstrate that the question of truth has been, and continues to be, the ultimate question.

Truth and Contemporary Culture

In our modern world, however, perhaps a more pertinent question than "What is truth?" would be "Is there truth?" A study by George Barna revealed that 66 percent of all Americans deny the existence of absolute truth.[7] Several factors contribute to this devaluation of truth, not the least of which are the dominant sociological processes that mark our time and the results of those processes on individual character. Sociologist Peter Berger, among many others, has suggested three dominant sociological trends in contemporary American culture that have shaped modern life and thought: secularization, pluralization, and privatization.[8] These three streams characterize the modern world.

---

5. For an overview of the pragmatic theory of truth, see Gertrude Ezorsky, "Pragmatic Theory of Truth," *The Encyclopedia of Philosophy* 6:427-430; see also William James, *Pragmatism* (New York: Longman's, Green, 1907), 75-78, 198-209, and 218-223.

6. Other theories would include the semantic theory of truth (assertions about truth are in a metalanguage and apply to statements of the base language) and the performative theory of truth (the assertion of truth is the performative act of agreeing with a given statement), see W. L. Reese's article "Truth" in *Dictionary of Philosophy and Religion: Eastern and Western Thought* (New Jersey: Humanities Press, 1980), 588-590.

7. George Barna, *What Americans Believe* (Ventura: Regal, 1991), 83.

8. Peter Berger, *The Sacred Canopy: Elements of a Sociological Theory of Religion* (Garden City, N.Y.: Anchor/Doubleday, 1969). See also the treatment of these three streams of modernity in Andrew Walker's *Enemy Territory* (Lexington, Ky., Bristol, 1990). An excellent analysis can also be found in Robert Wuthnow's *The Struggle for America's Soul: Evangelicals, Liberals, and Secularism* (Grand Rapids: Eerdmans, 1989).

Secularization

Secularization is the process by which "sectors of society and culture are removed from the domination of religious institutions and symbols."[9] Through this process the church is losing its influence as a shaper of life and thought in the wider social order. As Richard J. Neuhaus phrased it, we live in a "naked public square."[10] For example, once the church was the dominant institution in every community, but now morality and truth are often the property of the media. Television may not tell you what to think, but it certainly tells us what to think about. Today we are exposed to an estimated 1,500 commercial messages per day, as we choose from over 10,000 magazines, 6,000 radio stations, and 400 television stations.[11] Howard K. Smith, former commentator for ABC Television, estimated that at least four-fifths of what the average citizen continues to learn about the world after leaving school "comes filtered through observations of the journalist."[12] Secularization has removed the truth of the gospel from the world's dialogue. Page Smith sarcastically remarks that in our modern world, "God is not a proper topic for conversation, but 'lesbian politics' is!"[13]

Privatization

The second mark of modernity that Berger suggests is "individualization," or "privatization," which Berger defines as follows:

> Privatized religion is a matter of the "choice" or "preference" of the individual or the nuclear family, *ipso facto* lacking in common, binding quality...this religiosity is limited to specific enclaves of social life that may be effectively segregated from the secularized sectors of modern society.[14]

An interpreter of Berger, Os Guinness, has defined privatization as that "process by which modernization produces a cleavage between the

9. Berger, *Sacred Canopy*, 107. See also David Martin, *A General Theory of Secularization* (Oxford: Blackwell, 1978), and Martin E. Marty, *The Modern Schism* (London: SCM, 1969).

10. Richard John Neuhaus, *The Naked Public Square: Religion and Democracy in America* (Grand Rapids: Eerdmans, 1984).

11. George Barna, *The Frog in the Kettle: What Christians Need to Know About Life in the Year 2000* (Ventura: Regal, 1990), 53.

12. Fred Fedler, *An Introduction to the Mass Media* (New York: Harcourt Brace Jovanovich, 1978), 8. On the impact of technology on contemporary culture, see O.B. Hardison, Jr., *Disappearing Through the Skylight: Culture and Technology in the Twentieth Century* (New York: Viking, 1989).

13. Page Smith, *Killing the Spirit: Higher Education in America* (New York: Viking, 1990), 5. Similar sentiments can be found in Allan Bloom, *The Closing of the American Mind: How Higher Education Has Failed Democracy and Impoverished the Souls of Today's Students* (New York: Simon and Schuster, 1987).

14. Berger, *Sacred Canopy*, 133-134; compare Peter Berger, Brigitte Berger, and Hansfried Kellner, *The Homeless Mind* (Harmondsworth, Eng.: Penguin, 1974), chapter 3.

public and the private spheres of life and focuses the private sphere as the special arena for the expansion of individual freedom and fulfillment."[15] The origin of this dynamic was the church's acceptance during the seventeenth and eighteenth centuries of the claim of science to the throne of public, factual truth.[16]

The practical dynamic of this stream of modernity is that one's personal faith is often suspended in relation to business, politics, or even marriage and the home. This trend was evident to historian Theodore Roszak who, after travelling to America, remarked that Christian faith in America was "socially irrelevant, even if privately engaging."[17] At its worst, privatization makes the "truths" of any faith—including the Christian faith—simply a matter of personal preference.[18]

Pluralization

The final stream within modernity, according to Berger, is "pluralization," that "the man in the street is confronted with a wide variety of religious and other reality-defining agencies that compete for his allegiance or at least attention."[19] Again, Guinness offers a good interpretation of Berger's thought, writing that pluralization is that "process by which the number of options in the private sphere of modern society rapidly multiplies at all levels, especially at the level of world views, faith and ideologies."[20]

Berger speaks of the traditional role of religion as a "sacred canopy" covering the contemporary culture. Today that canopy is gone, replaced instead by millions of small tents.[21] For example, Barrett's *World Chris-*

---

15. Os Guinness, *The Gravedigger File: Papers on the Subversion of the Modern Church* (Downers Grove: InterVarsity Press, 1983), 74; compare Thomas Luckmann, *The Invisible Religion* (New York: Macmillan, 1967). Perhaps the best investigation into this dynamic of modernity was offered by Robert Bellah, and others, in *Habits of the Heart: Individualism and Commitment in American Life* (San Francisco: Harper and Row, 1985). A recent chronicle of America's privatization of faith can be found in Phillip L. Berman's *The Search for Meaning: Americans Talk About What They Believe and Why* (New York: Ballantine, 1990).

16. On this, see the analysis offered by Lesslie Newbigin in *The Gospel in a Pluralist Society* (Grand Rapids: Eerdmans, 1990).

17. Theodore Roszak, *Where the Wasteland Ends* (Garden City, N.Y.: Anchor, 1973), 412.

18. See John Naisbitt and Patricia Aburdene, *Megatrends 2000: Ten New Directions for the 1990's* (New York: William Morrow, 1990), for contemporary society, "Spirituality, Yes. Organized Religion, No", 275. A similar point is made by Barna, *The Frog in the Kettle*, 41-42, 117.

19. Berger, *Sacred Canopy*, 127. The historical background to this stream of modernity is illuminated by Nathan O. Hatch's *The Democratization of American Christianity* (New Haven: Yale, 1989).

20. Guinness, *Gravedigger*, 93.

21. Guinness, *Gravedigger*, 94. The idea of religion as a canopy serves as the motif for Martin E. Marty's recent exploration of modern American religion, *Modern American Religion: The Irony of It All, 1893-1919* (Chicago: University of Chicago Press, 1986), the first of four projected volumes on twentieth-century American religion.

tian Encyclopedia lists over twenty thousand denominations, with over two-thousand in the United States alone. The process of pluralization means far more than a simple increase in the number of "faith options." Gilkey is correct when he observes that "many religions have always existed;" what is unique is a "new consciousness" that "entails a feeling of rough parity, as well as diversity, among religions. By parity I mean at least the presence of both truth and grace in other ways."[22] Harold O. J. Brown adds that pluralism can mean many and varying convictions, including "value pluralism, namely, that all convictions about values are of equal validity, which says in effect that no convictions about values have any validity."[23]

The result of this process is the devaluation of truth. Leith Anderson notes that pluralism creates a mindset that all people should universally accept diversity to the point that all values are relative.[24] The sheer number of choices and competing ideologies suggests that no one perspective or religious persuasion has the inside track on truths about God and the supernatural. This encourages what Malise Ruthven calls "The Divine Supermarket," a smorgasbord mentality in regard to the construction of personal beliefs.[25] Barna uses the technical term "syncretism."[26] As a result, Christianity becomes simply one of many competing worldviews, no better or worse than another, existing in the milieu of civilization.[27]

The Four Marks of Modernity

If secularization, privatization, and pluralization are the three processes of modernity, what have been the results of these processes? These three streams have, according to conventional wisdom, produced four values which characterize modernity: moral relativism, autonomous individualism, narcissistic hedonism, and reductive naturalism.[28] As Tho-

---

22. Langdon Gilkey, *Through the Tempest* (Minneapolis: Augsburg Fortress, 1991), 21.

23. Harold O.J. Brown, "Evangelicals and Social Ethics," *Evangelical Affirmations*, ed. Kenneth S. Kantzer and Carl F. H. Henry (Grand Rapids: Academie/Zondervan, 1990), 279.

24. Leith Anderson, *Dying for Change: An Arresting Look at the New Realities Confronting Churches and Para-Church Ministries* (Minneapolis: Bethany House, 1990), 31-32.

25. Malise Ruthven, *The Divine Supermarket: Shopping for God in America* (New York: William Morrow, 1989).

26. Barna, *Frog in the Kettle*, 141. By syncretism, Barna means the "mix and match" mentality of pulling together different threads in various religions to create a personal religion that suits an individual taste.

27. The process of pluralization itself leads to the individuation which underlies the process of privatization. The reason for this is that inherent within pluralism is differentiation, and diversity inevitably leads toward individuation. On this, see Benton Johnson, "Modernity and Pluralism," *Pushing the Faith: Proselytism and Civility in a Pluralistic World*, ed. Martin E. Marty and Frederick E. Greenspahn (New York: Crossroad, 1988), 14.

mas Oden observes, "Modernity is not just a time but a set of passions, hopes, and ideas, a mentality that prevails."[29]

Moral Relativism. "Moral relativism" as a value states that what is moral is dictated by a particular situation in light of a particular culture or social location. The usual phraseology is "what is true for you is true for you, and what is true for me is true for me." The breakdown of morals is almost epidemic; recent studies reveal that lying is now a trait of American character and that one-third of all married men and women have had at least one affair.[30] Allan Bloom's statement has almost become legendary: there "is one thing a professor can be absolutely certain of. Almost every student entering the university believes, or says he believes, that truth is relative."[31]

Autonomous Individualism. "Autonomous individualism" as a value espouses that the individual person is autonomous in terms of destiny and accountability. Ultimate moral authority is self-generated. We ultimately answer to no one but ourselves. Thus our choices are ours alone, determined only by our personal pleasure. As Oden notes, the "key to 'hairesis' (root word for 'heresy') is the notion of choice—choosing for oneself, over against the apostolic tradition."[32]

Narcissistic Hedonism. In Greek mythology, Narcissus, upon passing his reflection in the water, became so enamored with himself that he lost thought, fell in the water, and drowned. The value of "narcissistic hedonism" is the classic "I, me, mine" mentality that places personal pleasure and fulfillment at the forefront of concerns. The popular ethical expression of this mindset is simply this: "if it makes you happy, and it doesn't hurt anyone else, then it's 'okay.'" Such a philosophy offers no basis for refraining from seeking personal happiness simply because another's welfare may be jeopardized.

Reductive Naturalism. "Reductive naturalism" as a value states that what can be known is only that which can be empirically verified. In other words, what is real is that which can be seen, tasted, heard, smelled, or touched. This is basically the view of empiricism. If it cannot be examined in a tangible, scientific manner, then it is not simply unknowable; it is also meaningless. The verdict such a view imposes on religious claims is self-evident.

---

28. These four marks were first suggested to my thinking by Langdon Gilkey in *Naming the Whirlwind* (Indianapolis: Bobbs-Merril, 1969), and most recently by Thomas C. Oden's *After Modernity . . . What? Agenda for Theology* (Grand Rapids: Academie/Zondervan, 1990).

29. Oden, *After Modernity . . . What?*, 52.

30. See James Patterson and Peter Kim, *The Day America Told the Truth: What People Really Believe About Everything That Really Matters* (New York: Prentice-Hall, 1991).

31. Bloom, *The Closing of the American Mind*, 25.

32. Oden, *After Modernity . . . What?*, 74, compare 157.

In the midst of this cultural milieu, Christians have "truth to tell," as Lesslie Newbigin reminds us.[33] Few groups within Christendom have recognized this challenge as passionately as American Evangelicals, and it is to their history we now turn.

---

33. Lesslie Newbigin, *Truth to Tell: The Gospel as Public Truth* (Grand Rapids: Eerdmans, 1991).

Chapter Two

AMERICAN EVANGELICALISM

Martin Marty has noted that to look at American religion and to overlook Evangelicalism "would be comparable to scanning the American physical landscape and missing the Rocky Mountains."[1] The meaning of the term "Evangelical" has evolved over time. In contemporary usage in the United States it refers to theologically conservative Protestants as well as to a small but increasing number of Roman Catholics.

To understand modern American Evangelicalism, one must understand its formative influences. The word itself comes from the Greek word *euangelion*, which is used in the New Testament to represent the "gospel," or "good news" of the life and ministry of Jesus Christ. "Evangelical" was not a self-conscious term that the church of the first century used. Rather it became historically important when certain groups of Protestants seized upon it during the Protestant Reformation to distinguish themselves from Roman Catholics.[2]

---

1. Martin E. Marty, *A Nation of Behavers* (Chicago: University of Chicago, 1976), 80.

2. For a good discussion on the use of the term in secular Greek, the Old Testament, and the New Testament, see U. Becker, "Gospel, Evangelize, Evangelist," *The New International Dictionary of New Testament Theology, vol. 2,* ed. Colin Brown, translated with additions and revisions from the German *Theologisches Begriffslexikon zum Neuen Testament* (Grand Rapids: Regency Reference Library, 1976, 1986), 107-115; also note Gerhard Friedrich's discussion in "euangelizomai, *euangelion, proeuangelizomai, euangelistes"* in *Theological Dictionary of the New Testament,* 10 vols., ed. Gerhard Kittel, trans. by Geoffrey W. Bromiley (Grand Rapids: Eerdmans, 1964), 2:707-737.

Three historical events take prominence in the shaping of American Evangelicalism: the Protestant Reformation of the sixteenth century, eighteenth-century Evangelical revivals, and the controversy between Fundamentalists and Modernists of the late nineteenth and early twentieth centuries.[3] The latter of these three formative influences is given the most attention, for it was American Fundamentalism's clash with Modernists that gave birth to contemporary American Evangelicalism.

The Protestant Reformation of the Sixteenth Century

The Protestant Reformation of the sixteenth century, especially English Puritanism, can be seen as a formative influence on contemporary American Evangelicalism.[4] Since, however, the Reformers denied starting a new church. Much of what American Evangelicals believe about God, Jesus Christ, humanity, sin, and the eternal world is owed to the Catholic tradition from which the Reformers eventually separated.[5]

Evangelicals do, however, join in the Reformation restatement of the gospel.[6] While giving no challenge to the orthodox tradition of early Christianity, the Reformers rejected the medieval doctrines regarding salvation and the church.[7] Four major distinctions can be observed

---

3. That Evangelicalism has been shaped by these three significant periods of modern Christianity is discussed at length by Bruce L. Shelley in "Evangelicalism," *Dictionary of Christianity in America*, ed. Dániel G. Reid, Robert D. Linder, Bruce L. Shelley, and Harry S. Stout (Downers Grove: InterVarsity, 1990), 413; this article is one of the best general introductions available regarding the history and shape of American Evangelicalism in a brief article format.

4. Perhaps the most accessible introduction to the history of the Reformation is Roland H. Bainton's *The Reformation of the Sixteenth Century* (Boston: Beacon, 1952, 1985); see also George H. Williams, *The Radical Reformation* (Philadelphia: Westminster, 1962).

5. An excellent introduction to the theological underpinnings of the Reformation is found in Timothy George's *Theology of the Reformers* (Nashville: Broadman, 1988), which examines Reformation thought through the lens of four major reformers of the sixteenth century: Martin Luther, Huldrych Zwingli, John Calvin, and Menno Simons; see also Jaroslav Pelikan, *The Christian Tradition, Volume Four: Reformation of Church and Dogma, 1300-1700* (Chicago and London: University of Chicago, 1984); Alister E. McGrath, *Reformation Thought: An Introduction* (New York: Basil Blackwell, 1988); Francois Wendel, *Calvin: Origins and Development of His Religious Thought*, trans. by Philip Mairet (Durham: Labyrinth Press, 1963).

Indispensable primary sources include Martin Luther's *The Bondage of the Will*, trans. by Henry Cole (Grand Rapids: Baker, 1976) and John Calvin's *Institutes of the Christian Religion* (two vols.), trans. by Henry Beveridge (Grand Rapids: Eerdmans, 1983); The *Library of Christian Classics*, 26 vols. (London and Philadelphia, 1953-1970), presents writings from all the leading Reformers in volumes XV-XXVI.

6. On this, see Bernard L. Ramm's *The Evangelical Heritage* (Waco: Word, 1973), especially chapter 2, "Evangelical Theology Belongs to Reformation Theology," 23-40.

7. These distinctions were those present at the time of the Protestant Reformation. The many changes that have resulted from Vatican II have significantly modified many of the theological disagreements that existed during the sixteenth century.

between the Reformers and their Catholic heritage that Evangelicals continue to share. The first distinction concerned the issue of salvation (soteriology). The Catholic tradition asserted that justification comes through a combination of faith and good works. The Reformers countered that justification is through faith in Christ alone. The second point of tension was the issue of religious authority. The Roman Church insisted that religious authority is a sacred institution established by Jesus Christ on Peter and his successors (the bishops of Rome). Reformation doctrine held that all truth necessary for faith and behavior is found in one source (the Bible, the written word of God). A third area of disagreement was the doctrine of the church (ecclesiology). Catholic theology at the time of the Reformation held that the true church is the sacred hierarchial and priestly institution that Jesus Christ founded on Peter, the first pope, and on the apostles, the first bishops. The theology of the Reformers saw the true church not as a sacred hierarchy, but as a community of faith in which all true believers share the priestly task. The final major area of division was over the subject of Christian living. The monastic way of life was thoroughly entrenched in Catholic practice and thought. The Reformers understood the essence of Christian living as serving God in one's calling (whether it be in secular or ecclesiastical life). These four Reformation understandings remain in the mainstream of contemporary American Evangelical theology.[8] Nonetheless, these distinctions explain why the term "evangelical" was used at the time of the Reformation to designate such individuals as Lutherans and their attempt to renew the church on the grounds of the authoritative Word of God, and why still later it was applied collectively to Lutheran and Reformed communities in Germany

Eighteenth-Century Evangelical Revivals

During the seventeenth century the vigorous defense of the gospel in the Protestant Reformation was replaced by an "unyielding spirit of Protestant orthodoxy." Throughout Northern Europe, Protestantism was accepted but was relatively lifeless.[9]   A series of renewal movements changed the face of traditional Protestantism and gave a new meaning

---

8. Summarizing Reformation distinctives in this manner in relation to Evangelicalism was suggested to me by Richard Mouw, "Theological and Ethical Dimensions of American Evangelicals," the Southern Baptist Theological Seminary, Louisville, Ky., speech delivered and recorded, April 21, 1988, and by Bruce Shelley's aforementioned article, "Evangelicalism," in *Dictionary of Christianity in America;* see also Ramm, *Evangelical Heritage,* 24-38; Philip Schaff, *Creeds of Christendom* (New York and London: Harper and Brothers, 1877), 3, 206-207.

9. Shelley, "Evangelicalism," *Dictionary of Christianity in America,* 414.

to the term Evangelical: that of being "born again." McLoughlin writes that revivalism is the "Protestant ritual (at first spontaneous, but, since 1830, routinized) in which charismatic evangelists convey 'the Word' of God to large masses of people who, under this influence, experience what Protestants call conversion, salvation, regeneration, or spiritual rebirth."[10]

The phrase "born again" was not an invention of eighteenth-century revivalism. It dates to Jesus' words recorded in John 3 in the New Testament with use in the Reformation period as well as the German pietistic era. As a phrase denoting spiritual regeneration, and thus prone to a broad and imprecise usage in general discourse, "born again" has generally come to mean "any Christian who exhibits intensity or overt self-identification or a keen sense of divine presence, or one who attributes causation to God for events in personal life or in the historical and natural processes."[11]

The first renewal of revivals rose in Germany within a movement termed Pietism. German Pietists stressed a sincere faith through Bible study, prayer, and the nurture and fellowship of the church as a supportive community of faith.[12] In Northern Germany Pietism expanded through a refugee group from Moravia called the Moravian Brethren under the leadership of Count Nicholas von Zinzendorf. In other areas of Europe, Pietism merged with the Anabaptist tradition to create the Mennonite and German Brethren traditions of faith.[13] One of the greatest contributions Pietism made to Evangelicalism was through its influence on John Wesley, who became the most prominent spokesperson for England's great spiritual awakening.[14] The American colonial counterpart to the Methodist revival in the British Isles has become known as

---

10. William G. McLoughlin, *Revivals, Awakenings, and Reform: An Essay on Religion and Social Change in America, 1607-1977* (Chicago and London: University of Chicago, 1978), xiii. McLoughlin gives what is perhaps the single best introduction to eighteenth century evangelical revivalism.

11. C. D. Weaver, "Born Again," *Dictionary of Christianity in America*, 177; see also George, *Theology of the Reformers*, 311.

12. Jacob Spener's *Pia Desideria*, ed. and trans. Theodore G. Toppert (Philadelphia: Fortress, 1964), was clearly the book that established the program for Pietism; F. Ernest Stoeffler is the individual who has given the most attention to the subject of Pietism in recent years: *The Rise of Evangelical Pietism* (Leiden: E. J. Brill, 1965); *German Pietism During the Eighteenth Century* (Leiden: E. J. Brill, 1973); and as editor, *Continental Pietism and Early American Christianity* (Grand Rapids: Eerdmans, 1976). See also William G. McLoughlin, "Pietism and the American Character," *American Quarterly* 17 (Summer 1965), 163-186; Dale Brown, *Understanding Pietism* (Grand Rapids: Eerdmans, 1978).

13. A good introduction to the Anabaptist tradition can be found in *Spiritual and Anabaptist Writers: Documents Illustrative of the Radical Reformation* ed. George Huntston Williams and Angel M. Mergal, The Library of Christian Classics (Philadelphia: Westminster, 1957).

14. On Wesley, see Stanley Ayling's *John Wesley* (London: Collins, 1979); A. C. Outler, ed., *John Wesley* (New York: Oxford University Press, 1964).

the Great Awakening.[15] Appearing first in the 1720s as a series of regional awakenings under the preaching ministry of George Whitefield (a friend of John Wesley), these regional revivals coalesced into a Great Awakening that can be said to have lasted until the American Revolution.[16] As Harry S. Stout has noted, these revivals "mark the beginning of popular evangelicalism in the American churches."[17] This had a decisive impact on American religion, for the

> Great Awakening, by increasing piety, increased proportionately dissatisfaction with rigid and especially political control of spiritual affairs. Pietism is invariably associated with that which is voluntary and personal, as it is antagonistic toward that which is compulsory and cultural—in the name of Christ.[18]

This Evangelical call for an immediate and instantaneous conversion to Christ continued throughout the nineteenth century in camp meetings, revivals, and classrooms all across America.[19] The leadership of such Evangelicals as Timothy Dwight (president of Yale), revivalist Charles Finney at Oberlin, and circuit-riding preacher Peter Cartwright helped to install Evangelical Christianity as the dominant faith in America before the Civil War.[20] Sydney Ahlstrom calls this the "golden age of democratic evangelicalism" and writes that "evangelical Protestant churches, with their message and methods tuned to the patriotic aspirations of a young nation, reached their high point of cultural influence."[21]

---

15. See Jonathan Edwards, "A Faithful Narrative" (1737), "Distinguishing Marks of a Work of the Spirit of God" (1741), and "Some Thoughts Concerning the Present Revival" (1742) in *The Works of Jonathan Edwards*, vol. 4 (New Haven: Yale University Press, 1957) which offer excellent primary sources regarding the Great Awakening. See also Perry Miller and Alan Heimert, eds., *The Great Awakening: Documents Illustrating the Crisis and its Consequences* (Indianapolis: Bobbs-Merrill, 1967) and Richard L. Bushman, ed., *The Great Awakening: Documents on the Revival of Religion* (Chapel Hill: Institute of Early American History and Culture/University of North Carolina Press, 1969/1989). A good general overview on a popular level can be found in Keith Hardman's "God's Wonderful Working: The First Great Awakening," *Christian History*, vol. 8, no. 3, Issue 23, 12-23, and in Harry S. Stout's article, "The Great Awakening," 494-496, in *Dictionary of Christianity in America*. See also Alan Heimert, *Religion and the American Mind* (Cambridge: Harvard University, 1966); Edwin S. Gaustad, *The Great Awakening in New England* (New York: Harper and Row, 1957); Perry Miller, *Jonathan Edwards* (New York: William Sloane, 1949).

16. On Whitefield, see Harry S. Stout, *The Divine Dramatist: George Whitefield and the Rise of Modern Evangelicalism* (Grand Rapids: Eerdmans, 1991), as well as Arnold A. Dallimore, *George Whitefield: The Life and Times of the Great Evangelist of the Eighteenth-Century Revival*, 2 vols., (Westchester, Ill: Cornerstone, 1980).

17. Stout, "Great Awakening," 494.

18. Gaustad, *Great Awakening*, 110.

19. On this, see Nathan O. Hatch, *The Democratization of American Christianity* (New Haven: Yale University Press, 1989); Shelley, "Evangelicalism," *Dictionary of Christianity in America*, 414.

20. Shelley, "Evangelicalism," 415.

21. Sydney E. Ahlstrom, *A Religious History of the American People* (New Haven: Yale University Press, 1972), 387.

William McLoughlin has said that the story of American Evangelicalism during the nineteenth century is the story of America itself. He contends that Evangelical religion

> lay behind the concept of rugged individualism in business enterprise, laissez faire in economic theory, constitutional democracy in political thought, the Protestant ethic in morality, and the millennial hope in the manifest destiny of white, Anglo-Saxon, Protestant America to lead the world to its latter-day glory.[22]

During the critical years between the Civil War and World War I, Evangelicalism was dethroned as the reigning religious perspective of American society, largely due to the clash between Fundamentalists and Modernists during the nineteenth and early twentieth centuries.[23]

American Fundamentalism

The term "Fundamentalist" or "Fundamentalism" was probably first coined by Curtis Lee Laws in the Baptist paper, *The Watchman Examiner*, in 1920.[24] According to Laws, Fundamentalists were those who were ready "to do battle royal for the Fundamentals."[25]

Origins of Fundamentalism

Discussions of the origins of Fundamentalism have been filled with as much diversity and disagreement as Fundamentalism itself. Stewart Cole's *The History of Fundamentalism* (1931) and Norman Furniss' *The Fundamentalist Controversy, 1918-1931* (1954) explored the origins of Fundamentalism in terms of a reaction to modernity. Both works were unsympathetic to Fundamentalism and tended toward caricature. They ignored much of its background.[26] Ernest Sandeen explored a more theological basis for understanding Fundamentalism.[27] For Sandeen,

---

22. William G. McLoughlin, "Introduction," in *The American Evangelicals, 1800-1900: An Anthology*, ed. William G. McLoughlin (Gloucester, Mass.: Peter Smith, 1976), 1.

23. Shelley, "Evangelicalism," 415.

24. Curtis Lee Laws, "Convention Side Lights," *The Watchman-Examiner*, July 1, 1920, a name which perhaps drew on the publication of *The Fundamentals* (Los Angeles, Ca: The Bible Institute of Los Angeles, 1917), a series of 12 volumes which intended to put forth the orthodox Christian faith (discussed below); the best collection of primary sources concerning American Fundamentalism can be found in *Fundamentalism in American Religion 1880-1950*, edited by Joel A. Carpenter with advisory editors Donald W. Dayton, George M. Marsden, Mark A. Noll, and Grant Wacker, a 45-volume facsimile series reproducing all major primary sources in relation to the history of American Fundamentalism (New York: Garland Publishing).

25. Laws, "Convention Side Lights."

26. As noted by Bill J. Leonard, "The Origin and Character of Fundamentalism," *Review and Expositor*, vol. 79, 1.c. no. 1 (Winter 1982), 5.

27. Ernest Sandeen, *The Roots of Fundamentalism* (Grand Rapids: Baker, 1970).

millennialism and Princeton Theology were the catalysts of Fundamentalism.[28]   Millennialism is characterized by the belief that a period of unprecedented peace and righteousness will reign upon the earth, usually associated with the return of Christ. Postmillennialists believe that the present age will be gradually transformed into the millennium through natural means, such as religious revival and social reform. Premillennialists believe that the golden age will come only after the current age is destroyed through supernatural means, such as the Second Coming of Christ.[29] Due to individuals such as J. Nelson Darby and events like the Niagara Bible Conferences (most notably the 1878 Conference), dispensational, pre-tribulation, pre-millennial theology was spread. Throughout the second half of the nineteenth century a plethora of prophetic conferences spread millennialist ideas.

Dispensationalism divided history into seven periods, with the current period categorized as the period of "Grace." The tribulation, seven years of Satanic rule through the anti-Christ, will end in a thousand-year millennium where Christ will rule. The church will be raptured, or "caught up" (from the latin word *rapio*) to be with Christ, prior to the tribulation.[30] Sandeen argued that America in the nineteenth century was "drunk on the millennial."[31]

Sandeen's second catalyst, Princeton Theology, was born in Princeton Theological Seminary under Archibald Alexander and Charles Hodge and their students, Archibald Alexander Hodge, B. B. Warfield, and J. Gresham Machen. Machen's *Christianity and Liberalism* (1923) continues to serve as an excellent and persuasive introduction to Princeton Theology.[32] Together they argued for the infallibility of Scripture

---

28. Sandeen, *Roots*, xix; Sandeen writes that millennialism gave life and shape to the fundamentalist movement so that Fundamentalism should not be understood apart from the history of millennialism.

29. See Timothy Weber, "Millennarian Movements," *Dictionary of Christianity in America*, 738-739; see also Leonard I. Sweet, "Millennialism in America: Recent Studies," *Theological Studies* 40 (September 1979), 510-531.

30. This was popularized during the 1970s through Hal Lindsey's *Late Great Planet Earth* (Grand Rapids: Zondervan, 1971), which as of 1978 had over 9,800,000 copies in print and was the best-selling book in America during the 1970s. See George M. Marsden, *Fundamentalism and American Culture: The Shaping of Twentieth Century Evangelicalism, 1870-1925* (Oxford: Oxford University, 1980), 239, note 11; see also Nathan O. Hatch, "Evangelicalism as a Democratic Movement," *Evangelicalism and Modern America*, ed. by George Marsden (Grand Rapids: Eerdmans, 1984), 78-79.

31. Sandeen, *Roots*, 42.

32. See also Machen's *The Virgin Birth of Christ* (Grand Rapids: Baker, 1930); for other representatives of Princeton Theology, see Benjamin B. Warfield's *The Inspiration and Authority of the Bible* (Phillipsburg, N.J.: The Presbyterian and Reformed Publishing Company, 1948); Charles Hodge, *Systematic Theology*, 3 vols. (Grand Rapids: Eerdmans, reprinted 1989); a good introduction to Princeton Theology is found in *The Princeton Theology, 1812-1921*, ed. by Mark A. Noll (Grand Rapids: Baker, 1983).

and a rationalistic system of thought, largely based on Thomas Reid and the philosophical school of Scottish Common Sense Realism.[33]

C. Allyn Russell explored a different thesis concerning Fundamentalism's origin, arguing that the energy behind Fundamentalism was Protestant Liberalism.[34] Russell's work was helpful in exemplifying the theological differences between the leaders of Fundamentalism, thus tempering Sandeen's contention that a theological animity undergirded and energized the entire movement.

George Marsden argues for four main streams which fed into Fundamentalism: first, the revivalistic empire of D. L. Moody (and revivalism in general); second, the onslaught of modernity, breeding an ambivalence toward culture; third, the holiness movements (especially the British-born Keswick movement); and finally, with Sandeen, pre-tribulational, pre-millennial, dispensationalist theology, although Marsden doubts that "premillennialism was really the organizing principle."[35] Perhaps the best conclusion is that of Bill J. Leonard, who notes that the study of Fundamentalism "reveals the complexity and diversity of the movement," and therefore concludes that premillennialism and Princton Theology "were but elements of an even broader base which included revivalism, moralism, individualism, and a strong reaction to Modernism."[36] Leonard is correct about the complexity of the movement and the many diverse streams which flowed into its origin and character. Still, we would agree that the major emphasis has to be given to Fundamentalism as a reaction to modernity. Basically, Fundamentalism was a

---

33. Scottish Common Sense philosophy is part of what Henry May in *The Enlightenment in America* (New York: Oxford, 1976), xvi and 307-362, called the "didactic" category of the Enlightenment. It opposed both skepticism and revolution but wanted to save some ideas from what it saw as the debacle of the Enlightenment. Among ideas accepted were the intelligible universe, clear and certain moral judgments, and progress. Thus Locke, Newton, Montesquieu, science, progress, intellectual freedom, and republicanism were good; but Voltaire, Hume, Rousseau, religious skepticism, frantic innovation, undisciplined emotions, and the French Revolution were bad. These distinctions had to be made through rational argument and not just through appeals to biblical or other authority. May argues that the "didactic" Enlightenment was part of a significant "counter-Enlightenment" and was the primary mode in which the Enlightenment was assimilated by the American culture of the nineteenth century.

In light of these concerns, Donald A. Carson has suggested that the dependence of the Princetonians on Scottish Common Sense Realism is not to be overstated. Common Sense Realism affected a large number of writers and thinkers during this period, thus removing a necessary connection between Common Sense Realism and Princeton theology. Carson also maintains that Hodge criticizes the Realists at many decisive points, thus demonstrating that he was not held hostage to their views. Finally, Carson posits that inerrancy is not paradigmatically dependent on Common Sense Realism. Letter received from Donald A. Carson, Professor of New Testament, Trinity Evangelical Divinity School, Deerfield, Illinois, January 30, 1991.

34. C. Allyn Russell, *Voices of American Fundamentalism* (Philadelphia: Westminster, 1976), 15.

35. Marsden, *Fundamentalism*, 5.

36. Leonard, "The Origin and Character of Fundamentalism," *Review and Expositor,* 14.

retreat from everything perceived to threaten the bastions of what was understood to be true and orthodox.[37]

Theology of Fundamentalism

Three areas can be examined in regard to determining the theology of Fundmentalism.[38] First, the Presbyterian General Assembly in 1910, produced what has become known as the "Five Points" of Fundamentalism: the deity of Christ; His virgin birth and miracles; the inspiration and infallibility of Scripture; Christ's penal death for our sins; and His physical resurrection and personal return.[39] Fundamentalists considered these five areas to be under direct attack from secular society and from within the contemporary church. The second source for Fundamentalist theology is the *Scofield Bible* (published in 1909). Selling over 2,000,000 copies, this annotated "study Bible" is blatantly pre-tribulational, pre-millennial, and dispensational. Sandeen has called this work "perhaps the most influential single publication in millennial and fundamentalist historiography."[40] Finally, a series of twelve volumes published between 1910-1915 called *The Fundamentals* both represented and shaped Fundamentalist theology.[41] Written by an impressive team of American and British scholars, these volumes were mailed free of charge to pastors, teachers, Sunday School workers, and laypersons across the United States. Over one-third of the essays defended Scripture, and the vast majority had the theme of the authority of God in Scripture over and against the authority of science.

Fundamentalist's theology largely reacted to Liberalism's accomodation to the modern world. Langdon Gilkey has delineated Liberalism's compromise as follows: (1) the change of the conception of Christian truth from that of divinely given and so infallible propositions about reality into a system of human, and so relative, symbols; (2) the change of the understanding of Christian doctrine from eternal statements of unchanging validity to relative human statements of Christian truth for

---

37. Martin E. Marty sounds this theme in *Modern American Religion, Volume 1: The Irony of It All, 1893-1919* (Chicago: The University of Chicago Press, 1986), noting that the Fundamentalist movement was decisively "countermodern" (see chaps. 10 and 11); see also H. Richard Niebuhr, *Christ and Culture* (New York: Harper, 1951), 45-82.

38. Many areas beyond these three can be examined for insight into the theology of the American Fundamentalist movement, such as the annual Niagra Bible Conferences that began in 1876; these three are cited only as representative examples.

39. Marsden, *Fundamentalism*, 117; J. I. Packer, *"Fundamentalism" and the Word of God* (Grand Rapids: Eerdmans, 1958), 28.

40. Sandeen, *Roots*, 222.

41. Recently re-published as *The Fundamentals: The Famous Sourcebook of Foundational Biblical Truths*, ed. by R. A. Torrey, and others, updated by Charles L. Feinberg, and others, with biographical introductions by Warren W. Wiersbe (Grand Rapids: Kregel, 1990); originally published with Charles Erdman as editor as *The Fundamentals* (Los Angeles, Ca.: The Bible Institute of Los Angeles, 1917).

their time, cultural situation, and needs; (3) the change of the understanding of Christian life from that of a life directed by divine rules of
holiness to that of a life devoted to the present human community in
terms of justice, freedom, and security; (4) finally, Liberalism conceived
of the Christian as primarily obligated to show love and tolerance to all,
regardless of another person's religious persuasion.[42] As Bernard Ramm
has written, this inevitably led to a "collision" with Evangelical theology.[43]

Fundamentalist Clash with Modernists

Fundamentalism became increasingly militant in the years surrounding World War II.[44] Sandeen has suggested that the animosity which
filled many Americans during that era spilled over and created the holy
war between Modernists and the Fundamentalists.[45] Fundamentalists
indeed experienced "profound ambivalence toward the surrounding culture."[46] Three major concerns occupied the Fundamentalists during this
time.[47] First, the influx of millions of immigrants and their various
worldviews. Many of these were professing Roman Catholics, Lutherans,
and Jews, none of whom shared the Puritan and revivalistic traditions of
America and American Evangelicalism. In three decades these immigrants changed the face of religion in America.[48] The second concern
which occupied Fundamentalists was the radical shift in contemporary
thought. The Scopes Trial typified such conflicts as the "city" versus the
"country," progress versus supposed ignorance, and most certainly Modernism versus Fundamentalism.

The "Scopes" trial, as it has become known, revolved around a
teacher who was charged and found guilty of violating the Tennessee
anti-evolution law. Though Fundamentalists "won" on the issue of evolution, some contend that their movement as a whole earned nothing
but ridicule. This interpretation is based largely on the cross-examina-
tion of William Jennings Bryan by Scope's attorney Clarence Darrow,

---

42. Langdon Gilkey, *Naming the Whirlwind: The Renewal of God-Language* (Indianapolis: Bobbs-Merrill, 1969), 76-77; see also L. Harold DeWolf, *The Case for Theology in
Liberal Perspective* (Philadelphia: Westminster, 1959).

43. Ramm, *The Evangelical Heritage*, 75-102.

44. Marsden, *Fundamentalism*, 141.

45. The term "Modernist" will refer to those in traditional Protestant denominations
who welcomed the fast-paced changes in American society and tried to adapt the Christian
faith accordingly. Modernists tried to retain the traditional Protestant hold on America by
modifying the traditional doctrines of the Christian faith to reconcile them with science,
evolution, and religious pluralism; see Shelley, "Evangelicalism," *Dictionary of Christianity
in America*, 415.

46. Marsden, *Fundamentalism*, viii; also, see above note 44.

47. These three concerns are common in regards to discussing the history of Fundamentalism, as noted by Shelley's article, "Evangelicalism," 413-416.

48. Shelley, "Evangelicalism," 415.

one of the most gifted attorneys in the nation. Bryan was unable to defend the Bible on the most simplistic points.[49]

Alhough Darwin's *Origin of Species* (1859) did not directly challenge Christianity, popular speculation about the book's doctrine of evolution tended to discount the traditional explanation of the origin of life and the personal God behind the universe. Men and women began to think in terms of process, progress, and evolution as opposed to creation, miracles, and new birth.[50]

The third concern which occupied the Fundamentalists was higher criticism. Higher criticism is the term used to describe the study of Scripture from the standpoint of literature, as opposed to "lower criticism," which deals with the text of Scripture and its transmission. Higher criticism has three main concerns: (1) detecting the presence of underlying literary sources in a work; (2) identifying the literary types that make up the composition; and (3) conjecturing on matters of authorship and date.[51] For Fundamentalists, this criticism undermined the idea that the Bible was special revelation, left the Christian minister bereft of a supernatural gospel, and provided little basis for the Evangelical experience of the new birth.[52] It has therefore been suggested that a "systematic theology of biblical authority which defended the common evangelical faith in the infallibility of the Bible had to be created."[53]

Higher Criticism was also associated with German liberalism in education and was therefore one of the many reasons evangelist Billy Sunday quipped that if you turned hell upside down, you would find "Made

---

49. Marsden has written in *Fundamentalism*, 184, that the trial brought an "outpouring of derision. The rural setting . . . stamped the entire movement with an indelible image," that of the anti-intellectual, Southern farmer. This is not to say that the national response (including the media) to the Scopes trial at the time of the trial did not side with the Fundamentalist perspective.

50. Shelley, "Evangelicalism," 415; on Darwin's theories, see *The Origin of Species by Means of Natural Selection*, vol. 49 ed. by Robert Maynard Hutchins. (Chicago: Encyclopaedia Britannica, 1952), where the summation of his argument is presented on 230-243, and *The Descent of Man and Selection in Relation to Sex* in *The Great Books of the Western World*, vol. 49 ed. Robert Maynard Hutchins 243 (Chicago: Encyclopaedia Britannica, 1952).

51. On this, see R. K. Harrison, "Higher Criticism," *Evangelical Dictionary of Theology*, 511-512; an excellent introduction to the area of biblical criticism can be found in Richard N. Soulen's *Handbook of Biblical Criticism*, 2nd ed. (Atlanta: John Knox, 1981).

52. Shelley, "Evangelicalism," 415; see also Timothy Weber's article, "The Two-Edged Sword: The Fundamentalist Use of the Bible" in *The Bible in America*, ed. Nathan O. Hatch and Mark A. Noll (Oxford: Oxford University, 1982), 101-120.

53. Sandeen, *Roots*, 106; this view has been rejected by Evangelical scholars such as John D. Woodbridge and Randall H. Balmer, see "The Princetonians and Biblical Authority: An Assessment of the Ernest Sandeen Proposal," *Scripture and Truth*, ed. by D. A. Carson and John D. Woodbridge (Grand Rapids: Academie/Zondervan, 1983), 251-279. Woodbridge and Balmer contend that a systematic theology of biblical authority stressing inerrancy of the original manuscripts was relatively commonplace by 1850 and far from an invention of Princeton theologians.

in Germany" stamped on the bottom.[54] In such a context it is not surprising that Fundamentalists entered into a holy war and began to equate their success with the future of Western Civilization.[55] This strong and emotive response to these three concerns, along with countless others, formed what Thomas Kuhn has called a "paradigm shift" of astronomical proportions.[56] Kuhn argues that science progresses not through the accumulation of new "facts" but through "paradigm conflicts" which exist between divergent world views. When two perspectives use radically different models and presuppositions, communication breakdown and conflict is inevitable. Weber has suggested that this type conflict took place in the nineteenth century between the older "mechanical" model and the newer "organic" view of things—a shift from "Baconianism" to "Darwinism."[57] Marsden notes that Kuhn's theory helps explain and clarify the Fundamentalist experience during this time of American History.[58]

Fundamentalist Retreat into Institutionalization

After the 1920's, Fundamentalism entered into a period perhaps best termed a "retreat into institutionalization." The retreat was hastened by the winsome appeal for tolerance from the Modernist camp, as found in Harry Emerson Fosdick's sermon, "Shall the Fundamentalists Win?"[59] Marsden writes that the ideal of tolerance was regarded as almost sacred in most American churches, thus making this response to Fundamentalism powerfully compelling.[60] This mood against Fundamentalism was aided greatly by the publication of Shailer Matthews' *The Faith of Modernism* (1924), an answer to J. Gresham Machen's *Christianity and Liberalism* (1923), and Sinclair Lewis' popular *Elmer Gantry* (1927) which parodied a Fundamentalist preacher.

---

54. Quoted in Ray H. Abrams, *Preachers Present Arms* (New York, 1933), 79, as quoted in Marsden, *Fundamentalism*, 142.

55. Marsden, *Fundamentalism*, 149.

56. Thomas S. Kuhn, *The Structure of Scientific Revolutions*, 2nd ed., enlarged (Chicago: University of Chicago, 1962, 1970); see also the similar contention of George Marsden, *Fundamentalism*, 215, and Timothy P. Weber in "The Two-Edged Sword," 101-20.

57. Weber, "Two-Edged Sword," 103.

58. Marsden, *Fundamentalism*, 215; see also James Davison Hunter, "The Evangelical Worldview Since 1890," *Piety and Politics: Evangelicals and Fundamentalists Confront the World*, ed. by Richard John Neuhaus and Michael Cromartie (Washington: Ethics and Public Policy Center, 1987), 19-54. Such an embrace of Kuhn's thinking in this regard should not be construed as a wholesale acceptance of Kuhn's entire system of thought, or even of Kuhn's conclusions based on his propositions. An excellent critique of Kuhn's proposals as used by Wentzel van Hysteen can be found in John S. Feinberg's "Rationality, Objectivity, and Doing Theology" Review and Critique of Wentzel van Huysteen's *Theology and the Justification of Faith* in *Trinity Journal*, vol. 10 New Series, no. 2 (Fall 1989), 161-184.

59. *The Annals of America*, vol. 14 (Chicago: Encyclopaedia Britannica, 1976), 325-330.

60. Marsden, *Fundamentalism*, 180.

Rather than engage culture, Fundamentalists retreated and sought areas where they could control doctrine, education, and morals. This often involved withdrawing from denominations to form their own alliances. Fundamentalist Harold Lindsell argues that Fundamentalists left the major denominations because they lost control of their ecclesiastical machinery to the Moderates.[61] There is little doubt that by the 1930s, Fundamentalists were "either outside the mainline structures or powerless minorities within them."[62] During this time, Fundamentalists explored what could happen if religion operated within and took advantage of the free enterprise system.[63] Their model was D. L. Moody's empire, although they could have looked to aspects of the Student Volunteer Movement as well.[64] Such educational institutions as Dallas Theological Seminary and Bob Jones University were founded as a result of this philosophy (founded in 1924 and 1926, respectively).[65]

Birth of Contemporary American Evangelicalism

Many Fundamentalists grew uneasy with the denominational separatism, social and cultural irresponsibility, and anti-intellectual stance that pervaded during the years of controversy with the Modernists.[66] These individuals branched off and formed the movement now known as con-

---

61. See Harold Lindsell, *The Battle for the Bible* (Grand Rapids: Zondervan, 1976), 85; another major impetus to the move was the dispensationalist theory of the inevitable apostasy of the church, typified by A. C. Gaebelein who as early as 1914 understood the doctrine of separation from the world as necessitating separation from the "worldly" church, see "The Present Day Apostasy," *The Coming Kingdom of Christ: A Stenographic Report of the Prophetic Bible Conference Held at the Moody Bible Institute of Chicago Feb. 24-27, 1914* (Chicago, 1914), 154, as quoted by Marsden, *Fundamentalism*, 127.

62. Richard F. Lovelace, *Dynamics of Spiritual Life* (Downers Grove: InterVarsity, 1979), 314.

63. This observation is related to the theme expounded by Sidney E. Mead in *The Lively Experiment* (San Francisco: Harper and Row, 1976) in regards to the rise and spread of American denominationalism. The same dynamics which allowed that "experiment" to take place afforded the Fundamentalist move outside of the denominational structure for religious free enterprise.

64. Marsden, *Fundamentalism*, 34.

65. On this organizational regrouping, see Joel A. Carpenter, "Fundamentalist Institutions and the Rise of Evangelical Protestantism, 1929-1942," *Church History* 49 (March 1980), 62-75.

66. Shelley, "Evangelicalism," *Dictionary of Christianity in America*, 415; see also Mark A. Noll, *Between Faith and Criticism: Evangelicals, Scholarship, and the Bible in America* (San Francisco: Harper and Row, 1986), 91-121.

temporary American Evangelicalism.[67] Carl F. H. Henry in *The Uneasy Conscience of Fundamentalism* (1947) warned of these excesses; nevertheless Henry still equated Fundamentalism with Evangelicalism. Later, in *Evangelical Responsibility in Contemporary Theology* (1957), Henry termed himself an Evangelical and associated Fundamentalism with a narrow-spirited polemicism.[68] Others who followed this new mindset and became significant leaders included evangelist Billy Graham,[69] Harold Ockenga, the pastor of Park Street Church in Boston, and Bernard Ramm, then a professor of philosophy at Bethel College and Seminary at St. Paul, Minnesota.[70] The formations of the National Association of Evangelicals in 1942,[71] Fuller Theological Seminary in 1947,[72] and *Christianity Today* magazine in 1956 helped to distinguish the two movements. Perhaps most decisive in the rise of Evangelicalism as a distinct movement from Fundamentalism was Billy Graham's 1957 New York City crusade. The basis of the Fundamentalist criticism of Graham involved his efforts to gain broad ecumenical support for this crusade, for Graham accepted the sponsorship of the local Protestant Council of

67. An introductory selection of the many works which give good general introductions and surveys of the history and thought of American Evangelicalism, beyond those already cited, include but are not limited to the following: Carol Flake, *Redemptorama: Culture, Politics, and the New Evangelicalism* (New York: Penguin, 1984); Douglas W. Frank, *Less Than Conquerors: How Evangelicals Entered the Twentieth Century* (Grand Rapids: Eerdmans, 1986); David E. Harrell, Jr., ed., *Varieties of Southern Evangelicalism* (Macon: Mercer University, 1981); George M. Marsden, *Understanding Fundamentalism and Evangelicalism* (Grand Rapids: Eerdmans, 1991); Ronald Nash, *Evangelicals in America: Who They Are, What They Believe* (Nashville: Abingdon, 1987); Richard Quebedeaux, *The Young Evangelicals: The Story of the Emergence of a New Generation of Evangelicals* (San Francisco: Harper and Row, 1974); Leonard I. Sweet, ed., *The Evangelical Tradition in America* (Macon: Mercer University, 1984); note especially Sweet's article, "The Evangelical Tradition in America," 1-86, which presents what is perhaps the best historiographical essay available on Evangelicalism up to 1984.

68. See Gabriel Fackre, "Carl F.H. Henry," *A Handbook of Christian Theologians*, enlarged ed., ed. by Dean G. Peerman and Martin E Marty (Nashville: Abingdon, 1984), 589, note 8.

69. On the life of Billy Graham during this period, see William Martin, *A Prophet with Honor: The Billy Graham Story* (New York: William Morrow, 1991).

70. Ramm was later Professor of Theology at the American Baptist Seminary of the West in Berkeley, California; of his many works, *After Fundamentalism* (San Francisco: Harper and Row, 1983) is perhaps his most complete attempt at moving beyond the Fundamentalist-Modernist controversy in regards to forging an Evangelical theology.

71. See James DeForest Murch, *Cooperation Without Compromise: A History of the National Association of Evangelicals* (Grand Rapids: Eerdmans, 1956), whose title speaks to the heart of much of the NAE's goal.

72. George Marsden provides an excellent history of Fuller Theological Seminary which also serves as a sequel and companion to his *Fundamentalism and American Culture* (1980) titled *Reforming Fundamentalism: Fuller Seminary and the New Evangelicalism* (Grand Rapids: Eerdmans, 1987); see also David Allan Hubbard, president of Fuller Theological Seminary, *What We Evangelicals Believe: Expositions of Christian Doctrine based on "The Statement of Faith" of Fuller Theological Seminary* (Pasadena, Ca.: Fuller Theological Seminary, 1979), a work offered in response to the charges of Harold Lindsell in *Battle for the Bible*.

Churches.[73] From this point forward the movement tended toward fragmentation as Fundamentalists separated themselves from Evangelicals. During the 1960s a related movement, the charismatic movement, added new vitality to American Evangelicalism.[74]

This new coalition gained national attention in 1976 when Jimmy Carter, a Southern Baptist and professed "born-again" Evangelical, was elected President of the United States. *Newsweek* magazine declared 1976 "The Year of the Evangelical."[75] Books such as Donald Bloesch's *The Evangelical Renaissance* (1973) and Dean M. Kelley's *Why Conservative Churches Are Growing* (1972) typified the Evangelical triumph in America.

This newfound prominence led to the desire among certain Evangelicals to shape contemporary culture and values. This was largely attempted through the political realm.[76] The late 1970s saw the formation of three organizations that would come to typify the emergence of a "Christian Right," or conservative Christian political activity which became associated with contemporary American Evangelicalism: the Christian Voice led by Gary Jarmin, the Moral Majority led by Jerry Falwell, and the (Religious) Roundtable led by Ed McAteer.[77] These groups

---

73. This split is discussed by Butler Farley Porter, Jr., "Billy Graham and the End of Evangelical Unity" (Ph.D. dissertation, University of Florida, 1976). See also Martin, *A Prophet with Honor*, 224.

74. For an introductory level discussion of the charismatic position in American Evangelicalism, see Ronald N. Nash, *Evangelicals in America*, 76-83; see also Martin E. Marty, *A Nation of Behavers*, 106-125; the cautious but sincere acceptance of charismatics by non-charismatic Evangelicals is exhibited by J. I. Packer's article, "Is the Charismatic Renewal, Seen in Many Churches Today, from God?," in the Series *Tough Questions Christians Ask*, ed. by David Neff (Wheaton: Victor Press/Christianity Today, Inc., 1989), 49-62; see also Donald W. Dayton, *Theological Roots of Pentecostalism* (Grand Rapids: Zondervan, 1988); John R. W. Stott, *Baptism and Fullness: The Work of the Holy Spirit Today* (Downers Grove: InterVarsity, 1975); Michael Green, *I Believe in the Holy Spirit* (Grand Rapids: Eerdmans, 1975); Harold B. Smith, ed., *Pentecostals from the Inside Out* (Wheaton: Victor/Christianity Today, 1990).

75. Kenneth L. Woodward with John Barnes in Texas, Laurie Lisle in New York and bureau reports, "Born Again: The Year of the Evangelical," *Newsweek* (October 25, 1976), 68-78.

76. On this, see Garry Wills, *Under God: Religion and American Politics* (New York: Simon and Schuster, 1990).

77. This relationship with politics was radically different from the older Fundamentalist attitude, which saw politics as akin to devilry, thus prompting Marsden to term this coalition "neo-fundamentalist," see George M. Marsden, "Unity and Diversity in the Evangelical Resurgence," *Altered Landscapes: Christianity in America, 1935-1985*, ed. by David W. Lotz, and others (Grand Rapids: Eerdmans, 1989), 72; see also "Fundamental Conflict on the Right," *Washington Post National Weekly Edition*, January 14, 1985, 6; Falwell defended his politicizing of Fundamentalist thought by saying "I can be true neither to my country nor my God if I separate my religious convictions from my political views," see "God and Politics," *Newsweek*, 17 September 1984, 28; for further discussion on Evangelicals and politics, see Mary Douglas and Steven M. Tipton, eds., *Religion and America: Spirituality in a Secular Age* (Boston: Beacon Press, 1982); Flake, *Redemptorama*, chapters 9-11; Neuhaus and Cromartie, eds., *Piety and Politics*; Richard John Neuhaus, *The Naked Public Square: Religion and Democracy in America* (Grand Rapids: Eerdmans, 1984); Richard V. Pierard, "The New Religious Right in American Politics," in *Evangelicalism*, ed. George Marsden, 161-174.

organized Evangelicals to support the 1980 election of Ronald Reagan to the presidency of the United States and to lend their voice to a host of issues, including school prayer, tuition tax credits, and the reversal of Supreme Court decisions such as "Roe v. Wade."[78] This politicization is still active, most notably through James Dobson and his parachurch ministry "Focus on the Family," which now publishes (under a division called "Family Research Council") a monthly newsletter titled *Washington Watch* that highlighs political concerns for Evangelicals along with instructions on how they can become actively involved in the political process.[79]

Two concerns fueled this politicization: first, an obsession, bordering on paranoia, with what was called "secular humanism."[80] Popularized as a tremendous threat to the continuing existence of Christianity by such Evangelical leaders as Francis A. Schaeffer, secular humanism was generally defined as the idea that humanity does not answer to any higher authority than humanity itself.[81] Inherent within this definition is the correlate that human beings are basically good or can become good by their own efforts. As a result, many Evangelicals understood secular

---

78. Roe v. Wade concerned legalized abortion. The issue of abortion is arguably the issue that most visibly blended right-wing politics and contemporary American Evangelicalism. For example, note the collaboration between Evangelical Francis A. Schaeffer and then Surgeon General of the United States, C. Everett Koop, for *Whatever Happened to the Human Race*, rev. ed. (Westchester, Ill.: Crossway, 1983), which argued against abortion, infanticide, and euthanasia and warned of the implications for American culture if they were not corrected; even more notable was the book by then President of the United States, Ronald Reagan, with afterwords by C. Everett Koop and Malcolm Muggeridge, *Abortion and the Conscience of the Nation* (Nashville: Thomas Nelson, 1984), a project initiated by Franky Schaeffer, son of Francis Schaeffer.

79. Dobson seems to be replacing individuals such as Jerry Falwell and even Billy Graham as the unofficial leader of Evangelical Christianity; see Peter Steinfels' "Radio Psychologist Is 'Rising Star' of Religious Right," *The Courier-Journal*, Sunday, 17 June 1990, editorial section, 1, 4; note also the recent "Williamsburg Charter," which celebrates the First Amendment's religious liberty clauses, signed on June 25, 1988, by over two hundred representatives led by Evangelical Os Guinness, executive director of the Williamsburg Charter Foundation—on this, see Samuel Rabinove, "Williamsburg Charter Fuels Debate," *The Christian Century* (November 9, 1988), 1007-1008; Kim A. Lawson, "A Fourth 'R'?," *Christianity Today* (December 9, 1988), 53.

80. See Harry Conn, *Four Trojan Horses of Humanism* (Milford, Mich.: Mott Media, 1982); Homer Duncan, *Secular Humanism: The Most Dangerous Religion in America* (Lubbock, Tex.: Missionary Crusader, 1980); James Hitchcock, *What Is Secular Humanism? Why Humanism Became Secular and How It Is Changing Our World* (Ann Arbor, Mich.: Servant Books, 1982); Robert Eugene Webber, *Secular Humanism: Threat and Challenge* (Grand Rapids: Zondervan, 1982).

81. See chapter 5 below on Schaeffer; two works by Schaeffer emphasized the danger of secular humanism in particular and heightened this interest among Evangelicals, *How Should We Then Live: The Rise and Decline of Western Thought and Culture* (Old Tappan, N. J.: Fleming H. Revell, 1976) and *A Christian Manifesto* (Westchester, Ill.: Crossway, 1981); see also the contribution to this concern among Evangelicals from Tim LaHaye, *The Battle for the Mind* (Old Tappan, N.J.: Fleming H. Revell, 1980).

humanism as that which sought to decide what was good and then to motivate humanity toward that goal without reference to God.[82]

The second concern which brought many evangelicals into the public arena was the vision of a "Christian America," perhaps popularized most widely by Evangelical authors Peter Marshall and David Manuel in *The Light and the Glory* (1977).[83] Marshall and Manuel held that America was founded as a Christian nation and flourished under the benevolent hand of divine providence, and that America's blessings will remain only as long as America is faithful to God as a nation.[84] A team of Evangelical historians attempted to lay this thesis to rest, but it is far from diminished as a popular framework for viewing American history among contemporary American Evangelicals.[85]

Contemporary American Evangelicalism

Rooted and shaped in the Reformation of the sixteenth century, the eighteenth-century Evangelical Revivals, and most recently in the controversy between Fundamentalists and Modernists, contemporary American Evangelicalism has a rich and varied history that has made definition problematic.[86] It can be concluded from the previous historical analysis that contemporary American Evangelicalism has gained its theology from the Reformation, its spirituality from eighteenth-century revivalism, and its concern for orthodoxy and intellectual engagement from the clash between Fundamentalists and Modernists in the early part of the twentieth century.[87]

---

82. The preoccupation among certain Evangelicals with "secular humanism" is not without warrant. The American Humanist Association, an organization boasting thousands, publishes the *Humanist* magazine and has issued forth *The Humanist Manifesto I* and *The Humanist Manifesto II*, ed. by Paul Kurtz (New York: Prometheus, 1973) which clearly sets forth their disbelief in God yet total enthusiasm for humanity.

83. Peter Marshall and David Manuel have since written a sequel to *The Light and the Glory* (Old Tappan, N.J.: Fleming H. Revell, 1977) titled *From Sea to Shining Sea* (Old Tappan, N.J.: Fleming H. Revell, 1986); the enormously popular writings of Francis A. Schaeffer, especially *A Christian Manifesto*, should be included in regard to the promotion of this thesis.

84. The idea of "chosenness" and special "blessing" from God has been a constant theme throughout the history of the United States, thus far from an Evangelical innovation; on this, see Conrad Cherry, ed., *God's New Israel: Religious Interpretations of American Destiny* (Englewood Cliffs, N.J.: Prentice-Hall, 1971).

85. Mark A. Noll, Nathan O. Hatch, and George M. Marsden, *The Search for Christian America*, expanded ed. (Colorado Springs: Helmers and Howard, 1989).

86. See *The Variety of American Evangelicalism*, ed. by Donald W. Dayton and Robert K. Johnston (Downers Grove: InterVarsity, 1991).

87. Note also the attempts which have been made at pulling together the various historical streams flowing into Evangelicalism in *The Evangelicals: What They Believe, Who They Are, Where They Are Changing*, ed. David F. Wells and John D. Woodbridge (Nashville: Abingdon, 1975), by George Marsden, "From Fundamentalism to Evangelicalism: A Historical Analysis," 122-142, and Sydney E. Ahlstrom, "From Puritanism to Evangelicalism: A Critical Perspective," 269-289. See also the articles by Leonard I. Sweet, "The Evangelical Tradition in America," 1-86, and Joel Carpenter, "The Fundamentalist Leaven and the Rise of an Evangelical United Front," 257-288, in *Evangelical Tradition*.

George Marsden does an admirable job of pulling the many diverse threads together in his essay "The Evangelical Denomination" which offers the following three-fold understanding of contemporary American Evangelicalism as a single phenomenon which involves the senses of (1) a conceptual unity that designates a grouping of Christians who fit a certain definition;[88] (2) an organic movement with some common traditions and experiences tending in some common directions; and (3) a transdenominational community with complicated infrastructures of institutions and persons who identify with "Evangelicalism."[89] It is in this sense that the terms *Evangelical* and *Evangelicalism* will be used throughout this study.[90]

The current state of American Evangelicalism is therefore best described as a "mosaic" or "kaleidoscope," a view shared by the Evangelical historian Timothy L. Smith, who along with his students has been working on a major collective historical study with the working title "The Evangelical Mosaic."[91] The major participants in the mosaic include: (1) Evangelical denominations;[92] and (2) parachurch organiza-

---

88. For example, Evangelical Christians typically emphasize the Reformation doctrine of the final authority of Scripture; the real, historical character of God's saving work recorded in Scripture; eternal salvation only through personal trust in Christ; the importance of evangelism and missions; and the importance of a spiritually transformed life.

89. George M. Marsden, "The Evangelical Denomination" in *Evangelicalism in Modern America*, vii-xix; another excellent source for determining Evangelical convictions is the covenant signed by approximately three thousand Evangelicals who gathered at Lausanne, Switzerland, in July 1974 for the Lausanne Congress on World Evangelization; see Shelley, "Evangelicalism," 416, and also E. A. Wilson, "International Congress on World Evangelization" (Lausanne, Switzerland, 1974)," 578-579, in *Dictionary of Christianity in America.*

90. Some have objected to the self-conscious use of the term *Evangelical* for one particular group within Christianity due to the rich, biblical history of the term. One such plaintiff has been Martin E. Marty, who, in his own words, has "only grudgingly yielded them their chosen designation" out of "sociological necessity"; see *Nation of Behavers*, 88; Donald W. Dayton, noting the variety within contemporary American Evangelicalism, advocates "giving up the word entirely," see "An Interview with Donald W. Dayton," *Faith and Thought* 1 (Spring 1983), 25.

91. Timothy L. Smith, "The Evangelical Kaleidoscope and the Call to Christian Unity," *Christian Scholar's Review* 15/2 (1986), 125-140; see Marsden, *Evangelicalism*, "Introduction: The Evangelical Denomination," viii and note 3, 175.

92. Bruce L. Shelley has identified at least seven Evangelical traditions in his article "Evangelicalism" in *Dictionary of Christianity in America*, 416: (1) Evangelicals in the Reformation tradition, primarily Lutheran and Reformed Christians; (2) Wesleyan Evangelicals, such as the Church of the Nazarene; (3) Pentecostal and charismatic Evangelicals, such as the Assemblies of God; (4) Black Evangelicals with their own distinctive witness to the gospel; (5) the counter-culture churches (sometimes called Peace Churches), such as the Evangelical Quakers and Mennonites; (6) several traditionally white Southern denominations, such as the Southern Baptists; (7) the spiritual heirs of Fundamentalism found in independent churches and many parachurch agencies.

tions.[93] Current estimates list up to twenty thousand separate para-church groups in America alone, including four of the ten largest Protestant missionary organizations in terms of staff and finances.[94] Parachurch organizations should be further categorized, thus creating the additional groupings: (3) the "Electronic Church;"[95] (4) Evangelical mission organizations;[96] (5) Evangelical publishing companies;[97] and (6)

---

93. Maurice Smith in his article "Parachurch Movements," *Missions USA* (October-December 1984), 145-149, has determined five types of parachurch groups: (1) tertiary organizations which promote a particular belief, such as Pentecostalism by the Full Gospel Businessman's Fellowship; (2) theme or role-oriented organizations which work with a particular theme, such as American Bible Society, Bread for the World, and Gideons International; (3) Evangelistic or missionary organizations such as Campus Crusade for Christ and the hundreds of missionary organizations; (4) media-oriented groups which make up what is often called the "Electronic Church;" and (5) spiritual growth centers, in which he places a number of Christian, sub-Christian, and/or non-Christian groups, including New Age organizations; this aspect of Evangelicalism must not be overlooked, for as Ronald Nash has written, "nowhere is Evangelicalism's transdenominational character more apparent than in its many parachurch organizations," *Evangelicals*, 30.

94. See Jerry White, *The Church and the Parachurch: An Uneasy Marriage* (Portland: Multnomah, 1983); Ron Wilson, "Parachurch: Becoming Part of the Body," *Christianity Today*, 24 (19 September 1980), 18; J. Alan Youngren, "Parachurch Proliferation: The Frontier Spirit Caught in Traffic," *Christianity Today*, 25 (6 November 1981), 6.

95. For example, the Christian Broadcasting Network (CBN), which according to a 1984 University of Pennsylvania study, is in 30 million homes with 13 million individuals watching Christian television regularly; see Richard N. Ostling, "Evangelical Publishing and Broadcasting," *Evangelicalism*, ed. Marsden, 46-55; Naisbitt and Aburdene; report in *Megatrends 2000*, 279-280, that before the publicizing of his affair with a prostitute, Jimmy Swaggart had broadcast in 140 countries weekly and in fifteen different languages. See also Stewart M. Hoover, *Mass Media Religion: The Social Sources of the Electronic Church* (Newbury Park: Sage Publications, 1988); Quentin Schultze, ed., *American Evangelicals and the Mass Media* (Grand Rapids: Academie/Zondervan, 1990); Quentin Schultze, *Televangelism and American Culture: The Business of Popular Religion* (Grand Rapids: Baker, 1991); Peter J. Daly, "Keeping the Faith in High-Tech America: Does Communion Over Cable TV Still Count?," *The Washington Post National Weekly Edition* (September 12-18, 1988), 21-22.

96. For example, the Wycliffe Bible Translators. On Evangelicals and missions, see Joel A. Carpenter and Wilbert R. Shenk, eds., *Earthen Vessels: American Evangelicals and Foreign Missions, 1880-1980* (Grand Rapids: Eerdmans, 1990); see Nash, *Evangelicals*, 33-34; one of the first products of the National Association of Evangelicals was the Evangelical Foreign Missionary Association; see Murch, *Cooperation Without Compromise*, 196, 202-203.

97. Examples of Evangelical publishers would include Zondervan, Word, Tyndale, Baker, and InterVarsity; as of 1986, there were 3,500 members of the Christian Booksellers Association; major Evangelical periodicals include *Christianity Today* and *Moody Monthly*; on this, see Ostling, "Evangelical Publishing," *Evangelicalism*, ed. Marsden, 46-55; Naisbitt and Aburdene report in *Megatrends 2000*, 292, that in 1987 alone sales among Christian booksellers topped $1.5 billion.

Evangelical colleges and seminaries.[98]

While organizational unity may be problematic as a result of the many denominations and parachurch organizations within the Evangelical mosaic, theological unity has been sought among Evangelicals, most recently in May, 1989.[99] Other affirmations of unity have been posited in "The Chicago Call" and "The Chicago Statement on Biblical Inerrancy," two documents put forth by groups of leading Evangelicals in an effort to sharpen Evangelical identity and foster Evangelical unity.[100]

Evangelicals will continue to wrestle with self-identity, as will all religious groups. Much of the conversation regarding what it means to be an Evangelical in the modern world will revolve around the crucial issue of the nature of truth.

---

98. Denominational Evangelical colleges and seminaries include Calvin College (The Christian Reformed Church), Trinity College and Trinity Evangelical Divinity School (The Evangelical Free Church), and Bethel College and Seminary (Baptist General Conference); non-denominational colleges and seminaries include Wheaton College, Gordon College and Gordon-Conwell Theological Seminary, Fuller Theological Seminary, Dallas Theological Seminary, and Westminster Theological Seminary. The fastest growing school is Jerry Falwell's Liberty University (formerly Liberty Baptist College) in Lynchburg, Virginia; see William C. Ringenberg, *The Christian College: A History of Protestant Higher Education in America* (Grand Rapids: Eerdmans and Christian University Press, 1984); Nash, *Evangelicals*, 37-38.

99. The affirmations put forth by this conference, including the various papers which were presented during the gathering, can be found in *Evangelical Affirmations*, ed. by Kenneth S. Kantzer and Carl F. H. Henry (Grand Rapids: Academie/Zondervan, 1990).

100. The "Chicago Call," representing eight themes in its final form, was the result of a gathering in Chicago, Illinois, of forty-five Evangelicals in May of 1977. A much larger group of Evangelicals put forth "The Chicago Statement on Biblical Inerrancy," under the organizational title "The International Council on Biblical Inerrancy," which first met in October of 1978. The "Chicago Statement" can be found in Ronald Youngblood, ed., *Evangelicals and Inerrancy* (Nashville: Thomas Nelson, 1984), 230-239, and Lewis Drummond, *The Word of the Cross* (Nashville: Broadman, 1992.) The "Chicago Call" can be found in *The Orthodox Evangelicals: Who They Are and What They Are Saying*, Robert E. Webber and Donald G. Bloesch, (Nashville: Thomas Nelson, 1978), 12-13.

Chapter Three

EVANGELICALS AND THE QUESTION OF TRUTH

The subject of truth has arguably been the fundamental concern for Evangelicals from the onset of their existence.[1] A self-conscious attempt by a group of Evangelicals to describe themselves opens with the following quotation from Blaise Pascal's *Pensees*: "Truth is so obscure in these times, and falsehood so established, that unless we love the truth, we cannot know it."[2] The quotation reflects the essence of Evangelical theology: from their perspective Evangelicals both love and possess the truth in a way distinctive from other faith traditions. Clark Pinnock writes that the goal of such conservative theology is to "give an authoritative and binding definition of God's truth in propositional form" and to

---

1. The best survey of the foundational roots of contemporary American Evangelicalism is George M. Marsden's *Fundamentalism and American Culture*; see also Douglas Jacobsen, "From Truth to Authority to Responsibility: The Shifting Focus of Evangelical Hermeneutics, 1915-1986 (Part I)," *TSF Bulletin*, vol. 10, no. 4 (March-April 1987), 8-15.

2. David F. Wells and John D. Woodbridge, eds. *The Evangelicals: What They Believe, Who They Are, Where They Are Changing* (Nashville: Abingdon, 1975).

teach "essential, fundamental truth that does not change in the midst of changing times."[3]

The thesis to be explored in this study is that the concept of truth in contemporary American Evangelical theology is largely the correspondence theory of truth, which understands truth to be that which corresponds with fact and is both objective and absolute. In other words, if a particular statement corresponds with the actual state of affairs, then that statement is "true."

While most Evangelicals would agree with a correspondence understanding of truth—that is, the truth of the Christian faith lies in its agreement with reality—great disagreement has risen on the nature of that correspondence. Some Evangelicals are "evidentialists;" they see value in supporting the claims of faith with specific evidences for external corroboration. This correspondence, to one degree or another, must be established by external verification. Biblical support for such a view is often found in such passages as John 5:36 and 1 Corinthians 15:17. The alternative school of thought is most often termed "presuppositional," and, as the name implies, this perspective views presuppositions as the decisive factor. Rather than establishing the truth of Christianity through external evidences, presuppositionalists maintain that facts cannot be interpreted apart from a conceptual worldview which dictates understanding and meaning. For their support, passages such as John 3:3; Romans 1:18-21, and 1 Corinthians 2:14 are often cited.

Beyond the divide over evidentialism and presuppositionalism, Evangelicals are also struggling with the issue of truth in terms of biblical inerrancy. Sociologist James Davison Hunter's study of the coming generation of American Evangelicalism has revealed that the theory of biblical inerrancy has "softened" and that the majority of those Evangelicals surveyed felt that some assertions in the biblical materials "were intended by the author to be historical or scientific in nature but may in fact be mistaken or contradictory."[4] Perhaps even more noteworthy is Hunter's discovery of growing support for the neo-orthodox positionthat advocates a subjectivist approach to bibli-

---

3. Clark Pinnock, *Tracking the Maze: Finding Our Way through Modern Theology from an Evangelical Perspective* (San Francisco: Harper and Row, 1990), 33.

4. James Davison Hunter, *Evangelicalism: The Coming Generation* (Chicago: University of Chicago, 1987), 23-25; see also Robert Brow's "Evangelical Megashift," *Christianity Today* (February 19, 1990), 12-17, which was accompanied by responses from Donald Carson, Clark Pinnock, David Wells, Robert Webber, and Donald Bloesch; also to be noted are the noteworthy changes in English Evangelicalism, as discussed by David Neff and George K. Brushaber in "The Remaking of English Evangelicalism," *Christianity Today* (February 5, 1990), 25-36.

cal interpretation as opposed to Evangelical theology's traditional objectivist approach.[5]

One of the more celebrated examples of this transition in Evangelical theology was Clark Pinnock's *The Scripture Principle* (1984). An Evangelical who had argued passionately for biblical inerrancy in previous publications,[6] Pinnock in this work departed from inerrancy while holding to the Bible's trustworthiness and authority.[7] Pinnock concluded that those who hold to inerrancy are "elevating reason over Scripture at that point."[8] His own description of his evolution is one that goes beyond Modernism and Fundamentalism to a form of postmodern orthodoxy.[9] Though Pinnock's epistemological transition has yet to attract a wide following within Evangelical theology, many now adjust the definitional meaning of biblical inerrancy to preserve its vibrancy in the face of such concerns.[10]

It would appear that those who embrace Evangelical theology have three choices: first, they can maintain previous conceptualizations of truth as correspondence; second, they can abandon that view completely for another conceptualization; or third, they can strive for a synthesis between the correspondence theory and views which take into

---

5. Hunter, *Evangelicalism*, 27; Hunter notes that the trend is toward "an accommodation of varying degrees to modern epistemology—philosophical rationalism, even shades of positivism" (46); Hunter makes the assessment that for the coming generation of Evangelicals, "religious truth devolves to religious opinion. The reality has been de-objectified" (47); see also Richard Quebedeaux, *The Young Evangelicals: The Story of the Emergence of a New Generation of Evangelicals* (San Francisco: Harper and Row, 1974), especially his chapter titled "Revolution in Orthodoxy," 73-135; note also Bernard Ramm, "Contemporary Divisions Among Evangelicals," in *The Evangelical Heritage* (Waco: Word, 1973), 137-140.

6. For example, see *A Defense of Biblical Infallibility* (Philadelphia: Presbyterian and Reformed, 1967) and *Biblical Revelation, the Foundation of Christian Theology* (Chicago: Moody, 1971).

7. See Rex A. Koivisto, "Clark Pinnock and Inerrancy: A Change in Truth Theory?," *Journal of the Evangelical Theological Society*, vol. 24, no. 2 (June 1981), 139-152, which concluded that Pinnock's concept of truth has changed from that of correspondence to a pragmatic theory of truth; this was followed by a cordial but ambiguous response from Pinnock, "A Response to Rex A. Koivisto," 153-156.

8. Clark H. Pinnock, *The Scripture Principle* (San Francisco: Harper and Row, 1984), 58.

9. See Pinnock's *Tracking the Maze: Finding Our Way through Modern Theology from an Evangelical Perspective* (San Francisco: Harper and Row, 1990).

10. The carefully delineated expression of biblical inerrancy found in such documents as the "Chicago Statement on Biblical Inerrancy" reflects this mindset, as does cautiously worded definitions such as the one David Dockery offers in "The Divine-Human Authorship of Inspired Scripture" in *Authority and Interpretation*, ed. Duane A. Garrett and Richard R. Melick, Jr. (Grand Rapids: Baker, 1987), 38-39; note also the recent Evangelical attention given to the reliability of language, observed by Mark A. Noll in *Between Faith and Criticism: Evangelicals, Scholarship, and the Bible in America* (San Francisco: Harper and Row, 1986), 148 and 233 note 10, as something that used to be a widely shared presupposition but is now carefully justified.

account the dynamics of such issues as an individual personal horizon and context.[11]

The choice from among these three options will have a decisive impact on Evangelical theology. The correspondence theory of truth is what lies behind the theory of inerrancy as the model for understanding the relationship between inspiration and Scripture; this theory gives Evangelical theology much of its distinctiveness.[12] In his exploration of the Evangelical subculture in America, Randall Balmer notes that those at Dallas Theological Seminary believe that the intellectual case for Evangelical theology "rests to a remarkable degree on the twin pillars of biblical inerrancy" and "of dispensational premillenialism."[13]

Ronald Nash rightly points out that it was in "conscious reaction to the neo-orthodox repudiation of revelation as a vehicle for truth or information" that Evangelical theologians like Gordon Clark, Cornelius Van Til, Carl F. H. Henry, Edward J. Carnell, and Kenneth Kantzer "began to emphasize the cognitive dimensions of God's revelation."[14] As a result, it would seem appropriate to begin this study with one of these foundational Evangelicals, Cornelius Van Til, who held to Scripture as a vehicle for truth.

---

11. All contemporary theologians have been forced to wrestle with the work of Hans-Georg Gadamer, who argued in *Wahrheit und Methode* that understanding is always interpretation in a "fusion of horizons" (Tubingen: J. C. B. Mohr, 1960); on this, see Josef Bleicher, *Contemporary Hermeneutics: Hermeneutics as Method, Philosophy and Critique* (London: Routledge and Kegan Paul, 1980), 108-140.

12. Stanley Obitts, "A Philosophical Analysis of Certain Assumptions of the Doctrine of the Inerrancy of the Bible," *Journal of the Evangelical Theological Society*, vol. 26, no. 2 (June 1983), 129-136; John Feinberg, "Truth, Meaning and Inerrancy in Contemporary Evangelical Thought," *Journal of the Evangelical Theological Society*, vol. 26, no. 1 (March 1983), 17-30; P. D. Feinberg, "The Meaning of Inerrancy," 287ff., and Norman L. Geisler, "Philosophical Presuppositions of Biblical Errancy," 307-334, *Inerrancy*, ed. N. L. Geisler (Grand Rapids: Zondervan, 1979); see the "Chicago Statement on Biblical Inerrancy," in *Evangelicals and Inerrancy*, ed. Ronald Youngblood (Nashville: Thomas Nelson, 1984), 230-239; see also Norman Geisler, "The Concept of Truth in the Inerrancy Debate," *Bibliotheca Sacra*, vol. 137, no. 548 (October-December 1980), 327-339; Nathan O. Hatch and Mark A. Noll, eds., *The Bible in America: Essays in Cultural History* (Oxford: Oxford University Press, 1982); Kern Robert Trembath, *Evangelical Theories of Biblical Inspiration: A Review and Proposal* (New York and Oxford: Oxford University, 1987).

13. Randall Balmer, *Mine Eyes Have Seen the Glory: A Journey into the Evangelical Subculture* (New York: Oxford University, 1989), 32.

14. Ronald H. Nash, "Truth by Any Other Name," *Christianity Today* (October 7, 1977), 17-23; note also the recent trend away from common sense rebuttals of various modernisms in the work of Paul Helm, Carl F. H. Henry, Alvin Plantinga, Anthony Thiselton, Nicholas Wolterstorff, and members of the recently established Society of Christian Philosophers, as mentioned in Mark Noll's *Between Faith and Criticism*, 147, 233 note 7.

Chapter Four

Truth and Presupposition: Cornelius Van Til

Cornelius Van Til was an Evangelical scholar in the Dutch Reformed tradition.[1] He is perhaps best known as a presuppositional apologist, one who felt that God's truth as revealed in Scripture is the necessary presupposition for any coherent system of thought.[2] Thus the best

---

1. While Van Til has been the main exponent of Dutch Reformed theology in America, Herman Dooyeweerd has served as its main representative on the European front as Professor of the Philosophy of Law at the Free University of Amsterdam; for the essence of his thought, known as the Philosophy of the Cosmonomic Law-Idea, see his *A New Critique of Theoretical Thought*, Eng. trans. in 4-vols. by David H. Freeman, and others (Amsterdam: H. J. Paris and Presbyterian and Reformed Publishing Company, 1953-58); note also the work of Gordon H. Clark on the American scene who argues for a form of deductive presuppositionalism, represented in such works as *A Christian View of Men and Things* (Grand Rapids: Eerdmans, 1952); *Thales to Dewey* (Boston: Houghton, Mifflin, 1956); and *Religion, Reason and Revelation* (Philadelphia: Presbyterian and Reformed, 1961).

2. The term "apologist" refers to the subject of apologetics, which is the enterprise of intellectually defending the Christian faith. A good introduction to Van Til's views on apologetics can be found in Jim Halsey's *For Such a Time as This: An Introduction to the Reformed Apologetic of Cornelius Van Til* (Phillipsburg, N.J.: Presbyterian and Reformed, 1976).

approach to articulating and defending the Christian faith was not through external evidence but through presenting Christianity's preeminence as a presupposed system of thought. J. Frame has contended that Van Til's presuppositional apologetic can be reduced to two primary assertions: (1) that human beings are obligated to presuppose God in all of their thinking, and (2) that unbelievers resist this obligation in every aspect of thought and life.[3] Van Til's system of thought continues to be a significant shaping influence on the academic life of Westminster Theological Seminary in Philadelphia, Pennsylvania, where he served as Professor of Apologetics until his retirement in 1975.

Biographical Background

Cornelius Van Til was born into a large family at Grootegast, The Netherlands, on May 3, 1895.[4] His family, devout Calvinists, immigrated to America in 1905 when Van Til was ten years old. On the basis of this immigration and subsequent citizenship Van Til, though born in The Netherlands, can be considered an American Evangelical.

The Van Til family chose to settle in Highland, Indiana, near the border of Illinois and the city of Chicago, where they supported themselves through farming. Van Til and his family were members of the Christian Reformed Church in North America, a small Reformed denomination, primarily of Dutch descent and centered in the Midwest. The Christian Reformed Church stresses the following: (1) heartfelt conversion and piety, although cast in covenantal rather than revivalistic terms; (2) confessionalism and orthodoxy as set by its three standards—the Belgic

---

3. See J. Frame, "Van Til and the Ligonier Apologetic," *Westminster Theological Journal* 47 (1985), 282; H. M. Conn, "Cornelius Van Til," *Dictionary of Christianity in America*, ed. Daniel G. Reid, Robert D. Linder, Bruce L. Shelley, and Harry S. Stout (Downers Grove: Intervarsity, 1990), 1211-1212; see also John C. Whitcomb, "Contemporary Apologetics and the Christian Faith, Part 1: Human Limitations in Apologetics," *Bibliotheca Sacra* (April-June 1977), 99-107.

4. Good introductory biographical articles on Cornelius Van Til can be found in D. F. Kelly's "Cornelius Van Til," *New Dictionary of Theology*, ed. Sinclair B. Ferguson, David F. Wright, and J. I. Packer (Downers Grove: InterVarsity, 1988), 704-705; Conn, "Cornelius Van Til," *Dictionary of Christianity in America*, ed. Daniel G. Reid, Robert D. Linder, Bruce L. Shelley, and Harry S. Stout (Downers Grove: InterVarsity, 1990), 1211-1212; Wesley A. Roberts, "Cornelius Van Til," *Reformed Theology in America: A History of Its Modern Development*, ed. D. Wells (Grand Rapids: Eerdmans, 1985), later published as *Dutch Reformed Theology* (Grand Rapids: Baker, 1989); in-depth treatments of Van Til's life and thought include J. Frame, *Van Til the Theologian* (Chattanooga: Pilgrim Publishing Co., 1976); E. R. Geehan, ed., *Jerusalem and Athens: Critical Discussions on the Philosophy and Apologetics of Cornelius Van Til* (Philipsburg, N.J.: Presbyterian and Reformed Publishing Co., 1971); Gary North, ed., *Foundations of Christian Scholarship: Essays in the Van Til Perspective* (Vallecito: Ross House Books, 1976); T. Notaro, *Van Til and the Use of Evidence* (Philipsburg, N.J.: Craig, 1980); D. Vickers, *Cornelius Van Til and the Theologian's Theological Stance* (Wilmington, Del.: Cross 1976); W. White, *Van Til, Defender of the Faith* (Nashville: Thomas Nelson, 1979).

confession (1561), the Heidelberg Catechism (1563), and the Canons of the Synod of Dort (1619); and (3) Christian cultural engagement. This final emphasis was most clearly articulated by the Dutch neo-Calvinist forbear Abraham Kuyper.[5]

As a result of his family's affiliation with the Christian Reformed Church, Van Til chose to attend Calvin College in Grand Rapids, Michigan, where he graduated with an B.A. degree. This was followed with a Th.M from Princeton Theological Seminary and a Ph.D. from Princeton University. At Princeton Theological Seminary he studied under such individuals as Geerhardus Vos, Casper W. Hodge, Robert Dick Wilson, Oswald T. Allis, and J. Gresham Machen. Van Til's Princeton education was also strongly influenced by B. B. Warfield,[6] Abraham Kuyper, and Herman Bavinck. Van Til has often been criticized for taking his systematic theology too uncritically from both Warfield and Bavinck.[7] In 1925 Van Til married a long-time friend, Rene Klooster (d. 1978), from his home-town in Indiana. Two years later Van Til was ordained by the Spring Lake Church of Classis Muskegon in Michigan, a Christian Reformed church which also called him to serve as their pastor. This position proved to be Van Til's first and only pastorate. Van Til accepted this call and spent one year in this role before accepting a position as Instructor of Apologetics in Princeton Theological Seminary (1928-1929). At the end of one year, Van Til was elected Professor of Apologetics in Princeton Theological Seminary by its Board of Directors. This election was not confirmed by the 1929 General Assembly due to the Assembly-authorized reorganization of the seminary. Princeton Theological Seminary was reorganized under what was perceived as a theologically more liberal board of directors, leading to the resignation of Robert Dick Wilson, Oswald T. Allis, and J. Gresham Machen. The new Board of Control asked Van Til to remain at Princeton, but he instead chose the position of Professor of Apologetics in the newly-formed Westminster Theologi-

---

5. On the Christian Reformed Church, see J. D. Bratt, "Christian Reformed Church in North America," *Dictionary of Christianity in America*, 259-260; J. D. Bratt, *Dutch Calvinism in Modern America* (Grand Rapids: Eerdmans, 1984); P. De Klerk and R. R. De Ridder, eds., *Perspectives on the Christian Reformed Church* (Grand Rapids: Baker, 1983); John H. Kromminga, *The Christian Reformed Church: A Study in Orthodoxy* (Grand Rapids: Baker, 1949).

6. Van Til later wrote an introduction to Warfield's *The Inspiration and Authority of the Bible* (Phillipsburg, N.J.: Presbyterian and Reformed, 1948), 8-68, though he disagreed with Warfield and the Princeton School of Theology in regards to the relation of systematic theology to apologetics; see Van Til's *An Introduction to Systematic Theology* (Philipsburg, N.J.: Presbyterian and Reformed Publishing Co., copyright den Dulk Christian Foundation, 1974), 2ff.

7. Edmund P. Clowney, "Preaching the Word of the Lord: Cornelius Van Til, V.D.M.," *Westminster Theological Journal* 46 (1984), 249.

cal Seminary in Philadelphia, Pennsylvania,[8] which vowed to carry on the conservative Reformed tradition of "Old Princeton." Van Til was instrumental in altering "Old" Princeton's tradition of evidentialism and commitment to the Scottish Philosophy of Common Sense to that of pre-suppositionalism.[9]

Van Til joined the Orthodox Presbyterian Church[10] shortly after its founding on June 11, 1936, as a result of the conflict at Princeton. J. Gresham Machen, along with several other professors, had left Princeton Theological Seminary to found Westminster Theological Seminary on the grounds that Princeton and the Presbyterian Church (USA) had departed from historic Christianity.

Van Til remained at Westminster Theological Seminary until his retirement in 1975. In 1987, Cornelius Van Til died at the age of ninety-two.

Description of Van Til's Concept of Truth

The concept of truth in the theology of Cornelius Van Til is rooted in his reformed presuppositionalism.[11] His concept can perhaps best be phrased in terms of "self-authenticating biblical claims" with all knowledge understood in terms of "analogy." Van Til's framework of truth is that which corresponds (from the human perspective only analogically) to God's truth as revealed in Scripture. The criteria of truth is that of coherence in that Christianity is the only framework that both gives rise

---

8. On this, see W. A. Hoffecker, "Princeton Theology," *Dictionary of Christianity in America*, 941-942; W. A. Hoffecker, *Piety and the Princeton Theologians* (Philipsburg, N.J.: Presbyterian and Reformed and Grand Rapids: Baker, 1981); Mark A. Noll, "The Founding of Princeton Seminary," *Westminster Theological Journal* 42 (Fall 1979), 72-110; Mark A. Noll, ed., *The Princeton Theology 1812-1921* (Grand Rapids: Baker, 1983); Mark Noll, "The Princeton Theology," *The Princeton Theology*, ed. David F. Wells (Grand Rapids: Baker, 1989), 30; J.C. VanderStelt, *Philosophy and Scripture: A Study in Old Princeton and Westminster Theology* (Marlton, N.J.: Mack, 1978); David F. Wells, *Reformed Theology in America* (Grand Rapids: Eerdmans, 1985), partially republished later as *The Princeton Theology* (Grand Rapids: Baker, 1989).

9. Evidentialism is a term which refers to a theory of apologetics that believes that the claims of the Christian faith should be verified by external evidence, such as historical and scientific evidence. Rather than appeal to the Christian faith as a presupposition, evidentialists believe that the common ground of evidence—available to the believer and the non-believer—is the place to begin.

10. On this, see S. T. Logan, "Orthodox Presbyterian Church," *Dictionary of Christianity in America*, 849; C. G. Dennison, ed., *The Orthodox Presbyterian Church, 1936-1986* (Philadelphia: Committee for the Historian of the Orthodox Presbyterian Church, 1986); C. G. Dennison and R. C. Gamble, eds., *Pressing Toward the Mark: Essays Commemorating Fifty Years of the Orthodox Presbyterian Church* (Philadelphia: Orthodox Presbyterian Church, 1986); Ned B. Stonehouse, *J. Gresham Machen: A Biographical Memoir*, 3rd ed. (Carlisle, Pa.: Banner of Truth Trust, 1987, copyright Westminster Theological Seminary), 446-508; White, *Defender of the Faith*, 111-118.

11. As Vickers comments in *Theologian's Theological Stance*, "Van Til's theology had to be what it is because his epistemology is what it is," 10.

to facts and adequately offers explanation for those facts. As Weaver has observed, "the common definition of truth, that truth is characteristic of propositions which correctly represent a state of affairs seems to fit well with the system of Cornelius Van Til."[12]

Van Til wrote that the "ultimate test for the relevancy of our hypotheses is therefore their correspondence with God's interpretation of facts."[13] Yet Van Til sought to avoid a correspondence concept of truth that allowed correspondence between an object and an idea and gave independent significance to either one.[14] Rather, both are part of a system of reality which must be presupposed before knowledge of any of the parts can be made known.[15] Van Til still wanted to define his system as correspondence, however, on the basis that it was a concept inherent with the presupposition of the truth of the system.[16] For example, when asked how he knew that what he believed was true, Van Til replied: "I am sure of my faith because its source is the Bible, the revealed Word of God."[17] To understand Van Til's concept of truth, therefore, is to understand his emphasis on presuppositional apologetics.

Emphasis on Presuppositional Apologetics

Presuppositionalism can be defined as the mandatory establishment of a particular world view or conceptual framework which is then used to approach and interpret all of reality.[18] As a result, "facts" as common

---

12. Gilbert B. Weaver, "The Concept of Truth in the Apologetic Systems of Gordon Haddon Clark and Cornelius Van Til" (Ph.D. dissertation, Grace Theological Seminary, 1967), 6.

13. Cornelius Van Til, *Christian-Theistic Evidences* (Philadelphia: Class Syllablus, Westminster Theological Seminary, 1961), 62; compare Gordon H. Lewis, *Testing Christianity's Truth Claims: Approaches to Christian Apologetics* (Chicago: Moody, 1976), 21.

14. Scott Oliphint, "The Consistency of Van Til's Methodology," *Westminster Theological Journal* vol. 52, no. 1 (Spring 1990), 35.

15. Cornelius Van Til, *A Survey of Christian Epistemology* (Nutley, N.J.: Presbyterian and Reformed, 1977), 4; this work is a retitled reprint of Van Til's 1932 *The Metaphysics of Apologetics*.

16. Van Til, *A Survey*, 2; see also Cornelius Van Til, "God and the Absolute" (Ph.D. diss., Princeton University, 1927), 37.

17. Cornelius Van Til as recorded by David E. Kucharsky, "At the Beginning, God: An Interview with Cornelius Van Til," *Christianity Today* (December 30, 1977), 415.

18. Van Til's most comprehensive presentation of presuppositional apologetics can be found in chapters 9 and 10 of *Defense of the Faith*, 3rd ed. (Philipsburg, N.J.: Presbyterian and Reformed Publishing Co., 1967). The 1967 paperback edition omits much of the debate between Van Til and other Christian Reformed authors found in the 1955 edition; Van Til was influenced along these lines methodologically by Calvin whose theological methodology was exegetical rather than speculative, leading Bernard Ramm to classify Calvin as the "god-father" of Van Til's system, see *Types of Apologetic Systems* (Wheaton: Van Kampen Press, 1953), 184. Ramm revised this work under the title *Varieties of Christian Apologetics* (Grand Rapids: Baker, 1962) where John Calvin was substituted for Van Til and Abraham Kuyper was inserted for Edward John Carnell under the section titled "Systems Stressing Revelation."

denominators of discourse are subordinate to an ultimate referent which makes those "facts" intelligible. Van Til writes:

> The method of reasoning by presupposition may be said to be indirect rather than direct. The issue between believers and non-believers in Christian theism cannot be settled by a direct appeal to "facts" or "laws" whose nature and significance is already agreed upon by both parties to the debate. The question is rather as to what is the final reference point required to make the "facts" and "laws" intelligible. The question is as to what the "facts" and "laws" really are. Are they what the non-Christian methodology assumes that they are? Are they what the Christian theistic methodology presupposes they are?[19]

Van Til asserts that the Christian faith cannot be defended apart from presuppositions derived from the Christian faith. Inherent within such a perspective is the corollary that one must therefore challenge the presuppositions of unbelief.[20] For Van Til, given anything that is meaningful "one can provide an account of the fact that it is possible only on the foundation of God's revelation in Jesus Christ, as witnessed by the Scriptures."[21]

As mentioned, two assertions are integral to Van Til's call for presuppositionalism: (1) the Creator-creature distinction that demands that human beings presuppose the self-attesting triune God in all their thinking; and (2) the reality that unbelievers will resist this obligation in every aspect of life and thought. The rationale for his presuppositionalism can be found in his view of the total depravity of humanity, a depravity which includes both human thought and reason. In light of this depravity the presupposition of the truth of Scripture over and against the knowledge of humanity is necessary to avoid surrendering the sovereignty of God. The actual presuppositions that Van Til asserts can be placed in two categories: (1) epistemological presuppositions; and (2) metaphysical presuppositions.[22]

Epistemological Presupposition. Epistemology is the branch of philosophy that concerns itself with human knowledge. Essentially, the epistemological question is "how do we know?" Therefore epistemological questions are raised as to which standard should be used in gaining knowledge and how decisions should be made about that knowledge.

---

19. Van Til, *Defense*, 100.

20. Robert D. Knudsen, "The Transcendental Perspective of Westminster's Apologetic," *Westminster Theological Journal* 48 (1986), 227; Knudsen rightly points out that today there is a wide spectrum of presuppositional apologetic noting that Van Til and the Westminster presuppositional apologetic is marked by its radicalness in regards to its beginnings and systematic formulation.

21. Knudsen, "Transcendental Perspective," 228.

22. Van Til states in *Defense* that to argue by presupposition "is to indicate what are the epistemological and metaphysical principles that underlie and control one's method," 99.

For Van Til, "no proposition about historical fact is presented for what it really is till (sic) it is presented as part of the system of Christian theism that is contained in Scripture."[23] The "self-attesting Christ of Scripture" is therefore the starting point for Van Til's entire system of thought.[24] The absolute truth and authority of Scripture is presupposed as a conceptual framework by which all discussion is framed and all knowledge is generated. Scripture is therefore the foundation of all knowledge.[25] The Reformed apologist, writes Van Til, must hold both "to the idea of absolute system and to that of genuine historic fact and historicity;" they must believe "truths of fact" because they are "truths of reason."[26] The truths of fact presented in Scripture must be what Scripture portrays them to be or else they are "irrational and meaningless altogether."[27]No true or meaningful knowledge exists outside of the knowledge of God, which is the only true knowledge available. Therefore the Bible is true because the Bible asserts its truthfulness.

On the nature of this truthfulness, Van Til affirms such ideas regarding the Bible as "fact," "absolute truth," "infallible," "verbal inspiration," "infallibly inspired," and "inerrant."[28] In regard to "apparent contradictions" in Scripture, Van Til would assert that these are only "seeming" contradictions, solved in God's omniscience.[29]

As a result, Van Til follows both Kuyper and Bavinck in stressing that Scripture is the objective principle of knowledge for the Christian.[30] He writes,

---

23. Van Til, *Defense*, 115.

24. Van Til, "My Credo," *Jerusalem and Athens*, 3; see also James M. Grier, Jr., "The Apologetical Value of the Self-Witness of Scripture," *Grace Theological Journal* (1980), 71-76.

25. Van Til stressed God's general revelation as well as God's special revelation, but rejected natural theology on the basis that it built a foundation for theology apart from the Bible; see Clowney, "Preaching the Word of the Lord," 251.

26. Van Til, *Defense*, 117; William S. Sailer in "Reformed Apologetics Revisited," *Evangelical Journal* 2 (1984), 23, notes that Van Til's contention that such convictions are necessary to be truly "reformed" is contested by a number of Reformed thinkers including J.O. Buswell and John H. Gerstner; for Buswell, see *A Christian View of Being and Knowing* (Grand Rapids: Zondervan, 1960); for Gerstner, see *Reasons for Faith* (Grand Rapids: Baker, 1967); compare Norman Geisler, *Christian Apologetics* (Grand Rapids: Baker, 1976), 7.

27. Van Til, *Defense*, 117.

28. On this, see chapter 12 of *Introduction to Systematic Theology*, Class Syllabus, Westminster Theological Seminary (Phillipsburg, N.J.: Presbyterian and Reformed, copyright den Dulk Christian Foundation, 1974); see also the second chapter of Van Til's *A Christian Theory of Knowledge* (Nutley, N.J.: Presbyterian and Reformed Publishing Co., 1969), 25-40; Kucharsky, "Interview," 20f.; see Van Til's introduction to B. B. Warfield's *The Inspiration and Authority of the Bible*, 3-68; note also the work of Van Til and his Westminster colleagues on this issue in *The Infallible Word: A Symposium*, 3rd rev. ed. (Phillipsburg, N.J.: Presbyterian and Reformed, 1946).

29. On this, see Weaver, "Concept of Truth," 40.

30. Roberts, "Cornelius Van Til," 78.

> I take what the Bible says about God and his relation to the universe as unquestionably true on its own authority. The Bible requires men to believe that he exists apart from and above the world and that he [God] by his plan controls whatever takes place in the world. Everything in the created universe therefore displays the fact that it is controlled by God, that it is what it is by virtue of the place that it occupies in the plan of God. The objective evidence of God and of the comprehensive governance of the world by God is therefore so plain that he who runs may read [sic]. Men cannot get away from this evidence. They see it round about them. They see it within them. Their own constitution so clearly evinces the facts of God's creation of them and control over them that there is no man who can possibly escape observing it. If he is self-conscious at all, he is also God-conscious.[31]

This assertion by Van Til is based on the first chapter of Paul's Letter to the Romans, a passage which appears repeatedly throughout Van Til's corpus as a justification that humanity has knowledge of God but suppresses that knowledge through their sinful desire.

Van Til argued for three types of epistemological consciousness, all are founded upon his Creator-creature distinctions: (1) Adamic consciousness; (2) unregenerate consciousness; and (3) regenerate consciousness.[32] "Adamic consciousness" refers to the state of Adam before the fall when he was engaged in receptively reconstructing and reinterpreting God's system of knowledge and truth on an analogical basis. "Unregenerate consciousness" alludes to humanity's mistaken and fruitless attempt to construct its own independent system disregarding God's revelation. "Regenerate consciousness" is the believer's thought as it is being restored to "Adamic consciousness," once again reinterpreting reality in submission to God's revelation. Van Til's system of thought and concept of truth cannot be understood apart from understanding his insistence that regeneration is prior to knowing.[33] These understandings should not be construed as Van Til's denial of a common created self-consciousness for all of humanity.[34] Rather, Van Til accentuated the organic unity of both general and special revelation, understanding that God's revelation extends not only to what is outside of humanity, but

---

31. Van Til, *Defense*, 195.

32. Van Til, *Defense*, 48-50; see also Van Til, *Introduction to Systematic Theology*, 25-30.

33. See Vickers, *Theologian's Theological Stance*, 12.

34. David L. Turner, "Cornelius Van Til and Romans 1:18-21: A Study in the Epistemology of Presuppositional Apologetics," *Grace Theological Journal*, vol. 2, no. 1 (Spring 1981), 49; note also the following from Van Til: "Both the men of Princeton and the men of Amsterdam constantly make this point plain. When they speak of the 'common consciousness' of man, they mean the sort of thing that Calvin means by the sense of deity. When they speak of the self-consciousness of man, they mean what Calvin means on the first page of the *Institutes* when he says that man knows himself in the same act whereby he knows God," see *Defense*, 297.

also to the human response to that revelation as enabled by the Holy Spirit.[35]

This approach can be called "transcendental" in that given any fact one must ascertain the presuppositions behind that fact which make the fact itself possible.[36] As Geisler observes,

> many followers of Van Til see his system as a kind of transcendental argument which contends that it is absolutely necessary to presuppose the divine revelation in the Bible before one can consistently think, communicate, do science, or make any sense out of life or this world.[37]

White notes that Van Til found his term "presupposition" in the writings of Immanuel Kant.[38] Post-Kantian metaphysicians gave Van Til the insight that "the given presuppositions of any philosophical position predetermined and governed much of its later outworkings."[39] Van Til and his followers are labeled correctly as "Kantians," but his dependence on Kant for certain insights reveals that when Van Til uses the term "presupposition" it is more than an epistemological axiom. Rather, it is an ontological (his term is "metaphysical") referent.[40] Ontology is a term from the Greek "ontos" ("being") and "logos" ("knowledge" or "word"). As a result, the term refers to the "knowledge of being." Perhaps the best way to phrase the "ontological question" is simply to ask "What is?"

Van Til's transcendentalism investigated what lies at the very foundation of the possibility of what is (being) and of meaning. Once established, the transcendental argument then moves from what "is" to the conditions underlying its possibility.[41] Van Til's epistemology is neither inductive nor deductive, "a priori" nor "a posteriori," but is presuppositional, based upon the objective truth claims of Scripture.[42] Vickers is

---

35. See Knudsen, "Transcendental Perspective," 228.

36. On this, see Scott Oliphint, "Jerusalem and Athens Revisited," *Westminster Theological Journal* 49 (1987), 65-90 (esp. 70-71); see also Hendrik G. Stoker, "Reconnoitering the Theory of Knowledge of Prof. Dr. Cornelius Van Til," *Jerusalem and Athens*, 35.

37. N.L. Geisler and P. D. Feinberg, *An Introduction to Philosophy* (Grand Rapids: Baker, 1980), 264.

38. White, *Defender of the Faith*, 74-75; on Kant, see *The Critique of Pure Reason, The Critique of Practical Reason*, and *The Critique of Judgment* in *The Great Books of the Western World*, vol. 42, ed. Robert Maynard Hutchins (Chicago: Encyclopedia Britannica, 1952).

39. White, *Defender of the Faith*, 74; see also Roberts, "Cornelius Van Til," 74.

40. Stephen R. Spencer, "Fideism and Presuppositionalism," *Grace Theological Journal* 8.1 (1987), 98; Spencer gives a good overview of how Kant influenced Van Til, see 97f; J. Frame notes that only after Kant could the logic of presuppositions be systematically investigated as it was, even before Van Til, by thinkers like Hegel, Marx, Kierkegaard, Wittgenstein, and Christian apologists such as James Orr, see "Van Til and the Ligonier Apologetic," 281.

41. Knudsen, "Transcendental Perspective," 228.

42. Roberts, "Cornelius Van Til," 78.

therefore correct in noting that to understand Van Til, one must understand that the epistemology is central to his theological stance.[43]

Metaphysical Presupposition. Metaphysics is a term which literally means beyond ("meta") physics.[44] It is the branch of philosophy concerned with ultimate reality. Here the subjects of universals, absolutes, and other such matters are explored.

The metaphysical question is raised in regards to whether all decisions are decisions of the self. Van Til contends that to debate any fact regarding the Christian faith would be to throw the whole claim of Christian theism into question.[45] "Without the presupposition of the truth of Christian theism no fact can be distinguished from any other fact."[46]

Thus the presupposition of the intelligibility of any fact in the world is presupposed by the actual existence of the God of Christian theism and the infallibility of Scripture.[47] No facts exist in any realm but, as Van Til insists,

> such as actually do exhibit the truth of the system of which they are a part. If facts are what they are as parts of the Christian theistic system of truth then what else can facts do but reveal that system to the limit of their ability as parts of that system? It is only as manifestations of that system that they are what they are.[48] I hold that belief in God is not merely as reasonable as other belief, or even a little or infinitely more probably true than other belief; I hold rather that unless you believe in God you can logically believe in nothing else.[49]

Thus no understanding of any fact can take place unless it is seen in right relation to Christ as Creator-Redeemer.[50] As Roberts notes, for Van Til the "ontological trinity is made the category of interpretation for all things and the final reference point in all human thinking."[51] Van Til proposes that God must be taken as the prerequisite of both the possibility and the actuality of the relationship between humanity's various concepts and propositions of knowledge, an "analogical replica" of the

---

43. See *Theologian's Theological Stance*, 12.
44. The term itself was generated as a result of an untitled book by Aristotle. Andronicus of Rhodes was classifying Aristotle's works, and titled the untitled book "the book beyond the Physics."
45. Van Til, *Defense*, 115.
46. Ibid.
47. Ibid., 118.
48. Ibid.
49. Cornelius Van Til, *Why I Believe in God* (Philadelphia: Prebyterian and Reformed, n.d.), 20.
50. Van Til, "My Credo," *Jerusalem and Athens*, 5.
51. Roberts, "Cornelius Van Til," 75.

system of knowledge which belongs to God.[52] No truth in human thought exists outside of these presuppositions.

Van Til's approach to metaphysical presuppositionalism was an "atomistic" approach to truth, a conveyance of Christian doctrine as fact only in piecemeal as human evidence and reason would allow. Van Til also rejected positivism, a "family of philosophies characterized by an extremely positive evaluation of science and scientific method."[53] Of equal concern was the granting of truth to individual propositions about reality independent of the truth of Christianity as a system. Van Til's overwhelming dissonance with non-presuppositional approaches was that such methods had "lost all power to challenge the non-Christian methodology."[54] Thus the Bible and the self-contained triune God are together posited as the final authority. He writes, "Fundamental to everything orthodox is the presupposition of the antecedent self-existence of God and his infallible revelation of himself to man in the Bible."[55] Pinnock writes that for Van Til, facts do not prove systems; rather, systems give meaning to facts.[56] As a result, the relationship between the Christian world view and the non-Christian world view is nothing less than a "head-on collision."[57]

Christian truth will always be nonsensical to the non-Christian mind, Van Til argues; therefore it is not something that can be "proved" to the satisfaction of humanity's sense of reason.[58] For Van Til, the following assumptions should not be conceded: (1) humanity is autonomous; (2) the space-time world is in some measure "contingent;" and (3) humanity can erect for itself its own epistemology in an ultimate sense.[59] Nothing can be allowed which would place humanity in the position of judge over the authoritative Word of God as found in the Bible.

The necessity of faith over reason is based on Van Til's assumption that humanity is totally depraved. For Van Til, the depravity of humankind extends to the whole of life, even to thoughts and attitudes.[60] For Van Til, reason is darkened by sin, in rebellion to God, and thus is sepa-

---

52. Van Til, *Defense*, 121; on Van Til's understanding of "analogical knowledge," see below.

53. W. L. Reese, "Positivism," *Dictionary of Philosophy and Religion: Eastern and Western Thought* (New Jersey: Humanities Press, 1980), 450-451; the most significant development of positivism came through the "Vienna Circle of Logical Positivists" to such a point that today the term "positivism" is virtually synonymous with "logical positivism."

54. Van Til, *Defense*, 122.

55. Van Til, *Introduction to Systematic Theology*, 1.

56. Clark Pinnock, *Tracking the Maze: Finding Our Way Through Modern Theology from an Evangelical Perspective* (San Francisco: Harper and Row, 1990), 44; Pinnock draws similarities between this position and that of philosophical idealism.

57. Van Til, *Defense*, 99.

58. Van Til, "My Credo," *Jerusalem and Athens*, 8.

59. "My Credo," 11.

60. Ibid., 19.

rated from the biblical revelation of God. Therefore if dogmatic conclusions are reached speculatively rather than exegetically in relation to Scripture, they are prone to error and deceit, subject to the reason of humanity. Van Til goes even farther, saying that any non-Christian epistemology, that is, any epistemology that does not begin with Christian presuppositions but rather with principles of reason, is "doomed to utter failure."[61] The Christian world view is reality, and to start apart from that reality results in intellectual frustration. Rather than rational autonomy, humanity is dependent upon God's knowledge for its own knowledge. Thus the only proof of the Christian position is that "unless its truth is presupposed there is no possibility of 'proving' anything at all."[62]

Van Til's Concept of Fact

Van Til's presuppositionalism speaks of providing the framework for that which gives "facts" meaning.[63] The concept of "fact" is central to Van Til's thought, though he does not offer a concise explanation of exactly what he means by the term. Bernard Ramm suggests that for Van Til, "fact" and "meaning" are virtually synonymous.[64] With this understanding, the meaning of everything stems from God with each individual fact attesting to the kind of God that He actually is. Thus God is not revealed by the facts themselves, but through the presupposition of the context of the belief-system as revealed in Scripture.[65] Therefore the ultimate "fact" is God, the Universal from which all other facts derive their meaning.[66] The only facts that exist are God-interpreted facts. Van Til's argument for this rests on his contention that there must be comprehensive knowledge somewhere if there is to be true knowledge anywhere,[67] so "brute facts" exist apart from the presupposition of Christian Theism. A "brute" fact is a fact which exists independent of God and His interpretation of that fact. Van Til does not oppose the use of facts in his appeal for the truth of Christian faith, only the appeal to brute facts. There are also no neutral or common facts, meaning a fact for which Christians and non-Christians have a common meaning. Propositions that have truth value are potential facts.[68] Only through Christian presuppositions can facts be recognized as facts. The method used to incor-

---

61. "My Credo," 16.
62. Ibid., 21.
63. Van Til, *Defense*, 100.
64. Ramm, *Types of Apologetic Systems*, 188.
65. Colin Brown, *Philosophy and the Christian Faith* (Downers Grove: InterVarsity, 1968), 249.
66. Van Til, *Systematic Theology*, 22; compare Ramm, *Types of Apologetic Systems*, 188.
67. Van Til, *Systematic Theology*, 194; cf. Cornelius Van Til, *Christian Apologetics*, Syllabus from Westminster Theological Seminary (Phillipsburg, N.J.: Presbyterian and Reformed, 1976), 23ff.
68. Ramm, *Types of Apologetic Systems,* 193.

porate these facts into daily existence is that of implication, an emphasis on the "process of relating those things (implicating, if you will) with which we come into contact to [with] the plan of God (transcendental)."[69]

Ramm notes that for Van Til, metaphysically all humans have all facts in common but epistemologically or ethically they have no facts in common.[70] Douglas Vickers gives a helpful commentary on this aspect of Van Til's thought:

> The believer and the unbeliever, we can say, are both surrounded by the totality of facts and fact structures and constellations of facts which are what they are because God has constituted them in the way He has, and which unavoidably, therefore, speak of God. The believer and the unbeliever both live in the same environment of God-constituted facts. In that sense they have everything in common metaphysically. The objective reality is the same for both of them. But epistemologically, as to their knowing ability or their knowledge capacity, they have nothing in common. For one is now a new man in Christ, to whom the truth and the ability to know the truth is mediated by the Holy Spirit whom Christ, in accordance with His promise, has sent precisely to lead men into truth.[71]

According to this understanding, any proposed fact which is contrary to Christianity is at best irrelevant.

Regarding science, Van Til contended that

> the assertions of philosophy and science can be self-consciously true only if they are made in the light of the Scripture. Scripture gives definite information of a most fundamental character about all the facts and principles with which philosophy and science deal. For philosophy or science to reject or even to ignore this information is to falsify the picture it gives of the field with which it deals. This does not imply that philosophy and science must be exclusively dependent upon theology for their basic principles. It implies only that philosophy and science must, as well as theology, turn to Scripture for whatever light it has to offer on general principles and particular facts"[72]

Thus Van Til wrote: "I would not talk endlessly about facts and more facts without ever challenging the non-believer's philosophy of fact."[73]

Analogical Knowledge. This analysis of Van Til's concept of truth has examined his presuppositionalism and his ideas regarding the term "fact." The final area to explore relates to Van Til's idea of analogical

---

69. Oliphint, "Van Til's Methodology," 34, n. 26; see Van Til, *Survey of Christian Epistemology*, 7.

70. Ramm, *Types of Apologetic Systems*, 196.

71. Vickers, *Theologian's Theological Stance*, 13.

72. Van Til, *Christian Apologetics*, 26.

73. Van Til, *Defense*, 199.

knowledge. Halsey writes that at "the very heart of Dr. Van Til's apologetic and therefore of his theology lies his notion of analogy."[74] This may not be an exercise in over-statement, for Van Til contended that the only knowledge available to humanity is "analogical knowledge." Van Til states that "our reasoning then must always and everywhere be truly analogical."[75] This knowledge is the attempt to think (analogically) God's thoughts after Him. Reality can be truly known for it is God's reality and God truly knows it. Human knowledge of this reality, however, is finite, for we are finite creatures and God's knowledge is infinite. Therefore, the distinction between Creator and created limits knowledge to that of analogical knowing. This translates into the idea that human knowledge is derived from and is dependent upon God's thought.[76]

> The system that Christians seek to obtain may, by contrast, be said to be analogical. By this is meant that God is the original and that man is the derivative. God has absolute self-contained system within himself. What comes to pass in history happens in accord with that system or plan by which he orders the universe. But man, as God's creature, cannot have a replica of that system of God. He cannot have a reproduction of that system. He must, to be sure, think God's thoughts after him; but this means that he must, in seeking to form his own system, constantly be subject to the authority of God's system to the extent that this is revealed to him.
>
> For this reason all of man's interpretations in any field are subject to the Scriptures given him. Scripture itself informs us that, at the beginning of history, before man had sinned, he was subject to the direct revelation of God in all the interpretations that he would make of his environment.[77]

Analogical knowledge leads Van Til to assert that we know the world truly, "though not comprehensively."[78] Indeed, the knowledge of humanity and that of God must not "coincide at any given point."[79] For Van Til, even the proposition "two plus two equals four" means something qualitatively different for God than it does for humanity. Truth must be established by correspondence in that our knowledge must correspond with God's thought, although without being identical.[80]

---

74. Jim Halsey, "A Preliminary Critique of Van Til: The Theologian" (a review article), *Westminster Theological Journal* 39 (Fall 1976), 120.

75. Van Til, *Survey of Christian Epistemology*, 203.

76. William S. Sailer, "Reformed Apologetics Revisited," *Evangelical Journal* 2 (1984), 18.

77. Van Til, *Christian Theory of Knowledge*, 16; see also *Defense*, 31-50; *Apologetics*, 9-11.

78. Van Til, *Defense*, 43.

79. Van Til, *Systematic Theology*, 171.

80. This aspect of Van Til's understanding of truth is also acknowledged by Sailer, "Apologetics Revisited," 19.

According to Van Til, this understanding of knowledge as being ana-logical extends even to human knowledge derived from revelation. Van Til's doctrine of analogy is built upon certain ontological considerations which he argues are derived from the Scriptures. Halsey notes that Van Til both begins with ontology and yet takes his ontology from the Scrip-tures, meaning that for Van Til the Bible not only gives the answers to our questions but also posits and defines the very questions them-selves.[81] Three key elements in this doctrine are important to note: (1) the ontological distinction between Creator and created, thus eliminating humanity's potential for univocal knowledge of such a being as God;[82] (2) humanity as derivative of God; and (3) lack of direct correspondence between divine knowledge and human knowledge. The term "univocal" is from the Latin "unus" ("one") and "vocare" ("to call"). If something is univocal, it has the same meaning in all uses. Van Til denies this, argu-ing instead for analogy, which is a relationship of similarity.

Van Til's commitment to analogy comes from the concern that univo-cal knowledge of the Creator could possibly lead, in principle, to humanity's ability to exhaust the knowledge of God.[83] To think analogi-cally entails: (1) thinking under the authority of the Scriptures; (2) being in covenant with God (by regeneration); and; (3) recognizing the finite, creaturely status of our thoughts; consequently, our reasoning (use of the law of non-contradiction) will accord with (1) above.[84] Univocal thinking is perceived as that which would: (1) reject the authority of God and His Word; (2) abrogate the covenant; and (3) shed the finite and temporal make-up of humanity via the enthroning of reason, mak-ing reason an eternal and the means by which humanity is raised to the level of the divine.[85] The means to such analogical knowledge is assisted by special revelation (the Scriptures) which serves as God's pre-interpretation. Thus while God's knowledge is comprehensive and ana-lytical, the knowledge of humanity is limited and analogical—yet genuine.[86] The precise nature of how this understanding works, how-ever, is not fully explicated by Van Til.

---

81. Halsey, "Preliminary Critique," 120-23.

82. Van Til, *Systematic Theology*, 181-185; for Van Til, this fundamental ontological distinction is essential and is most crucial for his doctrine of analogy; it is to be noted that for Van Til this is a qualitative difference, not a quantitative difference.

83. This is Halsey's contention, based on a "slippery slope" type of appeal, see "Pre-liminary Critique," 124f; it is important to note that when Van Til resists a positive appraisal of the term "univocal," he does not mean to reject the idea of the possibility of "literal."

84. Halsey, "Preliminary Critique," 125.

85. Ibid., 126; Van Til notes that "univocal reasoning itself leads to self-contradiction, not only from a theistic point of view, but from a non-theistic point of view as well," see *Survey of Christian Epistemology*, 205.

86. Turner, "Van Til and Rom. 1:18-21," 48.

Van Til's Criteria of Truth

As a result of Van Til's concept of truth as that which corresponds analogically to God's revealed truth in Scripture on the basis of epistemological and metaphysical presuppositions, his criteria of truth has been said to be largely that of coherence, non-contradiction, and meaningful relevance. These are established through the Bible, which is self-authenticating.[87] Perhaps it is better simply to say that Van Til's system entails a singular move in regard to the determination of truth, that of fideism.

Methodological Fideism

Van Til contends that nothing can be known outside of the presupposition of the reality of the living God as revealed in Scripture. Pinnock consequently characterizes Van Til's approach as "presuppositional fideism."[88] Geisler terms it a "methodological fideism."[89] No doubt Van Til holds that major religious beliefs are held as a matter of faith as opposed to a matter of reason or argument.[90] He writes:

> No proof for this God and for the truth of his revelation in Scripture can be offered by an appeal to anything in human experience that has not itself received its light from the God whose existence and whose revelation it is supposed to prove. One cannot prove the usefulness of the light of the sun for the purposes of seeing by turning to the darkness of the cave.[91]

For Van Til, "the ultimate test for the relevancy of our hypotheses is therefore their (the facts) correspondence with God's interpretation of facts."[92] Thus we are given a test for truth: that which corresponds with Christian presuppositions as found in the Word of God (the Bible).

---

87. See Lewis, *Testing Christianity's Truth-Claims*, 145-147; 290; Lewis argues that this is the case, against Van Til's own "protestations to the contrary." What can surely be said is that Van Til's critiques of the law of non-contradiction did not deny the principle, only its use; thus Lewis is correct in finding Van Til relying on the principle within his system. Halsey notes that Van Til's principle of analogy differs from univocal knowledge in that the principle of non-contradiction is often used to deny the ontological distinction between God and humanity and thus elevates reason inordinately. Rather than the point of identity between the mind of God and humanity being that of Scripture, it becomes reason (particularly the law of non-contradiction); see "Preliminary Critique," 126.

88. Pinnock, *Tracking the Maze*, 43.

89. Geisler, *Apologetics*, 56.

90. Though Van Til's supporters do not appreciate the label "fideistic" being applied to Van Til's system, they generally acknowledge that it is "one of the most frequent characterizations" of his presuppositional apologetic, for example see Spencer, "Fideism and Presuppositionalism," 89-99.

91. Van Til, *Defense*, 109.

92. Van Til, *Christian-Theistic Evidences*, 62.

As a result, traditional arguments for the existence of God are discarded as fallacious. Van Til rejects the notion that the task of Christian apologetics is to find some form of common ground with the non-Christian perspective. There is not and can not be any common ground in terms of knowledge, for the only rational thought process is that which presupposes Christian Theism. Colin Brown writes that for Van Til, the "best and only possible proof for the existence of such a God is that his existence is required for the uniformity of nature and for the coherence of all things in the world."[93] Van Til appeals to the image of God in humanity which produces an ineradicable "sensus deitatis" (sense of deity within humans).[94]

Norman Geisler suggests that fideists characteristically put forth the following tenets: (1) faith alone is the way to God; (2) truth is not found in the purely rational or objective realm, if it is there at all; (3) evidence and reason do not point definitively in the direction of God; (4) the tests for truth are existential, not rational; and (5) not only God's revelation but His grace is the source of all truth.[95] Is Van Til fideistic in this sense? Certainly Van Til opposes any form of autonomy in regarding human knowledge. No criterion of truth exists outside of the Word of God. God can only be known through the embrace of God's Word (the Bible)—an act of faith made possible through the miracle of regeneration.[96] Yet Van Til would reject the label of "mere" fideist, arguing that biblical Christianity is the only rational interpretation of the universe in which we live.[97]

> When we say that God is a mystery for us we do not mean that our knowledge of him is not true as far as it goes. When we say that God is "absolutely Other" we do not mean that there is not a rational relation between God and us. As God created us in accordance with his plan, that is, as God created us in accordance with his absolute rationality, so there must be a rational relationship from us to God. Christianity is, in the last analysis, not an absolute irrationalism, but an absolute "rationalism." In fact we may contrast every non-Christian epistemology with Christian epistemology by saying that Christian epistemology believes

---

93. Colin Brown, *Philosophy*, 248.

94. Cornelius Van Til, *The Reformed Pastor and Modern Thought* (Philadelphia: Presbyterian and Reformed, 1971), 6, 140, 151; see also Turner, "Van Til and Rom. 1:18-21," 46; for Van Til, it is the first chapter of Romans which forms the basis of his rejection of the traditional attempts to prove the existence of God because this passage implies that every human being has the idea of God already planted within, see Kucharsky, "Interview," 21.

95. Geisler, *Apologetics*, 58-59; though offered to suggest the concerns of those opposed to fideistic thinking, it is to be noted that it is unlikely that Van Til, nor many other fideists, would accept these characterizations.

96. Pinnock, *Tracking the Maze*, 43.

97. On this, see Kenneth Kantzer, "Unity and Diversity in Evangelical Faith," *The Evangelicals: What They Believe, Who They Are, Where They Are Changing*, ed. by David F. Wells and John D. Woodbridge (Nashville: Abingdon, 1975), 50.

in an ultimate rationalism while all other systems of epistemology believe in an ultimate irrationalism.[98]

Spencer notes that Van Til is arguing that in the realm of presuppositions and world views though "there are a number of ostensible alternatives, only one is in fact viable."[99] Van Til would also acknowledge the importance of what can be empirically demonstrated[100] and that which is consonant with scientific methodology.[101] Thus Van Til and the Westminster apologetic is argument, but argument that depends completely on the revelation of God.[102] Put another way, Van Til grants that reason is involved in all human thought, but he wants the criteria of truth that reason acknowledges to be that which is put forth and contained in Scripture.[103]

Van Til discusses fideism directly, dividing fideists into two classes: (1) consistent fideists who "hold that no defense of any sort is possible;" and (2) inconsistent fideists who contend that "Christianity may be scientifically, but cannot be philosophically, defended."[104] Van Til concludes that consistent fideists by seeking to withdraw from intellectual argument have "virtually admitted the validity of the argument against Christianity." "They will have to believe in their hearts what they have virtually allowed to be intellectually indefensible."[105]

Van Til therefore asserts that Christian truth must correspond to reality or "else the commitment is erroneous. Faith must have truth as its object."[106] Van Til states:

> Christianity meets every legitimate demand of reason. Surely Christianity is not irrational. To be sure, it must be accepted on faith, but surely it must not be taken on blind faith. Christianity is capable of rational defense.[107]

> There is objective evidence in abundance and it is sufficiently clear. Men ought, if only they reasoned rightly, to come to the conclusion that God exists. That is to say, if the theistic proof is constructed as it

98. Van Til, *Defense*, 41.

99. Spencer, "Fideism and Presuppositionalism," 94.

100. Van Til, *Survey of Christian Epistemology*, 7; see also his *Christian Theory of Knowledge*, 35.

101. Van Til, *Christian-Theistic Evidences*, x; later in this work he noted that the "Christian position is certainly not opposed to experimentation and observation," 57.

102. Thus rightly termed, as noted above, "transcendental;" see Knudsen, "Transcendental Perspective," 229.

103. On this, see J. Frame, "Van Til and the Ligonier Apologetic," 286, who writes "Reason is always involved in all human search for knowledge; but reason must always choose its standards, and that choice is fundamentally a religious one."

104. Van Til, *Christian-Theistic Evidences*, 35.

105. Ibid., 34.

106. Spencer, "Fideism and Presuppositionalism," 93.

107. Cornelius Van Til, *Common Grace and the Gospel* (Philadelphia: Presbyterian and Reformed, 1972), 184.

ought to be constructed, it is objectively valid, whatever the attitude of those to whom it comes may be.[108]

These and many other statements available from Van Til's corpus show that Van Til is not a "mere" fideist, one that denies the propriety of rational defense.[109] Therefore Van Til can be said to have agreed that Christianity is capable of rational proof, but he would have argued that the foundations of such proof must be closely examined in regard to presupposition and methodology.[110]

Critique of Van Til's Concept of Truth

Van Til offers a significant and distinctive contribution to contemporary American Evangelical thought in regard to the concept of truth. As Lewis notes in his survey of various approaches to Christian apologetics, "interaction with Van Til's apologetic is required by its highly controversial nature. If it is correct, every other writer considered in this book seriously compromises the Christianity he attempts to defend."[111]

Van Til's argument is marked by internal consistency to his own theology and system of thought. Positive elements include the need to examine the philosophical framework and presuppositions that accompany any formulation of knowledge. Who can doubt that the Christian faith presents a distinct world view? Van Til's goal to posit this world view in light of the living God and His revelation as found in the Bible is a difficult but noteworthy task. Van Til is consistent in his Calvinism, striving admirably within his system of thought to avoid the placement of any aspect of reality above the sovereign God, not to mention his insistence upon humanity's total and absolute depravity.

Any engagement with the work of Van Til, however, leaves the inquirer with questions regarding clarity and specificity. What exactly is Van Til's concept of truth? This analysis has put forth his own answer, namely that truth is that which corresponds analogically to God's revealed truth in Scripture; but this definition leaves much to obscurity. Colin Brown has noted that Van Til spends a "good deal of time reiterating points without really explaining them."[112] Related to this is an inad-

---

108. Van Til, *Common Grace*, 49.

109. Many have defended Van Til against this charge, including Knudsen, "Transcendental Perspective," 232; Spencer, "Fideism and Presuppositionalism," 93; G. L. Bahnsen, "Inductivism, Inerrancy, and Presuppositionalism," *Journal of the Evangelical Theological Society* 20 (1977), 292-295; Notaro, *Van Til and Evidence*; note also the impressive list of passages from Van Til's corpus, offered by J. M. Frame, in which his position concerning proofs are articulated, "The Problem of Theological Paradox," *Foundations of Christian Schola*, 301.

110. As noted by Knudsen, "Transcendental Perspective," 223-239.

111. Lewis, *Testing Christianity's Truth-Claims*, 144.

112. Brown, *Philosophy*, 249.

equate explication of how his concept actually works. Such omissions hinder Van Til's system of thought from adequately addressing many of the pressing issues concerning the nature of truth.

Evangelical interactions with Van Til's system of thought has raised many questions. The first concern among Evangelicals, primarily from the evidentialist camp, is that Van Til's method is circular in its reasoning. Evidentialists believe that it is important to support biblical claims with external evidence in order to engage the modern mind with the truth of the gospel. Van Til believed that the Bible is true because the Bible says that it is true. As a result of such presuppositionalism, Van Til stood firmly against the evidentialism of many Evangelicals such as Benjamin Breckinridge Warfield. Van Til argued that their approaches failed to challenge adequately the non-Christian view of knowledge and reality on the grounds that they allowed "sinners to be the ultimate judges of reality, and of arguing merely for the probability of Christianity."[113] Van Til and his followers would contend that the issue is not one set of personal presuppositions put forth against another set of personal presuppositions. It is rather the attempt to show that Christian presuppositions are necessary if one is to give an account of one's life and thought.[114] In other words, the opponents of Christianity—if consistent with his presuppositions—will not be able to give an account of their experiences. This brings in the criterion of coherence to justify the circular reasoning. Students of Van Til would add that if one could proceed from neutrality to truth then noncircular argument would be possible. Since that is not possible if one believes God alone is sovereign, circular reasoning (in one form or another) is inevitable for humans.[115] Critics of Van Til counter that Van Til's system, nonetheless, has left the faith defenseless by giving external verification a limited role at best.[116] Rather than provide a means to critique the prevailing non-Christian world view, Van Til's approach seems to assume the truth of a position which itself has yet to be proved. Theology, not apologetics, seems to be the outcome of such an approach.

A second concern among Evangelicals regarding Van Til's position is his paucity of exegetical work and the uncritical acceptance of previous interpretations within his stream of tradition. Even Van Til's supporters acknowledge this weakness in his theological construction.[117] The con-

---

113. Kelly, "Van Til," 704.

114. As argued by Knudsen, "Transcendental Perspective," 233.

115. On this, see J. Frame, "Van Til and the Ligonier Apologetic," 288.

116. For example, see Gordon R. Lewis, "Van Til and Carnell—Part I," *Jerusalem and Athens*, 359-361; see also Lewis, *Testing Christianity's Truth Claims*, 144-148; R. C. Sproul, J. Gerstner, and A. Lindsley, *Classical Apologetics* (Grand Rapids: Zondervan, 1984), 318ff.

117. William D. Dennison, *Paul's Two-Age Construction and Apologetics* (New York: University Press of America, 1985), 89f., notes that Van Til has a tendency to take possession of traditional interpretations, assuming that they are the best available; see also Turner's "Cornelius Van Til and Romans 1:18-21," 45-58, who notes that "biblical exegesis is not Van Til's forte," 47, thus giving rise to Turner's supportive exegetical effort.

cern is that Van Til not only avoids external verification for the Christian faith, but he also avoids internal verification as to the coherence of his system in regard to conversation with other Christian thought-systems and with the Scriptures as well.

A third concern, voiced by such Evangelicals as Arthur Holmes, is that individuals such as Van Til make presuppositions, perspectives, or world views the all-consuming difference in philosophical positions and thereby underestimate other differentiating factors.[118] One asks Van Til whether the biblical materials even purport to give such a systematic world view as a philosophical grid for interpreting all of reality and giving rise to all knowledge. Related to this is the tendency to view the Christian perspective or world view as a deductive or axiomatic system like geometry, and from this, to believe that human knowledge is limited to the propositions contained in the Bible or to propositions deduced from those in Scripture. This perspective concludes that if some proposition is not actually revealed in God's Word (the Bible), then it is unknowable by human beings.[119]

Some individuals embracing this view, such as Rousas Rushdoony, have been forced to go so far as to suggest the need for deducing disciplines such as mathematics and economics from the Bible.[120] On these grounds it has been suggested that Van Til's epistemology is the basis for the Christian Reconstructionist movement, which holds that God's civil and moral statutes as prescribed in Old Testament remain normative and binding and should be the basis for contemporary society.[121]

A fourth Evangelical concern is that Van Til's apologetic method, which denies that the non-Christian is able to arrive at any valid truth except on "borrowed capital" from a Christian world view, eliminates any point of contact between the Christian and the non-Christian. This was one of many points of tension between Van Til and such Evangelicals as Edward John Carnell.[122] Van Til himself writes that Carnell

---

118. Arthur F. Holmes, *All Truth Is God's Truth* (Grand Rapids: Eerdmans, 1977), 64.

119. On this, see Ronald H. Nash, *Faith and Reason: Searching for a Rational Faith* (Grand Rapids: Academie Books, 1988), 60-61, where Nash rightly points out that many commonsensical claims to knowledge can not be deduced as a true proposition from anything in the Bible; see also Arthur Holmes' similar concern in "The Philosophical Methodology of Gordon Clark," *The Philosophy of Gordon Clark*, ed. Ronald H. Nash (Philadelphia: Presbyterian and Reformed, 1968), 219.

120. Rushdoony's most important work is *The Institutes of Biblical Law* (Philipsburg, N.J.: Presbyterian and Reformed, 1973); for Rushdoony's writings on Van Til, see *By What Standard? An Analysis of the Philosophy of Cornelius Van Til* (Philipsburg, N.J.: Presbyterian and Reformed, 1958); *Van Til* (Philipsburg, N.J.: Presbyterian and Reformed, 1960).

121. On this, see H. Wayne House and Thomas Ice in *Dominion Theology: Blessing or Curse? An Analysis of Christian Reconstructionism* (Portland: Multnomah, 1988), 343f.

122. On this, and the many other points of tension between Carnell and Van Till, see Rudolph Nelson's *The Making and Unmaking of an Evangelical Mind: The Case of Edward Carnell* (Cambridge: Cambridge University, 1987), 44-45, 64.

was sure, as he told me during a whole day we spent together discussing these matters, that since I did not do justice to Aristotle's fourth book of the *Metaphysics*, my faith must be a blind faith. He was sure I could make no intelligible contact with the unbeliever.[123]

Inherent within this view is the repudiation of the law of non-contradiction, which Van Til saw as neither necessary nor sufficient. The law of non-contradiction states that "A" cannot be "Non-A." It should be remembered that it is not the actual principle of non-contradiction that Van Til repudiated, but its use by those who wished to dilute the Creator-created distinction and elevate reason as that which provides the meeting point between human knowledge and the mind of God. Van Til is unclear in what appears to be the simultaneous rejection and use of the law of non-contradiction. It is also unclear how Van Til's appropriation of the principle of non-contradiction coalesces with his disavowal of extra-biblical principles. For Van Til, a reliance upon the law of non-contradiction reduced God's truth to humanity's truth, which then would lead to the idea of human autonomy, an idea which Van Til rejected as unscriptural.[124] Yet this, too, raises problems in Van Til's system of thought. Clark argues that to hold to analogical truth alone inevitably leads to skepticism because humanity cannot know real truth, only an analogy of the truth.[125] Clark also argues that eternal principles, such as the law of non-contradiction, "are the prerequisites of all argumentation."[126] Robert Reymond, is similarly troubled by Van Til's denial that God's knowledge and humanity's knowledge fail to coincide at any point.[127] Reymond expresses further dismay that Van Til fails to make an effort to explain the qualitative difference between God's knowledge and humanity's knowledge. Van Til's insistence on the analogical relationship between God's knowledge and humanity's knowledge is seen by Reymond as the single greatest weakness in Van Til's apologetic system.[128] Reymond accuses Van Til of equivocism, based on Van Til's willingness to acknowledge that truth will probably appear as paradoxical

---

123. Cornelius Van Til, responding to Gordon Lewis' article, "Van Til and Carnell - Part I, *Jerusalem and Athens*, 368.

124. Kucharsky, "Interview," 418.

125. On this, see Clark's "The Bible as Truth," *Bibliotheca Sacra* 114 (April 1957), 157-170; "Apologetics," *Contemporary Evangelical Thought*, 159; it is to be noted that Van Til does not fully explicate how his understanding of analogy makes the move to certainty.

126. Gordon Clark, "Secular Philosophy (Wheaton Lecture I)," *The Philosophy of Gordon H. Clark: A Festschrift*, ed. by Ronald H. Nash (Philadelphia: Presbyterian and Reformed, 1968), 37; as noted in chapter 6 of this work, Carl F. H. Henry has voiced similar concerns.

127. Robert L. Reymond, *The Justification of Knowledge: An Introductory Study in Christian Apologetic Methodology* (Phillipsburg, N.J.: Presbyterian and Reformed, 1976), 100.

128. Raymond, *Justification of Knowledge*, 102; Reymond believes that if Van Til held to his views of analogical knowledge consistently it would be destructive of his system.

due to its analogical nature. Thus Raymond wonders aloud how such an "ardent a foe of Barthian irrationalism" could "come to the same conclusion concerning the nature of truth."[129]

Fifth, for many Evangelicals, the problematic nature of fideism looms large in Van Til's system of thought, this despite his many qualifications to the contrary. Norman Geisler notes six inadequacies within fideism concerning service as a method and test for truth: (1) the confusion between epistemology and ontology; (2) the failure to distinguish between belief "in" and belief "that" there is a God; (3) neglect to differentiate between the basis of belief in God and the support or warrant for that belief; (4) neglect and sometimes negation of the need for the propositional in its zeal to stress the personal; (5) the failure to understand the implications of the difference between the unavoidability of and the justifiability of presuppositions; and (6) the dilemma of whether fideism is making a truth claim or it is not.[130]

The essence of the problem of Van Til's fideism is that presuppositions are in and of themselves either true or false. Simply to proceed on the basis of one's own presuppositions without a rational defense tends to give the impression that the faith is irrational.[131] To be sure, Van Til would argue that his presuppositions are proven, not merely selected, but critics argue that their "proof" is at best indirect. Van Til's indirect proof is that the existence of God is necessary for the "uniformity of nature and for the coherence of all things in the world"; for Van Til, this is "absolutely certain proof."[132] This proof, however, is not able to satisfy humanity's sense of reason.[133] Therefore, Van Til is forced to say that argument by presupposition is "objectively valid" even if "subjectively unacceptable" to the unregenerate mind.[134]

---

129. Raymond, *Justification of Knowledge*, 105; while noting such similarities, Reymond does acknowledge the distinctions Van Til's concept retained, namely that for Van Til truth was still objectively present in biblical propositions while for Barth truth was essentially existential. Reymond's point is that they shared the idea that religious truth can appear paradoxical.

130. Norman Geisler, *Apologetics*, 61-64; in his exposition of major fideistic views, Geisler surveys Pascal, Kierkegaard, Barth, and Van Til, categorizing the latter as one who embraces "revelational fideism."

131. This is the concern of John Warwick Montgomery, "Once upon an a Priori," *Jerusalem and Athens*, 391; see also Clark Pinnock's article, "A Philosophy of Christian Evidences" in the same collection of essays; M. M. Hanna adds that "presuppositionalism" is only able to respond to inquiries as to the warrant for belief in terms of "obscurantistic fideism," see *Crucial Questions in Apologetics* (Grand Rapids: Baker, 1981), 56; agreeing with Hanna would be Sproul, Gerstner, and Lindsley who in *Classical Apologetics*, 304-309, argue that Van Til's apologetic has no place for reasoning with or giving evidence to unbelievers.

132. Van Til, *Defense*, 103.

133. Van Til, "My Credo," *Jerusalem and Athens*, 8.

134. Ibid., 104.

Finally, and perhaps most serious, is the question many Evangelicals are raising in the area of interpretation. If Scripture is the embodiment of God's truth through which we are able to acquire analogical knowledge, then how does one navigate through the difficult terrain of conflicting interpretations of those very biblical materials? In other words, how does one determine the correct analogical correspondence in light of the subjective interpretation of the text? Salier observes that Van Til's contentions regarding analogical knowledge demand an outside referent if it is to be maintained that our knowledge is in some sense and to some degree like God's knowledge.[135] Or as Nash states,

> How is a sincere disciple of Van Til supposed to know when his facts are God-interpreted? When they are consistent with the Scripture? Hardly, for the Bible says nothing about most of the facts in question. When our interpretation coincides with God's? Hardly, for we must never forget that there is no point of identity between the divine and human knowledge. I contend then that Van Til's use of "fact" is vacuous, since there is no way for man to know when his facts are God-interpreted.[136]

Van Til's response, seen by Pinnock as less than adequate, is his advocacy of the "Calvinian system of interpretation found in the Westminster Confession of faith as the only key to the proper interpretation of the Bible."[137] Elsewhere Van Til seems oblivious to the hermeneutical problem of subjective interpretation and his own emphasis on humanity's fallen-ness in regards to distorted reason. He states "Christian theism . . . holds that truth, though interpreted and reinterpreted, is still absolute."[138] In other words, when an individual thinks "normally," that is analogically, his re-interpretation will not introduce an element of subjectivity in such a way that the absoluteness of the truth with which he has come in contact is distorted.[139] Thus an infallible hermeneutic seems to be bestowed upon the regenerate person when encountered with the biblical materials.

Ramm's assessment is that Van Til fails to give a well-defined answer to this concern.[140] Put simply, Van Til leaves no room in his concept of truth for the serious hermeneutical issues his system generates. Without such concerns addressed, there are no adequate directions given as to how truth can be extrapolated from God's pre-interpretation of fact as given in Scripture. Further, Van Til does not effectively demonstrate a

---

135. Salier, "Apologetics Revisited," 19.
136. Ronald M. Nash, "Review of Van Til's *A Christian Theory of Knowledge*," *Christianity Today* (Jan. 16, 1970), 349.
137. Pinnock, *Tracking the Maze*, 44-45.
138. Van Til, *Systematic Theology*, 137.
139. Weaver, "Concept of Truth," 21; compare Van Til, *Systematic Theology*, 139.
140. Ramm, *Types of Apologetic Systems*, 208.

necessary jump exists from the establishment of all knowledge as derivative to the conclusion that all knowledge is therefore analogical.[141]

Summary

The concept of truth in the theology of Cornelius Van Til is that which is presupposed and independent of human verification. This is necessitated on the grounds of humanity's total depravity. Truth comes to humanity through God's revelation in Scripture. The message of Scripture is that which forms the idea of Scripture, hence the proclamation of its truth. Thus all biblical claims are self-authenticating. This truth is an analogical correspondence to God's knowledge, meaning it is faithful to God's truth but is qualitatively different and finite. For Van Til, truth ultimately consists in "correspondence to the internally self-complete nature and knowledge that God has of himself and of all created reality."[142]

Van Til's concept of truth raises many significant questions for those outside of Evangelicalism. The first broad question is the issue of common ground between the Christian and the non-Christian. Van Til's concept of truth, and arguably much within Evangelical theology, obliterates common ground between the Christian and the non-Christian. If biblical Christianity is the only rational interpretation of the universe in which we live, is it a complete one? What about the realms of science, mathematics, and psychology? If biblical Christianity as a rational interpretation of the universe does not address these areas, from where does their truth come? Perhaps this question could be stated more briefly in the following statement that many would embrace: not all truth is about God.[143]

A second question raised is Van Til's assumption of the Bible's truthfulness in terms of propositions, and that those propositional truths are given in a rational form that addresses all of reality. It is common, indeed perhaps characteristic, of Evangelical theology to assume that the truth of the Bible, God's truth, is given in propositional form. Even further, that propositional form is understood in terms of sentences—a view rejected by such scholars as George A. Lindbeck, who argues that sentences are not to be identified with propositions.[144] Moreover, Van

---

141. Related to this, in regard to whether knowledge is analogical, univocal, or equivocal, one could add that Van Til fails to demonstrate the necessity of derivative knowledge being relevant to whether the proposition is analogical of the source or shares univocal meaning with the source. This is noted by David Hoover, "For the Sake of the Argument" (unpublished paper presented at the annual meeting (1977) of the Evangelical Philosophical Society, 17), quoted in Sailer, "Apologetics Revisited," 19.

142. Van Til, *Apologetics*, 10.

143. It is to be noted that this is quite distinct from stating that not all truth is *of* God.

Til and many other Evangelicals would assert that the Bible's truthfulness goes beyond faith and ethics and enters the realms of science and history.[145] A fundamental question is whether this is indeed the case, or whether there are fields of knowledge to which the Bible does not speak.[146] Further, one must ask what role is given to personal experience?

Finally, what of the use of reason? Have Van Til and others within Evangelical theology adequately explained the dynamics between the use of reason and the noetic consequences of the fall? Are such disciplines as mathematics prone to error in the same way that unregenerate thinking apart from biblical revelation is prone to error? The broadest question of all must not be overlooked: is truth rational?

---

144. George A. Lindbeck, *The Nature of Doctrine: Religion and Theology in a Postliberal Age* (Philadelphia: Westminster, 1984), 67-69.

145. Most Evangelicals would assert this only in regard to those passages where the context intimates that the biblical author intended to speak to a historical or scientific issue in a factual manner. Evangelicals would insist that error here is disastrous to the authority of Scripture. Others insist that this is a concept of revelation and inspiration that is problematic.

146. An excellent introduction to various Evangelical "standpoints" in terms of scholarship can be found in Mark A. Noll's *Between Faith and Criticism: Evangelicals, Scholarship, and the Bible in America* (San Francisco: Harper and Row, 1986), 143-161.

Chapter Five

TRUTH AND
APOLOGETIC:
FRANCIS A. SCHAEFFER

Francis A. Schaeffer was an Evangelical who enjoyed wide popularity through books, lectures, and films. Schaeffer's enormous popularity can be gauged by many standards, such as the recognition by the secular media: he was called "missionary to the intellectuals" by *Time* and "Guru of Fundamentalism" by Kenneth L. Woodward in *Newsweek*. Woodward also noted that "he is the newest celebrity . . . Senate wives discuss his writings. . . . TV preachers vie to get him on their shows; evangelical magazines feature his craggy face on their covers, and at fundamentalist schools, students quote him almost as often as Holy Writ."[1] Schaeffer's books also were popular; for example, *How Should We Then Live* sold 40,000 copies in its first three months.[2] As Garry Wills has noted, it was not Schaeffer's critical acclaim that garnered his popularity; it was the fact that he offered a "refreshing initiation into cultural

---

1. "Missionary to the Intellectuals," *Time* (January 11, 1960), 48; Kenneth L. Woodward, "Guru of Fundamantalism" in *Newsweek*, (November 1, 1982), 88.
2. See "The Rise of Francis Schaeffer," *Eternity* (June 1977), 40-42, 59, an article which also mentions the large attendance at his accompanying seminars, which in 1976 included 6,600 attendees in Los Angeles alone.

criticism for those who had been encouraged to neglect secular concerns."[3] With his wife Edith, Schaeffer founded an international study center and Christian community, L'Abri Fellowship, which has branches in Switzerland, England, the Netherlands, Sweden, France, and the United States.[4]

Biographical Background

Francis August Schaeffer was born the only child of Francis August Schaeffer III and Bessie Williamson Schaeffer on January 30, 1912, in Germantown, Pennsylvania.[5] Schaeffer was intellectually inquisitive at an early age. At the age of eighteen he began to read the Bible along with his reading of Ovid, simply for comparison as a matter of curiosity. Six months later he became a Christian.[6]

In 1935 Schaeffer graduated magna cum laude with a B.A. degree from Hampden-Sydney College after leaving a brief period of study at Drexel Institute in Philadelphia where he had pursued engineering. One year later, on July 26, 1935, he married Edith Seville, the daughter of former missionaries to China who had returned to the United States. Later that same year he entered Westminster Theological Seminary in Philadelphia, Pennsylvania. J. Gresham Machen, along with several oth-

---

3. Garry Wills, *Under God: Religion and American Politics* (New York: Simon and Schuster, 1990), 321.

4. L'Abri is French for "the shelter;" L'Abri was designed to operate on four principles: (1) they would not ask for contributions but would rather make their needs known to God alone; (2) they would not recruit staff but would rely on God to send them the right people; (3) plans would be made day to day and not far ahead, in order to allow for God's sovereign guidance to lead them; (4) they would not publicize themselves but would trust the Lord to send them people truly seeking and in need; on this, see Christopher Catherwood, *Five Evangelical Leaders: John Stott, Martyn Lloyd-Jones, Francis Schaeffer, James I. Packer, Billy Graham* (Wheaton: Harold Shaw, 1985), 123.

5. Biographical background on the life and ministry of Francis A. Schaeffer is greatly aided by three works written by Schaeffer's wife, Edith, on their lives: *L'Abri* (Wheaton: Tyndale, 1969); *The Tapestry: The Life and Times of Francis and Edith Schaeffer* (Waco: Word, 1981) and *What Is a Family?* (Old Tappan, N.J.: Fleming H. Revell, 1975). Other articles and works which offer biographical information include Board, "The Rise of Francis Schaeffer," 40-42, 59; Stephen Board and Vernon C. Grounds, "An Evangelical Thinker Who Left His Mark: Francis A. Schaeffer IV: 1912-1984," *Christianity Today* (June 15, 1984), 60-63; Catherwood, *Five Evangelical Leaders*, 111-162; Lane T. Dennis, ed., *Francis A. Schaeffer: Portraits of the Man and His Work* (Westchester, Ill: Crossway, 1986); Lane T. Dennis, *Letters of Francis A. Schaeffer* (Westchester, Ill.: Crossway, 1985); George Marsden, "As We See It: Francis A. Schaeffer (1912-1984)," *The Reformed Journal* vol. 34, no. 6 (June 1984), 2-3; Louis Gifford Parkhurst, Jr., *Francis Schaeffer: The Man and His Message* (Wheaton: Tyndale, 1986); Ronald W. Ruegsegger, ed., *Reflections on Francis Schaeffer* (Grand Rapids: Academie, 1986); Philip Yancey, "Francis Schaeffer: A Prophet for Our Time?," *Christianity Today* (March 23, 1979), 655-659; Philip Yancey (interview), "Schaeffer on Schaeffer, Part I," *Christianity Today* (March 23, 1979), 660-662; Part II," *Christianity Today* (April 6, 1979), 731-736.

6. See Schaeffer, "Why and How I Write My Books," *Eternity* 24 (March 1973), 64.

ers previously associated with Princeton Seminary, had left to form
Westminster Theological Seminary. This newly formed seminary and
subsequent denomination, the Orthodox Presbyterian Church, soon
experienced dissent within its own ranks over the issues of eschatology,
Christian liberty, and denominational sectarianism. Carl McIntire led a
group including Schaeffer who broke from Westminster and Machen to
form Faith Theological Seminary and the Bible Presbyterian Church. In
1956 the majority of the Bible Presbyterian group removed McIntire and
as an alternative to Faith Seminary founded Covenant College and Seminary in St. Louis, Missouri, the current home to the Francis A. Schaeffer
Institute. The Bible Presbyterian Church would become the Evangelical
Presbyterian Church, then the Reformed Presbyterian Church, Evangelical Synod. It is now part of the Presbyterian Church in America. Schaeffer graduated from Faith Theological Seminary.[7]

Schaeffer was ordained as the first pastor of the newly formed Bible
Presbyterian denomination in 1938. That very year he began his ministry
as pastor of Covenant Presbyterian Church in Grove City, Pennsylvania,
where he served for three years. Schaeffer continued in the pastorate
following his tenure at Covenant, serving three different churches in
Pennsylvania and Missouri in just six years. In 1947 he moved to Europe
as a missionary with the Independent Board for Presbyterian Missions.[8]

Schaeffer first travelled throughout Europe for three months to evaluate the state of the church as a representative of the Independent Board
for Presbyterian Foreign Missions and as the American Secretary for the
Foreign Relations Department of the American Council of Christian
Churches. The Schaeffers moved to Lausanne, Switzerland, to become
involved with the Children for Christ ministry and to assist in the formation of the International Council of Christian Churches which was to
gather in Amsterdam in August, 1948.

During the winter months of 1951 Schaeffer went through a spiritual
crisis. He reconsidered his most basic Christian commitments and priori-
ties, emerging with a renewed certainty regarding Christianity and a new
direction concerning his own personal ministry. During this period
Schaeffer began to pursue his interest in philosophy and apologetics,
largely as a result of his friendship with Amsterdam art historian Hans
Rookmaker.[9]

---

7. On this, see Charles G. Dennison, and Richard C. Gamble, eds., *Pressing Toward the Mark: Essays Commemorating Fifty Years of the Orthodox Presbyterian Church* (Phila-delphia: Orthodox Presbyterian Church, 1986); Board, "Evangelical Thinker," 60; Marsden, "As We See It," 2-3.

8. In 1941 Schaeffer was elected moderator of the Great Lakes Presbytery of the Bible Presbyterian Church and also began serving as associate pastor of the Bible Presbyterian Church in Chester, Pennsylvania. In 1943 Schaeffer began serving as the pastor of the Bible Presbyterian Church in St. Louis, Missouri.

9. Board, "Evangelical Thinker," 60.

From this time forward Schaeffer began to grow in popularity. On furlough between 1953 and 1954, Schaeffer travelled across the United States, speaking 346 times during 515 days about the deeper spiritual life.[10] He was awarded an honorary Doctor of Divinity degree in May of 1954 by Highland College in Long Beach, California.

Schaeffer resigned from the Independent Board for Presbyterian Foreign Missions on June 5, 1955, a date which can also serve as the informal beginning of L'Abri Fellowship. Francis and Edith Schaeffer focused on this ministry until shortly before Francis' death in 1984. L'Abri's ministry began one weekend in 1955 when Schaeffer answered questions from some visiting friends of his daughter Priscilla. Captivated by the answers, they relayed their experience to others. Before long people were coming to L'Abri from all over the world.[11] L'Abri provided a place where confused young people with intellectual doubts and concerns could find an environment that would assist them in discovering answers. Three types of students came to L'Abri: (1) twentieth-century people, mainly of university age, troubled by modern thinking; (2) young people from Christian backgrounds who had turned against their faith; and (3) older Christian workers who wanted assistance in regards to the questions modern youth asked.[12]

L'Abri has been described as follows:

> A community where the questions arising out of 20th century life and thought are brought into contact with the answers provided by historical, biblical Christianity. We believe that there is objective Truth in the universe, beginning with the existence of the infinite, triune God of Scripture. We consider that the truth of Christianity is open to discussion, examination and verification and that *it encompasses the whole of reality.* On this basis of historical, biblical Christianity we believe that those who honestly seek after Truth will find it. Therefore, we pray that those who are seeking the Truth of the universe and not just a personal experience, and who have not been able to find what they need in other ways, will be brought here. We pray that God will order the comings and going of those people whom He would have be here, so that the combination of people at any given moment will be the most beneficial to all concerned.[13]

---

10. Schaeffer's *True Spirituality* in *The Complete Works of Francis A. Schaeffer,* vol. III is largely a product of his spiritual crisis in 1951 and of the talks he gave on this furlough. Throughout that work one can see a commitment to the certainty of the faith and an emphasis on sanctification and the work of the Holy Spirit.

11. On L'Abri, see Edith Schaeffer's two biographical volumes, *L'Abri* and *The Tapestry.*

12. See Catherwood, *Evangelical Leaders,* 127-128; Schaeffer, "Why and How I Write," 76.

13. Taken from personal correspondence which was sent in preparation for personal study at L'Abri at Chalet les Melezes in Huemoz, Switzerland, under the direction of Udo and Debbie Middelmann.

Os Guinness summarized L'Abri in this manner: "Truth mattered and people mattered; those were the two secrets of L'Abri."[14] An English L'Abri was founded after Schaeffer lectured at Oxford in 1958. The first of Schaeffer's twenty-three books, based upon a series of Wheaton College lectures, was published in 1968.[15] In 1971 Schaeffer received the honorary Doctor of Letters from Gordon College in Wenham, Massachusetts. In 1974 Schaeffer reacted to Kenneth Clark's civilization by starting the book and film *How Should We Then Live?* with his son Franky. This book contains the most comprehensive statement of Schaeffer's system of thought. Reception of the book led to a twenty-two city speaking tour in 1977. Schaeffer's excursion into this medium of communication drew criticism from many, even within the circle of L'Abri. They said he had abandoned the initial principles that guided L'Abri and that he was catering to his image as a "guru."[16] That same year Schaeffer helped found the International Council on Biblical Inerrancy. In 1979, Schaeffer wrote *Whatever Happened to the Human Race* with C. Everett Koop, Surgeon General of the United States. This was instrumental in drawing together the anti-abortion movement in the United States.[17]

In 1978 he was diagnosed as having lymphatic cancer at the Mayo Clinic in Rochester, Minnesota.[18] The last six years of Schaeffer's life were anything but unproductive in spite of his long and difficult battle

---

14. As quoted in Catherwood, *Evangelical Leaders*, 131.

15. Francis A. Schaeffer, *The God Who Is There* in *The Complete Works of Francis A. Schaeffer*, vol. I (Westchester, Ill.: Crossway, 1982); Ronald W. Ruegsegger has insightfully selected from among Schaeffer's writings and organized them for study (largely due to Schaeffer's tendency to repeat arguments and build upon previous writings) in the following three groupings: first, Schaeffer's self-conscious trilogy *The God Who Is There, Escape from Reason* in *The Complete Works of Francis A. Schaeffer*, vol. I, and *He Is There and He Is Not Silent* in *The Complete Works of Francis A. Schaeffer*, vol. I, all of which explore fundamental issues of philosophy and epistemology; second, *How Shall We Then Live*, a fulsome presentation of Schaeffer's system of thought, expanding from the aforementioned trilogy into areas of history, morals, and politics; third, *Whatever Happened to the Human Race?* in *The Complete Works of Francis A. Schaeffer*, vol. 5 and *A Christian Manifesto* in *The Complete Works of Francis A. Schaeffer*, Vol. 5 where Schaeffer turned toward the practical and politically oriented issues of the day, such as abortion and biblical inerrancy, see Ruegsegger, "Schaeffer's System of Thought," *Reflections*, 27-9. The most significant of Schaeffer's writings are indeed found in his first trilogy, recently reissued as *The Francis A. Schaeffer Trilogy: The Three Essential Books in One Volume* (Westchester, Ill.: Crossway, 1990). These will be the works most frequently cited throughout the text; invaluable insights into Schaeffer's system of thought can be found through the large number of cassettes, encompassing thousands of hours of lectures, available through Sound Word Associates, P.O. Box 2035, 430 Boyd Circle, Michigan City, IN 46360 (organized under "L'Abri Cassettes, Catalogue No. 5.").

16. See "Schaeffer on Schaeffer, Part II," 26; Catherwood, *Evangelical Leaders*, 146-149.

17. Wills writes that Schaeffer is the single individual most responsible for making abortion the galvanizing issue it has become, see *Under God*, 320. Randall Terry, activist founder of anti-abortion "Operation Rescue," says that to understand their organization, you must read Schaeffer's *A Christian Manifesto*, see Wills, *Under God*, 324.

18. On Francis Schaeffer's last days, see "God Is Giving Me New Opportunities," an interview with Edith Schaeffer, *Decision* (July-August 1985), 23-24.

with cancer. In 1979 the American headquarters of L'Abri was established in Rochester, Minnesota; in 1982 *The Complete Works of Francis A. Schaeffer* was published. This involved extensive re-editing, updating, and clarifying of many of his works. In 1983 he received an honorary Doctor of Laws degree from the Simon Greenleaf School of Law, and in 1984, Schaeffer went on a tour to ten Christian colleges in support of his last book, *The Great Evangelical Disaster.* He remained in the United States where he lived until his death on May 15, 1984, at his home in Rochester, Minnesota.[19]

Description of Schaeffer's Concept of Truth

The concept of truth in the theology of Francis A. Schaeffer is a correspondence theory of truth built upon the basis of antithesis with the ultimate referent existing in God's perfect knowledge. Such an understanding of truth, for Schaeffer, entails that such truth is revealed, absolute, and objective.

Truth as Antithesis

Schaeffer's first line from his first book is indicative of what occupied much of his intellectual life: "The present chasm between the generations has been brought about almost entirely by a change in the concept of truth."[20] What is this change? Schaeffer expressed it as follows:

> The basic one was that there really are such things as absolutes. They accepted the possibility of an absolute in the area of Being (or knowledge), and in the area of morals. Therefore, because they accepted the possibility of absolutes, though people might have disagreed as to what these were, nevertheless they could reason together on the classical basis of antithesis. They took it for granted that if anything was true, the opposite was false. In morality, if one thing was right, its opposite was wrong. This little formula, "A is A" and "If you have A it is not non-A," is the first move in classical logic. If you understand the extent to which this no longer holds sway, you will understand our present situation.[21]

---

19. Schaeffer's son, Franky, has attempted to continue many of his father's concerns in such works as *Addicted to Mediocrity* (Westchester, Ill.: Crossway, 1981), *A Time for Anger* (Westchester, Ill.: Crossway, 1982), and *Bad News for Modern Man* (Westchester, Ill.: Crossway, 1984) but with a very poor reception, largely due to the lack of an irenic spirit which tempered his father's strong convictions. On this, see Richard V. Pierard's "The Unmasking of Francis Schaeffer: An Evangelical Tragedy" in *The Wittenberg Door* 78 (April-May 1984), 27-31, who notes that the real undoing of Francis A. Schaeffer IV is Francis A. Schaeffer V.

20. Schaeffer, *God Who Is There*, 5; compare *Christian Manifesto*, 423-30.

21. Schaeffer, *God Who Is There*, 6.

If a statement is true, its opposite is not true. We must take this very seriously. . . . Unless we accept the modern twentieth-century concept that religious truth is only psychological truth, then if there is that which is true, the opposite is not true. Two religions that teach exactly opposite things may both be wrong, but they cannot both be right. We must act upon, witness, and preach this fact: what is contrary to God's revealed propositional truth is not true, whether it is couched in Hindu terms or traditional Christian terms with new meanings.[22]

This excerpt reveals the central idea of antithesis in Schaeffer's understanding of truth. It can be termed "propositional truth," or "truth which can be communicated in the form of a statement in which a predicate or object is affirmed or denied regarding a subject."[23] The idea of antithesis means "the concept that if a certain thing is true, the opposite is not true; or if a certain thing is right, the opposite is wrong."[24] According to Schaeffer, this must be presupposed, that is, it must be "accepted before the next step in logic is developed. Such a prior postulate consciously or unconsciously affects the way a person subsequently reasons."[25] For Schaeffer, the presupposition of antithesis as integral to the concept of truth is all-encompassing, for "Christianity demands antithesis, not as some abstract concept of truth, but in the fact that God exists, and in personal justification."[26] Failure to stand for this concept of truth—that of antithesis—was for Schaeffer "the great Evangelical disaster."[27]

Schaeffer should not, however, be construed as a "rationalist," especially when rationalist is defined as "someone who thinks man can begin with himself and his reason plus what he observes, without information from any other source, and come to final answers in regards to truth, ethics and reality."[28] Schaeffer did argue that good and sufficient reasons exist to know that the biblical claims are indeed true, largely on the grounds of an orderly universe and the "mannishness" of man. In other words, those aspects of humanity, such as significance, love, rationality, and the fear of non-being, separate human beings from animals

22. Francis A. Schaeffer, *The Church at the End of the Twentieth Century* in *The Complete Works of Francis A. Schaeffer*, vol. 4, 31-32.

23. Schaeffer, *God Who Is There*, 202; on propositional truth, see also *He Is There*, 345-9.

24. Schaeffer, *God Who Is There*, 184.

25. Ibid,, 201.

26. Ibid., 47; Schaeffer treats the philosophical necessity of God's existence in *He Is There*.

27. This formed the title for Schaeffer's last book, *The Great Evangelical Disaster*, see 37; Schaeffer coupled the rejection of antithesis with the raging debate on biblical inerrancy but by this time the focus of his attention was biblical inerrancy, see 143.

28. Schaeffer, *God Who Is There*, 183; this section of *God Who Is There* was added as an appendix to the original when Schaeffer's corpus was gathered for publication as a unit in 1982 to answer such questions, including the idea that he was putting forth his own "apologetic," which he denied; see Thomas V. Morris, *Francis Schaeffer's Apologetics: A Critique* (Chicago: Moody, 1976).

and machines and give evidence of humans being created in the image of a personal God. Schaeffer, in "contrast to the words rationalist or rationalism," argued for "rationality," which "concerns the validity of thought, or the possibility to reason."[29] Although rationality was obviously important to Schaeffer, he did not want it to "become exclusively so. Rationality," he wrote, "is not the end of the matter."[30] In fact, Schaeffer contended that "no one stresses more than I that people have no final answers in regard to truth, morals or epistemology without God's revelation in the Bible."[31] For example, Schaeffer wrote that a human being, "if he is only rationalistic, cannot really be sure that the sun is going to rise tomorrow morning; all he has is statistics and averages."[32] Schaeffer also rejected the label "Aristotelian," insisting that such a claim intimates that "thought in terms of antithesis was originated by Aristotle," which he claimed is erroneous.[33] Schaeffer contended that historic Christianity rested upon the presupposition of antithesis, and thus without it, is meaningless.[34] He wrote:

> If a clear and unmistakable emphasis on truth, in the sense of antithesis, is removed, two things occur: firstly, Christianity in the next generation as true Christianity is weakened; and secondly, we shall be communicating only with that diminishing portion of the community which still thinks in terms of the older concept of truth . . . If we do not communicate clearly on the basis of antithesis, many will respond to their own interpretation of the gospel, in their own relativistic thought-forms, including a concept of psychological guilt-feeling rather than of true moral guilt before the holy, living God . . . The unity of orthodox or evangelical Christianity should be centered around this emphasis on truth. It is always important, but doubly so when we are surrounded by so many for whom the concept of truth, in the sense of antithesis, is considered to be totally unthinkable . . . In such a setting the problem of communication is serious; it can only be overcome by negative state-

29. *God Who Is There*, 183; Schaeffer was less than consistent in his use of these terms. His definitions were not the traditional ones used by philosophers in epistemological discussions; on this see Kent R. Hill, "Francis Schaeffer (1912-1984): An Evaluation of His Life and Thought," in *Faith and Imagination: Essays on Evangelicals and Literature*, ed. by Noel Riley Fitch and Richard W. Etulain (Albuquerque, N.M.: Far West Books, 1985), 144-145.

30. *God Who Is There*, 123.

31. Ibid., 184.

32. Francis A Schaeffer, *Genesis in Space and Time* in *The Complete Works of Francis A. Schaeffer*, vol. 2, 105; nonetheless, Philip Yancey in "Francis Schaeffer: A Prophet for Our Time," 18, has observed that in Schaeffer's work one finds the "downplaying of the nonrational (not irrational) aspects of the gospel. Schaeffer seems to rely on the power of reasoning, as if the only way a person could come to Christ is by arguing himself into the Kingdom."

33. Thus Schaeffer rejects Heidegger's view to the contrary, which Schaeffer feels has no historic basis. For Schaeffer, antithesis is rooted not in Aristotle, but in reality; see *God Who Is There*, 184.

34. Ibid., 8.

ments that clearly say what we do not mean, so that the twentieth-century man understands the positive statements we do mean.[35]

Schaeffer held to this view on the grounds that "the basic antithesis is that God objectively exists in contrast (in antithesis) to His not existing."[36]

Presuppositionalism. The spectre of Schaeffer's former teacher at Westminster Theological Seminary, Cornelius Van Til, looms large in Schaeffer's presuppositionalism.[37] Schaeffer asserts that presuppositional apologetics would have arrested the move from the idea of absolutes to the idea of truth as relative.[38] Yet Schaeffer disagreed with Van Til on several points such as the possibility of common ground between the Christian and the non-Christian:

> There are no neutral facts, for facts are God's facts. However, there is common ground between the Christian and the non-Christian because regardless of a man's system, he has to live in God's world. If he were consistent to his non-Christian presuppositions he would be separated from the real universe and the real man, and conversation and communication would not be possible.[39]

Schaeffer also differed from Van Til in his stance that the presuppositions with which one begins are themselves open to verification. Schaeffer writes that "we cannot say, on the one hand, that we believe in the unity of truth and then, on the other hand, suddenly withdraw from the discussion and tell him to believe on blind authority."[40] For Schaeffer, the historic Christian faith is

---

35. *God Who Is There*, 195-196; throughout his writings, Schaeffer constantly stressed the importance of coupling this strong stand for antithetical truth with the personal practice of truth, stating that "in an age of synthesis, men will not take our protestations of truth seriously unless they see by our actions that we practice truth and antithesis in the unity we try to establish, and in our activities." See *God Who Is There*, 196, as well as *The Mark of the Christian*, contained in *The Complete Works of Francis A. Schaeffer*, vol. 4.

36. *God Who Is There*, 8.

37. For a discussion of Van Til's system of thought, see the previous chapter on Van Til; Schaeffer acknowledged his debt to his former teacher in "A Review of a Review," *The Bible Today* 42 (October 1948), 7-9, and in "Schaeffer on Schaeffer, Part 1," 21; beyond Van Til, Forrest Baird in "Schaeffer's Intellectual Roots," *Reflections*, 45-67, notes that Schaeffer borrows heavily from Princeton Theology and its primary spokesmen (Machen, Warfield, and Hodge) in regards to biblical inerrancy, religious experience, and separatism; Jack Rogers adds in "Francis Schaeffer: The Promise and Problem, Part I," *The Reformed Journal* 27 (May 1977), 15, that Schaeffer also takes the views that all persons think alike and that language is precise and literal and shares a universal grammar. Such a view stemmed from Thomas Reid and Scottish Common Sense Philsophy, discussed in chapter 1 of this text, 14.

38. See *God Who Is There*, 15.

39. Ibid.,138; Schaeffer notes that this idea was first presented in his article "A Review of a Review;" as with Van Til, Romans 1 is essential to this perspective and is quoted and exegeted in an accompanying footnote.

40. *God Who Is There*, 139; see also *Whatever Happened*, 391.

not a leap of faith in the post-Kierkegaardian sense because He is not silent, and I am invited to ask the adequate and sufficient questions, not only in regard to details, but also in regard to the existence of the universe and its complexity and in regard to the existence of man. I am invited to ask adequate and sufficient questions and then believe Him and bow before Him metaphysically in knowing that I exist because he made man, and bow before Him morally as needing His provision for me in the substitutionary, propitiatory death of Christ.[41]

Van Til would reject such an idea on the grounds that it elevated reason above revelation. As a result, Schaeffer is best placed in the apologetical category of verification[42] as opposed to Van Tillian presuppositionalism,[43] though Schaeffer himself resisted such categorizations.[44] When a student asked a question that began, "Since you are a presuppositionalist, rather than an evidentialist . . . ," Schaeffer replied, "I'm neither. I'm not an evidentialist or a presuppositionalist. You're trying to press me into the category of a theological apologist, which I'm really not. I'm not an academic, scholastic apologist. My interest is in evangelism."[45]

Schaeffer agrees with Van Til on the importance of presuppositions. He agrees that if non-Christians were consistent with their presuppositions, common ground between believers and non-believers would be non-existent. Schaeffer disagrees as to the amount of common ground available between the Christian and non-Christian on the basis of rational verification. Schaeffer's presuppositions, perhaps better termed "hypotheses," are not meant to be too ultimate to be verified.[46] Non-Christians are not consistent in applying their presuppositions, a product of common grace (a remnant of God's image in humanity), and therefore communication and intellectual persuasion can occur.[47] An example of Schaeffer's contention along these lines can be found in a parable

---

41. Schaeffer, *He Is There*, 352.

42. Schaeffer defines verification as the "procedure required for the establishment of the truth or falsity of a statement," see *God Who Is There*, 180.

43. On this, see Gordon Lewis' article, "Schaeffer's Apologetic Method" in *Reflections*, 69-104; see also Gordon Lewis, *Testing Christianity's Truth-Claims* (Chicago: Moody, 1976), 296-301; Kenneth C. Harper, "Francis A. Schaeffer: An Evaluation," *Bibliotheca Sacra* (April 1976), 138, who categorizes Schaeffer as an "inconsistent presuppositionalist;" Harold J. Franz, in an early review of Schaeffer's work, notes that Schaeffer's "appeal is no longer in a presuppositional frame," see "The God Who Is There," *Westminster Theological Journal* XXXII (November 1969-May 1970), 116. This contention regarding Schaeffer's apologetic approach is contested by Morris in *Schaeffer's Apologetics*, who argues for Schaeffer being a presuppositionalist, as well as Robert L. Reymond, *The Justification of Knowledge* (Nutley, N.J.: Presbyterian and Reformed, 1976), who argues that Schaeffer is representative of the empirical apologetic tradition.

44. Harper notes that in an interview Schaeffer showed extreme reluctance to answer questions regarding this subject, see Harper, "Schaeffer: An Evaluation," 138.

45. Rogers, "Schaeffer: Promise and Problem, Part 1," 12-13.

46. On this, see Lewis, "Schaeffer's Apologetic Method," 79.

47. On this, see Harper, "Schaeffer: An Evaluation," 138; Schaeffer, "A Review of a Review," 7-9; Schaeffer, *God Who Is There*, 129ff.

about a group of mountain climbers caught on a dangerous ledge with fog and darkness quickly closing.[48] The shout of a potential rescuer comes to their ears, claiming knowledge to save them from their predicament. Can the group trust this voice? Schaeffer argues that the group should ask questions of the rescuer first, and only after determining trustworthiness should they follow his guidelines to reach safety. Nonetheless, Schaeffer is hesitant to use traditional proofs for the Christian faith, tending rather to follow his presuppositionalism to point out the discrepancies in the presuppositions of non-Christian systems of thought. As Harper noted,

Schaeffer absorbs this largely negative approach by seeking to document the emptiness and despair inherent in contemporary culture and in its philosophical bases. Therefore, despite Schaeffer's continued insistence that Christianity is rational and has a rational basis for communication, he makes very little of this on a practical level.[49]

Schaeffer's insistence on using the negative approach of presuppositionalism was due to his being convinced that only Christians can live consistently with their presuppositions. The reason for this contention is that Schaeffer felt that only the biblical absolutes correspond to the reality of the universe and humanity.[50]

The Line of Despair. Schaeffer argued that the shift in modern thought regarding the rejection of antithesis as a presupposition can be traced to what he calls "the line of despair" (see following diagram):[51]

**Europe before 1890 and the
U.S. before 1935**

The line of despair_____

**Europe after 1890
U.S. after 1935**

---

48. Schaeffer, *He Is There*, 351-352.

49. Harper, "Schaeffer: An Evaluation," 139; a similar approach is noted by Harper in Gordon H. Clark, *A Christian View of Men and Things* (Grand Rapids: Eerdmans, 1960), where internal self-consistency is the only 'evidence' presented for Christianity and where the emphasis is on showing the weaknesses in alternative positions.

50. On this, see Rogers, "Schaeffer: Promise and Problem," 13.

51. Schaeffer, *God Who Is There*, 8-9; a much more elaborate schematization of Schaeffer's line of despair can be found in Ruegsegger's article, "Schaeffer's System of Thought," *Reflections*, 31.

"Above this line we find men living with their romantic notions of absolutes (though with no sufficient logical basis)," wrote Schaeffer, yet on this "side of the line, all is changed. Man thinks differently regarding truth."[52] Before the "line of despair" the common assumption was that truth was absolute; after the "line of despair" truth continued to be seen as absolute by Christians, but as relative by non-Christians.[53] Ruegsegger argues that Schaeffer really has two "lines" which are present in his thought: first, the line which indicates the shift from absolutism to relativism; second, the line which indicates the shift from reason to faith.[54] The first of these shifts is in the nature of truth: the second involves how we know truth. Ruegsegger calls the first line "the line of relativism," and the second "the line of despair."[55] These shifts have spread in three ways: (1) a geographic movement from Germany to the Continent, England, and the United States; (2) a social movement from intellectuals to the working class and then the middle class; and (3) a movement through the disciplines, beginning with philosophy, then moving to art, music, general culture, and then theology.

According to Schaeffer, the reason for this shift is that the "philosophers came to the conclusion that they were not going to find a unified rationalistic circle that would contain all thought, and in which they could live." Departing "from the classical methodology of antithesis, they shifted the concept of truth, and modern man was born."[56] Schaeffer terms this "antiphilosophy" and associates it with many of the modern forms of philosophy that have abandoned any attempt to find a rational unity to the whole of thought and life.[57]

Schaeffer pointed to Hegel as the principal philosopher for this transition.[58] "The German philosopher Hegel (1770-1831) . . . opened the door into the line of despair."[59] What Hegel changed,

---

52. *God Who Is There*, 8.

53. See Ron Ruegsegger, "Francis Schaeffer on Philosophy," *Christian Scholar's Review* 10 (1981), 240.

54. Ibid., 240f.

55. Ibid., 241.

56. Schaeffer, *God Who Is There*, 10; Schaeffer based such conclusions on the grounds that rationalism (or humanism, treated synonymously by Schaeffer, see the glossary, 202) is the unity within non-Christian thought; see also *Church At End of Century*, 73.

57. Schaeffer, *God Who Is There*, 199.

58. Essential writings of Hegel for study would include *The Philosophy of Right*, trans. with notes by T. M. Knox, *Great Books of the Western World*, vol. 46, ed. Robert Maynard Hutchins (Chicago: Encyclopedia Britannica, Inc., 1952); *The Philosophy of History*, trans. J. Sibree, *Great Books of the Western World*; *The Logic of Hegel*, trans. William Wallace, 2nd ed. (London: Oxford University Press, 1873); a secondary source which serves as an excellent introduction can be found in Frederick Copleston's *A History of Philosophy*, Book Three, vol. 7 (Garden City: Image Books, 1985), 159-247.

59. Schaeffer, *God Who Is There*, 13; this contention, among many made by Schaeffer, has been disputed; see Ruegsegger, "Schaeffer on Philosophy," 242-243.

was something more profound than merely one philosophic answer for another. He changed the rules of the game in two areas: epistemology, the theory of knowledge and the limits and validity of knowledge; and methodology, the method by which we approach the question of truth and knowing.[60]

Prior to Hegel, truth (in the sense of antithesis) was related to the idea of cause and effect, which produced a chain reaction which went straight on a horizontal line.[61] Hegel's formula of thesis, antithesis, and then synthesis, which in turn became a thesis, continuing as an ongoing dialectic, changed this understanding.[62] Schaeffer understood Hegel to say that absolute truth, as a result of this dialectical manner of thinking, is non-existent—only relativism remains. Following Hegel, aided by Soren Kierkegaard,[63]

> people gave up the concept of a rational, unified field of knowledge and accepted instead the idea of a leap of faith in those areas which make people distinctive as people—purpose, love, morals and so on. It was this leap of faith that originally produced the line of despair.[64]

According to Schaeffer, without the rational basis of antithesis, one can only engage in a "leap of faith" into meaning and truth.[65] For Schaeffer, this is the understanding of "modern man"; this is the "concept of truth by which we are surrounded. This is the spirit of the world to which we must say 'No,' no matter what face it puts on, including a theological one."[66] Without antithesis, argues Schaeffer, there is no ade-

---

60. Schaeffer, *Escape*, 233.

61. Schaeffer, *God Who Is There*, 13.

62. As Colin Brown notes, "it is customary to describe Hegel's view of the outworking of Spirit as a Dialectic (which is simply another word for process or dynamic pattern) of Thesis, Antithesis and Synthesis. But it has been pointed out that although Hegel makes occasional use of these latter terms, they are in fact more characteristics of Fichte. However, the basic idea is there, and the notion of Dialectic is paramount," see *Philosophy and the Christian Faith* (Downers Grove: InterVarsity, 1968), 121.

63. A case can be made that it was Kierkegaard, not Hegel, that Schaeffer sees as his main protagonist, intimated in *Church at the End of the Twentieth Century*, 14-75, and "Some Men Weep: The Tragic Loss of Our Era," *Christianity Today* 5 (May 22, 1961), 3-5. As Ruegsegger notes, Hegel may have been the doorway to the line of despair for Schaeffer, but Kierkegaard was the first to go underneath, see "Schaeffer on Philosophy," 243. Schaeffer, in his later years, saw Kierkegaard's separation of faith and reason in less absolute terms; see Ronald H. Nash, "The Life of the Mind and the Way of Life," *Schaeffer: Portraits*, 58, 224.

64. Schaeffer, *God Who Is There*, 43.

65. On the ground that faith has become divorced from justification, Schaeffer criticized Bultmann's separation of the existential Christ-encounter and the Jesus of history; see *God Who Is There*, 52. Harold O.J. Brown observed that Schaeffer's system, though not requiring a leap, demands a step of faith, and thus shares congruity with Kierkegaard's insights, see "Kierkegaard's Leap or Schaeffer's Step?," *Christianity Today* 28 (December 14, 1984), 82.

66. Schaeffer, *God Who Is There*, 31; for a discussion on what Schaeffer would see as the theological "leap," see *Escape*, 268-269.

quate base for truth. On these grounds Schaeffer rejected the "neo-orthodoxy" of individuals such as Karl Barth. They accepted the view that rationality and logic led to pessimism and instead of turning to the concept of antithesis turned to a non-rational and non-logical "upper story" of faith as "an optimistic leap without verification or communicable content."[67] Schaeffer defined the "upper story" as that which, in modern thinking, deals with significance or meaning, but which is not open to contact with verification by the world of facts (the "lower story"). Such attempts have given up a unified field of knowledge and offer instead a system which is not open to verification.[68]

Schaeffer argues that the teaching of Hegel, Kierkegaard, Immanuel Kant, and Jean Jacques Rousseau has turned the whole theory of knowledge upside down.[69] The definitional status of truth itself has been revolutionized. Schaeffer determined that the problem is so deep that

> people today live in a generation that no longer believes in the hope of truth as truth. That is why I use the term "true truth" in my books, to emphasize real truth. This is not just a tautology. It is an admission that the word truth now means something that before these four men would not have been considered truth at all. So I coined the expression "true truth" to make the point, but it is hard to make it sharp enough for people to understand how large the problem really is.[70]

Truth as Revealed

Schaeffer contended that the Bible is necessary for finding final answers regarding truth, morals, or epistemology. To support special revelation's position as that which conveys authoritative truth, Schaeffer argued vociferously for the inerrancy of the Bible. In 1977 he helped to found the International Council on Biblical Inerrancy. Schaeffer's passion for the cause of biblical inerrancy can be sensed in what he wrote for the folder distributed to call for the conference:

> Unless the Bible is without error, not only when it speaks of salvation matters, but also when it speaks of history and the cosmos, we have no foundation for answering questions concerning the existence of the universe and its form and the uniqueness of man. Nor do we have any

---

67. Schaeffer, *God Who Is There*, 53, 202; Schaeffer argues that Kierkegaard, with his leap, opened the door to existentialism in general, and Barth, with his leap, opened the door to the existentialistic leap in theology, followed by Reinhold Niebuhr and Paul Tillich, see *God Who Is There*, 55.

68. Ibid., 55; by verification, Schaeffer means the procedure required for the establishment of the truth or falsity of a statement, see 202.

69. For a detailed discussion of this, see Schaeffer's *How Should We Then Live?*, 165-182.

70. Schaeffer, *He Is There*, 312-313.

moral absolutes, or certainty of salvation, and the next generation of
Christians will have nothing on which to stand.[71]

"What we claim as Christians," wrote Schaeffer, "is that when all of
the facts are taken into consideration, the Bible gives us true knowledge
although not exhaustive knowledge."[72] More specifically, Schaeffer
insisted concerning the Bible that

> wherever it touches upon anything, it does so with true truth, but not
> with exhaustive truth. That is, where it speaks of the cosmos, science,
> what it says is true. Likewise, where it touches history, it speaks with
> what I call true truth—that is, propositional, objective truth.[73]

In using the term inerrancy, Schaeffer defended:

> Because of the widely accepted existential methodology in certain parts
> of the evangelical community, the old words "infallibility," "inerrancy"
> and "without error" are meaningless today unless some phrase is added
> such as: the Bible is without error not only when it speaks of values,
> the meaning system and religious things, but it is also without error
> when it speaks of history and the cosmos.[74]

It is important to note that Schaeffer did not construe the Bible as the
systematic presentation of the unity of truth. For Schaeffer, the emphasis
on the unity of truth is not ultimately related to orthodoxy, the Creeds,
or even to Scripture. "The Bible, the historic Creeds, and orthodoxy are
important because God is there, and, finally, that is the only reason they
have their importance."[75] The unity of truth exists as a result of the
existence of God and who He is; Christian truth is that which is in relationship to what exists and ultimately to the God who exists.[76]

Schaeffer did note that Christianity itself is a system "which is com-
posed of a set of ideas which can be discussed."[77] By "system," Schaeffer did not mean a "scholastic abstraction;" he felt that the Bible does
not set out "unrelated thoughts. The system it sets forth has a beginning
and moves from the beginning in a noncontradictory way."[78] Schaeffer
has written that it contains "all the answers to all the intellectual questions to all of life."[79]

---

71. *Church at End of Twentieth Century,* 103.
72. *Genesis,* 22-3.
73. Ibid., 52.
74. Francis A. Schaeffer, *No Final Conflict* in *The Complete Works of Francis A. Schaeffer,* vol. 2, 146; see also Schaeffer's similar contention is his address delivered at the International Congress on World Evangelization in Lausanne, Switzerland, July, 1974, partially
reprinted as "Schaeffer on Scripture," *Christianity Today* 19 (August 29, 1975), 29.
75. *God Who Is There,* 157.
76. Ibid., 157.
77. *Escape,* 268.
78. Ibid., 268.
79. "Why and How I Write," 64.

This truth is also propositional, for it has been given to us in propositional form (the Bible). The propositional form of truth in the Bible also assists Schaeffer's contention that humanity's rationality is part of the image of God retained from creation after the fall.

Truth as Absolute

Schaeffer argued passionately throughout his writings for truth being that which is absolute. As quoted previously, of all the presuppositions upon which historic Christianity rests,

> the basic one was that there really are such things as absolutes. They accepted the possibility of an absolute in the area of Being (or knowledge), and in the area of morals. Therefore, because they accepted the possibility of absolutes, though people might have disagreed as to what these were, nevertheless they could reason together on the classical basis of antithesis.[80]

Schaeffer defines what he means by "absolute" as follows: "A concept which is not modifiable by factors such as culture, individual psychology or circumstances, but which is perfect and unchangeable."[81] For Schaeffer, such a term is "used as an antithesis of relativism."[82] In other words, "there are certain unchangeable facts which are true. These have no relationship to the shifting tides."[83] The "shifting tides" to which Schaeffer refers are related to such variables as historical setting, personal life-situation, or cultural setting which might be used to suggest that what was true at one point in time in a given situation might not be true at another point in time in a given situation. Schaeffer saw this dynamic taking place in some areas of knowledge, but denied that it could take place in regard to God's revealed truth as recorded in Scripture. Truth as absolute was essential for Schaeffer. He warned,

> once we begin to slip over into the other methodology—a failure to hold on to an absolute which can be known by the whole man, including what is logical and rational in him—historic Christianity is destroyed, even if it seems to keep going for a time.[84]

Without truth as absolute, there are no absolutes—except society, which becomes absolute by default.[85]

---

80. *God Who Is There*, 6.
81. Ibid., 199.
82. Ibid.
83. *Escape*, 269.
84. *God Who Is There*, 47.
85. *How Should We Then Live?*, 224.

Truth as Objective

Truth is objective. This is decisive for Schaeffer's system of thought. The Christianity's evangelistic efforts depend upon it. Non-Christian individuals must understand that Christianity's proclamation announces objective truth—truth that exists in reality apart from subjective appropriation. Truth is objective because it is truth both to God and humanity.[86] This contention is based upon Schaeffer's belief in biblical inerrancy.[87] Schaeffer wrote:

> As we get ready to tell the person God's answer to his or her need, we must make sure that the individual understands that we are talking about real truth, and not just about something vaguely religious which seems to work psychologically. We must make sure that he understands that we are talking about real guilt before God, and we are not offering him merely relief for his guilt-feelings. We must make sure that he understands that we are talking to him about history, and that the death of Jesus was not just an ideal or a symbol but a fact of space and time. If we are talking to a person who would not understand the term "space-time history" we can say: "Do you believe that Jesus died in the sense that if you had been there that day, you could have rubbed your finger on the cross and got a splinter in it?" Until he understands the importance of these three things, he is not ready to become a Christian.[88]

Thus Schaeffer, in regards to the Christian faith, would argue that "we are talking about objective truth related to reality and not just something within our own heads."[89] With this contention Schaeffer perceived himself as standing against the Hegelian emphasis on truth as synthesis (the "both-and") and its accompanying relativism.[90]

Schaeffer's Criteria of Truth

Schaeffer has a two-fold criterion of truth which extends from what has already been explored at length, and therefore will only be discussed briefly: (1) truth involves a statement that must be non-contradictory and able to give an answer to the phenomenon in question; (2) one must be able to live consistently with the theory. With these two assertions, Schaeffer suggests that philosophical proof, scientific proof, and religious truth follow the same rules. This moves Schaeffer beyond mere correspondence with empirical data to a position demanding logical non-contradiction, empirical fit, and existential authenticity.[91]

---

86. *Whatever Happened*, 392.
87. *Church at End of Twentieth Century*, 103-110. Not only was this based upon biblical inerrancy, but Schaeffer's biblical inerrancy was based upon his belief in the objectivity of truth.
88. *God Who Is There*, 139; see also the introductory chapters in *Genesis*.
89. *God Who Is There*, 179.
90. *Escape*, 233.
91. See Lewis, "Schaeffer's Apologetic Method," 101.

Non-Contradictory

For Schaeffer, the first step in the nature of proof is that the "theory must be noncontradictory and must give an answer to the phenomenon in question."[92] For example, does the "Christian answer conform to and explain what we observe concerning man as he is (including my knowledge of myself as a man)?"[93] What is argued in this criteria is a correspondence to reality as well as a view toward coherence as a system.

Able to Live Consistently with Theory

The second step in Schaeffer's understanding of the criteria for truth is that we "must be able to live consistently with our theory."[94] In other words, does it provide meaning and a sense of worth to the individual, or does it lead to despair?[95] Such an emphasis on viability has led at least one observer to place Schaeffer in the camp of pragmatism.[96]

Schaeffer's criteria of truth are largely concerned with coherence. Within that construct the concept of truth is one of correspondence. What is put forward as true must correspond with what is true according to God's truth. Facts are true according to correspondence; the system is true based on the criterion of coherence.

Critique of Schaeffer's Concept of Truth

Francis Schaeffer, describing himself often as "simply an old-fashioned evangelist,"[97] has received extensive criticism from the Evangelical community. Even a cursory reading of Schaeffer's critics reveals resentment and even envy relative to publisher's blurbs on Schaeffer's status as an intellectual, to his popularity with main-stream Evangelicals, to his style of dress, and even to the pictures of modern art with Schaeffer in the foreground. Such attitudes did not enhance Schaeffer's favorable reception by many in Evangelical and non-Evangelical academia. This criticism seemed to grow more intense with each publication.[98] Often such criticisms have revealed more about Schaeffer's reviewers

---

92. *God Who Is There*, 121.

93. Ibid.

94. Ibid.

95. Ibid., 121-122.

96. Norman Geisler, *Christian Apologetics* (Grand Rapids: Baker, 1976), 110-111; compare Lewis, "Schaeffer's Apologetic Method," 83.

97. Board, "Evangelical Thinker," 60.

98. For example, reviews of Schaeffer's early work, such as *The God Who Is There*, received enthusiastic responses from Clark Pinnock, "Breakthrough for Evangelicals," *Christianity Today* 13 (January 3, 1969), 24 and Arthur Holmes, "The God Who Is There," *HIS Magazine* 29 (February 1969), 26. Richard Pierard has noted that the publication of *How Should We Then Live?* began the negative criticism largely as a result that its promotion begged engagement and was found wanting; see "Unmasking," 29.

than they do about Schaeffer's works.[99] His arguments have been criticized on the grounds of factual inaccuracy and methodological error;[100]
his conclusions on the grounds of over-generalization;[101] his ministry
and life on the grounds of catering to publicity;[102] his projects on the
grounds of attempting what only an omniscient expert could hope to
achieve;[103] and his politics on the grounds that they were tied too
closely to right-wing Republican politics with a blurring between faith
and the American flag.[104] Many supporters have come to Schaeffer's
defense on these and other criticisms,[105] including Schaeffer himself.[106]
This critique must sidestep these discussions of Schaeffer's life and ministry to concentrate on Evangelical reactions to Schaeffer's concept of
truth.

Schaeffer wrote with clarity and passion. He attempted to combine all
branches of knowledge in his theological and philosophical reflections.
His writings were instrumental in the evangelization of many individuals
and served to interest many Evangelicals in the larger issues of truth.

Yet Evangelicals have received Schaeffer's concept of truth with concerns that go to the heart of his system of thought. First, such Evangeli-

---

99. W. Stanford Reid, "How Should We Then Live," *Westminster Theological Journal*
XL (Fall 1977-Spring 1978), 380.

100. Stephen T. Davis, "How Should We Then Live? A Review," *The Evangelical
Quarterly* 50 (April-June 1978), 109-112, who noted that Schaeffer's arguments were "over-
simplified, that his interpretation of Western philosophy was suspect in several places, and
that the oracular, almost dogmatic pose he struck . . . was hard to swallow." G. Thomas
Stadler, "Renaissance Humanism: Francis Schaeffer Versus Some Contemporary Scholars,"
Fides et Historia XXI:2 (June 1989), 4-20, stated that "Schaeffer's presentation of Renaissance humanism is incorrect and fails to take into account the best current scholarship in
the field" (4). Woodward, "Guru of Fundamentalism," quoted Evangelical Wheaton professor Arthur Holmes, "We . . . use Schaeffer as an example how not to do philosophy," and
Mark Noll, also professor of Wheaton, added, "The danger is that people will take him for
a scholar, which he is not . . . " see 88.

101. David W. Gill, "Jacque Ellul and Francis Schaeffer: Two Views of Western Civilization," *Fides et Historia* XIII:2 (Spring-Summer 1981), 23-37, notes in regards to Schaeffer's over-generalizations that it is important not to miss the forest for the trees, but the
forests do have trees! (35); see also Marsden, "As We See It," 2-3; Woodward, "Guru of
Fundamentalism," 88.

102. Discussed at some length by Catherwood, *Evangelical Leaders*, 146ff.

103. This criticism came out most ardently with the publication of *How Should We
Then Live?*, for example in George Giacumakis, Jr. and Gerald C. Tiffin's "Francis Schaeffer's New Intellectual Enterprise: Some Friendly Criticisms," *Fides et Historia* IX:2 (Spring
1977), 52-58, where there is the added fear that this will be mistakenly used as a text for
the study of western civilization.

104. W. Merwin Forbes, "Review Article: A Christian Manifesto," *Grace Theological
Journal* 4.2 (1983), 303-309; Ronald A. Wells, "Whatever Happened to Francis Schaeffer,"
The Reformed Journal," 33 (May 1983), 10-13.

105. Board, "The Rise of Francis Schaeffer," 40-42, 59; Catherwood, *Evangelical Leaders*, 146-156; Dennis, "Schaeffer and His Critics," *Schaeffer: Portraits*, 99-126.

106. For example, Schaeffer answers his critics in regards to over-generalizations and
commercialization in "Schaeffer on Schaeffer, Part 1," 20, and on his wooden acceptance
of Princeton Theology in the same article, 21; on his ties to right-wing politics and even
the wearing of knickers, Schaeffer responds in "Schaeffer on Schaeffer, Part II," 23.

cals as Arthur Holmes have observed that Schaeffer fails to make the distinction between reason serving as a capacity for understanding and reason as a capacity for proving universally true propositions.[107] Kierkegaard attempted to escape the latter, not the former, and it can be argued that only the former is demanded by Christian thought.

Second, Schaeffer's concept of truth blends epistemology with metaphysics. Is epistemological objectivity necessary for metaphysical objectivity? Schaeffer answers in the affirmative, but therein lies the blurring between metaphysics and epistemology. Holmes rightly points out that there can be epistemological subjectivity and metaphysical objectivity, allowing Kierkegaard's emphasis on personal appropriation and God's objective existence.[108] In light of this one can also critique Schaeffer's equation of universals with absolutes, again a confusion between the metaphysical and the epistemological. As Ruegsegger observes, the "absolute-relative contrast is an epistemological contrast whereas the universal-particular contrast is a metaphysical one, and it does not serve the interest of conceptual clarity to run the two categories together."[109]

Third, Schaeffer's concept of antithesis attempts to defend Christian presuppositions against contradictories, but is deficient in its defense against its contraries. Ruegsegger notes that two propositions are contradictories if they cannot both be true and they cannot both be false, while two propositions are contraries if they cannot both be true although they might both be false.[110] In other words, to defend the notion that a personal God created the universe over and against the view that it was created by an impersonal being says nothing to the contention that this personal God who created the universe is the triune God of the Christian Bible. This would seem to weaken the usefulness of the view as a means to convey Christianity as truth to the modern world. Christianity is not defended or even necessarily evangelistically articulated merely on the grounds that its contradictory has been shown to be problematic.[111] This then is a weakness made especially apparent in Schaeffer's criteria of truth, which is largely that of cohesiveness.[112] Gordon H. Clark, responding to this criticism of Schaeffer, argues that if

107. On this, see Arthur F. Holmes, *All Truth Is God's Truth* (Grand Rapids: Eerdmans, 1977), 47.

108. Ibid., 5-6.

109. Ruegsegger, "Schaeffer on Philosophy," 247; see also Jack Rogers, "Francis Schaeffer: The Promise and the Problem," Part 2, *The Reformed Journal* 27 (June 1977), 16; William A. Hendricks, "He Is There and He Is Not Silent," *Southwestern Journal of Theology*, XV:1 (Fall 1972), 139.

110. Ruegsegger, "Schaeffer on Philosophy," 249.

111. Schaeffer could have sharpened his definition of non-contradiction, for as Lewis observes, not every "opposite" is a contradictory; see "Schaeffer's Apologetic Method," 81.

112. Levit, "Schaeffer's Apologetic Method," 94.

one proves a contradictory false, "the contrary must also be false."[113] Yet
Clark offers this only as a "semi-defense," noting that it is not enough to
assert the trustworthiness of sensory experience in order to discredit
skepticism; one must define sensation, prove that there are "uninter-
preted elements in the mind, show how these can be combined into
perceptions, and then develop concepts without assuming, what is actually false, that all men have sensory images."[114] Schaeffer wants to show
the correspondence of the Christian faith to reality through antithesis,
but his approach only allows coherence and existential plausibility and
meaningfulness.

A fourth concern among some Evangelicals toward Schaeffer is that
antithesis as the sole insight into the nature of truth fails to take into
account the changing nature of language and thought and leaves no
room for ambiguity, paradox, or relativism.[115] To some Evangelicals, this
is problematic in the face of many recent developments in science and
society.[116]

Schaeffer made statements that hinted at the allowance for some
aspect of relativism regarding the application of biblical truth where
clear, absolute statements are not forthcoming on a particular issue. For
example, note the following analogy:

> The Bible doesn't and we therefore cannot give absolutes. All we can
> do is produce principles, and then the individual has to decide under
> the leadership of the Holy Spirit for himself how to apply those princi-
> ples to the situation. Conceivably the Holy Spirit could lead one person
> to apply them one way, and another person to apply them slightly dif-
> ferently and they would be equally right.[117]

Schaeffer writes that "we have no right to set absolutes unless they
can be shown directly from Scripture,"[118] but such statements beg the

---

113. Gordon H. Clark, "A Semi-defense of Francis Schaeffer," *Christian Scholar's
Review* 11 (1982), 148; Clark's article is a direct reply to Ruegsegger's "Schaeffer on Philosophy;" Ruegsegger responded that this does not address the essence of his argument, that
even if proving the contradictory also disproves the contrary, it does not prove the specific
assertions of Christian faith, namely that the personal God is the God of the Bible and not
Zeus or Thor; see "A Reply to Gordon Clark," *Christian Scholar's Review* 11 (1982), 150-152.

114. Clark, "Semi-defense," 149.

115. A concern expressed by Wells, "Whatever Happened," 10-13, especially in the
area of ambiguity; see also Hill, "Francis Schaeffer," 137-171.

116. For example Einstein's theory of relativity and Heisenberg's uncertainty principle
which have seemed to establish relativism in science. In other words, one must at least
allow for the possibility that the eighteenth century view of science as a completely pre-
dictable cause and effect system is problematic. On this, see Rogers, "Promise and Problem, Part 2," 16; as Hendricks notes, Schaeffer "asserts that all things which are known
must be known in a uniform way," which Hendricks asserts is Aristotelian, see "He Is
There," 139.

117. "Schaeffer on Schaeffer, Part II," 23.

118. Ibid.

question of *who* determines *where* the Bible *has* spoken absolutely, and in what way to which context.

A fifth concern among certain Evangelicals is that Schaeffer fails to acknowledge the difficulties inherent within the subject-object split in the subjective appropriation of knowledge. Not only is exhaustive knowledge an impossibility, but the determinants of "true" knowledge are also suspect in regards to interpretive subjectivity. In other words, if the Bible is the embodiment of truth, the enormous dilemma of hermeneutics rears its head. How does one determine what that body of truth proclaims in the contemporary context.[119] As with Van Til, this does not negate Schaeffer's concept of truth, but much work in hermeneutics needs to be done to allow this concept to remain useful.

A sixth concern is that while Schaeffer does not equate a commitment to biblical authority with a "leap of faith," the brevity of his remarks in this area might lead one to conclude that this is indeed the case.[120] If accepted on the basis of geometric reasoning, what role does the effect of the fall play on human reason? If human beings are subject to total depravity, logical consistency would dictate that this depravity would extend to the faculties of reason. This raises the question, if this critique is valid, of whether Schaeffer's contention of Christianity's rational coherence is weakened. If humanity's reason is not depraved (Aquinas), or only partially depraved (Calvin), on what basis does Schaeffer take his stand between natural theology and materialism?[121] Schaeffer contended that humanity's reason was indeed fallen and objected to Aquinas, arguing that to say that reason is not fallen would be to make it autonomous (independent from God).[122] Still Schaeffer argued that a reasonable God made the universe, and that humanity, through reason, can hope to discover its nature.[123] This is a point of tension in Schaeffer's system which simply is not resolved.

Summary

Francis Schaeffer's concept of truth is that of ultimate correspondence with reality as revealed through God's revelation in an infallible Scripture. The specific concept of correspondence involves antithesis. For

---

119. Franz, "The God Who Is There," 114-116, one of the few early reviews of Schaeffer's work which was thoroughly negative, points out that "we are told always to distinguish biblical truth from human argument . . . but the presuppositional approach of the author makes no such distinction."

120. Pinnock, "Schaeffer on Modern Theology," *Reflections*, 176.

121. Such was the nature of a question posed to Schaeffer by Philip Yancey, answered ambiguously at best, in "Schaeffer on Schaeffer, Part II," 26.

122. On this, see Ruegsegger, "Schaeffer's System of Thought," *Reflections*, 28f.

123. Schaeffer, *Escape*, 30-31.

Schaeffer, truth is, therefore, propositional, objective, and absolute. This correspondence is to make ample use of various processes of verification and reason, although he contends that unless one works within a Christian world view true knowledge will not be found. Only the Christian framework provides the necessary coherence to approach all of reality.

Many substantive questions present themselves as a result of Schaeffer's concept of truth, not the least of which is his contention that truth is universal and absolute. Few within the Christian faith would deny this from an ontological perspective, but Schaeffer's insistence upon it epistemologically is uniformly contested outside of Evangelical theology.[124] Schaeffer's view demands that monumental questions related to the Creator-created distinction and the subjective appropriation of knowledge be answered.

Second, Schaeffer presents a rationalism that is seemingly devoid of faith, a truncated expression of the dynamics of the divine-human relationship. Even if some understanding of biblical propositionalism is accepted, the role of faith is raised concerning the acceptance of those propositions. This leads to the broad and essential question of what reason can achieve in regard to the issue of certainty. Schaeffer puts few limits on reason's worth in this area, a conclusion far from accepted in many theological circles. Inherent within this optimistic view of reason are Schaeffer's own presuppositions which become problematic when opposed to a differing set of presented presuppositions. A fundamental question is how reason can be effectively used for the discovery and verification of truth in light of differing presuppositions which arguably determine the outcome of the reasoning process.

Finally, the issue of biblical authority must be raised. Schaeffer insists on a view of biblical inerrancy that points the nature of its religious truth in propositional form, intending to convey factual, historical truth in all it narrates. This view demands verifiability before truth can be asserted. The concern is also voiced that such a move is more in debt to Enlightenment ideals of empiricism and positivism than to the actual biblical materials. The question must, therefore, be asked as to whether such a position is fair to the biblical narrative, the biblical intent, and the biblical context. Further, the question must also be raised as to whether verification would change the scriptural message, for meaning is far from inherent in verification.

---

124. Hill notes that opposition is coming increasingly from within Evangelical theology, see "Francis Schaeffer," 157-164.

Chapter Six

TRUTH
AND REASON:
CARL F. H. HENRY

Carl F. H. Henry is an Evangelical theologian who has experienced prominence in both academic and popular circles. He is the author of a widely referenced and respected Evangelical systematic theology.[1]

Biographical Background

Carl Ferdinand Howard Henry was born on January 22, 1913, in a small apartment in Manhattan, New York, to parents who had immigrated

---

1. Henry's six-volume systematic is *God, Revelation and Authority*, vols. 1-4 (Waco: Word, 1976-1983). Although referred to as a systematic theology throughout this text, it is to be noted that these six-volumes deal primarily with only three doctrines: revelation, God, and religious authority. In spite of many notable omissions, such as ecclesiology, Henry may nonetheless be said to have provided a systematic approach to Christian theology. Henry's concern with systematic theology has been present throughout his academic career. *Basic Christian Doctrines* (reprinted, Grand Rapids: Baker, 1962), first published as a series of articles in *Christianity Today*, was intended by Henry as editor to provide a comprehensive systematic overview of the Evangelical faith (ix).

from Germany.[2] The family's original name was Heinrich, but it was changed due to the anti-German sentiment prevalent in America during World War I. Henry was baptized and confirmed in an Episcopal congregation at an early age. Henry's early adolescence was not particularly religious;[3] rather he was devoted to secular journalism.[4]

In 1933, Henry experienced a three-hour conversation with a friend which ended in his conversion to the Christian faith and subsequent indoctrination into Evangelical Christianity and the Baptist denomination. Understanding a new calling for his life, Henry enrolled in Wheaton College in 1935, earning both an A.B. and M.A. degree. Henry's educational pursuits then led him to Northern Baptist Seminary for what would eventually result in both a B.D. and Th.D. degree. Ordained in 1941, Henry served two churches before accepting a teaching position at Northern.[5] At Wheaton Henry developed relationships which would figure importantly into his life in later years, such as those with Harold Lindsell, Edward J. Carnell, Paul Jewett, and Billy Graham. Perhaps the most important contribution Wheaton made to Henry's life was his mentor, Gordon Clark, a Presbyterian who influenced Henry toward the rationality of the Christian faith.[6]

Henry's academic career has involved serving the vanguard of Evangelical educational institutions while exhibiting a prolific gift for writing. His first major work has been called the "manifesto of neo-evangelical-

---

2. Henry is the author of an autobiography which is invaluable for biographical background *Confession of a Theologian* (Waco: Word, 1986); see also J. D. Douglas, "Carl F.H. Henry," *New Dictionary of Theology*, ed. Sinclair B. Ferguson, David F. Wright, and J. I. Packer (Downers Grove: InterVarsity Press, 1988), 291; Gabriel Fackre, "Carl F.H. Henry," *A Handbook of Christian Theologians*, enlarged ed., ed. Dean G. Peerman and Martin E. Marty (Nashville: Abingdon, 1984), 583-607; R. Albert Mohler, Jr., "Carl F.H. Henry," *Baptist Theologians*, ed. Timothy George and David S. Dockery (Nashville: Broadman, 1990), 518-538; Ronald H. Nash, *Evangelicals in America* (Nashville: Abingdon, 1987), 89-90; Bob Patterson, *Carl F. H. Henry* in the series *Makers of the Modern Theological Mind* (Waco: Word, 1983); D. M. Roark, "Carl Ferdinand Howard Henry," *Dictionary of Christianity in America*, ed. Daniel G. Reid, Robert D. Linder, Bruce L. Shelley, and Harry S. Stout (Downers Grove: InterVarsity, 1990), 520-521.

3. See Henry, *Confessions*, 17-18.

4. Henry was a sportswriter during high school and after graduation worked as a reporter for the *Islip Press*, graduating to the position of editor at the *Smithstown Star* and then the *Port Jefferson Tribune*. Henry's journalistic experience also included serving as a regional reporter for the *New York Tribune*.

5. Henry served as a student pastor at Humboldt Park Baptist Church and then as an interim pastor at First Baptist Church of Elmhurst, Illinois.

6. Clark's Calvinism was out of step with many in Wheaton's community and eventually forced him to take a position at Butler University in Indianapolis. Clark would later teach at Covenant College in Tennessee. Clark's works include *A Christian Philosophy of Education* (Grand Rapids: Eerdmans, 1946); *A Christian View of Men and Things* (Grand Rapids: Eerdmans, 1952); *Karl Barth's Theological Method* (Nutley: Presbyterian and Reformed, 1963); *The Philosophy of Science and Belief in God* (Nutley: Craig, 1972); *Religion, Reason and Revelation* (Nutley: Presbyterian and Reformed, 1961); *Thales to Dewey* (Boston: Houghton Mifflin, 1957); see also R. H. Nash, ed., *Philosophy of Gordon Clark: A Festschrift* (Philadelphia: Presbyterian and Reformed, 1968).

ism" as it critiqued separatism, unyielding orthodoxy, and a failure to engage social issues.[7] In 1947 Henry was invited to serve as a founding faculty member of Fuller Theological Seminary in Pasadena, California, where he taught as professor of philosophy and theology. During Fuller's first year he served as acting dean.[8] At the time of his appointment to Fuller, Henry was also completing a Ph.D. degree at Boston University under Edgar Brightman, a personalist philosopher.[9] This would prove to be Henry's last earned degree, bringing the total to five, though numerous honorary degrees would follow. Henry's writings during his years at Fuller covered a wide range, including theology, philosophy, and ethics.[10] Henry would later serve as president of the Evangelical Theological Society (1967-1970) and the American Theological Society (1980-1981). He founded the Institute for Advanced Christian Studies, which produces literature with the secular university audience in mind.

In 1955 he took a leave of absence from Fuller that resulted in becoming the editor of *Christianity Today* in 1959. This was a new journal which would become "the most influential organ of American evangelicalism."[11] Henry served as editor for twelve years, creating a periodical which "expressed unswerving commitment to evangelical distinctives yet sought to show their relevance to contemporary social issues and to demonstrate

---

7. Carl F. H. Henry, *The Uneasy Conscience of Modern Fundamentalism* (Grand Rapids: Eerdmans, 1947); compare Fackre, "Carl F.H. Henry," 584.

8. On Fuller's beginnings and subsequent history, see George Marsden, *Reforming Fundamentalism: Fuller Seminary and the New Evangelicalism* (Grand Rapids: Eerdmans, 1987).

9. Personalism is a philosophical position which takes the concept of "person" as that which is ultimate, thus opposing both pantheism and materialism. The term itself was first used by Schleiermacher, and later by Fuerbach in order to characterize the position that God is a person rather than an abstract principle. Marsden rightly notes that one of the influences of personalism on Henry was his idea of a "mind" controlling an age, a concept evident in many of the titles of his books, such as *Remaking the Modern Mind*, 2nd ed. (Grand Rapids: Eerdmans, 1948) and *The Christian Mindset in a Secular Society* (Portland: Multnomah, 1984): see *Reforming Fundamentalism*, 79.

10. During his years at Fuller (1947-1957), Henry produced an impressive display of works which established him as a winsome and compelling advocate of Evangelical thought, such as *Notes on the Doctrine of God* (Boston: W. A. Wilde, 1948); *Remaking the Modern Mind*, *Giving a Reason for Our Hope* (Boston: W. A. Wilde, 1949); *The Protestant Dilemma: An Analysis of the Current Impasse in Theology* (Grand Rapids: Eerdmans, 1949); *Fifty Years of Protestant Theology* (Boston: W. A. Wilde, 1950); *The Drift of Western Thought* (Grand Rapids: Eerdmans, 1951); *Glimpses of a Sacred Land* (1953); his published dissertation from Boston University, *Personal Idealism and Strong's Theology* (Wheaton: Van Kampen, 1951); *Christian Personal Ethics* (Grand Rapids: Eerdmans, 1957); and *Evangelical Responsibility in Contemporary Theology* (Grand Rapids: Eerdmans, 1957).

11. Fackre, "Carl F.H. Henry," 585; *Christianity Today* was created to be an intentional rival to the more liberal *The Christian Century* and was originally conceived by Billy Graham and Harold John Ockenga; see D. G. Tinder, "Christianity Today," *Dictionary of Christianity in America*, 262.

the intellectual viability of evangelical faith."[12] Henry strove to put Evangelical Christianity forward as something intellectually tenable and socially mindful, and also as a movement united in common causes and convictions.[13] "Key 73," an ecumenical effort among Evangelicals which began in the World Congress on Evangelism in 1966 in Berlin, was an example of this effort. "Key 73" was sponsored by *Christianity Today* and chaired by Henry, with evangelist Billy Graham as honorary chairman.

Henry's tenure as editor of *Christianity Today* ended in 1968 under less than desirable circumstances, an "involuntary termination after twelve years of sacrificial labor."[14] Henry emphasized Evangelicalism's need for social and political involvement, evidenced early on in such works as *The Uneasy Conscience of Modern Fundamentalism* and later in such articles as "Evangelicals in the Social Struggle," which first appeared in the pages of *Christianity Today* and later as a chapter in *The God Who Shows Himself* (1966). This emphasis was not shared by J. Howard Pew, principal financier of *Christianity Today*. A rather lengthy chain of events and unfortunate miscommunication between Henry, Pew, Harold John Ockenga, and Nelson Bell resulted in Henry's dismissal as editor, announced January 5, effected July 1, 1968.[15]

After a few years in Cambridge, England,[16] Henry became professor-at-large at Eastern Baptist Theological Seminary in Philadelphia, where he served until 1974. He then devoted himself almost entirely to writing and

---

12. Fackre, "Carl F. H. Henry," 585-586; for a good introduction to the writings found in *Christianity Today* during Henry's time as editor, see *Christianity Today*, ed. Frank E. Gaebelein (New York: Pyramid Books, 1968), an anthology of articles, editorials, news, book reviews, and even cartoons drawn from *Christianity Today's* first ten years of publication (the original title of this anthology was *A Christianity Today Reader* published in 1967 by Meredith Press).

13. On this see Henry's *Evangelicals at the Brink of Crisis: Significance of the World Congress on Evangelism* (Waco: Word, 1967); E. A. Wilson, "World Congress on Evangelism," *Dictionary of Christianity in America*, 1273; note also Henry's edited works which attempted to unite Evangelical thought, such as *Contemporary Evangelical Thought* (New York: Harper and Bros., 1957); *Revelation and the Bible* (Grand Rapids: Baker, 1958); *The Biblical Expositor*, 3 vols. (Philadelphia: A. J. Holman, 1960); *Basic Christian Doctrines*; *Christian Faith and Modern Theology* (New York: Channel, 1964); *Jesus of Nazareth: Saviour and Lord* (Grand Rapids: Eerdmans, 1966); *Fundamentals of the Faith* (Grand Rapids: Zondervan, 1970); *The Identity of Jesus* (Nashville: Broadman Press, 1992).

14. Henry, *Confessions*, 281; Henry's relationship with the journal seems to have recovered from this episode, evidenced by a recent "celebratory surprise and reunion" hosted by early *Christianity Today* staffers in Chesapeake Bay (letter from Carl Henry, Christmas, 1990).

15. See Henry, *Confessions*, 264-287; see also Marsden, *Reforming Fundamentalism*, 160, 260, 288, who cites Henry's concern from the very beginning over the clash of his political and economical convictions with those of Pew's; on Pew, see R. L. Petersen, "John Howard Pew," *Dictionary of Christianity in America*, 894-895, and M. Sennholz, *Faith and Freedom: The Journal of a Great American, J. Howard Pew* (1975).

16. It was during this time in England that Henry devoted himself to the research and reflection which laid the groundwork for his six-volume *God, Revelation and Authority*.

lecturing for World Vision, Inc., an Evangelical agency focusing on social service. With a global platform, Henry emerged as "a kind of world evangelist—'the thinking man's Billy Graham,' as he is sometimes called."[17]

Henry continues to shape the hearts and minds of Evangelicals around the world through his lectures and books,[18] remaining an engaging and articulate ambassador for Evangelical Christianity.[19] The majority of Henry's scholarly lectures are given at Trinity Evangelical Divinity School where he serves as Visiting Professor of Biblical and Systematic Theology. He travels widely as a Lecturer-At-Large for Prison Fellowship Ministries, an inter-denominational Evangelical para-church organization founded by Charles Colson. Henry delivered the 1989 Rutherford Lectures at Edinburgh, "Presuppositionalism and Theological Method," recently published in a book titled *Toward a Recovery of Christian Belief*.[20]

Only in 1993, when Dr. Henry turns 80, is there the possibility of full retirement.[21] As Bob Patterson has noted, Henry may be called the unofficial spokesperson for the entire contemporary American Evangelical tradition.[22]

Description of Henry's Concept of Truth

The concept of truth is central to his system of thought and is most fully treated in his prolegomena,[23] a concept that is central to his system

---

17. Fackre, "Carl F.H. Henry," 587.

18. Recent works by Henry include "American Evangelicals in a Turning Time," *Theologians in Transition*, The Christian Century "How My Mind Has Changed" Series, ed. James M. Wall (New York: Crossroad, 1981), 41-49; "Biblical Authority and the Social Crisis," *Authority and Interpretation: A Baptist Perspective*, ed. Duane A. Garrett and Richard R. Melick, Jr. (Grand Rapids: Baker, 1987), 203-20; *Carl Henry at His Best* (Portland: Multnomah, 1990); *The Christian Mindset in a Secular Society; Christian Countermoves in a Decadent Culture* (Portland: Multnomah, 1986); *Conversations with Carl Henry: Christianity for Today* (Lewiston, N.Y.: Edwin Mellen, 1986); *Evangelical Affirmations*, ed. with Kenneth Kantzer (Grand Rapids: Zondervan, 1990); "Liberation Theology and the Scriptures," *Liberation Theology*, ed. Ronald H. Nash (Grand Rapids: Baker, 1988), 187-202; *Toward a Recovery of Christian Belief* (Westchester, Ill: Crossway, 1990); *Twilight of a Great Civilization: The Drift Toward Neo-Paganism* (Westchester, Ill.: Crossway, 1988); "Where Will Evangelicals Cast Their Lot?," *This World* 18 (1987), 3-11; and *The Identity*, a major Christology, *The Identity of Jesus of Nazareth* (Nashville, Broadman Press, 1992).

19. The author studied under Dr. Henry during the summer of 1988 at the Southern Baptist Theological Seminary for a seminar covering his system of thought titled "God, Revelation and Authority." Dialogue and correspondence with Dr. Henry has been personally rewarding and invaluable for this chapter.

20. The final lecture, not published in this volume, is forthcoming in *The Scottish Bulletin of Evangelical Theology*, a journal published by the Rutherford House.

21. Letter received from Carl F. H. Henry, November 18, 1990.

22. Patterson, *Carl F. H. Henry*, 9.

23. Henry's theological prolegomena is contained largely in the first volume of his systematic, *God, Revelation and Authority*, vol. 1; the concept of truth is most fully treated in chapters 13 and 14, titled "The Method and Criteria of Theology (I)," 213-224, and "The Method and Criteria of Theology (II)," 225-244; also to be noted is Henry's *Toward a Recovery of Christian Belief*, which in his own words "from first to last . . . interacts with the truth-issue" (letter received from Carl F.H. Henry, November 18, 1990).

of thought. He wrote that "the fundamental issue remains the issue of truth, the truth of theological assertions. No work on theology will be worth its weight if that fundamental issue is obscured."[24]

For Henry, Christians must indicate their conviction that Christianity is "distinguished above all by its objective truth, and must adduce the method of knowing and the manner of verification by which every man can become personally persuaded."[25] Christianity is perceived as having entered the world in the name of the living God of truth to proclaim Jesus Christ as the "unique and final revelation of God's truth."[26] As a result, Christianity's theological method should be "predicated on the priority of divine revelation."[27] Henry contends that one of the basic issues in Christian theology is the "character of revelation as truth and not simply as act."[28] According to Henry, logic is on the side of such a revealed religion. Non-Christian alternative world views are decisively rejected as false, and non-Christians are seen to have ignored or rejected rationally convincing considerations which point to the logical truth of the Christian faith. As a result,

> since the viability of theology hangs on the truth or falsity of its affirmations, discussion of the ways of knowing theological truth, and of the criteria appropriate to judging theological claims, is imperative. The evangelical's first task is to insist upon the truth . . . the next task is to identify truth and indicate how one can recognize and be assured of it.[29]

Henry then proceeds to express his response to these concerns in the following thesis:

---

24. Henry, *God, Revelation and Authority*, 1:14; as early as 1946 in *Remaking the Modern Mind* Henry was arguing that philosophical discussions were the central issues and concerns of contemporary religion, a conclusion not surprising when one notes that the volume is dedicated to the following three "Men of Athens:" Gordon Clark, Harry Jellema, and Cornelius Van Til.

25. Henry, *God, Revelation and Authority*, 1:213; note also Henry's response to those who would deny objectivity on grounds of cultural relativity in "The Cultural Relativizing of Revelation," *Trinity Journal* 1 NS (1980), 153-164.

26. "The Cultural Relativizing," 214.

27. "The Cultural Relativizing," Henry's critique of mediating systems can be traced to his work under Edgar Brightman at Boston University in regard to A. H. Strong's attempt to mediate between orthodoxy and liberalism, an attempt perceived as a failure by Henry, largely due to its dependence on modern critical philosophy and post-Kantian epistemology. Henry perused the theological landscape and discovered three rival theological methods, that of Tertullian, Aquinas, and Augustine. Tertullian was seen to be the figure who represented the abandonment of reason, Aquinas the elevation of reason, and Augustine the appropriate *via media*. See *Remaking the Modern Mind*, 219-239, especially 223, 233, and 238; note the brief but solid discussion along these lines in Mohler, "Carl F. H. Henry," *Baptist Theologians*, 523-525.

28. Carl F. H. Henry, *Frontiers in Modern Theology: A Critique of Current Theological Trends* (Chicago: Moody, 1966), 65.

29. *Frontiers in Modern Theology*, 215.

Divine revelation is the source of all truth, the truth of Christianity included; reason is the instrument for recognizing it; Scripture is its verifying principle; logical consistency is a negative test for truth and coherence is a subordinate test. The task of Christian theology is to exhibit the content of biblical revelation as an orderly whole.[30]

Henry separates this comprehensive statement of theological method into six statements, four of which will be used in this examination as a means to investigate more fully the concept of truth operative in his systematic.[31]

1. God in His revelation is the first principle of Christian theology, from which all the truths of revealed religion are derived.[32] "If we are authorized to say anything at all about the living God," wrote Henry, "it is only because of God's initiative and revelation."[33] Thus the basic epistemological foundation is divine revelation, a revelation that is "rational communication conveyed in intelligible ideas and meaningful words, that is, in conceptual-verbal form."[34] To argue that we have revelation of the triune God means divine revelation must be intelligible.[35] Truth has its source in God's divine revelation and can, therefore, be classified as that which holds objective cognitive validity.[36] As a result, humanity can have cognitive knowledge of transcendent realities.

---

30. *Frontiers in Modern Theology*, as a result, it is not surprising that Henry understands the task of theology to be that of expositing and elucidating the content of Scripture in an orderly way, the repetition, combinating, and systematization of the truth of revelation in its propositionally given biblical form; see 238.

31. The final two statements of Henry's method are not germane to the specific discussion of the concept of truth operative in his theological methodology. These two statements are as follows: (1) The proper task of theology is to exposit and elucidate the content of Scripture in an orderly way, see *God, Revelation and Authority:* 1:238-240; (2) The theology of revelation requires the apologetic confrontation of speculative theories of reality and life, see *God, Revelation and Authority*, 1:241-244.

32. Henry, *God, Revelation and Authority:* 1:215; so for Henry, the question of Scripture is really a question concerning God, for if one believes "in a sovereign divine mind and will, in God who personally speaks and conveys information and instruction, then the presuppositions of scriptural inspiration lie near at hand," see *God, Revelation and Authority*, 3:428.

33. Ibid., 2:8.

34. *God, Revelation and Authority*, 12; without this, argues Henry, we have no more than a natural theology available from which to operate; see *The Protestant Dilemma*, 113-114. Even further, "if man's ideas and concepts of the divine are simply products of his own creative consciousness, and imply no claim to literal truth about the objective nature of God, is there any compelling reason to regard the moral transcendence of God any less than His metaphysical (or indeed His epistemological) transcendence as anything less other or more than symbol or myth? The renunciation of rational divine revelation can only lead to moral as well as theoretical agnosticism about God-in-Himself" see "The Nature of God" in *Christian Faith and Modern Theology*, 86-87, see also 89-90; 92-93.

35. *God, Revelation and Authority*, 5:51; Henry thus seeks to avoid what he perceives to be a weakness in Kant's understanding, namely that the case for theism is no longer founded upon knowledge, but upon a faith-construct in an area where knowledge is assumed to be impossible, see *Notes on the Doctrine of God*, 48.

36. *God, Revelation and Authority*, 1:44.

Henry's theological method is deductive rather than inductive. Empiricism and existentialism have penetrated Evangelical theology far too deeply for Henry's liking.[37] Autonomous human postulation, according to Henry, leaves no room for metaphysical truth.[38] Henry consciously distances himself from many contemporary Protestant theologians, arguing that they have forfeited the external miraculous and the cognitive and propositional nature of divine revelation. This is an epistemic slide into despair he feels began with

> Kant's postulational divinity, Friedrich Schleiermacher's God-only-in-relation-to-us, Albrecht Ritschl's value-judgment religious experience, and Karl Barth's nonpropositional person-revelation, all of which share subjective faith in a religious reality that allows no objectively valid propositional truth.[39]

Ontologically, Henry certainly understands the priority of the living God before His revelation, but here Henry is concerned with epistemology. Embracing the Augustinian motto *"credo ut intelligam,"* Henry asserts that one must believe in order to understand. The triune God remains the ontological axiom of the Christian faith, but divine revelation is to be understood as the foundational epistemological axiom "from which all other truths are deduced."[40] Henry does not see this position as having its basis "merely in philosophical presuppositionalism," but rather as anchored in "God's self-revelation."[41] Thus we have far more than a speculative first-principle, vulnerable to charges of fideism, but rather something which is affirmed "in view of the self-revealing activity of God."[42] Henry argues that evidentialists who dismiss presuppositionalists as fideists detach faith from reason and link it with presumption, to which Henry asserts that appealing to faith in no way repudiates public reason or logic.[43]

Revelation, both general and special, is historically grounded with irreducible historical facets. Henry acknowledges that the events of the creation narrative are of such a nature that records of them cannot be classified as historical in the strict sense on the grounds that they antedate humanity and human writing, but for Henry that is far different from saying that they cannot convey factual information through divine disclosure. To deny this element "emasculates the Christian religion."[44]

---

37. Henry, *Toward a Recovery,* x.
38. *God, Revelation and Authority,* 1:95.
39. Ibid., 57.
40. Ibid., 1:219; see also *Toward a Recovery,* 59.
41. *God, Revelation and Authority,* 1:219; compare 1:14.
42. Ibid., 1:219.
43. See *Toward a Recovery,* 38-40.
44. See *God, Revelation and Authority,* 1:68, compare 1:163,2:311-334. Henry is clear, however, in his assertion that historical investigation in no way serves as a sufficient method of knowing the truth of revelation; rather "divine revelation is the epistemic source and Scripture the methodological principle of the Christian interpretation of history"; see *God, Revelation and Authority,* 2:320.

Henry is therefore rejecting mere evidentialism or an appeal to empirical considerations alone for his epistemology. To allow this would be to participate in the reduction of external reality to impersonal categories. Henry rejects beginning with "particulars and then moving to universals"; rather he advocates postulating a universal explanatory principle which is subject to verification.[45] According to Henry, the Bible will not allow a "total correlation of reality, reason, meaning and progress with the providence of empirical scientific methodology."[46] Henry notes that this reduces reality to the categories of what is empirically identifiable. He associates such reduction with the existential despair inherent within the counter-culture movement of the 1960s. He writes that "instead of challenging the technocratic correlation of the real and the rational solely with what corresponds to empirical scientific methodology, disaffiliated youth reached for an inner mystical reality, transcending scientific method, which they hoped would provide anchorage for human values."[47] An appeal to transcendent revelation is in order, for without a reliance on revelational authority, the meaning and significance of events such as the Resurrection could never be established.[48]

Henry holds to the priority of revelation on the conviction that

> the basic axiom of every system is undemonstrable, that is, cannot be deduced from some still higher or prior knowledge, since the whole system of theorems and propositions is dependently suspended upon this primary axiom. The axioms of the Christian system of truth are not presuppositions shared in common with secular thought. Christian doctrines are not derived from experimental observation or from rationalism, but from God in his revelation.[49]

Thus while acknowledging the validity of both general and special revelation,[50] Henry finds that in Scripture an "authorized summary of all God's revelation—in the universe, in redemptive history, in Jesus of Nazareth—is divinely provided for us in inspired form."[51] The Bible "openly publishes man's predicament and God's redemptive remedy in the form of objectively intelligible statements." This results in "epistemo-

---

45. *Toward a Recovery*, 37.

46. *God, Revelation and Authority*, 1:117.

47. Ibid, compare Henry's introduction to *Quest for Reality: Christianity and the Counter Culture* (Downers Grove: InterVarsity Press, 1973), n.p. as well as his comments on 160.

48. Henry, *God, Revelation, and Authority*, 1:221.

49. Ibid., 1:223; compare 1:245, where Henry asserts that one cannot have a logically coherent system, which Christianity claims to be, without a dependance on undemonstrated axioms.

50. By general revelation, Henry means the "disclosure of God's eternal power and glory through nature and history," and by special revelation, "the disclosure of God's redemptive purpose and work"; see *God, Revelation, and Authority*, 1:223; compare 2:69-76, where Henry argues for the unity of all revelation, though not in regard to form.

51. *God, Revelation, and Authority*, 1:223.

logical priority over general revelation" because Scripture as an inspired literary document "republishes the content of general revelation objectively, over against sinful man's reductive dilutions and misconstructions of it."[52] Here Henry finds himself in direct tension with Barth whom he interprets as arguing that theological truth is contrary to the natural capacity of human language. Henry, along with his mentor Gordon Clark, states, "If language is the product of sin, conditioned by man's perverted nature and unsuitable even when revelation grasps it, there arises the question whether God himself would or could use it . . . it would matter little whether God's Word is language or not."[53] Henry concedes that the biblical materials do not offer an "extended treatise" on religious epistemology, thus never identifying one "single correct system of epistemology," and therefore it would be "unjustifiable to identify any one scheme as biblical."[54]

It can be maintained that the final choice for humanity is between an epistemology (fashioned on God's divine self-revelation) or nihilism, "between the Logos of God and the ultimate meaninglessness of life and the world."[55]

Christian theology is based on its own presuppositions derived from revelation.[56] As a result, the "task of Christian leadership is to confront modern man with the Christian world life view as the revealed conceptuality for understanding reality and experience."[57]

This can be maintained, says Henry, for "in the Christian view, God's mind and will are the source of all truth, of mathematics, of logic, of law, and of cosmic order."[58]

2. Human Reason is a divinely fashioned instrument for recognizing truth; it is not a creative source of truth.[59] Henry does not wish to evade "the demand for verification and tests for truth" and wishes to reject "any correlation of revelation with the irrational."[60] At the same time, Henry does not want to grant autonomous reason the ability to fashion metaphysical truth apart from God's revelation:

---

52. Ibid., 1:223.

53. See *God, Revelation, and Authority*, 3:287 (it is important to note that Henry is not here arguing that the "words we use are identical with the objects they designate," 3:289); note also a similar discussion by Henry on Barth in *Frontiers in Modern Theology*, 68-69; on Henry's interpretation and reaction to Barth, see Richard Albert Mohler, Jr., "Evangelical Theology and Karl Barth: Representative Models of Response" (Ph.D. dissertation, The Southern Baptist Theological Seminary, 1989), 107-134; Gregory C. Bolich, *Karl Barth and Evangelicalism* (Downers Grove: InterVarsity Press, 1980).

54. *God, Revelation, and Authority*, 1:224.

55. Ibid., 1:41; compare 1:91, where Henry writes that the "intellectual depletion of philosophical rationalism is an open invitation to despair."

56. *God, Revelation, and Authority*, 3:282.

57. Ibid., 1:43.

58. *Toward a Recovery*, 70.

59. *God, Revelation, and Authority*, 1:225; compare 2:73.

60. Ibid., 1:225.

> The superiority of reason over all other proposals for gaining informa-
> tion about the ultimately real world has been asserted from antiquity.
> The rationalistic method of knowing considers human reasoning as the
> only reliable and valid source of knowledge.[61]

In making this assertion, Henry stresses that "revealed religion," to
which he subscribes, "gives no quarter to the idealistic illusion that
human reason is intrinsically capable of fashioning eternal truth."[62]
Henry sees human reason as inadequately equipped, apart from divine
revelation, to "unravel all the enigmas of life."[63] He writes:

> To say that man's mental powers are virtually divine contradicts both
> the basic Christian axiom that God in his transcendent revelation is the
> only source of truth and its related emphasis, namely, that finite and
> fallen man even though gifted with the divine image is dependent
> upon revelation. When human reasoning is exalted as the source of
> truth, then the content of truth is soon conformed to the prejudices of
> some influential thinker or school of scholars, or it may be conformed
> to the current consensus of opinion, sometimes dignified by the
> expression 'the universal human consciousness.' Christian theology
> denies that the human mind or human reasoning is a creative source of
> revelational content; its proper role is not to fashion revelation or truth,
> but rather to recognize and elucidate it.[64]

Truth is therefore that which is derived from God's self-revelation, for
God is the embodiment of all truth. Henry's concern is that reason not
be elevated above or to the same level as God's special revelation and
thus perhaps stand in judgment upon God's special revelation in terms
of viability. The fear is that "truth and the good become merely what the
pack or the herd wills," placing truth in the realm of "mood" or "temper-
ament."[65] Revelation is seen as that which purges philosophical understandings from the mind of the theologian. Ultimately, Henry warns, this
will lead to a form of pragmatism as an epistemological truth-princi-
ple.[66] Thus human reason explicates the truth of special revelation, but
in no form is it to be construed as generating such truth. Henry asserts
that to allow reason a role of generation an absolute truth apart from
divine revelation "arrogantly overlooks the creatureliness and sinfulness
of man."[67] Therefore "Christian religion assigns a critical and indispens-

---

61. Ibid., I:85.
62. Ibid., I:225-6.
63. Ibid., I:226.
64. Ibid.
65. *God, Revelation, and Authority*, I:41.
66. Ibid., I:41.
67. See Henry, *Drift of Western Thought*, 96.

able role to reason," granting legitimacy to human reasoning such as "employed in syllogisms and other valid forms of implication."[68]

It is important to note that Henry affirms the use of reason, not rationalism, the latter being defined as "human reasoning deployed into the service of premises that flow from arbitrary and mistaken postulations about reality and truth."[69] Henry dismisses this outright.[70] Rather, "Christian theology unreservedly champions reason as an instrument for organizing the data and drawing inferences from it, and as a logical discriminating faculty competent to test religious claims."[71] Such a perspective does not leave Henry enamored with theologians who ignore rational objections to the Christian faith. The Christian faith has truth and reason on its side and should thus be noted for its "intelligible confrontation of the issues."[72] It is time to "recall reason once again from the vagabondage of irrationalism and the arrogance of autonomy to the service of true faith."[73] Henry holds to this presuppositional approach on the grounds that presuppositionless thinking is a misnomer.[74] All thinking is

68. Henry, *God, Revelation, and Authority*, 1:226; Henry rejects the "prevalent notion that the rules of logic —simply because Aristotle first consistently expounded them —are culture-relative"; rather they are indispensable, for "apart from the law of noncontradiction" there can be no insistence upon the truth of revelation, see *God, Revelation, and Authority*, 4:59; see also his discussion of Western modes of thought and non-Western modes, a distinction that Henry finds erroneous in regard to principles of reason in *Toward a Recovery*, 108-110.

69. Henry, *God, Revelation, and Authority*, 1:226; Henry writes that the decisive question concerning the "interrelation between theology and philosophy is derived from revelation, or whether human reasoning is elevated as a secondary instrument of revelation— and hence considered another final authority—alongside the Word of God," see 199.

70. Thus the remark by William Abraham in *The Coming Great Revival* (San Francisco: Harper and Row, 1984), 37, that *God, Revelation and Authority* is "over three thousand pages of turgid scholasticism" which offers only a "dead and barren orthodoxy decked out in a magnificent display of learning" can be classified misreading of Henry's careful embrace of reason. Note also the misunderstanding of Thomas Reginald McNeal, who argued that Henry is a Thomist and that his theological method represents a "rationalistic theological methodology dominated by the priority of reason over faith that places reason above faith" see "A Critical Analysis of the Doctrine of God in the Theology of Carl F.H. Henry" (Ph.D. dissertation, Southwestern Baptist Theological Seminary, 1986), 1. What Henry proposes is not rationalism, but rationality, the reasonableness of the Christian faith.

71. Henry, *God, Revelation, and Authority*, 1:226; note also Henry's conviction that "Evangelical confidence in the ontological significance of reason makes possible a positive, courageous approach to science," see *Evangelical Responsibility in Contemporary Theology*, 73. For Henry, reason that is "fully informed" makes for successful engagement with contemporary philosophy; see *Remaking the Modern Mind*, 238.

72. *God, Revelation, and Authority*, I:14.

73. Ibid., I:43.

74. Henry notes that "no historian and no scientist approaches historical or physical events without presuppositions," see *God, Revelation, and Authority*, 1:261; "Science continually works within undemonstrable postulates; without them, the scientific enterprise itself would collapse . . . the scientist believes in order to know," see *Contemporary Evangelical Thought*, 262; see also Henry's article "The Ambiguities of Scientific Breakthrough" in *Horizons of Science: Christian Scholars Speak Out* (San Francisco: Harper and Row, 1978), 87-116, a collection which Henry also served as editor, and *The Drift of Western Thought*, 92, where Henry rejects the limitation of knowledge to the scientific method. Perhaps Henry's most focused discussion of presuppositionalism and his theological method, and certainly his most current, is found in *Toward a Recovery*, 37-60.

based on presuppositions; it is simply a question of which presuppositions one chooses to begin the process. For Henry, the presuppositions can be stated in characteristically direct fashion: "revelation is the source of all truth, . . . reason the instrument for recognizing it, the Bible . . . the Christian verifying principle."[75] So presuppositions are inescapable while the issue of distinguishing between valid and invalid assumptions is to be attended.[76]

Though a presuppositionalist, Henry seeks to incorporate the central insights of the evidentialist camp. He accepts the importance of verification but refuses to sacrifice the inherent concerns of the presuppositionalist position, namely the a priori contention of theism and the truth of God's revelation in Scripture. Henry feels his presuppositionalism withstands the concerns against presuppositionalist theology, that presuppositionalist theology (1) exaggerates the noetic consequences of the fall of humanity; (2) denies the existence of any "common ground" between believers and nonbelievers; and (3) bows to the demands of a coherence theory of truth.[77] For Henry, the fall of humanity does not mean that human beings cannot comprehend God's special revelation prior to the regenerative work of the Holy Spirit. Instead, it is humanity's will, as opposed to reason, that is affected most pervasively.[78] He writes:

> While revealed religion insists that man as created is inescapably conscious of God and of his transcendently ordered cosmos, that is, of the incomparable power and deity of the Cosmic Planner, his response to the revealed God known in his revelation is broken and evasive. Man can indeed know the God of creation and created reality—not exhaustively, to be sure, but nonetheless truly. Yet as sinner he frustrates the divine revelation that penetrates into his very mind and conscience, and in significant respects also dilutes and even suppresses the revelation in created reality. For all that, man even as sinner is aware of the living God and of created reality as a divinely given order and as an arena of divine disclosure, even if he throws himself athwart this revelation and responds to it obliquely.[79]

Henry asserts that if humanity's reason was perverted in the fall, then "no rationally persuasive case could be mounted for or against anything

---

75. Henry, *God, Revelation, and Authority*, 1:232; it is to be noted that Henry's concern was the speculative notion that divine revelation is never communicated objectively, but only subjectively through submissive response, an assumption that Henry rejects as out of step with the historic Christian view that divine revelation is objective intelligible disclosure; see *Frontiers in Modern Theology*, 78-81, where Henry speaks of the necessary controlling presuppositions of the Christian faith and the danger of the subjective view.

76. Henry, *Toward a Recovery*, 42-45.

77. These very concerns were expressed by John Gerstner to Henry in a public dialogue at Trinity Evangelical Divinity School in Deerfield, Illinois, in November of 1974, see Henry, *God, Revelation and Authority*, 1:226.

78. Henry, *God, Revelation, and Authority*, 1:226.

79. Ibid., 160.

whatever."[80]   Henry believes that it is very important to maintain the distinction between "the individual who bears the 'imago Dei' by creation and the schematized response he makes to the revelation of God and his created reality."[81]

Instead of categorizing human thinking as regenerate and unregenerate, the division is better seen as valid and invalid. "Revelation lifts human reason beyond restrictions of intellect limited by finitude and clouded by sin through the knowledge it conveys of man's Maker and Redeemer."[82] The laws of logic remain intact as a capacity given by God to humanity for the appropriation of true knowledge. Indeed, Henry argues that "in contemplating the divine image in man, it should be clear that the rational or cognitive aspect has logical priority."[83] This line of reasoning proceeds from the conclusion that if fallen humanity cannot know the truth, then it cannot have knowledge concerning God.

Such a reduction necessarily leads to skepticism concerning the spiritual realm. Yet skepticism itself is self-refuting, argues Henry, since it claims to know that we cannot know. Moreover, Scripture refutes the view that humanity is without knowledge of God, considering all of humanity guilty of rebellion against God (compare Rom. 1:18-32). The survival of rational competence after the fall is a necessity for people to communicate intelligible truth, appropriate such communication, and find it meaningful.[84] Henry states that "there is but one system of truth, and that system involves the right axiom and its theorems and premises derived with complete logical consistency."[85] As a result, the possibility of ascertaining God's truth comes through divine revelation, and that divine revelation is accessed through the use of reason, a created capacity of both thought and speech which enables rational knowledge and interaction.[86] "Man's rationality," writes Henry, "is therefore one

---

80. Ibid., 227; for Henry, an example of an unacceptable noetic effect of the fall would be an immunity to the rational validity of the basic categories of logic, such as the law of contradiction.

81. Ibid., 160; Henry's doctrine of the "imago Dei" is discussed at length, 2:124-142.

82. *God, Revelation, and Authority,* 1:201.

83. Ibid., 2:125.

84. Henry, *God, Revelation, and Authority,* 2:136.

85. Ibid., 1:227, compare 14; such a system, argues Henry, does not "require a presuppositionalist to extrapolate an entire system of theology conformable to a coherence theory of truth, nor does it necessitate a denial of all common ground between the believer and the unbeliever," 1:227.

86.   Henry asserts that if it is true that logic is objective rather than subjective, and that there can ultimately be only one set of rules for understanding and for the criteria of truth, then the Christian doctrine of creation provides the best explanation of the objectivity of logic and of the fact that human beings share this fundamental conceptual structure; see *God, Revelation, and Authority,* 5:351.

span of the epistemological bridge whereby he knows theological truth."[87]

For Henry this cognitive element of God's revelation allows God's truth to be meaningfully embraced and communicated. In this respect it is like any other form of truth.[88] The distinction between theological truth and other forms is that "theological truth is divinely authorized, infallibly certain, and biblically attested; all other claims for truth are subject to correction and at most are but probable."[89] Henry does not feel that individuals can commit to faith in Christianity solely on the grounds of theoretical argument; he does feel Christians can "demote and demolish nonrevelational counterclaims."[90] Therefore, truth is that which persuades and convinces.

3. The Bible is the Christian's principle of verification. Henry's system is built on the conviction that the Bible is the inspired Word of God and therefore serves as the "proximate and universally accessible form of authoritative divine revelation."[91] This revelational truth is "intelligible, expressible in valid propositions, and universally communicable"[92] with the Logos as the mediating agent.[93] If revelation is nonpropositional, it cannot be intelligible, much less true or false. He writes, "If revelation is a communication of sharable truth, it will consist of sentences, propositions, judgments, and not simply of isolated concepts, names or words. To be sure, concepts and words are instrumentalities of God's disclosure; divine revelation is conceptual and verbal."[94] For Henry, only propositions "have the quality of truth."[95] Henry defines a propositional statement as the association of a predicate with a subject, thus being an "intelligible, logically formed statement, a declarative sentence that is either true or false."[96] Aware that the Bible contains a variety of literary

---

87. Ibid., 1:227; anti-intellectual theologians who "claim that the content of revelation is, as such, rationally unchallengeable should understand that the price of such privilege can only be the forfeiture of any claim to truth." See *God, Revelation and Authority*, 3:280.

88. Ibid., 1:200.

89. Ibid., 1:228.

90. Ibid.

91. Ibid., 1:229.

92. Ibid. Henry is well aware of the many objections to propositional revelation; see 3:429-438.

93. Henry, *God, Revelation, and Authority*, 3:203-215; according to Henry, the Logos of God as scripturally identified is "personal, intelligible communication centered in the transcendent Christ as the sole mediator of divine revelation"; 3:212, and "the mind of God incarnate in Jesus Christ whose very speech is truth and spirit and life, the written Scriptures . . . whereby the eternal Christ now rules in truth over the family of faith"; 3:215.

94. See *God, Revelation, and Authority*, 3:429; *The Protestant Dilemma*, 55, 97.

95. *God, Revelation, and Authority*, 3:430.

96. See "The Concerns and Considerations of Carl F.H. Henry," *Christianity Today* (March 13, 1981), 20, where he also writes that by propositional revelation he does not mean "simply that the Bible is written in meaningful sentences—as most books are—but that God has revealed himself intelligibly and rationally in units of human speech involving sentences, words, and syntax that Scripture attests, and thus gives us an inspired literary document" (20); see also Fackre, "Carl F. H. Henry," 591.

forms and mediums of revelation, Henry stands by the "overwhelming virtue" of the term "propositional revelation" in that it serves to demonstrate that we have a "body of truth, however transmitted, which originates with God and which provides the subject matter of theology."[97]

To those who dismiss the prospect of propositional truth, Henry counters that their very denial is itself propositional.[98] It is not argued that "words as isolated units of speech" are in and of themselves either "fallible or infallible," but rather that truth is a "property of sentences or statements" with words serving as "meaningful referents in a logical, propositional context."[99] The use of language to convey meaning and especially authorial intent is decisive for Henry, a view supported by other scholars, such as E. D. Hirsch in *Validity in Interpretation* (1967) and *The Aims of Interpretation* (1976). Henry wants to separate meaning from significance, attributing meaning to the text and significance to the individual relationship between the meaning and the reader.

This contention therefore argues against Christian truth being culture-bound or time-constrained.[100] God's revelation is intelligible, and the Bible serves as a universally valid criterion of meaning and truth.[101] For Henry, "the permanent significance of Scripture is clear from 2 Timothy 3:16, where its values are enumerated in terms of teaching truth and refuting error."[102] As a result, "a verifiability or controllability postulate is wholly appropriate to Christian theology."[103] At this point Henry wishes to guard against Christian truth being perceived as that which is subjective and incommunicable beyond its national or cultural borders. Henry states that the truth-content of theology "can be investigated—as can that of astronomy and botany and geology—quite apart from the moral character of the technical scholar and his interest or disinterest in a new way of life."[104]

Inspired Scripture is therefore normative in all matters of religion and ethics. Henry writes that the Bible is not a textbook on science or on history, but that "attention to the Bible's statements bearing on the physical sciences and history . . . will enable its readers to avoid many misconceptions to which empirical inquiry remains ongoingly vulnerable."[105] This

---

97. See "The Authority and Inspiration of the Bible," *The Expositor's Bible Commentary*, vol. 1, ed. Frank E. Gaebelein (Grand Rapids: Regency Reference Library, 1979), 23.

98. "Authority and Inspiration," 455-481.

99. *God, Revelation, and Authority*, 4:46.

100. Ibid., 4:53.

101. *God, Revelation, and Authority*, 1:192; the notion that "truth is a feature only of language determined solely by grammatical rules" is rejected by Henry as based on the presupposition that "there is no reality beyond language itself, or that if there is we cannot know it," see *God, Revelation, and Authority*, 3:448-9.

102. Ibid., 3:46.

103. Ibid., 1:229.

104. Ibid.

105. Ibid., 1:232.

brings up Henry's position on biblical inerrancy,[106] a doctrine that Henry objects to being elevated above the assertion that the Bible is inspired and authoritative.[107]

The Bible is perceived as the "reservoir and conduit of divine truth" and as that which serves as the "authoritative written record and interpretation of God's revelatory deeds, and the ongoing source of reliable objective knowledge concerning God's nature and ways."[108] He writes:

> In its original form the prophetic and apostolic witness, oral and written, had the special quality of inerrancy. Inerrancy pertains only to the oral or written proclamation of the originally inspired prophets and apostles. Not only was their communication of the Word of God efficacious in teaching the truth of revelation, but their transmission of that Word was error-free. Inerrancy does not extend to copies, translations or versions however. Yet copies may be said to be infallible in that these extant derivatives of the autographs do not corrupt the original content but convey the truth of revelation in reliable verbal form, and infallibly lead the penitent reader to salvation . . . if error had permeated the original prophetic-apostolic verbalization of the revelation, no essential connection would exist between the recovery of any preferred text and the authentic meaning of God's revelation.[109]

For Henry, biblical faith cannot be disengaged from a conviction that the Bible's historical details are indeed historically factual and the statements asserted objectively true.[110] If the Bible is to be comprehensively

---

106. The fourth volume of Henry's systematic, *God, Revelation, and Authority* is devoted almost entirely to the subject of biblical inspiration, inerrancy, and infallibility; important sections include discussions on the literal truth of Scripture (103-128), the meaning of inspiration (129-161), the inerrancy of Scripture (162-195), the meaning of inerrancy (201-210), infallibility (220-255), and hermeneutics (272-367); publications edited or written by Henry in support of biblical inerrancy can be found as early as *Revelation and the Bible* (1958), 7-10, and continue with such articles as "Authority and Inspiration," 3-35 and "Who are the Evangelicals?," *Evangelical Affirmations*, 69-94.

107. Henry, "Concerns and Considerations," *Christianity Today*, 19; in this article Henry attempts to distance himself from Lindsell's *The Battle for the Bible* (Grand Rapids: Zondervan, 1976), which Henry felt made the following mistakes: (1) elevated inerrancy over authority and inspiration; (2) eclipsed the important issues of revelation and culture, hermeneutics, and propositional revelation; (3) wrongly created distrust over all but a small handful of conservative institutions; and (4) through overstatement made it easy for opponents of inerrancy to gain an undeserved sympathy for their views. Henry's perspective is that inerrancy should be viewed as a mark of Evangelical consistency as opposed to Evangelical authenticity, see *Evangelicals in Search of Identity* (Waco: Word, 1976), 48-56, where Henry notes that "the real question is whether, once scriptural errancy is affirmed, a consistent evangelical faith is maintained" (55) and that the "duty of evangelical enterprise requires something higher than invalidating every contribution of evangelicals who halt short of that commitment" (56); see also "Theology and Biblical Authority: A Review Article," *Journal of the Evangelical Theological Society* 19 (1976), 315-323; "Authority and Inspiration," 4-5; *Confessions*, 365; *Conversations with Carl Henry*, 23-30; Marsden, *Reforming Fundamentalism*, 288.

108. Henry, *God, Revelation, and Authority*, 2:13.

109. Ibid., 2:14-15.

110. Ibid., 3:96.

trustworthy, then there must not be the possibility of error.[111] More pointedly, "if we declare the category of inerrancy to be irrelevant for Scripture, can we any longer contend for the truth of Scripture?"[112]

An inerrant Bible is decisive, then, for Henry's understanding of Scripture as that which provides the principle of verification. Humanity must be able to judge the truth of the Christian faith prior to Christian commitment or the non-believer cannot be held responsible for rejecting the truth of the Christian faith. The nature of this verification, however, is another matter. Henry disallows logical positivism or laboratory science as acceptable verificational criteria. With his mentor Gordon Clark, Henry feels that what is required is only that the propositions under consideration be capable of being tested by anyone who is sufficiently attentive in order to determine the conformity of the church's language about God to its biblical criterion.[113] God has revealed Himself intelligibly to humanity in such a way that all of humanity can both understand and appreciate the truth of that revelation. They can then choose to respond with faith or disobedience. The verifying principle in this matrix is Scripture. Henry writes that

> the specially inspired prophetic-apostolic proclamation is the basis of the church's distinction between canonical and noncanonical writings and constitutes a standard for verifying Christian truth-claims as authentic and authoritative.[114]

The rejection of merely an empirical approach is advanced on the basis that feeling reveals more about ourselves than about God, and that our perceptions reveal more about sense realities than the supersensible. Henry wants an approach that reveals truth about supernatural realities, not just perceptible realities.[115] In regard to the doctrine of analogy, Henry finds difficulty with its failure to "recognize that only univocal assertions protect us from equivocation; the very possibility of analogy founders unless something is truly known about both

---

111. Ibid., 4:170.

112. Ibid., 4:177; "I remain unpersuaded that any theological movement can dramatically affect the course of the world while its own leaders undermine the integrity of its charter documents, or while its spokespersons domestically exhaust all their energies in internal defense of those documents," "American Evangelicals in a Turning Time," *Theologians in Transition*, 45.

113. *God, Revelation and Authority*, 1:230; compare Gordon Clark, *Karl Barth's Theological Method* (Nutley, N.J.: Presbyterian and Reformed, 1963), 60-61.

114. *God, Revelation, and Authority*, 2:13.

115. Ibid., 1:85; in agreement with his mentor Gordon Clark, Henry "bluntly challenges the validity of the empirical method in science . . . however useful scientific laws are, they cannot be true"; see *Contemporary Evangelical Thought*, 270; Henry is more than willing to have science serve as a "negative check against false exegesis, and as a complement and supplement to the biblical data," but in no way is it to be allowed to "fix the content of the biblical revelation of nature"; see *Contemporary Evangelical Thought*, 272.

analogates."[116] Henry asserts that the basic difficulty with the analogical method of determining the divine attributes of God is "its denial that the terms used of God and man have univocal meaning."[117]

Instead, God is defined by divine revelation.

4. *Logical consistency is a negative test for truth and coherence a sub-ordinate test.*[118] At this juncture it would be wise to raise the question of the validity of various tests for truth. Such a question finds Henry wholly supportive of tests for truth. For example, Henry asserts that

> tests of truth will not only serve to refute as spurious the natural man's objections, but also show that the alternatives they propose do not hold up and lead rather to skepticism. Rational tests will also exhibit the logical and psychological superiority of the Christian revelation as a world view that best meets all human needs.[119]

"Without noncontradiction and logical consistency, no knowledge whatever is possible."[120] Henry states his case in strong terms: "whatever violates the law of contradiction cannot be considered revelation: . . . The God of biblical revelation is the God of reason, not Ultimate Irrationality; all he does is rational."[121] For Henry, the denial of the law of contradiction blurs the distinction between what is true and what is false. Only "persuasive rational evidence unmasks the inconsistencies of other views and exhibits the rational consistency of Christian claims."[122] If the Christian faith is not logically consistent, it is not tenable for the non-Christian even to consider. "The axioms of any system are testable for the consistency or inconsistency with which they account for relevant data," writes Henry, and therefore the "axioms lose explanatory power if theorems deduced from them are shown to be logically inconsistent."[123] Truths must not contradict each other, and derived theorems must be self-consistent. Rational consistency as a test for truth is necessary for presuppositionalism to avoid lapsing into fideism.[124]

Logical consistency alone is prey to several objections, not the least of which is that it does not move the discussion to the point of deter-

---

116. *God, Revelation, and Authority*, 4:118; such a view distances Henry from the perspective of Cornelius Van Til, who understood analogy as the only form of knowledge (see chapter on Van Til).

117. Ibid., 5:87; for Henry, such a denial cannot consistently avoid agnosticism and skepticism.

118. Here Henry distances himself again from Cornelius Van Til, who while holding to a coherence theory of truth, exempted Christian revelation from logical self-consistency.

119. Henry, *God, Revelation, and Authority*, 1:232; Henry asserts that the biblical theist does not, because of his belief in the biblical miraculous, "rule out all tests of truth and fact, but rather insists on adequate warrants," see *God, Revelation, and Authority*, 4:340.

120. Ibid., 1:232; see also *Toward a Recovery*, 52-54.

121. *God, Revelation, and Authority*, 1:233.

122. Ibid..

123. *Toward a Recovery*, 80.

124. Ibid., x.

mining whether any one logically cohesive system is more correct than another. Henry counters this objection with his categorization of logical consistency as a negative test for truth. If it were considered a positive test for truth, it would legitimate a host of conflicting views which begin from diametrically opposed presuppositions.[125]

While Henry would deny being an adherent of a correspondence theory of truth, his resistance to that label is epistemological, not ontological, in orientation. Henry wishes to avoid the pitfall of evidentialism in terms of apologetics and epistemology. What Henry ultimately offers is a modification of the correspondence theory of truth. Its modification notes that if "the human mind cannot know reality itself, but only what corresponds to it, the consequence would seem to be skepticism."[126] In other words, if we cannot know reality, then what corresponds to that reality will not be very helpful. Henry holds to a correspondence understanding of truth in terms of divine revelation, which gives us reality in true correspondence. He states that "if there is no point of identity in what God and man may know . . . then man has no truth about God."[127] Favorably quoting Clark, Henry points out that if no proposition "means to man what it means to God, so that God's knowledge and man's knowledge do not coincide at any single point, it follows by rigorous necessity that man can have no truth at all."[128] In deference to the coherence view of truth, Henry holds that "truth is a consistent system, and that all facets of it (including all facts) have meaning as a part of that system."[129] Attempts at interpretation which try to engage life and reality apart from the base of revelation will prove inadequate, logically inconsistent, and even false.[130] Henry insists that the truth of revelational theism is the most consistent and coherent explanation of empirical data. This is something very different than professing to validate the core-commitments of Christian theism wholly on empirical grounds," an exercise which Henry discounts.[131] Thus the Christian faith does not offer mathematical or speculative certainty, but rather spiritual assurance. Divine authority eliminates the rational gap between probability and certainty.[132]

---

125. *God, Revelation, and Authority*, 1:234-235; see also *Toward a Recovery*, 86-87.

126. *God, Revelation, and Authority*, 1:237.

127. *God, Revelation, and Authority*, 2:54.

128. Ibid., 2:55; compare Gordon Clark, "Apologetics," in *Contemporary Evangelical Thought*, 159.

129. Henry, *God, Revelation, and Authority*, 1:237.

130. Ibid.

131. Ibid., 1:238.

132. *Toward a Recovery*, 59.

Critique of Henry's Concept of Truth

Carl F. H. Henry is a persuasive thinker who presents his ideas with compelling force. He is consistent in his method and clear in his style. He interacts knowledgeably with a wide range of contemporary views as well as ancient and modern thinkers. He has presented the case for presuppositionalism, the centrality of revelation, and the use of reason in a manner that has gained both wide respect and a careful hearing.

Nonetheless, fellow Evangelicals have engaged Henry's system of thought and have come away with questions and concerns, largely related to his presuppositions and the nature of his theological method. The first question from Evangelicals for Henry is as follows: On what basis does Henry's epistemological principle prohibit reason from human self-discovery of God's truth apart from special revelation? It is certainly granted that special revelation is indeed special, but does it need to be exhaustively exclusive? Can it not simply serve as that which gives the parameters for truth, providing the basis for further, non-contradictory truth discoveries, while remaining coherent to the special revelation? Though such truths need not be placed on the same level as that of special revelation, it can be asked whether Henry's refusal to allow reason a creative role is necessary.

A second concern is the viability of Henry's use of reason as an overarching hermeneutic for accessing the truth of the biblical materials. Hans Frei has correctly noted that one's hermeneutic must attend to the nature of the narrative at hand.[133] Does the nature of the biblical narrative allow Henry's hermeneutic?[134] Has he joined Enlightenment rationalism too closely with the idea of special revelation, thus construing special revelation too exclusively in terms of propositions? Henry is right in that he does not want to confuse such categories as "myth" with that which purports to be intentionally cognitively informative,[135] but does his employment of reason as the divinely given instrument for recognizing truth violate this concern? Many Evangelicals would argue that it does, contending that Aristotelian categories of logic are used as an artificial hermeneutical grid which the biblical materials are forced to pass through in violence to their nature. Bernard Ramm insists that Henry's emphasis on non-contradiction may be fine for those elements within Scripture that are propositional, but Ramm points out that not all of the

---

133. Hans Frei, *The Eclipse of Biblical Narrative* (New Haven: Yale University Press, 1974).

134. Henry has engaged narrative theology in the following articles: "Narrative Theology: An Evangelical Appraisal," *Trinity Journal* 8 NS, No. 1 (Spring 1987), 3-19; "Where Will Evangelicals Cast Their Lot?," *This World* 18 (1987), 3-11, a response to Mark Ellingsen, *The Evangelical Movement: Growth, Impact, Controversy, Dialog* (Minneapolis: Augsburg, 1988).

135. *God, Revelation, and Authority*, I:65-66.

Bible is of that genre. Therefore, Henry is in error if he attempts to force all of Scripture into the propositional mode—not to mention that if Henry cannot do this, then "he has to admit that there is more to revelation than propositions and therefore other criteria of truthfulness must be used along with the law of non-contradiction."[136]

Henry acknowledges that some scholars feel such an emphasis binds God to rational criteria, ignores paradox, and refuses mystery. Henry answers that he has no wish to deny such dimensions to God, or to reduce God to the canons of reason. He finds, however, that without the cognitive emphasis "man has no basis for discriminating between mysteries, paradoxes and contradictions . . . it is necessary to avoid the divorce of faith and logic."[137] Nonetheless, despite Henry's desires, certain Evangelicals affirm the critique that his system leaves little room for the mysterious, paradoxical, and contradictory (from the finite perspective) in regard to theological insight and construction.[138] In ruling out such forms of knowing as analogy, insisting instead on univocal language and knowledge, Henry may not give enough respect to the divide between the finite and the Infinite, which arguably demands some form of analogical knowledge in certain areas. Without room for these elements, the charge that God has become limited to the capacity of human reason is left unanswered.[139]

A third concern begins with the claims that reason is that which is divinely given in order to recognize the truth and that the noetic effects of the fall did not do damage to this activity. Is it not an enormous burden to place on the fallen will to make it account for the vast compromise of the legitimate and proper use of reason by non-Christian humanity? Henry asserts that "revelation lifts human reason beyond restrictions of intellect limited by finitude and clouded by sin through

---

136. See "Carl Henry's Magnum Opus," review of Carl Henry, *God, Revelation and Authority*, vols. 1 and 2 (Word), *Eternity*, XXVIII (March 1977), 62; note also the informed and insightful discussion of difficulties with the idea of propositional revelation by Kevin J. Vanhoozer, "The Semantics of Biblical Literature," *Hermeneutics, Authority, and Canon*, ed. D. A. Carson and John D. Woodbridge (Grand Rapids: Academie, 1986), 56-75.

137. *God, Revelation, and Authority*, 1:232-233; Henry finds support for such a contention from Norman L. Geisler and Ronald M. Brooks in *Come Let Us Reason: An Introduction to Logical Thinking* (Grand Rapids: Baker, 1990).

138. See Donald Bloesch, *Essentials of Evangelical Theology*, vol. 2 (San Francisco: Harper and Row, 1979), 267-268.

139. Even one as "Aristotelian" as Mortimer Adler, who became a Christian in 1984, confesses to the "mystery" of the "triune nature of the godhead and the incarnation of God in the dual nature of the person Jesus Christ," see *Truth in Religion: The Plurality of Religions and the Unity of Truth* (New York: Macmillan, 1990), 18. In an interview with Terry Muck, associate professor of comparative religion at Austin Presbyterian Theological Seminary, Adler makes the following comment: "My chief reason for choosing Christianity was because the mysteries were incomprehensible. What's the point of revelation if we could figure it out ourselves? If it were wholly comprehensible, then it would be just another philosophy"; see "Truth's Intrepid Ambassador," *Christianity Today* vol. 34, no. 17 (November 19, 1990), 34.

the knowledge it conveys of man's Maker and Redeemer."[140] However, does this not demand an infallible hermeneutic? To be sure, Henry notes that the point "is not that Christian scholars can attain infallibility in this life," and that too often "the distinction is forgotten between the canonical content of revelation and systems derived from it for which absolute claims are made," but nonetheless, one could argue that Henry's system still does not address the criticism.[141] Similarly, if empirical scientific knowledge is less than objective,[142] on what grounds is reason free of subjective error when approaching the Scriptures? Is reason totally free from the effects of sin? If the fall has affected humanity, Henry's system would seem to demand that reason in regard to the use of logic is exempt from its consequences. Henry would certainly assert that it is not, but he does speak of reason being "fully informed";[143] yet if not untainted, to what degree is reason corrupted, and how does that affect Henry's use of reason as that which recognizes the truth of revelation? If the Christian mind is enlightened in a way that the unregenerate mind is not, then is this not a gift as opposed to a higher operation of reason? As Patterson observes, Henry will respond to these criticisms by saying that revelation is a disclosure of higher truth that stands in continuity with rational truth.[144] Yet here again is the concern of hermeneutical method in regard to appropriation. Though Henry admirably sees the rules of language and reason as the way beyond the impasse, these concerns remain; logical deduction may be sound but not infallible in the hands of the sinful human. Therefore, it might be warranted to say that Henry places too much confidence in the role of reason.

Fourth, one must acknowledge the many concerns of the Evangelical evidentialist camp, perhaps most formally marshalled against Henry by John Warwick Montgomery.[145] Montgomery's concern is that Henry has jettisoned the facticity of the Christian argument in his abandonment of empirical verifiability and falsifiability.[146] The charges are circular rea-

---

140. *God, Revelation, and Authority*, 1:201.

141. Ibid., 1:240.

142. Ibid., 1:121.

143. *Remaking the Modern Mind*, 238; in *Toward a Recovery*, 110, Henry states that "not even humanity's Fall into sin has annuled the law of contradiction. The noetic effect of sin is serious, for it hinder's man's disposition to meditate on the proper content of human thinking. But it does not deform or destroy the components of logic and reason. Propositions that were universally true before the Fall and belong to God's propositional revelation remain so ongoingly despite the Fall." This is a different assertion than that which sees reason as a means of recognition of those propositional truths which remain free from the consequences of the Fall.

144. Patterson, *Carl F. H. Henry*, 167.

145. John Warwick Montgomery, *Faith Founded on Fact: Essays in Evidential Apologetics* (Nashville: Thomas Nelson, 1978), whose introductory essay is a polemic against Henry's presuppositionalist methodology in *God, Revelation and Authority*. See also *Evidence for Faith: Deciding the God Question*, ed. John Warwick Montgomery (Dallas: Probe/Word, 1991).

146. *Faith Founded on Fact*, xviii.

soning, fideism, and a weakened apologetic. Most feared by Montgomery is Carl Henry's contention "that empirical facts—and in particular historical facts—are incapable of establishing the Christian case."[147] Contrary to Henry's assertion that facts are in and of themselves neutral, divorced from meaning and in need of significance, Montgomery states that it is facts which ultimately arbitrate interpretations.[148] Montgomery concludes that Christians need not return to a "nineteenth-century aprioristic religious metaphysic" when philosophy has made "tremendous strides in the direction of truth-testing and verification. One can confidently rely on fact to support faith."[149] Henry's response remains the same: "empirical science is never able to reach absolute truth, because its observational data are incomplete. Worse yet, it cannot even deal with the supernatural or with moral absolutes, for these fall outside its area of competence."[150] For Henry, God reveals Himself to humanity, as opposed to humanity discovering God on its own. Henry answers the charge of circular reasoning—that is, reason does not verify revelation, revelation is the source of all truth, yet revelation serves as its own verifying principle—on the grounds that all reasoning is circular. The argument that the Christian system is circular "because it sets out what needs first to be proved would apply to all systems, since no system exists without basic axioms. The fact is, all arguments involve circularity."[151] Evidentialists point to such lines of thinking and claim that fideism and anti-intellectualism are inevitable results.[152] A related apologetic concern for those elements of the coherence theory of truth present in Henry's thought is that it would seem to demand proving every opposing system incoherent before Christianity could stand firm as the most coherent system. There is no doubt that if Christianity is true as a system, then deductions from axioms diametrically opposed to Christianity

---

147. Ibid., xix.

148. Ibid., xxii.

149. Ibid., xxv.

150. Henry, *Christian Countermoves in a Decadent Culture*, 140; see also *Toward a Recovery*, 50; it should not be forgotten that in such contentions Henry is revealing his dependence on Augustine's apriorism, meaning that truth is found primarily in the intellect, unmixed with anything empirical and validated independently of all impressions of sense, see Patterson, *Carl F. H. Henry*, 70, Patterson also discusses the debate between Henry and Montgomery on 82.

151. Henry, *Toward a Recovery*, 90.

152. Such is the claim against Henry by R. C. Sproul, John Gerstner, and Arthur Lindsley, *Classical Apologetics: A Rational Defense of the Christian Faith and a Critique of Presuppositional Apologetics* (Grand Rapids: Academie, 1984), see especially 336-338; responses to such charges from Henry are certainly noteworthy, but the defense of presuppositionalism given by Ronald H. Nash, *The New Evangelicalism* (Grand Rapids: Zondervan, 1963), 131-143; Alvin Plantinga, "Advice to Christian Philosophers," *Faith and Philosophy*, vol. 1, no. 3 (July 1984), 253-271; and Kelly James Clark, *Return to Reason* (Grand Rapids: Eerdmans, 1990) are just as engaging.

are false, but proving such a conclusion is an enterprise that would be monumental and arguably impossible.[153]

Fifth, the question is raised as to whether Henry's reliance upon syllogistic logic for the discovery of truth actually leaves out the truth question. It is possible to exercise the canons of logic with rigor and consistency and yet leave the question of truth far behind. As Dr. William L. Hendricks, professor of systematic theology at The Southern Baptist Theological Seminary is often known to point out in class lectures on this subject, the syllogism "Nobody likes crying babies, all babies cry, therefore nobody likes babies" may be good formal logic, but it is patently false in its conclusion because the major premise is false. Here is a challenge to formal logic itself, not to mention a deductive methodology, as a means to knowing.

Finally, does Henry's reliance upon non-contradiction in his concept of truth along with his allegiance to biblical inerrancy forge a problem regarding historical and critical issues in relation to the text in hand? Even if regarded as biblical difficulties rather than errors and contradictions, how these concerns fit into Henry's system of truth is not fully explicated.[154] Biblical criticism is a formidable obstacle for any theological method which rests heavily on a propositional understanding of the revealed truth of God.[155]

Summary

In Carl F. H. Henry's system of thought, divine revelation is the epistemic base for all truth. This specially revealed truth is recognized, understood, and appropriated through the use of reason, a divinely given gift for just such a purpose. A presuppositionalist approach is advocated as opposed to one built on empirical evidence. Henry accepts verification and the use of reason, but he does not see reason as being capable of creating truth on its own. The Bible is the Christian principle of verification and is normative, authoritative, and inerrant. Henry employs logical consistency as a negative test for truth and coherence as a subordinate test. The law of contradiction is viewed as essen-

---

153. Clark Pinnock voiced his concern about Henry's system in *Tracking the Maze*, 47; Henry answers in *Toward a Recovery*, 81, that we can only grapple with known systems that are leading competitors for the hearts and minds of humanity.

154. Bernard Ramm expressed this concern *After Fundamentalism: The Future of Evangelical Theology* (San Francisco: Harper and Row, 1983), 26-27. He accused Henry as one who "stumbles because he glosses biblical criticism;" it would appear that this is also a concern of Patterson, see *Carl F.H. Henry*, 113-114, 162-163.

155. Evangelicals who have attempted a non-inerrantist approach in light of such concerns can be found in I. Howard Marshall, *Biblical Inspiration* (Grand Rapids: Eerdmans, 1982); Jack B. Rogers and Donald K. McKim, *The Authority and Interpretation of the Bible* (San Francisco: Harper and Row, 1979).

tial. A type of correspondence is accepted in terms of divine revelation corresponding to actual fact, with the system of Christian truth being a coherent whole. For Henry, the entire history of Western thought is seen as that which is founded upon biblical theism, logic, verificatory criteria, and shared verbal signification. His system of thought defends that understanding of history.[156]

Such a concept of truth raises many significant, broad questions which relate to those from within the Evangelical community, as well as some which are germane to those who do not embrace certain Evangelical convictions. First, the question of whether rational, propositional truth is what constitutes God's truth as revealed in Scripture is a much debated assertion.[157]

Second, even if one embraces Henry's contentions, the limits of language itself pose decisive questions and concerns. If one is convinced that truth can be paradoxical, for instance, such truth resists confinement within human language. As Hill notes, "to expect too much from language runs the risk of unnecessarily confining truth."[158] The many hermeneutical concerns related to a proposal such as Henry's are also to be noted.[159] Such concerns might voice that Henry's system limits God to the limits of our reason through his insistence on univocal language, and that Enlightenment rationalism is being used indiscriminately and out of context as a framework for truth.[160]

---

156. Henry, *Toward a Recovery*, 30.

157. For example, note the view of religious truth represented in the collection of essays titled *Phenomenology of the Truth Proper to Religion*, ed. Daniel Guerriere (Albany: State University of New York Press, 1990), which represents the whole spectrum of phenomenology, and such insights into the nature of Scripture as offered by Paul J. Achtemeier in *The Inspiration of Scripture* (Philadelphia: Westminster, 1980).

158. Kent R. Hill, *Faith and Imagination*, ed. Noel Riley Fitch and Richard W. Etulain (Albuquerque: Far West Books, 1985), 162.

159. An introduction to these issues can be found in Richard E. Palmer, *Hermeneutics* (Evanston: Northwestern University Press, 1969).

160. Many significant works warrant attention regarding the subject of truth as it relates to reason, including, but not limited to, the following: Robert J. Ackerman, *Belief and Knowledge* (Garden City: Doubleday, 1972); A. J. Ayer, *The Problem of Knowledge* (London: Macmillan, 1956); Jonathan Dancy, *An Introduction to Contemporary Epistemology* (Oxford: Basil Blackwell, 1985); Michael Devitt, *Realism and Truth* (Oxford: Basil Blackwell, 1984); Brian Ellis, *Truth and Objectivity* (Oxford: Basil Blackwell, 1990); G. W. F. Hegel, *Faith and Knowledge*, trans. Walter Cerf and H. S. Harris (Albany: State University of New York Press, 1977); Paul Helm, *The Varieties of Belief* (New York: Humanities Press, 1973); Basil Mitchell, *The Justification of Religious Belief* (London: Macmillan, 1973); Basil Mitchell, *Philosophy of Religion* (Oxford: Oxford University Press, 1971); R. W. Newell, *Objectivity, Empiricism and Truth* (London: Routledge and Kegan Paul, 1986); Alvin Plantinga and Nicholas Wolterstorff, *Faith and Rationality* (Notre Dame: University of Notre Dame, 1983); John L. Pollock, *Contemporary Theories of Knowledge* (New Jersey: Rowman and Littlefield, 1986); Bertrand Russell, *An Inquiry into Meaning and Truth* (New York: W. W. Norton, 1940); Harvey Siegel, *Relativism Refuted* (Dordrecht: D. Reidel Publishing, 1987); Richard Swinburne, *Faith and Reason* (Oxford: Clarendon, 1981); Ralph C. S. Walker, *The Coherence Theory of Truth* (London: Routledge, 1989).

Third, the deconstructionist concern is the limitation, even disavowal, of human knowing's creative contribution to the question of truth. Fourth, the relationship with science might be seen as tenuous or even false on the grounds of Henry's disavowal of empiricism. Though Henry's refutation of the evidentialist approach to Christian apologetics may be persuasive to some thinkers, it is a firmly entrenched mindset in many quarters that any system of thought must have some means by which to dialogue with such concerns. Finally, the issue of biblical criticism must be fully engaged for Henry's system to enjoy wide viability among non-Evangelical thinkers.

Chapter Seven

TRUTH AND GOD'S TRUTHFULNESS: MILLARD J. ERICKSON

Millard J. Erickson is an Evangelical theologian within the Baptist tradition. Erickson served as vice-president, dean, and professor of theology at Bethel Theological Seminary in St. Paul, Minnesota, before joining the faculty of Southwestern Baptist Theological Seminary in Fort Worth, Texas.

Biographical Background

Millard J. Erickson, the youngest of four children, was born on June 24, 1932, in Stanchfield, Minnesota.[1] His father came to the United States from Sweden with a large group of relatives when he was six months old. Erickson's mother is also of Swedish descent, born in the United

---

1. Biographical information on Millard Erickson is greatly assisted through two excellent articles by David S. Dockery, "Millard J. Erickson: Baptist and Evangelical Theologian," *Journal of the Evangelical Theological Society*, vol. 32, no. 4 (December 1989), 519-532, and "Millard J. Erickson" in *Baptist Theologians*, ed. Timothy George and David S. Dockery (Nashville: Broadman Press, 1990), 640-659; see also Leslie R. Keylock, "Evangelical Leaders You Should Know: Meet Millard J. Erickson," *Moody Monthly* (June 1987), 71-73.

States only months after her family had arrived from Sweden. The family supported itself from a 106-acre farm, living without the luxury of electricity until Erickson was in high school.

Erickson's education began in a one-room school house a mile and a half from his home. An athletic student, Erickson earned high school letters in football, basketball, and baseball. He graduated valedictorian from Braham High School out of a class of 38 students in 1949.

Baptist roots run deep for the Erickson family. His grandparents regularly carried their two daughters on their backs for eleven miles to their church in order to worship. Millard Erickson's father served as a lay pastor of a Baptist church for five years. Erickson's Baptist background is that of the Baptist General Conference, a Baptist denomination that originated in the Evangelical revivals of the nineteenth century with specific roots in Swedish Pietism. Characteristics of this denomination include a simple biblical faith, intentional evangelism, repudiation of formalism, and a demand for a clergy that demonstrated regeneration.[2] Such a background was a great influence on Erickson in his decision against the University of Minnesota for Bethel College. His background continues to serve as an influence on his theological system of thought.[3]

Prior to his first semester of college, Erickson received an opportunity to preach on a Wednesday evening in his home church, impressing his pastor enough to warrant a suggestion that Erickson consider entering the ministry as a vocation. That seed continued to grow in Erickson's heart and mind, blossoming one Thursday in a Bethel chapel service when a speaker emphasized the need for pastors. Understanding that God had called him, Erickson decided the following Saturday to answer that call and serve as a minister.

Seeking exposure to non-Christian perspectives, Erickson left Bethel after two years to study philosophy at the University of Minnesota, graduating Phi Beta Kappa in 1953. He then pursued studies at Bethel Theological Seminary and transferred to Northern Baptist Theological Seminary in Chicago, Illinois. At Bethel, Erickson met and began to date Virginia Nepstad. They were married on August 20, 1955. During this

---

2. On this, see J. E. Johnson, "Baptist General Conference," *The Dictionary of Christianity in America*, ed. Daniel G. Reid, Robert D. Linder, Bruce L. Shelley, and Harry S. Stout (Downers Grove: InterVarsity Press, 1990), 113-114; N. Magnuson, *How We Grew: Highlights of the First Hundred Years of Conference History* (1988).

3. Dockery notes that "Erickson's theological thought and method have been shaped by his Baptist beliefs and practices," see "Millard Erickson," *Journal of the Evangelical Theological Society*, 520; this view is shared by W. C. Young in his review of *The New Evangelical Theology* in *Foundations*, no. 12 (1969), 95-96. Erickson has also been involved in Baptist work outside of the Baptist General Conference, serving in various positions with the Baptist World Alliance and as a visiting professor at several Baptist seminaries, such as the Southern Baptist Theological Seminary in Louisville, Kentucky.

time Erickson was pastor of the Fairfield Avenue Baptist Church.[4] Following his study at Northern, Erickson entered the University of Chicago for a master's degree in philosophy, graduating in 1958. He then enrolled in the joint program between Garrett Theological Seminary and Northwestern University for a Ph.D. in systematic theology.

During this time Erickson accepted a call as pastor of Olivet Baptist Church in Minneapolis, Minnesota, ministering as pastor while completing Ph.D. examinations. His dissertation was on the "new Evangelical theology," represented by such figures as Carl F. H. Henry, Bernard Ramm, and Edward John Carnell.[5] Dockery rightly notes that this "new movement" provided the context for Erickson's theology.[6] Completing his doctorate in 1963, Erickson left Olivet Baptist Church in 1964 to become a professor of Bible and apologetics at Wheaton College in Wheaton, Illinois.[7] By 1967 Erickson was chairman of the Department of Bible and Philosophy. He left Wheaton for Bethel Theological Seminary in the summer of 1969 to accept a position as professor of theology. Erickson remained at Bethel, serving as executive vice-president, dean, and professor of theology, until 1992, when he was named to the faculty of Southwestern Baptist Theological Seminary in Fort Worth, Texas.

Erickson is best known for what Clark Pinnock has called a "magnum opus,"[8] a three-volume systematic theology titled *Christian Theology*. Erickson conceived the volume out of the need for an up-to-date textbook in systematic theology for his students. Finding none available, Erickson took it upon himself to publish such a work for classroom use, devoting over 4,000 hours to its completion. Erickson's hopes were to offer a "recent introductory textbook written from an evangelical perspective."[9] His family simply calls it "the book."[10] The organization and conclusions of the book are described by Erickson as "classical orthodoxy" with a postcritical approach to the Scriptures.[11] The first volume

---

4. Described by Keylock as a "melting pot urban congregation" near Chicago, "Meet Millard J. Erickson," *Moody Monthly*, 72. Fairfield Avenue Baptist Church ordained Erickson on March 21, 1957.

5. This dissertation was re-written and published as *The New Evangelical Theology* (New Jersey: Fleming H. Revell, 1968). On the "new" Evangelicalism, see chapter 1 of this dissertation, 22-25.

6. Dockery, "Millard Erickson," *Journal of the Evangelical Theological Society*, 521.

7. Ibid., 520; Erickson has remained a dedicated churchman, having served in almost forty churches as an interim pastor.

8. Clark H. Pinnock, "Erickson's Three-Volume Magnum Opus," *TSF Bulletin*, vol. 9, no. 3 (January-February 1986), 29-30.

9. See Millard J. Erickson, *Christian Theology*, 3 vols. (Grand Rapids: Baker, 1983, 1984, 1985; one-volume edition published, 1986), 9.

10. Keylock, "Meet Millard Erickson," *Moody Monthly*, 73.

11. Erickson, *Christian Theology*, 10-11; an example of the application of Erickson's method can be found in "Principles, Permanence, and Future Divine Judgment: A Case Study in Theological Method," *Journal of the Evangelical Theological Society*, vol. 28, no. 3 (September 1985), 317-325.

is dedicated to Bernard Ramm,[12] the second to William Hordern,[13] and the final installment to Wolfhart Pannenberg.[14] The project has been well-received among Evangelicals[15] and is enhanced by a companion dictionary of theological terms[16] and an earlier three volumes of selected readings in Christian theology, thus providing a comprehensive

---

12. Bernard Ramm is retired professor of systematic theology at American Baptist Seminary of the West, Berkeley, California, and served as Erickson's first theology professor at Bethel. Erickson's apologetic method was greatly informed by Ramm, though it was shaped most largely by Edward John Carnell, see Dockery, "Millard Erickson," *Journal of the Evangelical Theological Society*, 520, as well as "Millard Erickson," *Baptist Theologians*, 642.

13. Hordern is currently president of Lutheran Theological Seminary, Saskatoon, Saskatchewan, and served as Erickson's mentor in the doctoral program at Northwestern University and Garrett Theological Seminary, now Garrett Evangelical Theological Seminary. Dockery notes that Erickson gained "a concern for clarity of thought as well as a writing style worthy of emulation" from Hordern, see "Millard Erickson," *Journal of the Evangelical Theological Society*, 521. Erickson contributed a chapter on narrative theology, "Narrative Theology: Translation or Transformation?," for a festschrift in tribute to Hordern titled *Festschrift: A Tribute to Dr. William Hordern*, ed. Walter Freitag (Saskatoon, Saskatchewan: University of Saskatchewan, 1985), 29-39.

14. Erickson spent a sabbatical in 1976 with Pannenberg, a German theologian, at the University of Munich. Erickson had gained an appreciation and respect for Pannenberg prior to this sabbatical, evidenced by an insightful article titled "Pannenberg's Use of History as a Solution to the Religious Language Problem" in *Journal of the Evangelical Theological Society*, vol. 17, no. 2 (Spring 1974), 99-105, where Erickson applied Pannenberg's concept of revelation as history into various areas of doctrine. Dockery records Erickson's comment regarding Pannenberg that the German theologian is "in a league by himself"; see "Millard Erickson," *Journal of the Evangelical Theological Society*, 521.

15. Positive reviews of Erickson's work predominate in Evangelical reactions, see L. Russ Bush, "Review," *Southwestern Journal of Theology*, vol. XXVII, no. 2 (Spring 1985), 62-63; Charles L. Chaney, "Review," *Review and Expositor*, vol. LXXXIII, no. 1 (Winter 1986), 134-135; Charles L. Chaney, "Review," *Review and Expositor*, vol. LXXXIV, no. 3 (Summer, 1987), 541-542; Robert H. Culpepper, "Review," *Faith and Mission*, vol. III, no. 1 (Fall 1985), 96-97; Bruce Demarest, "Review," *Journal of the Evangelical Theological Society*, vol. 29 (1986), 236-237; John S. Feinberg, *Trinity Journal*, vol. 5 NS (1984), 208-217; Stanley J. Grenz, "Review," *Christian Scholar's Review*, vol. XIV, no. 1 (1984), 86-87; Stanley J. Grenz, "Review," *Christian Scholar's Review*, vol XVI, no. 1 (1986), 93-96; F. R. Howe, "Review," *Bibliotheca Sacra*, vol. 143, no. 569 (January-March 1986), 75-76; David Landegent, "Review," *Reformed Review*, vol. 39, no. 2 (Winter 1986), 121; David Landegent, "Review," *Reformed Review*, vol. 40, no. 1 (Autumn 1986), 67-68; Ralph W. Vunderlink, "Review," *Calvin Theological Journal*, vol. 20, no. 2 (November 1985), 291-295; Ralph W. Vunderlink, "Review," *Calvin Theological Journal*, vol. 22, no. 1 (April 1987), 139-144; David Wells, "A Capable, Usable Text," *Eternity*, vol. 38, no. 2 (February 1987), 41; finally, note the careful and sustained engagement of Erickson's work by David S. Dockery, who reviewed the three volumes sequentially in *Grace Theological Journal*, vol. 5, no. 2 (Fall 1984), 302-303; *Grace Theological Journal*, vol. 7, no. 1 (Spring 1986), 140-142; and in *Grace Theological Journal*, vol. 8, no. 2 (Fall 1987), 295-296. Dockery found much to celebrate, especially in the first two volumes, stating that "the evangelical community will be in debt to Millard Erickson for years to come" with the series becoming "a standard textbook in evangelical seminaries and colleges"; see Dockery, "Review," *Grace Theological Journal*, 296.

16. Millard J. Erickson, *Concise Dictionary of Christian Theology* (Grand Rapids: Baker, 1986); see review by this author in *Criswell Theological Review*, vol 3, no. 1 (Fall 1988).

package for theological reflection and instruction.[17] Erickson has added to his substantive theological corpus through works on ethics,[18] eschatology,[19] salvation,[20] and Christology.[21]

Description of Erickson's Concept of Truth

"Theology," writes Erickson, "is biblical. It takes as the primary source of its content the canonical Scriptures of the Old and New Testaments."[22] The greatest degree of authority for theology is reserved for the direct statements of Scripture. Theology employs the "insights of other areas of truth, which it regards as God's general revelation,"[23] but Erickson contends that "any truth, no matter where you find it, is divine truth."[24] Therefore the "first task of apologetics will be to ask the question of the truth of Christianity,"[25] understanding that truth is that which "accords with reality or is genuine."[26] As a result, Erickson posits a form of correspondence for his theory of truth, meaning that view which holds that "truth is a quality of ideas that agree with or accurately reflect that to which they refer."[27] Further explanation of what Erickson means

---

17. The three volumes, with Erickson serving as editor, are as follows: *The Living God: Readings in Christian Theology* (Grand Rapids: Baker, 1973); *Man's Need and God's Gift: Readings in Christian Theology* (Grand Rapids: Baker, 1976); and *The New Life: Readings in Christian Theology* (Grand Rapids: Baker, 1979). Erickson intended his systematic theology, *Christian Theology*, to be "supplemented" by these three volumes, see *Christian Theology*, 9.

18. Millard J. Erickson, *Relativism in Contemporary Christian Ethics* (Grand Rapids: Baker, 1974).

19. Millard J. Erickson, *Contemporary Options in Eschatology* (Grand Rapids: Baker, 1977).

20. Erickson has produced two popular works dealing with soteriology: *Salvation: God's Amazing Plan* (Wheaton: Victor, 1978), and *Responsive Faith* (Arlington Heights: Harvest, 1987).

21. Millard J. Erickson, *The Word Became Flesh: A Contemporary Incarnational Christology* (Grand Rapids: Baker, 1991).

22. *Christian Theology*, 21; compare 21-25.

23. *Christian Theology*, 21; Erickson notes that "there has been a growing awareness, partly through the rise of the 'new hermeneutic,' that it is not possible to formulate a theology simply on the basis of the Bible. Issues such as how the Bible is to be conceived of and how it is to be approached in interpretation must be dealt with;" see 64; Erickson's hermeneutical sensitivities in this area are acknowledged to flow from his interaction with Anthony Thiselton's *The Two Horizons: New Testament Hermeneutics and Philosophical Description* (Grand Rapids: Eerdmans, 1980).

24. *Christian Theology*, 305; such a view, Erickson continues, "virtually obliterates the traditional distinction between special revelation and general revelation." Prominence, however, is clearly given to special revelation as found in the Scriptures.

25. Millard J. Erickson, "Apologetics Today: Its Task and Shape," *Bethel Seminary Journal*, vol. XVIII, no. 1 (Autumn 1969), 2; this article was reprinted in two installments in *Christianity Today* as "The Potential of Apologetics" (July 17, 1970), 6-8, and "The Potential of Apologetics," (July 31, 1970), 13-15.

26. *Concise Dictionary*, 171.

27. *The Word Became Flesh*, 310.

by this definition of truth, as well as its divine nature, will first be pursued by a discussion of his understanding of God's truthfulness.

God's Truthfulness: Genuineness, Veracity, and Faithfulness

Foundational to Erickson's concept of truth is his understanding of the truthfulness of God. "In the ultimate analysis . . . God Himself is the authority in belief and conduct."[28] Erickson maintains that there are three dimensions of the truthfulness of God: genuineness, veracity, and faithfulness. Genuineness is "being true"; veracity is "telling the truth"; and faithfulness is "proving true."[29] For Erickson, all are related to the idea of God's "integrity."[30]

Genuineness. When Erickson speaks of genuineness as "being true," he is referring to the most basic dimension of God's truthfulness.[31] "God is real," writes Erickson. "He is not fabricated or constructed or imitation, as are all the other claimants to deity."[32] According to Erickson, "this is a large part of his truthfulness."[33] The attributes of God are not simply embodied by God; rather "He actually is those attributes."[34] Erickson's ontological base is that God "is."

Veracity. Veracity is the second dimension of God's truthfulness. "God represents things as they really are."[35] The Bible claims that God does not lie (I Sam. 15:29; Titus 1:2; Heb. 6:18). Erickson uses these passages to maintain not only that God does not lie, but that God cannot lie.[36] God's very nature prohibits the possibility of lying. Erickson uses this understanding of God's nature in light of His omniscience to conclude that everything God tells us is truth.[37] Therefore God can always be trusted; He cannot unknowingly tell an untruth; and His knowledge of the truth is exhaustive. Related to this is the practical subject of honesty, for the "God of truth is best served by the presentation of the truth"; [38] thus God's followers will strive to be truth-tellers.

Faithfulness. Erickson discusses "faithfulness" as a dimension of God's truthfulness. By the use of the term faithfulness, Erickson is posit-

---

28. *New Evangelical Theology,* 48.

29. *Christian Theology,* 289.

30. Ibid.

31. Ibid.

32. Ibid., 290; Erickson looks to Jer. 10; John 17 for biblical support, as well as 1 Thess. 1:9; 1 John 5:20; Revelation 3:7; 6:10.

33. *Christian Theology,* 290.

34. Ibid.

35. Ibid.

36. Ibid. Erickson writes, "Lying is contrary to his [God's] very nature."

37. Ibid.

38. *Christian Theology,* 291.

ing the idea of "proving true."[39] This is a function of God's unlimited power and capability. Faithfulness intimates that God "never has to revise his word or renege on a promise."[40] In God's dealings with humanity, His truthfulness exhibited as faithfulness is manifest.

Special Revelation as Personal and Propositional

The truthful God has made truth known through both general and special revelation.[41] For Erickson, the primary objective of special revelation is relational.[42] It's primary purpose is not to enlarge the general scope of knowledge, for the knowledge "about" is for the knowledge "of."[43] In other words, the primary result of special revelation is knowledge about God.[44] This special revelation is built on general revelation.[45]

For Erickson, special revelation contains elements that are both personal and propositional. By including both elements, he hopes to avoid the dichotomy between special revelation as that which conveys propositional truth and as that which elicits personal faith and commitment.[46] Revelation is not defined only as an actual occurrence, or the "revealing," but also as the product, or the "revealed."[47] In other words, both the Exodus from Egypt and the biblical narrative describing that Exodus can be understood as revelation. Thus the Bible can be termed "revelation,"[48] asserting that "'the Bible says' is equivalent to 'God says.'"[49]

---

39. Ibid. Erickson writes: "If God's genuineness is a matter of his being true and veracity is his telling of the truth, then his faithfulness means that he proves true."

40. Ibid. Supportive biblical passages put forth by Erickson include Num. 23:19, 1 Thess. 5:24, 1 Cor. 1:9, 2 Cor. 1:18-22, 2 Tim. 2:13, and 1 Pet. 4:19.

41. Erickson's definition of special revelation is as follows: "God's manifestation of himself at particular times and places through particular events, for example, the exodus and Isaiah's vision in chapter 6; also, the Scriptures"; see *Concise Dictionary*, 144. The actual modes of special revelation are historical events, divine speech, and the incarnation, see *Christian Theology*, 181-191.

42. *Christian Theology*, 176.

43. Ibid.

44. Ibid., 191; this knowledge is "real, objective, rational information communicated from God to man." Whereas the purpose of revelation is the communication of divine truth from God to humanity, inspiration relates more to the relaying of that truth from the first recipients of it to other persons; see 200.

45. Erickson understands "general revelation" to be that revelation which is available to all persons at all times, particularly through the physical universe, history, and the makeup of human nature; see *Concise Dictionary*, 143. Special revelation goes beyond general revelation in regards to its clarity, intensity, and detail; see *New Evangelical Theology*, 50.

46. Erickson identifies the reduction of special revelation to its personal element with neoorthodoxy but also contends that the view has been widespread throughout the rest of the twentieth-century theological scene as well, see *Christian Theology*, 191.

47. *Christian Theology*, 196-197.

48. Methodologically, he attempts to avoid the impasse of beginning with God (the object of knowledge) or special revelation (the means of knowledge) by presupposing both God and His special revelation together, see *Christian Theology*, 32-33. Both are presupposed as part of a basic thesis, from which one proceeds to develop the knowledge which flows from this thesis, assessing the evidence for its truth. For Erickson, the self-revealing God is a singular presupposition from which theological construction begins.

49. *New Evangelical Theology*, 50.

Revelation as Personal. When Erickson states that special revelation is personal, he is asserting that Scripture is not a set of universal truths such as one finds in the axioms of Euclid's geometry, but rather it is "a series of specific or particular statements about concrete occurrences and facts."[50] This special revelation is "anthropic" in nature, "coming in human language and human categories of thought and action."[51] The "personal" dimension which is present when one speaks of special revelation includes the "presentation of a person."[52] The response to this personal special revelation is the act of personal trust and commitment.

Erickson credits Soren Kierkegaard's distinction between objective and subjective truth with the view that special revelation is personal.[53] Therefore, the focus for Kierkegaard was not on objective truth and knowledge but on subjective truth and personal relationship. While Erickson holds to a personal element, he wishes to avoid subjectivism. He feels subjectivism is inherent when special revelation is reduced to the merely personal realm. As a result, he brings in the idea of special revelation as not only personal, but also propositional.

Revelation as Propositional. Erickson holds to a personal dimension of special revelation, but he does so in tandem with the idea that special revelation is propositional—the idea that God has communicated factual information about Himself.[54] Truth is thus seen not only as a personal response, but also as "a quality of propositions."[55] The response to such propositional special revelation is the believing of those truths. The idea of non-propositional special revelation would intimate that God has not revealed such truths, but rather only reveals Himself.[56] Agreeing with Carnell, Erickson contends that "all vital faith rests upon general faith. General faith is believing a fact; vital faith is trusting in a person."[57] Erickson does not feel that a personal view of special revelation provides a sufficient basis for faith. For Carnell and other propositionalists,

---

50. *Christian Theology,* 178.

51. Ibid.

52. Ibid., 191. Erickson points out that neoorthodoxy's mistake in regard to the appropriation of this personal dimension was to maintain that theology is not a set of doctrines that have been revealed, but rather the church's attempt to express what it has found in God's revelation.

53. Ibid., 193; According to Erickson, Kierkegaard contended that in seeking objective truth one attempts to define an item by putting it into finite classes, which inevitably limits the item and makes it finite. The aim of gaining objective information about an item is basically to bring it under one's control. Kierkegaard thus felt that if we conceive our knowledge of God as basically objective (propositional), we are making Him into something less than God. We are making Him a thing, or an object.

54. Erickson, *Concise Dictionary,* 143.

55. *Christian Theology,* 56; here Carl Henry's influence on Erickson's theological system is apparent.

56. *Concise Dictionary,* 143.

57. *Christian Theology,* 193; compare Edward John Carnell, *The Case for Orthodox Theology* (Philadelphia: Westminster, 1959), 29-30.

faith is believing in certain affirmations about God and then placing trust in the God so defined.

This communication of factual information from God about God is through analogical language, which Erickson perceives as being "midway between univocal and equivocal language."[58] By analogical language, Erickson means terms which are qualitatively the same with differences of degree rather than of kind.[59] He writes:

> While God cannot show us Himself as He really is, if the revelation is to be real knowledge and in any way a map of Himself, it must be analogical. This means that God selects those elements, or factors, from our realm of experience which bear a resemblance to the truth about Himself. While they are not perfect replicas of God, they are nonetheless adequate reproductions. Their relationships to the original is more like that of a sketch or a cartoon than a blueprint or a portrait. There is a certain analogy between some elements of man's knowledge and some portions of God's truth, and God employs the analogy for His purposes.[60]

Therefore, our knowledge of God is true and genuine but not exhaustive. Erickson writes that "in analogical usage there is always at least some univocal element."[61] Thus Erickson wishes to keep a univocal element within his emphasis on analogical language, for "whenever God has revealed himself, he has selected elements which are univocal in his universe and ours."[62] It is God, therefore, who makes such knowledge possible, for God selects the components and is knowledgeable of both sides of the analogy. This avoids the problem created if humanity, by its own unaided reason, seeks to understand God by constructing an analogy involving God and humanity, for such an enterprise would involve two unknowns.[63] Such an analogy, however, cannot be verified independently, therefore, remains a presupposition and a matter of faith that corresponds to the truth God is portraying.[64]

---

58. *Christian Theology*, 179. A univocal understanding of language entails that a term is employed in only one sense, or carries the same meaning in its several senses. It stems from latin "unus" ("one") and "vocare" ("to call"). Perhaps a more contemporary term would be "synonymn" An equivocal understanding of language entails the idea that a term used in two senses carries the same meaning when, in fact, the term possesses completely different meanings. It stems from the latin "aequus" ("equal") and "vocare" ("to call").

59. Ibid., 180; see also *Concise Dictionary*, 11.

60. *New Evangelical Theology*, 52.

61. *Christian Theology*, 179.

62. Ibid., 180.

63. Ibid., 180-181.

64. Ibid.,181. "In this respect," writes Erickson, "the theologian working with special revelation is in a situation similar to that of the empiricist, who cannot be certain that his sensory perceptions accurately correspond to the objects they are purported to represent." In theory, however, Erickson argues that it is possible to offer evidence to conform or verify these affirmations, see 194.

Special Revelation as Personal and Propositional. So Erickson concludes that revelation is not "either personal or propositional; it is both/ and. What God primarily does is to reveal himself, but he does so at least in part by telling us something about himself."[65] This lays the basis for Erickson's unitary dimension to truth, discussed below, and his move from God's truthfulness to a concept of truth as correspondence via analogical language made concrete in the special revelation of Scripture.

With his understanding of God's truthfulness and his idea of special revelation as that which is both personal and propositional, Erickson uses his concept of truth to elucidate various dimensions of the nature of truth. According to Erickson, the dimensions of truth are factual, objective, unitary, and logical.

Factual Dimension of Truth

By factual, Erickson contends that special revelation as presented in the Bible conveys factual information or factual truth. This brings in Erickson's understanding of biblical inerrancy and what he means by the term "fact." Both, however, must be discussed in light of Erickson's concept of inspiration.

Inspiration. Whereas revelation is the communication of divine truth from God to humanity, inspiration relates more to the relaying of that truth.[66] "Inspiration guarantees that what the Bible says is just what God would say if he were to speak directly."[67] Erickson holds to the Bible's inspiration largely on the grounds of its own self-declaration. However, he denies circularity in this assertion, stating that such a claim does not assert that the testimony of Scripture settles the matter as to its inspiration, but rather that it is something taken into consideration as part of the process of formulating a hypothesis regarding the nature of Scripture.[68] This perspective has a more nuanced presentation than an earlier contention that the "conservative's presentation of the message" rests upon the tacit syllogism: "Whatever the Bible teaches is true; This is something that the Bible teaches; Therefore, this is true."[69] The Bible is to be treated as a historical document and is to be allowed to plead its own case.[70] When this is done, Erickson feels that it will be found that

---

65. Ibid., 196. The charge against religious language made by analytical philosophy is taken seriously by Erickson, but answered by noting analytical philosophy's prescriptive nature, its overly sharp distinctions between different types of language, its naturalistic assumptions (Erickson maintains that it should not preclude language having supraempirical reference), and the inadequacy of merely descriptive, nonprescriptive treatments; see 50. See also the entire chapter "Theology and Its Language," 127–149.

66. *Christian Theology*, 200; Erickson writes that revelation is "God's making his truth known to man. Inspiration preserves it, making it more widely accessible"; see 246.

67. Ibid., 246.

68. Ibid., 201; see also *New Evangelical Theology*, 58.

69. "Apologetics Today," *Bethel Seminary Journal*, 3.

70. *Christian Theology*, 201.

the uniform testimony of Scripture is that the Bible has originated from God and is God's message to humanity.

Erickson also contends that one's view of God's working has a direct influence on one's views of inspiration. If a more immanent view of God's activity is maintained, then there tends to be more emphasis on the human role in the production of Scripture. If a more transcendental understanding of God's working is held, then inspiration will be seen as a more miraculous and unique occurrence.[71] What inspiration means apart from its factuality is another matter. At this point Erickson's understanding of inerrancy comes into play.[72]

Inerrancy. Erickson offers a carefully defined understanding of biblical inerrancy:

> The Bible, when correctly interpreted in light of the level to which culture and the means of communication had developed at the time it was written and in view of the purposes for which it was given, is fully truthful in all that it affirms.[73]

Therefore, inerrancy pertains to what is affirmed rather than what is reported. The truthfulness of Scripture is judged in terms of what the statements meant in the cultural settings in which they were expressed. The Bible's assertions are fully true when judged in accordance with the purposes for which they were written, with the exactness varying according to the intended use of the material. Reports of historical events and scientific matters are in phenomenal rather than technical language, and difficulties are not prejudged as indications of error. This doctrine does *not* assert, what type of material the Bible will contain, how we are to interpret passages, or the maximum amount of specificity that will be present. Rather, "our doctrine of inerrancy maintains merely that whatever statements the Bible affirms are fully truthful when they are correctly interpreted in terms of their meaning in their cultural setting and the purpose for which they were written."[74]

---

71. On this, see Erickson's "Immanence, Transcendence, and the Doctrine of Scripture," *The Living and Active Word of God: Studies in Honor of Samuel J. Schultz*, ed. Morris Inch and Ronald Youngblood (Winona Lake: Eisenbrauns, 1983), 193-205; see also "Biblical Inerrancy: The Last Twenty-Five Years," *Journal of the Evangelical Theological Society*, 391-392.

72. Erickson is careful to note the significant objections to the formulation of a theory of inspiration. His writings on this subject reflect these insights; see *Christian Theology*, 203-207. Erickson also carefully notes the various methods in constructing such a theory, such as Warfield's emphasis on what the biblical writers themselves say about inspiration and Beegle's suggestion to look at what the Bible is actually like. Erickson embraces both insights, but places priority on what the biblical materials assert about the nature of inspiration; see 207-210.

73. *Christian Theology*, 233-234.

74. Ibid., 238.

Erickson proposes that a view of full inspiration logically entails the inerrancy of Scripture, and is a corollary of the doctrine of inspiration.[75] He acknowledges that this view is closely aligned to that of Everett F. Harrison.[76] Erickson recognizes the many problem areas related to the concept of biblical inerrancy,[77] but he maintains that if one can show that the Bible is not fully truthful, the classical Christian view of inspiration would be in jeopardy.[78] This is different from the "domino" theory, the idea that if the Bible is "false in one" then it is "false in all." A more accurate summary of Erickson's position would be "false in one, uncertain in all."[79] Erickson's concern is that if the Bible can be shown to be in error in those areas where claims can be checked, there is no basis for holding to its dependability in areas where one cannot verify what it says. This line of thinking precludes the idea that the Bible is inerrant in matters of faith but not in history. "Thus a thoroughgoing functionalism . . . must be regarded as untenable."[80] Erickson attempts to add support to this view by contending that factual inerrancy has held a rich heritage throughout Christian history.[81]

In affirming such inerrancy for the Bible, Erickson distinguishes himself somewhat from authorial intent,[82] a view he acknowledges as the

75. Ibid., 225, 229.

76. Millard J. Erickson, "A New Look at Various Aspects of Inspiration," *Bethel Seminary Journal*, vol. XV, no. 1 (Autumn 1966), 22. On Harrison's view of inspiration, see "The Phenomena of Scripture," *Revelation and the Bible*, ed. Carl F. H. Henry (Grand Rapids: Baker, 1958), 235-250; see also Harrison's *Introduction to the New Testament*, 2nd ed. (Grand Rapids: Eerdmans, 1971).

77. Millard J. Erickson, "Problem Areas Related to Biblical Inerrancy," *The Proceedings of the Conference on Biblical Inerrancy* (Nashville: Broadman, 1987), 175-189. Erickson outlines eight primary problem areas for those who hold to biblical inerrancy: the problem of (1) the text, (2) lexical research, (3) definition of error, (4) parallel accounts, (5) chronology, (6) the use of non-canonical sources by canonical writers, (7) scientific type scripture references, and (8) ethics. In this article Erickson also discusses the problems which result from misunderstandings of inerrancy, such as overlooking the variety of material in Scripture, failing to see a biblical statement in its cultural context, and identifying inerrancy and interpretation. Erickson also addressed this conference on the subject of "Implications of Biblical Inerrancy for the Christian Mission," 223-236.

78. *Christian Theology*, 225.

79. Ibid., 227.

80. Ibid., 56. Also, see *New Evangelical Theology*, 145.

81. Erickson acknowledges the work of J. Rogers and D. McKim, who in *The Authority and Interpretation of the Bible: An Historical Approach* (San Francisco: Harper and Row, 1979) argued that the historic position of the church has been biblical infallibility in areas of faith and practice but not biblical inerrancy in areas of facticity, but Erickson asserts with John D. Woodbridge in *Biblical Authority: A Critique of the Rogers/McKim Proposal* (Grand Rapids: Zondervan, 1982) that factual inerrancy holds a rich heritage. For Erickson's interaction with this discussion, see "Biblical Inerrancy: The Last Twenty-Five Years," *Journal of the Evangelical Theological Society*, vol. 25, no. 4 (December 1982), 388.

82. A position present in Carl Henry's system of thought (see chapter on Henry) and posited by E. D. Hirsch, *Validity in Interpretation* (New Haven: Yale University Press, 1967). Erickson's ambivalence toward authorial intent is somewhat out of step with his definition of inerrancy, particularly the contention that the inerrancy of the biblical narrative is to be construed in "view of the purposes for which it was given."

general Evangelical insistence.[83] Rather, Erickson emphasizes the assertions or affirmations of Scripture, not the intention of the speaker or writer.[84] However, Erickson extends his understanding of inspiration to include verbal inspiration, even to the choice of words. This is not seen by Erickson as a dictation model, but rather as the ability to "think the thoughts of God."[85] For Erickson, authorial intent unduly restricts the meaning of a passage to one central intention. Erickson contends that authorial intent can fail to take into account the insights that have arisen from twentieth-century psychology's understanding of the unconscious.[86]

Fact and Error. In terms of what constitutes error, Erickson maintains that "statements in Scripture which plainly contradict the facts (or are contradicted by them) must be considered errors."[87] Therefore the relationship between the Bible and history, with all of its ensuing questions and difficulties, must be engaged.[88] For "while history alone cannot verify the truth, there can be no verification without history either."[89] In this contention Erickson is employing a modified form of the verifiability principle, but "without the extreme dimensions which prove to be the undoing of that criterion as it is applied by logical positivism; for in the present case the means of verification are not limited to sense data."[90] For Erickson, many of the apparent errors in Scripture appear erroneous "because of a misunderstanding of what Scripture involves. When more stringent demands are placed upon it than are appropriate to its nature and purpose, it will seem to contain mistakes."[91]

This discussion is of great importance to ascertain Erickson's concept of truth. He writes:

> there has been a growing awareness among evangelicals that logically prior to the understanding of Scripture and its statements is a set of presuppositions affecting what is meant by any of those statements, and

---

83. Erickson, "Biblical Inerrancy: The Last Twenty-Five Years," *Journal of the Evangelical Theological Society,* 394. This article does not put forth a critique authorital intent and even intimates approval of the use of authorial intent as a hermeneutical device. As this article antedates what appears to be a critique of authorial intent in *Christian Theology,* it may be conjectured that Erickson is moving toward a greater appreciation of authorial intent in his own hermeneutical reflections.

84. *Christian Theology,* 234.

85. Ibid., 218.

86. Ibid., 235.

87. Ibid., 239. "Facts" here seem to mean that which has been established by some form of empirical evidence or common-sensical observation.

88. Ibid., 84; Erickson writes that "the view of faith and reason espoused in this text [*Christian Theology*] will not permit the question of the relationship between the contents of the Bible and historical reality to be ignored or settled by presumption."

89. Ibid., 139. By history, Erickson means those events which have occurred and can be investigated as to their occurrence.

90. Ibid., 239.

91. *New Evangelical Theology,* 78.

even what is to be understood by an assertion such as "The Bible is inerrant." There is the realization that a theological construction is based on, and expressed in terms of, certain philosophical conceptions.[92]

He then asserts that

in particular there has been a growing awareness that the issue of inerrancy depends to a considerable extent on the theory of truth that one adopts. When one speaks of the Bible infallibly accomplishing the purpose for which it was written, this frequently indicates a functionalist or pragmatist view of truth as contrasted with the correspondence view of truth found in the stricter view of factual inerrancy.[93]

Erickson's view of inerrancy is clearly dependent upon the correspondence theory of truth.[94] In distancing himself from the functionalist approach, often based on the commonly held distinctions between Greek and Hebrew mentalities, Erickson agrees with James Barr's assessment that this distinction has been overstated.[95] Erickson seeks to add support to his correspondence understandings of truth, and thus to his understanding of factual inerrancy, on the grounds that "the Hebrews were more concerned with questions of factual correctness than they have sometimes been credited with being."[96] Erickson maintains that to object to factual inerrancy on the basis that "this is not the Hebrew way of thinking is now seen to represent an eisegetical reading back of twentieth-century existentialism, imposing it on the Hebrew mentality."[97]

The Objective Dimension of Truth

Having maintained the factual dimension of truth, built upon God's truthfulness and the nature of special revelation, Erickson argues that truth also contains an objective dimension apart from subjective appropriation. In using the term "objective knowledge," Erickson means "knowledge of phenomena which exist independent of the knower."[98] By "objective truth," Erickson means "facts about phenomena external to

---

92. "Biblical Inerrancy: The Last Twenty-Five Years," *Journal of the Evangelical Theological Society*, 389.

93. Ibid., 390.

94. In regard to the pragmatic or "intentional" view of truth, Erickson maintains that such a view sacrifices metaphysical truth as well as the idea of truth as absolute, see *Christian Theology*, 43. Erickson does applaud pragmatism, however, in its attention to the important link between ideas and actions, see 44.

95. James Barr, *The Semantics of Biblical Language* (London: Oxford University Press, 1961), 161-205.

96. "Biblical Inerrancy," 391.

97. Ibid.

98. *Concise Dictionary*, 118.

the person; in the thought of Soren Kierkegaard, facts which, while correctly describing external phenomena, do not really affect the knower."[99] Positing an objective dimension to truth distinguishes Erickson's system of thought from that of existentialism and its tenets regarding subjectivity:

> Generally speaking, existentialism classifies truth into two types. Objective truth is involved when an idea correctly reflects or corresponds with the object signified. Objective truth applies in scientific-type endeavors. Subjective truth, on the other hand, is not a matter of correspondence with the object known, but rather of the effect of that object and idea on the knowing subject. Where the object evokes great inward passion or subjectivity, there is truth. This is the really important type of truth [for the existentialist]; it involves knowing persons rather than things.[100]

For Erickson, however, existentialism fails to justify the choice of one particular object to relate to in faith, as well as the difficulty of supporting its values and ethical judgments.[101]

Erickson posits the world view of objectivism. "By this it is meant that there are objective measures of the true, the good, and the right."[102] According to William Hordern, there are two approaches to contemporizing theology: transformers and translators.[103] Translators of theology "feel a need for re-expressing the message in a more intelligible form, but intend to retain the content."[104] Transformers, on the other hand, "are prepared to make rather serious changes in the content of the message in order to relate it to the modern world."[105] In stressing the objective nature of truth, Erickson seeks to avoid the categorization of

---

99. *Concise Dictionary*, 118.

100. *Christian Theology*, 46.

101. Ibid., 47.

102. Ibid., 55; see also his introduction to *Relativism in Contemporary Christian Ethics*, which states that "the most crucial issue raised . . . is the problem of objectivity in ethical judgments," xiii. This work is an interesting complement to Erickson's theological constructions in *Christian Theology* in regard to cultural backgrounds for non-objective viewpoints, such as relativity theory in physics, non-Euclidean geometries, cultural relativism, historical criticism of the Bible, form criticism, nonpropositional revelation, and existentialism, see *Relativism in Ethics*, 1-33.

103. William Hordern, *New Directions in Theology Today, Vol. 1: Introduction* (Philadelphia: Westminster, 1966).

104. *Christian Theology*, 113.

105. Ibid. On Erickson's appropriation of Hordern's categories of "transformers" and "translators," as well as Erickson's desire to remain in the "translator" camp, see Erickson's contribution to Hordern's festschrift, "Narrative Theology: Translation or Transformation?," *Festschrift to Hordern*, 29-39. Erickson's answer to whether narrative theology is translation or transformation is "that all depends" (35), basing his evaluations largely on the hermeneutical use of story (36). Those who use narrative heuristically, however, are marked as transformers (39).

"transformer" in this theological system of thought. The view of the "translator," according to Erickson, is that

> Here modern man is made the measure of truth. Since truth is to a large extent considered relative, man today is the judge of what is right and wrong. In no real sense is there the idea of a revelation from God which somehow is the source and criterion of truth. Thus, there is nothing normative outside of human experience, nothing which could sit in judgment upon man's ideas.[106]

Such a perspective is rejected by Erickson. He holds objectivity as a dimension for truth, or for the role of "translator."

> The translator maintains that man is not the measure of what is true. Truth generates from above, from a higher source. It is God who speaks and man who is on trial, not the other way around. If transformation is needed, it is man, not the message, that must be transformed.[107]

By stressing objectivity as a dimension of truth, Erickson should not be understood to be maintaining a form of scholastic orthodoxy in regard to the Bible's objectivity. Erickson dismisses this view outright, holding rather to a combination of "the objective word, the written Scripture, together with the subjective word, the inner illumination and conviction of the Holy Spirit."[108] This combination constitutes the authority for the Christian faith.

Yet Erickson will argue for the content of the Bible as "objectively the Word of God."[109] In so doing he consciously distances himself from the neoorthodox position, which Erickson understands as that which fails to see revelation primarily in terms of the communication of information, but rather as the presence of God Himself. Rather than the Word of God becoming the Word of God through encounter, Erickson maintains that "what these writings say is actually what God says to us, whether or not anyone reads, understands, or accepts them."[110] In other words, the Bible's "status as revelation is not dependent upon anyone's response to

---

106. *Christian Theology*, 114; this seems to be the essence of Erickson's critique of the "new hermeneutic," the theological method of moving from experience of reality to theology, see 1004-1005.

107. Ibid., 117; compare Hordern, *New Directions*, 146-147. Erickson notes that translators tend not to raise the issue of truth, see *Festschrift to Hordern*, 30. In *Relativism in Ethics* Erickson posits that the absolutist tendency in Protestant Christian faith stems from the doctrine of verbal-plenary inspiration.

108. Ibid., 251.

109. Ibid., 252.

110. Ibid., 252-253.

it."[111] Inherent within this view is the idea that the Bible has "a definite and objective meaning which is (or at least should be) the same for everyone."[112] This, too, is in reaction to the neoorthodox view which Erickson feels holds to the idea of "no revealed truths . . . how one person interprets an encounter with God may be different from another . . . even the interpretations given to events by the authors of Scripture were not divinely inspired."[113] Erickson asserts that

> since the words of Scripture are objectively God's revelation, one person can point to the content of the Bible in seeking to demonstrate to another what is the correct understanding. The essential meaning of a passage will be the same for everyone, although the application might be different for one person than for another.

> Further, since the Bible does have an objective meaning which we come to understand through the process of illumination, illumination must have some permanent effect. Once the meaning is learned, then (barring forgetfulness) we have that meaning more or less permanently. This is not to say that there cannot be a deepened illumination giving us a more profound understanding of a particular passage, but rather that there need not be a renewing of the illumination, since the meaning (as well as the revelation) is of such a nature that it persists and can be retained.[114]

The Unitary Dimension of Truth

In understanding truth as unitary, Erickson maintains that all truth is God's truth and is, therefore, divine in nature. Whereas Carl F. H. Henry seemingly discounts empirical knowledge as a source for truth, Erickson embraces it, unwilling to see any branch of knowledge as outside of God's truth.[115]

---

111. *Christian Theology*, 253. Erickson writes that the "new Evangelicals would insist strenuously that one of the results of special revelation is genuine knowledge of God. Neo-orthodoxy has stressed the idea of revelation being an encounter with God, rather than communication of information about God. The new evangelicals, however, would say that these two are not to be separated, but rather must be conjoined. The statement, 'What God reveals is God, not information about Himself,' is answered by the query, 'But how does He reveal Himself?' and the rather forthright reply, 'He reveals Himself by communicating the truth about Himself.' This becomes the basis for a personal encounter"; see *New Evangelical Theology*, 56.

112. *Christian Theology*, 253.

113. *Christian Theology*, 253. Erickson notes in another place that neoorthodoxy has a dialectical understanding of truth operative in its theological methodology, that within ideas or reality there is tension, polarity, and paradox; this is contrasted with a more logistic method which proceeds from premises to conclusions, on this see "Presuppositions of Non-Evangelical Hermeneutics," *Hermeneutics, Inerrancy, and the Bible*, ed. Earl D. Radmacher and Robert D. Preus (Grand Rapids: Academie/Zondervan, 1984), 608-609.

114. *Christian Theology*, 253.

115. These distinctions are symptomatic of Evangelicalism's divide over presuppositionalism and evidentialism, a divide Erickson attempts to circumnavigate by embracing both presuppositionalism and evidentialism in complimentary fashion.

Rather than there being one kind of truth (objective) in regard to scientific matters, and another type (subjective) in matters of religion, truth has something in common in all areas. Truth is a quality of statements or propositions which agree with the ways things are.[116]

Erickson maintains that God and reality "are what they are independently of anyone's perceiving, understanding, appreciating, or accepting them."[117] Therefore, truth is not dependent upon the knower's reaction, although this is seen as important. Erickson desires to omit any type of subjective idealism.

The Logical Dimension of Truth

Existentialism's emphasis on existence over essence is critiqued by Erickson in large part due to its irrationalism.[118] In conscious alignment with Carl F. H. Henry, Edwin Ramsdell, and Arthur Holmes, Erickson states that the Christian theologian is not to embrace irrationalism, but rather is

> to utilize the capacity of reasoning given him by God to work out the implications of the revealed body of truth. In other words, he philosophizes from the position of perspective created by the divine revelation. In this respect . . . my position maintains that the biblical world view is the starting point and framework for all intellectual endeavor . . . Christian theology is perspectival.[119]

For Erickson, logic is "applicable to all truth."[120] Some areas are "clothed in mystery" and may, therefore, be "beyond our ability to understand all of the relationships involved," no areas "are believed to be inherently contradictory."[121] Indeed, what God has communicated is "rational, cognitive truth."[122] Abandoning this contention would necessitate the abandoning of coherent thought, or at least the communication of coherent thought.

Erickson is careful, however, to distance himself from the idea that reason is the means of biblical interpretation. His concern is that if rea-

---

116. *Christian Theology*, 55.

117. Ibid.

118. Ibid., 45.

119. Ibid., 54; Erickson's embrace of Henry at this juncture points to *God, Revelation, and Authority: The God Who Speaks and Shows* (Waco: Word, 1976). Vol. 1:198-201; Edwin Ramsdell's work in this area is *The Christian Perspective* (New York: Abingdon-Cokesbury, 1950); Arthur Holmes' contribution can be found in *Faith Seeks Understanding* (Grand Rapids: Eerdmans, 1971), 46-47.

120. *Christian Theology*, 55.

121. Ibid., 55-56; the assumption of an antithetical relationship between faith and reason is perceived by Erickson to be at the root of the sharp distinction between "Historie" and "Geschichte," which in turn goes back to Kierkegaard's distinction between objective and subjective thinking, all of which are perspectives which Erickson rejects, see 103-104.

122. *Relativism in Ethics*, 134.

son becomes the means of biblical interpretation, "is not reason, rather than the Bible, the real authority, since it in effect comes to the Bible from a position of superiority?"[123] Erickson is also hesitant to join those who celebrate reason as the essence of divinity and the nature of the image of God in humanity.[124] As a result he draws a distinction between legislative authority and judicial authority and then uses this distinction as a "good way to think of the relationship between Scripture and reason."[125] Scripture is the supreme legislative authority, giving us the content of our belief and our code of behavior and practice. Reason, however, does not participate in the giving of content or the discovery of truth. Its role is akin to judicial authority in that it assists the determination of the meaning of a message and then assesses its truthfulness. This epistemology is termed "authoritarian rationalism."[126]

Erickson's Criteria of Truth

Two criteria for truth come forward in Erickson's theology: first, albeit brief, pragmatic evidence; second, and much more extensively, logical evidence.

Pragmatic Evidence. Erickson contends that no matter how impressive the reasons offered for the truthfulness of a statement or system, "man is not too likely to commit himself to it unless he sees its practical usefulness."[127] Although formally acknowledged by Erickson, this criterion of truth is not exposited much further than this in his published writings. Thus the discussion of logical evidence as a criteria of truth will be explored at length.[128]

Logical Evidence. Erickson welcomes philosophical theology in the enterprise of systematic theology.[129] Building upon his idea that truth has a logical dimension, he contends that philosophy scrutinizes the meaning of terms and ideas which are employed in the theological

---

123. *Christian Theology*, 256-257.

124. Ibid., 499-500. Erickson agrees with David Cairns, *The Image of God in Man* (New York: Philosophical Library, 1953), 57, that the text of Scripture never identifies what qualities within humanity might be the image of God and that such ideas as the ancient Greek notion of reason as the answer is nonbiblical; see *Christian Theology*, 512. On the subject of depravity, Erickson posits that the fact of total depravity is that humanity "is utterly unable to do anything to save himself or to extricate himself from his condition of sinfulness"; see 803.

125. *Christian Theology*, 257.

126. *New Evangelical Theology*, 149.

127. Ibid., 136.

128. Erickson's lack of attention to this category, although heartily acknowledged as important, seems to be due to its shortcomings as an apologetic argument for the Christian faith, since psychology can offer alternative explanations for these phenomena of experience that do not rely on the truthfulness of the object of belief; see *New Evangelical Theology*, 139.

129. *Christian Theology*, 27.

enterprise, as well as criticizing theological arguments and sharpening a theological message for clarity.[130] Even further, Erickson states that philosophy, in restricted scope, weighs the truth claims of theology and consequently gives part of the basis for accepting the message theology proclaims.[131] In an important footnote, Erickson states that

> although philosophy cannot prove the truth of Christian theology, it can evaluate the cogency of the evidence advanced, the logical validity of its arguments, and the meaningfulness or ambiguity of the concepts. On this basis philosophy offers evidence for the truth of Christianity, without claiming to prove it in some conclusive fashion. There are philosophical and historical evidences which can be advanced, but not in such a way as to offer an extremely probable induction.[132]

Apparently Erickson wants to maintain the viability of philosophy for the theological enterprise, but not in such a way that theology becomes the handmaiden of philosophy. Revelation, not philosophy, should supply the content of theology. Theology is to be independent of any particular philosophical system.[133] "Philosophy should be thought of primarily as an activity, philosophizing, rather than as a body of truths."[134] Complete or exact proof, however, is not possible in theology.[135] "Probability is the best that can be hoped for. Yet one must not be content with showing the plausibility of a conception," Erickson continues, for "it is necessary to demonstrate that this option is preferable to the alternatives."[136] Therefore "faith, once engaged in, enables us to reason and to recognize various evidences supporting it. This means that faith is a form of knowledge; it works in concert with, not against, reason."[137]

---

130. *Christian Theology*, 57; Erickson maintains, for example, that we "do well to consider any . . . assertion to be the conclusion of a syllogism, and to ask what are the premises of that syllogism."

131. Ibid., 27-28.

132. Ibid., 28; Erickson, 57, adds that "philosophy also makes us aware of the necessity of testing truth claims. Assertions by themselves are not sufficient grounds for us to accept them; they must be argued. This involves asking what kind of evidence would bear upon the truth or falsity of the issue under consideration, and when an appropriate type and a sufficient amount of evidence would be present. There also needs to be assessment of the logical structure of each argument, to determine whether the claimed conclusions really follow from the support offered for them."

133. *Christian Theology*, 53.

134. Ibid., 56.

135. Erickson, "Apologetics Today," *Bethel Seminary Journal*, 10.

136. *Christian Theology*, 58; Erickson states that "whenever we critique a view different from our own, we must use valid objective criteria. There would seem to be two types: the criteria which a view sets for itself, and the criteria which all such views must meet (universal criteria)." For religious language, this criterion involves internal consistency and coherence.

137. Ibid., 941.

Erickson's acceptance of logical evidence and his use of philosophy lead to his specific criteria for truth. Borrowing categories from Frederick Ferre, Erickson posits two classes of criteria, external and internal, with two criteria in each class.[138] The first of the internal criteria is consistency, or the "absence of logical contradiction among the symbols in the system."[139] Erickson states that the "Christian religion has a set of fundamental theological propositions which form an interrelated non-contradictory system of religious truth."[140] The second internal criterion is coherence, intimating that consistency within a system is inadequate by itself, but that there needs to be "genuine unity."[141] Erickson notes that certain idealists, including Evangelical Gordon Clark, have attempted to make these internal criteria the sole basis for assessing the truthfulness of a theory.[142] Erickson discounts this assertion, stating that "if Christianity is indeed to be judged as empirically meaningful it must meet the external criteria as well."[143] The first of these is applicability, meaning that it "must correspond with and serve to explain some reality."[144] The second external criterion is adequacy. Erickson contends that "since a world-view is intended to be a conceptual synthesis, it must in theory be capable of accounting for all possible experience."[145] He writes that "there can never be any conflict between the Bible, properly interpreted, and natural knowledge, correctly construed."[146] Erickson concludes by asking two rhetorical questions:

> If these criteria are fulfilled by a particular world-view, then may we not claim truth for the system? If it serves more effectively than alternative models to cast light upon our experience—moral, sensory, aesthetic, and religious—may we not conclude that reality itself is best described and interpreted by this particular model?[147]

---

138. Frederick Ferre, *Language, Logic, and God* (New York: Harper and Row, 1961), 162-163.

139. *Christian Theology*, 143; Erickson notes that this is but a negative test for truth.

140. *New Evangelical Theology*, 139; as with previous Evangelicals studied in this work, here Erickson embraces Aristotle's Law of Contradiction.

141. *Christian Theology*, 144.

142. Ibid. On Clark, see *A Christian View of Men and Things* (Grand Rapids: Eerdmans, 1952), 29-31.

143. *Christian Theology*, 144; Erickson's contention is that although knowledge is not gained exclusively through our sense experience, its meaning is seized on an empirical basis. On this, see also *New Evangelical Theology*, 143.

144. *Christian Theology*, 144; in *New Evangelical Theology*, 143-56, Erickson exposits this contention along the lines of historical evidence, supernatural evidence, and metaphysical evidence.

145. *Christian Theology*, 145.

146. *New Evangelical Theology*, 200.

147. *Christian Theology*, 145; such a perspective is more Augustinian than Thomistic in regard to its apologetic stance; see *New Evangelical Theology*, 130.

Erickson contends that the language of Christian theology is cognitively meaningful, "for its truth status is as a metaphysical system. Its truthfulness can be tested by the application of the several types of criteria."[148]

Critique of Erickson's Concept of Truth

Erickson has written a widely used and accessible systematic theology which offers a sound and balanced introduction to traditional Christian faith from a Protestant Evangelical perspective. It engages divergent viewpoints with fairness, giving reasoned evaluations of their strengths while respectfully noting problems which are perceived to be less than helpful to theological construction. It is carefully organized, demonstrating Erickson's thoughtful interaction with contemporary issues. Erickson's irenic tone and winsome presentation of classical orthodoxy has won his entire corpus a respected hearing from its intended audience as well as from those outside contemporary American Evangelical life. His careful scholarship and effective writing style combine to form a theology which is both captivating and compelling.

Evangelical concerns have been voiced, however, about various aspects of Erickson's concept of truth. First, some feel his nuanced understanding of biblical inerrancy has made the term inconsequential. Clark Pinnock, for example, chides Erickson for even using the term "inerrancy" with such a wide array of qualifications.[149] Pinnock feels Erickson's definition is so broad that it can be asked rhetorically, "What legitimate objection could any Christian have to Erickson's definition of inerrancy?"[150] Culpepper shares this concern regarding the number of qualifications placed on the term "inerrancy," saying that Erickson thus appears to take back "with his disclaimers what his positive statements seem to be affirming."[151] Grenz adds that Erickson's doctrine of inerrancy is "less than convincing when Scriptural phenomena force him to stretch the concept to the breaking point."[152] An interesting exception is

---

148. *Christian Theology*, 146; Erickson adds that "when one makes the basic presupposition described in chapter 1 (God and his self-revelation) and works out the system that follows from that by implication, that system can be regarded as cognitively meaningful."

149. Pinnock, "Erickson's Magnum Opus," *TSF Bulletin*, 30.

150. Clark Pinnock, *The Scripture Principle* (San Francisco: Harper and Row, 1984), 78-79, a work which was dedicated to Erickson along with Donald Bloesch and Gabriel Fackre.

151. Robert H. Culpepper, "Review of *Christian Theology*, Vols. 1 and 2," *Faith and Mission*, vol. 3, no. 1 (Fall 1985), 97.

152. Stanley J. Grenz, "Review of *Christian Theology*, Vol. 1," *Christian Scholar's Review*, vol. 14, no. 1 (1984), 86.

Dockery, who feels that Erickson does not go far enough in his nuancing of inerrancy.[153]

A second critique has been voiced over the decisive omissions in Erickson's system of thought that relate directly to this central assertion, such as canonicity and the relationship of canonicity to inspiration, authority, and hermeneutics.[154] This is not only a critique of Erickson, but of Evangelical theologians in general, for though the subject has been explored by Evangelicals, it has not been in light of recent discussions regarding canonical criticism.[155] Feinberg suggests that Erickson should have at least discussed "why the Bible contains the books it does and not others, and whether the canon of Scripture is closed or not."[156]

Dockery offers a third criticism in that Erickson's system of thought seems to "reject paradox in theological thinking."[157] This concern is related to Pinnock's critique of Erickson's rationalism. Pinnock feels that Erickson seems to "rest the issue of validation, not upon the narrative of the gospel, but upon verbal revelation as a kind of rational axiom."[158] Pinnock's problem with this approach is that in this view, "Christian theology would not differ essentially from Islamic theology."[159] Pinnock senses something foundationally wrong with this approach, asking, "Do we really wish to compare sacred books with the Muslim, or to contrast good news with bad news?"[160] Feinberg's concern for Erickson's rationalism is the importance given to empirical knowledge, writing that "Erickson appears too much to make the data of science the touchstone for the interpretation of Scripture rather than the reverse."[161]

A fourth concern raised by Peter Rhea Jones is methodological in nature and deals with Erickson's holding for biblical inerrancy. Jones notes that Erickson's methodology "insists upon making the doctrinal text primary . . . but . . . admits that there is no explicit doctrinal text for inerrancy. It must be inferred."[162] Jones is concerned that Erickson is

---

153. Dockery, "Review of *Christian Theology*, Vol. 1," *Grace Theological Journal*, 303. Dockery writes that Erickson's "view of full inerrancy may not sufficiently express all necessary nuances articulated by the 1978 Chicago Statement."

154. Dockery, "Millard Erickson," *Baptist Theologians*, 653.

155. Evangelical treatments include such standard works as R. Laird Harris, *Inspiration and Canonicity of the Bible* (Grand Rapids: Zondervan, 1957), as well as the more recent by F. F. Bruce, *The Canon of Scripture* (Downers Grove: InterVarsity Press, 1988). For an introduction to the issues surrounding canonical criticism, see Terrence J. Keegan, *Interpreting the Bible: A Popular Introduction to Biblical Hermeneutics* (New York: Paulist Press, 1985), 131-144.

156. Feinberg, "Review of *Christian Theology*, Vol. 1," *Trinity Journal*, 5 NS (1984), 211; compare similar concerns voiced by Landegent, "Review of *Christian Theology*" 1:121.

157. Dockery, "Millard Erickson," *Baptist Theologians*, 653.

158. Pinnock, "Erickson's Magnum Opus," *TSF Bulletin*, 30.

159. Ibid.

160. Ibid.

161. Feinberg, "Review of *Christian Theology*" 1:212.

162. Peter Rhea Jones, "Response to Millard J. Erickson," *Proceedings of the Conference on Biblical Inerrancy*, 191.

willing to "draw the doctrine of inerrancy from inferences but not willing to accept inferences from the phenomena."[163] Jones argues that had Erickson found a text which taught inerrancy explicitly, his case would have been more logically sound.[164] Erickson uses phenomenological approaches to defend inerrancy, but he discounts phenomenological approaches in demonstrating inerrancy.

Equally telling is Jones' critique of Erickson's definition of error. Jones contends that Erickson's definition of error should correspond with his definition of inerrancy. Jones charges Erickson with lessening "the problems and difficulties at the expense of broadening the definition."[165] Jones posits that Erickson holds to a firm understanding of inerrancy with intellectual honesty only through the excessive qualification of the term "error." Yet Jones acknowledges that what is perhaps most operative in Erickson's formulations is a desire to "define inerrancy in terms of Biblical intentions rather than modern precision."[166]

Finally, Gordon Lewis expresses concern over Erickson's hermeneutics, namely that Erickson overstates the "gap between the biblical and contemporary cultures."[167] Lewis does not feel that Erickson takes Hirsch's distinction between meaning and significance into account as fully as he should, especially Hirsch's understanding that meaning is conveyed by a text through authorial intent and that significance refers to a relationship between that meaning and another person, time, or situation. Lewis feels such an appropriation by Erickson would have minimized the gap Erickson maintains between the world of Scripture and our contemporary culture.

---

163. "Response," 191.

164. It is to be noted, however, that Richard R. Melick, also delivering a response to Erickson's address at the 1987 Proceedings of the Conference on Biblical Inerrancy in Ridgecrest, North Carolina, states that inerrancy as an inference is sound theologically on the grounds that the biblical writers assumed the inerrancy of Scripture. Melick also notes that many theological categories cannot be found in Scripture, yet are accepted as adequate by most theologians. See Melick, "Response," *Proceedings of the Conference on Biblical Inerrancy*, 199.

165. Jones, "Response," *Proceedings of the Conference on Biblical Inerrancy*, 192; here Jones looks to I. Howard Marshall for similar concerns. In *Biblical Inspiration* (Grand Rapids: Eerdmans, 1982), 72, Marshall writes that inerrancy is "in danger of dying the death of a thousand qualifications." Jones muses that Erickson, along with Clark Pinnock, Donald Bloesch, and the Chicago Statement on Biblical Inerrancy are perhaps proposing a "limited inerrancy," which is perhaps a contradiction in terms.

166. Ibid. This is indeed Erickson's position, writing that "the nature of that inerrancy is now understood in terms of what these writers were evidently doing . . . this does not require verbal exactness, identical ordering or accounts, or the possession of the exact words spoken by Jesus"; see "Biblical Inerrancy: The Last Twenty-Five Years," *Journal of the Evangelical Theological Society*, 392-393.

167. Gordon R. Lewis, "A Response to Presuppositions of Non-Evangelical Hermeneutics," *Hermeneutics, Inerrancy, and the Bible*, 617-619.

Summary

The concept of truth in the theology of Millard J. Erickson is that of correspondence, though Erickson's failure to give this concept a detailed discussion has engaged many philosophical questions inherent in its usage. Erickson assumes the correspondence theory of truth throughout his corpus, mentioning it as the evangelical position in distinction with various other theories of truth. Yet Erickson fails to offer a direct discussion of the concept itself or of his rationale for holding to its tenets other than brief comments regarding the problems inherent in the denial of Aristotle's Law of Contradiction, which can be held distinct from the correspondence theory of truth.[168] Erickson also turns to the necessity of the correspondence theory of truth in critiquing the neopragmatist perspective, writing that we "require something approximating the correspondence theory of truth." The referent for this correspondence is God, whose truthfulness is marked by genuineness, veracity, and faithfulness. All truth is, therefore, divine in its nature. From this presupposition, Erickson moves to truth as correspondence through revelation, which marks the communication of this truth to humanity, taking the form of general and special revelation. Special revelation is both personal and propositional in its nature, though it places a decided emphasis on the propositional element of special revelation. The language of special revelation is analogical with a univocal element. The dimensions of truth involve that which is factual, objective, unitary, and logical.

Several broad questions surface in relation to Erickson's system of thought.[169] First, Erickson seems to confuse metaphysics and epistemology. In other words, he asserts that objective truth exists, and that such truth corresponds with reality, rooted in God's ontological truthfulness. Yet the leap from metaphysical objectivity to epistemological objectivity results in a confusion of categories that is far from helpful to theological construction. However this appears to be Erickson's theological move regarding the objective dimension of truth. The need for further explication in this area is heightened by recent deconstructionist assertions about the ontology of relativism. Their perspective is that an onto-noetic analysis intimates that truth is relative because meaning is contextual and being is relational. Put more succinctly, "contextualized meaning and relational meaning join in relative truth disclosed through symbolic awareness."[170] If this critique is accepted, and if metaphysical and epis-

---

168. Erickson, *The Word Became Flesh*, 331.

169. Not mentioned here to avoid redundancy from other chapters, but equally relevant to Erickson's system of thought, is the question of whether rational, propositional truth is that which constitutes the nature of God's self-disclosure in Scripture. A second large question regards the limits of language in regard to such issues as paradox and mystery.

170. Mark C. Taylor, *Deconstructing Theology*, American Academy of Religion Studies in Religion, no. 28 (New York: The Crossroad Publishing Company and Scholars Press, 1982), 57.

temological categories are not to be confused, can any claim to objectivity be made? Is coherence the only theory of truth then available, and if so, can any positive case for truth be constructed?[171] Erickson has responded by asserting that in his judgment, it is extremely difficult to separate metaphysics and epistemology and to assign priority to one over the other. "To arrive at a conclusion about the nature of what is known," he writes, "one must have a conception of how knowledge is gained. Conversely, in order to know how we know, there must be some conception of the nature of the objects known."[172]

Second, if truth is that which corresponds to God, then the issue regarding a referent becomes paramount. If revelation is looked to as the referent, the interpretation becomes all-encompassing. This raises countless hermeneutical issues,[173] such as how the Spirit's illumination guides into correct interpretation of the Bible's objective truth, not to mention the perennial problem of human depravity. The issue of human depravity for rationalistic systems of thought is the degree that human depravity affects humanity's reasoning abilities. This is a highly significant issue for any system which gives a lofty role to reason. Perhaps the main concern is this: in stressing the objective dimension of truth, Erickson fails to engage the enormous difficulties regarding the appropriation of that objective truth, hence blurring the relation between metaphysical and epistemological objectivity. Here is where many hermeneutical questions are posed regarding subjective appropriation of objective truth. Erickson makes great use of the category of "translator" as opposed to "transformer," but such a perspective must take into account that even translation demands the use of cultural and temporal categories.

Third, Erickson's rationalistic approach to Christian theology and propositional understandings of special revelation are challenged on many fronts, such as from those embracing the ideas and insights of narrative theology.[174] The phenomenological approach to what constitutes

---

171. That this is indeed the case is proposed by Gordon D. Kaufman in *An Essay on Theological Method*, American Academy of Religion Studies in Religion, no. 11, rev. ed. (Missoula, Montana: Scholars Press, 1975, 1979), 75-76. Kaufmann believes the truth question for theological statements is valid, but only in terms of coherence and pragmatic usefulness. Kaufmann, 75, writes that "the most a theologian can do is attempt to show that the interpretation of the facts of experience and life, which he or she has set forth, holds within it greater likelihood than any other for opening up the future into which humankind is moving."

172. Erickson, *The Word Became Flesh*, 520, n. 16.

173. Note the many questions raised by such works as Hans-Georg Gadamer's *Truth and Method*, 2nd rev. ed. (New York: Crossroad, 1990).

174. Note the many penetrating essays in *Why Narrative?*, ed. Stanley Hauerwas and L. Gregory Jones (Grand Rapids: Eerdmans, 1989). Note also such figures as George Lindbeck who posits the idea of nonpropositional revelation in *The Nature of Doctrine* (Philadelphia: Westminster, 1984), making doctrine "second-order" truth claims which affirm nothing about extra-linguistic or extra-human reality, thus making intrasystematic rather than ontological truth claims.

truth in religion also poses several questions to Erickson's rationalistic system, especially in its contention that objectivity means presence-for the subject, and subjectivity means presence-toward the object.

Fourth, reliance on empirical knowledge has been challenged throughout the history of modern philosophy, certainly from Descartes forward, and thus raises many questions about the reliability of sense-experience. Present within Erickson's system of thought is the Enlightenment understanding of fact and evidence, thus intimating an evidentialist or classical foundationalist view of knowledge.[175] This has been severely critiqued in a new and growing movement advocating a "reformed epistemology" in Christian philosophy.[176] This is a decisive question about Erickson's embracing of Ferre's external criteria for truth. Related to these questions is Erickson's attempt to embrace both evidentialism and presuppositionalism, a relationship which is never fully explicated.[177] Stating that they should be mutually conjoined is vastly different than demonstrating the nature of how this can and should be achieved.

Fifth, in regard to Erickson's division between legislative and judicial authority, it is unclear how this protects Erickson's system from the elevation of reason to a plane above revelation, for it would seem that the role given to reason—even as judicial authority—determines that which is to be accepted as truth, and thus determines the content of truth. Consequently, it would seem to engage in legislative authority as well.

A sixth question is in regard to Erickson's use of analogical language. The question is simple: How can we know by analogy unless we have a sure foundation for knowing that there actually is an analogy? Erickson

---

175. Evidentialism means that one holds to a particular belief because there is good evidence for that belief. Classical foundationalism is that view which holds that a particular belief is rational if and only if that belief is self-evident, evident to the senses, or incorrigible, or inferable from a set of beliefs that are self-evident, evident to the senses, or incorrigible. Erickson might vehemently deny many of the consequences and tenets of classical foundationalism, but his embrace of empirical knowledge as a "truth-check" makes him vulnerable to this charge and its accordant difficulties for theological construction.

176. A good introduction to this critique can be found in Kelly James Clark's *Return to Reason: A Critique of Enlightenment Evidentialism and a Defense of Reason and Belief in God* (Grand Rapids: Eerdmans, 1990); see also Alvin Plantinga, "Reason and Belief in God," *Faith and Rationality*, ed. Alvin Plantinga and Nicholas Wolterstorff (Notre Dame: University of Notre Dame Press, 1983). These two works espouse a view known as "reformed epistemology," a theory of knowledge, belief, and rationality which is "person-relative," a perspective which borrows largely from Thomas Reid and the philosophical school of common-sense realism. Against foundationalism and evidentialism, the contention of those who hold to a "reformed epistemology" is the view of knowledge that sees belief in God as its own foundation, as properly "basic" in and of itself.

177. Most endeavors of this nature are unsatisfactory, such as Robert L. Reymond, *The Justification of Knowledge: An Introductory Study in Christian Apologetic Methodology* (Phillipsburg: Presbyterian and Reformed Publishing Co., 1976), which discounts inductive apologetic methods while attempting to make amends for some of Van Til's fideistic tendencies.

answers this directly by stating that "we do not have any independent knowledge of it. The revelation itself includes the disclosure that God has chosen expressions and concepts that are analogical."[178] This answer, however, can be challenged on the grounds of circular reasoning. Erickson's system also lacks a clear explanation of the exact relationship between univocal and analogical language and a detailed discussion on the apparent dismissal of equivocal language. The question of how one can hold to a univocal element in analogical language in an ontological sense remains a pressing concern.

---

178. Erickson, *New Evangelical Theology*, 53.

Chapter Eight

TRUTH
AND THEOLOGY:
DONALD G. BLOESCH

Donald G. Bloesch is an Evangelical theologian who has been
described as the "most brilliant, creative evangelical writing in systematic theology."[1] Bloesch currently serves as the Professor of Systematic
Theology at Dubuque Theological Seminary.

Biographical Background

Donald G. Bloesch was born on May 3, 1928, in Bremen, Indiana, to
a deeply religious family of Swiss immigrants.[2] His father was the pastor
of a German Evangelical Church, and both of Bloesch's grandfathers
had come to the United States from Switzerland to serve as missionaries

---

1. Leslie R. Keylock, "Evangelical Leaders You Should Know: Meet Donald G. Bloesch,"
Moody Monthly (March 1988), 61.

2. Biographical introductions to Bloesch are essentially limited to Keylock's article,
"Meet Donald Bloesch," *Moody Monthly*, 61-63, and his own *Theological Notebook: Volume
I, 1960-1964* (Colorado Springs: Helmers and Howard, 1989), which is described in the
preface, vii, as a "kind of spiritual journal focusing on my thoughts rather than my activities."

to German-speaking immigrants.[3] Bloesch's father used to drive the great ethicist Reinhold Niebuhr around in a horse and buggy when Niebuhr was trying to support himself selling books. The Niebuhrs and Bloeschs have remained family friends.[4]

The Bloesch family moved to the Chicago suburb of Monee, Illinois, where Bloesch accepted the Christian faith as his own, writing that "it was there that I first came to know the Lord in a personal, experiential way."[5] Bloesch's childhood was marked with intellectual promise, evidenced by his attempt to write a history of the world while still in grade school.

Feeling a call to ministry as early as high school, Bloesch enrolled in Elmhurst College where he received his B.A. degree in philosophy.[6] Elmhurst students interested in pursuing the ministry traditionally went to Eden Theological Seminary in St. Louis, Missouri. Bloesch selected the Chicago Theological Seminary, which had offered him a full scholarship instead. Attending Chicago Theological Seminary for his Bachelor of Divinity degree also allowed Bloesch immediately upon graduation to enter a Ph.D. program at the University of Chicago.[7] During his seminary study, Bloesch discovered neo-orthodoxy, not considering "any of the leading conservative evangelical theologians in America as viable options."[8]

Bloesch was eventually pointed toward Evangelicalism through several influences, the first being his maternal grandmother. Bloesch writes that his maternal grandmother "was probably the most important spiritual influence on me in my early years. She was a godly Swiss woman who lived with us and often gave me devotional literature that played a critical role in my spiritual maturation."[9] The second influence toward Evangelicalism came through Moody Memorial Church. Bloesch's father sought to expose his children to a wide variety of worship and practices. This included a visit during a family vacation to Moody Memorial, a church associated with the Moody Bible Institute, an Evangelical training institution founded in the late nineteenth century. Bloesch felt more at home at Moody than at other churches. The third major influence that

---

3. The German Evangelical Church merged with the Reformed Church, becoming the Evangelical and Reformed Church, which then merged with the Congregational Church to form the United Church of Christ, of which Bloesch is an ordained minister.

4. Donald G. Bloesch, *Theological Notebook*, xi.

5. Keylock, "Meet Donald Bloesch," *Moody Monthly*, 61.

6. Elmhurst College is a denominational school affiliated with the United Church of Christ, founded in 1871, and located in Chicago's western suburbs.

7. Bloesch characterized Chicago Theological Seminary as an institution which espoused an "extreme liberal theology," though he appreciated Daniel Day Williams' effort to relate his liberal theology to the life of the church. See Keylock, "Meet Donald Bloesch," *Moody Monthly*, 62.

8. Keylock, "Meet Donald Bloesch," 62.

9. Ibid.

moved Bloesch toward Evangelicalism was the ministry of Inter-Varsity Christian Fellowship, a transdenominational, Evangelical parachurch group which focuses on campus ministry. Bloesch was exposed to Inter-Varsity during his doctoral studies at the University of Chicago.

Though buoyed throughout his doctoral study by the fellowship and support of the local chapter of Inter-Varsity, Bloesch encountered several setbacks during his course of study. With a dissertation virtually completed in apologetics, Bloesch saw his adviser leave for another university. Beginning a new thesis under a new adviser was understandably traumatic. Bloesch rose to the occasion, completing a new thesis on Reinhold Niebuhr's apologetical system of thought. During his oral exams, Bloesch encountered a professor who vowed that "no fundamentalist would ever graduate while he was in office."[10] Fortunately the rest of Bloesch's examining committee passed him "with hearty congratulations."[11] Bloesch's time of study at the University of Chicago exposed him to an impressive array of scholars, including Charles Hartshorne, Daniel Jenkins, Wilhelm Pauck, Jaroslav Pelikan, and the aforementioned Daniel Day Williams. Beyond his postdoctoral work at Oxford, Bloesch has also studied at Basel and Tubingen. Such travels have enabled him to study under Karl Barth, Hans Kung, and Leonard Hodgson. Beyond his B.A., B.D., and Ph.D., Bloesch holds an honorary doctor of divinity degree from Doane College.

Throughout his doctoral studies, Bloesch served as pastor of St. Paul's Church in Richton Park, Illinois. In 1956, upon graduation of the University of Chicago, Bloesch went to England for a year of postdoctoral study at Oxford University. During this period of study, Bloesch travelled to Switzerland, France, Italy, and Germany. His study of monasticism during this period highlighted his concern for renewal in mainline denominations, such as his own United Church of Christ.[12] Upon his return to the United States, Bloesch accepted a one-year appointment to the University of Dubuque Theological Seminary in Dubuque, Iowa, an appointment which has become a thirty-two-year tenure. Bloesch later discovered that he had received this appointment on the assumption that because his degree was from the University of Chicago he would provide a liberal counterpart to a neo-orthodox theologian currently serving on the faculty.[13]

---

10. Keylock, "Meet Donald Bloesch," 63.

11. Ibid.

12. This concern has continued in Bloesch's life, spawning such works as *Centers of Christian Renewal* (Philadelphia: United Church Press, 1964); *The Invaded Church* (Waco: Word, 1975); and *The Reform of the Church* (Grand Rapids: Eerdmans, 1970).

13. On this, see Keylock, "Meet Donald Bloesch," *Moody Monthly*, 63.

In the summer of 1958 Bloesch travelled to Geneva. There he met a young woman working on her doctorate in eighteenth-century French literature at the University of London. Donald Bloesch married Brenda Mary Jackson in November, 1962, at St. Paul's House in Chicago, a home for the elderly where Bloesch's father was resident chaplain. After teaching French at the University of Dubuque for several years, Mrs. Bloesch now works alongside her husband as a research associate and copy editor.

Bloesch has proved to be a prolific writer, authoring over 25 books and almost 300 published articles and book reviews.[14] The most comprehensive statement regarding his system of thought can be found in his two-volume systematic theology.[15] The first of these two volumes is dedicated to Bloesch's wife, Brenda; the second is dedicated to the Anglican Evangelical John R. W. Stott, rector emeritus of All Souls Church in London, England, and president of the London Institute for Contemporary Christianity. Donald Bloesch is a past president of the American Theological Society and is an advisor to renewal groups within mainline denominations.

Description of Bloesch's Concept of Truth

Donald Bloesch differs from other theologians in this study in that he offers a concise and purposeful exploration of the concept of truth in the context of a detailed exploration of the relationship between philos-

---

14. Beyond those previously mentioned, a selection of Bloesch's books include but are not limited to the following: *The Battle for the Trinity: The Debate over Inclusive God-Language* (Ann Arbor: Vine Books, 1985); *The Christian Life and Salvation* (Grand Rapids: Eerdmans, 1967); *The Christian Witness in a Secular Age* (Minneapolis: Augsburg, 1968); *The Crisis of Piety: Essays Toward a Theology of the Christian Life* (Colorado Springs: Helmers and Howard, 1988); *Crumbling Foundations: Death and Rebirth in an Age of Upheaval* (Grand Rapids: Academie/Zondervan, 1984); *The Evangelical Renaissance* (Grand Rapids: Eerdmans, 1973); *Faith and Its Counterfeits* (Downers Grove: InterVarsity Press, 1981); *Freedom for Obedience: Evangelical Ethics in Contemporary Times* (San Francisco: Harper and Row, 1987); *The Future of Evangelical Theology: A Call for Unity Amid Diversity* (Colorado Springs: Helmers and Howard, 1988); *Is the Bible Sexist? Beyond Feminism and Patriarchalism* (Westchester: Crossway, 1982); *Light a Fire* (St. Louis: Eden, 1975); *The Struggle of Prayer* (San Francisco: Harper and Row, 1980); *Wellsprings of Renewal: Promise in Christian Communal Life* (Grand Rapids: Eerdmans, 1974). Edited works include but are not limited to the following: *The Orthodox Evangelicals*, co-edited with Robert Webber (Nashville: Thomas Nelson, 1978); *Servants of Christ: Deaconesses in Renewal* (Minneapolis: Bethany Fellowship, 1971). Bloesch has contributed articles to such published reference works as the *Beacon Hill Dictionary of Theology*, ed. Richard S. Taylor (Kansas City: Beacon Hill, 1983), the *Evangelical Dictionary of Theology*, ed. Walter Elwell (Grand Rapids: Baker, 1984), and the *Holman Bible Dictionary*, ed. Trent C. Butler (Nashville: Holman Bible Publishers, 1991).

15. Donald G. Bloesch, *Essentials of Evangelical Theology, Volume 1: God, Authority, and Salvation* (San Francisco: Harper and Row, 1978), and *Essentials of Evangelical Theology, Volume 2: Life, Ministry, and Hope* (San Francisco: Harper and Row, 1978).

ophy and theology.[16] Bloesch is currently working on a project, unavailable at the time of this writing, which will undoubtedly prove essential reading for a research project of this nature.[17]

Donald Bloesch perceives two general approaches to the concept of truth throughout Western thought. These two approaches are the philosophical and the theological.[18] These categories will provide the framework for a discussion of the concept of truth in his system of thought. Bloesch begins by stating that theology must be open to the insights of philosophy while being critical of the philosophic proclivity to include all things in a conceptual framework.

Philosophy and Truth

Bloesch discusses four main categories for the concept of truth operative in philosophy: the correspondence theory of truth, the coherence theory of truth, the pragmatic theory of truth, and what he calls the "mystical" or "intuitive" theory of truth.

The Correspondence Theory of Truth. The first philosophical theory of truth that Bloesch sets forth for analysis is the correspondence theory of truth, defined truth as that which "signifies the correspondence of an idea and its object. Truth is said to lie in a correlation or agreement between concept and thing."[19] Bloesch associates this perspective regarding the nature of truth with empiricism and modern realism. He further posits that the correspondence theory of truth generally presupposes a "dualistic view of reality; there is the world of ideas or universals and that of things or particulars."[20] In what he terms the "more idealistic type" of philosophy, correspondence means the "conformation of appearance to reality."[21]

Bloesch is willing to grant that Christian theologians can speak of correspondence, but when they do, "they have in mind the correspondence of our thinking and the meaning of the Gospel."[22] Bloesch is quick to

---

16. Donald Bloesch, *The Ground of Certainty: Toward an Evangelical Theology of Revelation* (Grand Rapids: Eerdmans, 1971). The concise discussion regarding truth is found in chapter 7, "The Meaning of Truth," 126-139. This small section will necessarily be used out of proportion to Bloesch's extensive theological corpus due to the specific nature of this study, serving as the framework for explicating Bloesch's concept of truth operative in his system of thought. It is to be noted that Bloesch refers to *The Ground of Certainty* as that work which expounds his theological methodology, laying the groundwork for the theology of revelation manifest in his two-volume systematic, *Essentials of Evangelical Theology;* see *Essentials,* 1:xii.

17. Letter received from Donald G. Bloesch, January 10, 1991. The subject of the forthcoming work is "Holy Scripture." The final chapter concerns the meaning of truth and is tentatively titled "Truth in Biblical and Philosophical Perspective."

18. Bloesch, *Ground of Certainty,* 126.

19. Ibid., 128-129.

20. Ibid., 129.

21. Ibid.

22. Ibid.

add that the "Gospel is not an object at our disposal but rather a personal message addressed not simply to the mind but to the heart of man, that is, the very center of his personality."[23] Thus correspondence for those holding to biblical faith is "not simply an agreement between our ideas and the Gospel but a conforming of our total life-orientation to the demands of the Gospel."[24] Bloesch admits that this includes our thought-world, but states that "reason must not be viewed as a correlative of revelation but instead as a servant of revelation."[25] He writes:

> Truth for the Christian is not so much the factual as the eventful . . . truth is not external history as such but God in history, history seen through the eyes of God, history seen in the perspective of divine revelation.[26]

So Bloesch's understanding of correspondence is substantively different than secular philosophical musings on the subject, for a correspondence understanding of truth takes place "when our minds are brought into accordance with the mind of Christ; then our judging accords with reality."[27] Bloesch concludes by affirming that the correspondence understandings of truth may have a place in the Christian doctrine of God, for God always corresponds to Himself, meaning that He is faithful to His Word and to His covenant. "Through the gift of faith there can be a partial correspondence between man's knowledge and God's but not an equation, since God remains hidden ("deus absconditus") even in his revelation."[28]

The Coherence Theory of Truth. The second philosophical theory of truth for which Bloesch offers an analysis is the coherence theory of truth, defined as that which maintains that "the meaning of the part can only be understood through the whole."[29] Stated differently, "a proposition is said to be true if it fits into an all-encompassing logical system."[30]

Bloesch categorizes adherents to this theory as those who tend toward monism, the idea which "holds that thought and reality are one and the same."[31] Bloesch contends that the most consistent type of monism is absolute idealism, but he finds that all idealism has monistic tendencies and usually rests its case upon rational coherence.[32]

---

23. *Ground of Certainty,* 129.
24. Ibid.
25. Ibid.
26. Ibid.
27. Ibid., 130.
28. Bloesch, *Essentials,* 1:75.
29. Bloesch, *Ground of Certainty,* 130.
30. Ibid.
31. Ibid.
32. Ibid.

Bloesch's theological concern with this approach is that we "cannot perfectly resolve the antinomies and contradictions of life in any system of meaning; there are some mysteries that simply cannot be comprehended and must be accepted on faith alone."[33] Bloesch contends that although we can show that the suprarational affirmations of faith give meaning to the seeming contradictions that run through life and history, the "absolute synoptic perspective lies outside our grasp."[34] The reason for this is that the truth of faith "is suprarational as well as rational."[35]

Bloesch's appropriation of this theory is that "the meaning of the part can be understood only through the meaning of the Word," but Bloesch argues that this "is not identical with the whole of the reality that is generally experienced but which enters our reality from the beyond."[36] What is at stake for Bloesch is the preservation of those things and events that are "absolutely unique and therefore cannot be coordinated into any rational system," such as the event of God becoming human in Jesus Christ.[37] Bloesch contends that these cannot be placed into a rational system because they are incomparable and unrepeatable, thereby eluding rational comprehension. Other distinctions exist between a "biblical" or "theological" approach to truth and the coherence theory. The logic of deduced conclusions is opposed to the theologian's effort to discover meaning from the written and oral testimony to a particular historical revelation, and the implicative system inherent within idealistic philosophy is opposed to the open-ended and paradoxical nature of the Christian faith where seemingly contradictory affirmations are held together in creative tension rather than resolved into a higher synthesis. Bloesch's concern is that the coherence view does not allow faith to reject logical conclusions which may be implied but are not warranted in the light of the total biblical witness. Put simply, Bloesch does not find the mysteries of the faith amenable to syllogistic reasoning or what Emil Brunner called "straight-line" inference.[38]

The Pragmatic Theory of Truth. The pragmatic theory of truth is defined by Bloesch as that which says "truth is a matter of fulfilling genuinely human needs and solving the perplexing problems in life."[39] According to the pragmatist, "that which works to satisfy our deepest

---

33. *Ground of Certainty,* 131.
34. Ibid.
35. Bloesch, *Essentials,* 1:18.
36. Bloesch, *Ground of Certainty,* 131. By the "Word" Bloesch does not mean "the universal Logos that resides in all things" but rather "the Word become flesh, the event of God becoming man in Jesus Christ."
37. Ibid.
38. Ibid., 132.
39. Ibid.

needs and integrate our experience is true."[40] In this view the method of discovering truth is "trial and error;" the goal is "satisfaction."[41]

Bloesch understands the pragmatic theory of truth to be largely empirical in that it does not appeal "to any reality that transcends experience."[42] It is also contextual in that it tries to see "every problem in its concrete social and behavioral setting."[43] Finally, it can be said to be existential in that it holds that truth is discovered not "by detached observation but by total human involvement."[44]

Bloesch concedes that this view of truth is the dominant view in contemporary American culture. He writes that "not timeless truth but workable truth is the concern of most Americans."[45] Bloesch agrees that theologians must be pragmatists, but only to a point. Human beings have needs, and the Christian faith speaks of meeting those needs. However it is liberation which is offered rather than integration or satisfaction. It is "He who works" rather than "that which works." The call is often to "self-denial" rather than "self-fulfillment." Bloesch summarizes:

> Pragmatic philosophy still retains the classical Greek notion of ideas that are true, though it seeks to relate these to the work-a-day world in which men find themselves. Christian theology, on the other hand, understands truth primarily in terms of the person of Jesus Christ and His self-revelation. Granted that we might have true ideas about a person, we cannot actually know him until he addresses us and thereby actually reveals himself to us.[46]

The Mystical Theory of Truth. The final philosophical theory of truth that Bloesch explores is what he terms the "mystical" theory, sometimes called the "intuition" theory. "Here the locus of truth is an identification with essential being or the whole of reality."[47] The criterion of truth is "immediacy; the experience of truth is self-verifying in character."[48]

The mystical approach does not find truth in either historical event or external authority, but rather "in the depths of one's soul."[49] Bloesch cites the German mystic Meister Eckhart (about 1260-1327) as one who attached more importance to the birth of the Son in the soul than to the historical incarnation of Christ. Bloesch finds common ground in mysticism in that Christian theology also affirms a "transcending of the subject-object cleavage in faith."[50] He desires to distinguish mystical

---

40. *Ground of Certainty*, 132.
41. Ibid.
42. Ibid., 133.
43. Ibid.
44. Ibid.
45. Ibid.
46. Ibid.
47. Ibid., 134.
48. Ibid.
49. Ibid.
50. Ibid.

approaches to truth from that of Christian theology's approach in that "instead of an identity with some primal reality behind the dualism of subject and object, Christian faith envisions a subject-Subject relationship."[51] Put another way, whereas Christian theology "views the knowledge of God as something given in revelation, mysticism tends to see truth hidden in the depths of the soul and waiting only to be discovered."[52]

Bloesch concludes his analysis of these four philosophical approaches to the meaning of truth by stating that the correspondence and pragmatic theories tend to share affinities with the cosmological philosophy of religion, whereas the coherence and mystic theories are more closely aligned with the ontological approach.

> In the cosmological approach knowledge of God is attained by looking at the outside world and inferring the existence of God from His effects in nature. In the ontological approach ultimate reality or God is to be found by looking within the soul and discovering there an awareness of the unconditional or an idea of perfection.[53]

Bloesch uses Paul Tillich's understandings for the differences between the cosmological and ontological approaches.[54] Bloesch contends the "correspondence and pragmatic theories gain a hearing in the circles of empiricism and naturalism whereas the coherence and mystical theories find their natural home in idealism and mysticism."[55]

Theology and Truth

Having explored the correspondence, coherence, pragmatic, and mystical theories of truth—finding much to commend and critique in all of them—Bloesch posits that the theological understanding of truth is distinct from all philosophical understandings of truth.[56] Indeed, he maintains that when the philosophical understanding of truth has pene-

---

51. *Ground of Certainty*, 134.
52. Ibid., 135.
53. Ibid.
54. Paul Tillich, "The Two Types of Philosophy of Religion," *Union Seminary Quarterly Review*, 1 (May 1946), 3-13. Bloesch critiques Tillich, however, in that he does not feel Tillich has overcome his dependence upon idealistic philosophy and thereby fails to give an authentically biblical understanding of Christ, see *Ground of Certainty*, 136.
55. Bloesch, *Ground of Certainty*, 135.
56. In finding strengths and weaknesses present in each of the four philosophical views surveyed, Bloesch might be revealing his own contention that "truth is many-sided, and the various aspects of truth must be held together in dialectical tension," a view he recorded in his own theological notebook of musings in mid-summer of 1964, see *Theological Notebook* 1:183. Such a statement is pregnant with theological import for any system of thought, and one would have liked to have seen this statement explicated in the discussions contained in *Ground of Certainty*. As this latter work antedates the recorded words in volume one of Bloesch's *Theological Notebook*, it may be that Bloesch moved away from this neoorthodox contention regarding the nature of truth.

trated the Christian faith, it has served only to provide a static under-standing of truth as opposed to the "dynamic biblical conception of truth."[57] The theological approach to truth must not be confused with either the cosmological or the ontological approach to the philosophy of religion. Bloesch writes that in

> biblical theology truth is a liberating word with power given in a divine-human encounter; it is not an idea or principle that can be discovered or conceived. Truth is God in action, God revealing His will and purpose to mankind.[58]

Biblical Terms for Truth. In making such a claim regarding the nature of theological truth, Bloesch draws heavily from the biblical words for truth, such as the Old Testament terms "'emeth" and "'emunah."[59] These terms speak of God's faithfulness and resoluteness. Bloesch sees truth operating at this level in the Old Testament, as well as the idea that God's word and works are reliable and trustworthy and that humanity is to enter into the truth of God by keeping God's commandments and conforming to God's will. Bloesch also takes refuge in the New Testament term for truth, "aletheia." While he acknowledges that the term has a more cognitive dimension than "'emeth" or "'emunah," he posits that it retains the ethical and mystical dimensions present in the Old Testament. Bloesch is also willing to admit that an ontological dimension to truth can be found in the biblical terms for truth, but primarily in reference to divinity.

Existential Truth. Building on the biblical terminology related to the idea of truth, Bloesch understands the New Testament materials to present a view of truth in terms of personal encounter and participation. He writes that "in order to be in the truth, one must do the truth. In order to have the truth one must receive the truth."[60] In other words, "knowing the truth is not so much an intellectual matter as a matter of personal salvation."[61] As a result, Bloesch's understanding of the biblical concept of truth is vastly different than the Hellenistic mind which conceived of truth "as the unchangeable order of reality or as eternal being."[62] Bloesch states that "truth in the New Testament is identified not with the most universal (whether this be process or being) but with the historical fact Jesus Christ."[63] The position presented by Bloesch is a

---

57. Bloesch, *Ground of Certainty*, 126. He writes, 21, "I believe that the attempted synthesis between faith and philosophy has been detrimental to both religion and culture."
58. Ibid.
59. This discussion of biblical terms for truth takes place in *Ground of Certainty*, 126-127.
60. *Ground of Certainty*, 126.
61. Ibid., 137.
62. Ibid., 127.
63. Ibid.

"biblical evangelicalism that seeks to hold in balance objective revelation and subjective decision."[64]

Therefore, Bloesch contends that the biblical concept of truth "is
understood as a divine word or act by which men are inwardly
changed."[65] Truth is not "an unveiling of a primal Being, as Heidegger
contends, but the self-revelation of a living God in a particular person
and in a decisive series of events in history."[66] From this Bloesch posits
that the biblical notion of truth "cannot be known apart from decision
and commitment: therefore it can be said to be more existential than theoretical."[67] This is not to say that Bloesch is an existentialist, however, for
he writes, "Truth is not to be found in a venture that entails absolute
uncertainty (as in existentialism) nor in a feeling of absolute dependence
(as in the mysticism of Schleiermacher); instead it is to be found in an
absolute receptivity towards its Object, the living Christ."[68] Thus reason
can only "bow before the mystery of this truth; it cannot grasp or possess
it. The truth of faith can be known, but it cannot be comprehended."[69]

As a result, Bloesch is quite adamant in his stance that human reason
is not the basis for certainty. The basis for certainty for the Christian faith
and theology is divine revelation.[70] Bloesch does not mind saying that
his position is much closer to fideism than rationalism, but he also states
that in contradistinction to radical fideists he does not "see a divorce
between faith and reason but the conversion of reason by faith."[71] For
Bloesch, there is nothing wrong in the search for truth as long as we
"search in the light of God's revelation and not in the darkness engen-
dered by a reason sufficient unto itself."[72] Bloesch asserts that the
proper theological method is "reason in the service of revelation to the
greater glory of God."[73] Therefore, faith can be said to contradict "the

---

64. *Control of Certainty*, 187.

65. *Ground of Certainty*, 127.

66. Ibid. Bloesch understands Heidegger's position to be "partly a return to and partly a
correction of the Greek philosophical meaning of truth" with affinities toward mysticism. For
Heidegger's position, see *Existence and Being* (Chicago: Regnery, 1949), 117-167, 292-324.

67. *Ground of Certainty*, 127.

68. Ibid., 136.

69. Ibid., 127. On such grounds Bloesch critiques Gordon H. Clark rather severely,
see 183-185. For a good introduction to Clark's understanding of reason and the Christian
faith, see *The Philosophy of Gordon H. Clark*, ed. by Ronald H. Nash (Philadelphia: Presbyterian and Reformed, 1968).

70. *Ground of Certainty*, 70.

71. *Ground of Certainty*, 187. Bloesch is not claiming to be a fideist, but rather is
stressing which pole of the spectrum he finds most conducive to theological reflection and
construction. In another place he writes that "Evangelical theology is not to be confused
with fideism. The former makes revelation its criterion, whereas the latter absolutizes faith.
Moreover, for evangelical theology revelation is not to be accepted blindly, but rather is to
be weighed in the light of its own evidence"; see *Theological Notebook* 1:128.

72. *Theological Notebook* 1:128.

73. *Essentials* 1:18. See also Bloesch's continued concern in this area in *Essentials*,
2:267-69.

arrogance of reason but not the basic structure of reason."[74] Along with Barth, Bloesch maintains that to appeal to common ground with non-Christian thought is suspect. An apologetic defense of the faith can silence criticism, but not facilitate the decision of the faith. Bloesch contends that traditional apologetics has gone astray in its tendency to perceive intellectual doubt as the main barrier to Christian faith.[75]

Bloesch's distinction between philosophical and theological truth is clear: whereas the philosophical understanding of truth is envisioned in terms of an idea, the theological understanding of truth is seen in terms of a Person. Philosophers have in mind "discursive, propositional truth arrived at by analysis and experimentation . . . either right conception or right perception . . . an idea that either corresponds with the object-world or mirrors the whole of reality."[76] The knowledge of God in Christian theology, rather, is that of "personal acquaintance."[77]

Bloesch does not exclude propositional truth, but rather he places propositional truth "in the service of personal truth. Secular or philosophical meanings of truth can sometimes be appropriated by the church, but they will be transformed in the process."[78] Theology does not need philosophy "as a foundation, nor as a superstructure, but as an instrument and a tool."[79] Ideas, then, are true insofar as they "point beyond themselves to the One who is the Truth."[80] In this sense Bloesch can speak of truth as ontological as well as personal, objective in basis yet subjective in appropriation, open to revision as well as that which is irrevocable.

Truth and Scripture

The definition Bloesch offers regarding truth begs for investigation as to how this concept relates to his understanding of truth and Scripture. Our examination of Bloesch's system of thought will involve the nature of Scripture, biblical inerrancy, and the Christological hermeneutic Bloesch advances for theological construction.

---

74. *Ground of Certainty*, 196-197.

75. Ibid., 198-199.

76. Ibid., 128. Bloesch adds that philosophical knowledge is akin to scientific knowledge, in that it is a knowledge derived from self-evident principles and factual experience. Here Bloesch draws from Henri Renard in the foreword to M. R. Holloway's *An Introduction to Natural Theology* (New York: Appleton-Century-Crofts, 1959), ix.

77. *Ground of Certainty*, 128. Bloesch writes, 136, that "theology is oriented about the God-Man, not an abstract idea of God.

78. Ibid., 128.

79. *Theological Notebook*, 1:231.

80. *Ground of Certainty*, 137. Bloesch does not identify our ideas and God's ideas. Bloesch rejects this idealist perspective. He argues for at best a correspondence or analogical relationship.

The Nature of Scripture. "Evangelical theology appeals to the authority of Scripture because it sees Scripture as the written Word of God."[81] Bloesch's understanding of the Word of God encompasses both person and act to the point of being equated with God in action.[82] Bloesch asserts that the "truth about God and man cannot be discovered nor conceived; it must be revealed."[83] Outside of this revelation "man exists in untruth."[84] Secular philosophy may incidentally reflect the truth of God, but its overall orientation is decisively human centered. The truth that theology proclaims is "the ground of truth that the philosopher may occasionally stumble upon in his reflection."[85] For Bloesch, revelation signifies not only the acts of God in past biblical history but also "the biblical interpretation of these acts. It also includes the inward illumination of the Holy Spirit in the present by which we become convinced of the truth of the biblical witness."[86] Scripture is not, however, the only channel of truth. In an interesting use of terms, Bloesch contends that while Scripture is the only "source" of truth, there are many "channels" of truth. He writes that "there is but one wellspring, but there are also many pipes that contain the water of life to the church in every age."[87]

Therefore, when Bloesch speaks of the Word of God, he is not positing the Bible as such but the truth to which the Bible attests.[88] The objective dimension of revelation "signifies the disclosure of meaning in the historical events mirrored in the Bible and also in the Biblical testimony itself."[89] The subjective pole is that which "refers to the mystical or inward illumination of the Holy Spirit."[90] The criterion of authority for the Christian is not the "objective Word of God as such, but rather the Word of God proclaimed and also received and obeyed."[91]

Bloesch maintains that the Bible is a "trustworthy and unfailing guide because the light of God's countenance shines upon it and because the Spirit grants illumination to the community of faith."[92] In what has become known as the "Chicago Call," Bloesch and several other Evangelicals proposed the following affirmation regarding biblical fidelity:[93]

---

81. *Essentials* 1:51.
82. *Ground of Certainty*, 128.
83. Ibid., 136.
84. Ibid., 138.
85. Ibid., 139.
86. Ibid., 88.
87. *Theological Notebook* 1:184.
88. *Ground of Certainty*, 12.
89. Ibid., 70.
90. Ibid.
91. Bloesch, *Theological Notebook* 1:26.
92. *Ground of Certainty*, 74.
93. The "Chicago Call" is not to be confused with the "Chicago Statement on Biblical Inerrancy," a document conceived by a much larger group of Evangelicals under the organizational title "The International Council on Biblical Inerrancy" resulting in a much more explicit statement regarding the nature of biblical inspiration as that of inerrancy.

> We deplore our tendency toward individualistic interpretation of Scripture. This undercuts the objective character of biblical truth, and denies the guidance of the Holy Spirit among his people through the ages.
>
> Therefore we affirm that the Bible is to be interpreted in keeping with the best insights of historical and literary study, under the guidance of the Holy Spirit, with respect for the understanding of the historic church.
>
> We affirm that the Scriptures, as the infallible Word of God, are the basis of authority in the church. We acknowledge that God uses the Scriptures to judge and to purify his Body. The church, illumined and guided by the Holy Spirit, must in every age interpret, proclaim and live out the Scriptures.[94]

This statement reveals how many Evangelicals have found in Karl Barth a "fresh interpretation of biblical authority, which enables us to contend for the primacy of biblical revelation. . . and . . . acknowledge the rightful place for the historical investigation of Scripture."[95] This statement also reveals how Bloesch and other Evangelicals wish to distance themselves from a "rationalistic biblicism" where an "absolute identification is made between the words of the biblical text and the truth of revelation."[96]

For Bloesch, the Word of God is not simply the letter or text itself but the divine meaning imbedded in the text which is unveiled only by the Holy Spirit. The concern is that positing a direct identity between Scripture and revelation could lead to bibliolatry. Therefore, an indirect identity is put forth in such a way that God's Word is not the Bible in and by itself but it is the correlation of Scripture and Spirit. Bloesch wants to hold to the divine inspiration of Scripture and even the infallibility of Scripture "without reducing its truth to a datum available to human perception."[97] He affirms a "union but not a fusion between the divine content and its worldly form."[98] As a result, Bloesch has little interest in defending a "naive biblical literalism" where the "credibility of the Bible rests upon the edibility of Jonah."[99] The better course for Evangelicalism

---

94. Robert E. Webber and Donald G. Bloesch, eds., *The Orthodox Evangelicals: Who They Are and What They Are Saying* (Nashville: Thomas Nelson, 1978), 12-13. The "Chicago Call," representing eight themes in its final form, was the result of a gathering in Chicago, Illinois, of 45 Evangelicals in May of 1977 which resulted in a "call to Evangelicalism . . . back to historic Christianity" (from the Preface).

95. Bloesch, "Karl Barth: Appreciation and Reservations," *How Karl Barth Changed My Mind*, 127.

96. Bloesch, *The Evangelical Renaissance*, 21.

97. *The Evangelical Renaissance*, 21.

98. *The Future of Evangelical Christianity*, 119. Bloesch states that "Fundamentalism has placed the accent on the words" of the Bible at the expense of the Bible's meaning and power.

99. *The Evangelical Renaissance*, 28.

is to stem the tide of irrationalism and subjectivism "by emphasizing the particularity and objectivity of the historical revelation in Jesus Christ."[100] The Bible's authority is clearly dependent on Jesus Christ, and it is His Spirit that "guarantees the trustworthiness of its witness."[101]

Biblical Inerrancy. The nature of Scripture is important background to Bloesch's reinterpretation of the concept of biblical inerrancy.[102] Bloesch maintains that inerrancy and infallibility can be posited of the Bible, but only if rightly understood. A view of inerrancy that seeks a rationally guaranteed authority, for example, is rejected. Bloesch maintains that inspiration "conveys the truth that the writers were guided in their selection of words and meanings so that their overall witness is reliable and trustworthy"[103] in regard to that which concerns "the will and purpose of God made known in Jesus Christ."[104] The biblical writers were so "guided by the Spirit that what was actually written had the very sanction of God himself."[105] Therefore "inspiration refers to the divine election and guidance of the biblical prophets for the express purpose of ensuring the trustworthiness and efficacy of their witness through the ages."[106] To affirm the Bible's infallibility is to assert that "Scripture does not lead astray, it does not deceive."[107] This is maintained by Bloesch as the classical "sacramental" view of Scripture, which sees the Bible as a "divinely appointed channel, a mirror, or a visible sign of divine revelation."[108]

Bloesch feels that a return to this view would overcome the current impasse in Evangelical circles regarding the authority of Scripture.[109]

Yet Bloesch also maintains that the dual authorship of Scripture should be kept in the vanguard of all formulations of biblical inspiration such as inerrancy. It is both "the very Word of God and the very word of man."[110] To emphasize the humanity of the Bible at the expense of its

---

100. *The Evangelical Renaissance*, 28. Bloesch adds, 29, however, that "evangelicals would do well to eschew the opposite danger of objectivism, for the God of the Bible is not available to human perception but can only be discerned by faith."

101. Ibid., 56.

102. On this, see Bloesch's article "Crisis in Biblical Authority," in *Theology Today*, vol. 35 (April 1978-January 1979), 455-462.

103.   Bloesch, *The Evangelical Renaissance*, 55. Note, however, that this is very different for Bloesch than affirming that biblical propositions are themselves revealed, a view he discounts, see *Essentials* 1:76. There is a propositional element, but it is virtually subsumed under the polydimensional sense of truth as an event of God.

104. Donald G. Bloesch, "The Sword of the Spirit; The Meaning of Inspiration," *Reformed Review*, vol. 33, no. 2 (Winter 1980), 66.

105. Bloesch, *Essentials* 1:54-55.

106. *Essentials.* He writes that "in our view inspiration is both conceptual and verbal, since it signifies that the Spirit was active both in shaping the thoughts and imagination of the biblical writers and also in guiding them in their actual writing."

107. "Sword of the Spirit," *Reformed Review*, 66.

108. *The Future of Evangelical Christianity*, 118.

109. *Essentials*, 2:270-5.

110. Ibid., 1:52.

divinity is to have an "ebionitic view of Scripture." To emphasize the divine nature of the Bible disregarding its human dimension is to have a "docetic view of Scripture." The terms "ebionite" and "docetic" are used by Bloesch in reference to the early church heresies regarding the Person of Christ. The docetics did not want to acknowledge the full humanity of Jesus, while the ebionites were hesitant to acknowledge the full divinity of Jesus. The early church decided to reject this dichotomy and put forth a "both/and" perspective on the Person of Christ.

Bloesch does not desire to give up inerrancy and infallibility when applied to Scripture, but he does believe "that we need to be much more circumspect in our use of these and related terms. Scripture is without error in a fundamental sense, but we need to explore what this sense is."[111] To posit that the Bible does not err means that "whatever Christ teaches in Scripture is completely true. Scripture is without error in its matter, i.e., in its basic teaching and witness."[112] In other words "it does not err in what it affirms concerning the law and Gospel, the two sides of the revelation of God. It does not err in what the Holy Spirit intends to teach us in and through the biblical text, and this teaching extends to truth about man and the world as well as the truth about salvation."[113] Bloesch adds in a footnote that "this includes not only its testimony concerning God and salvation, but also its interpretation of man, life and history. But this does not imply perfect factual accuracy in all details as the extreme literalist holds."[114] Indeed, "verbal inspiration must not be confused with perfect accuracy or mechanical dictation."[115] It is the doctrine or message of Scripture which is inerrant, and that inerrant message is hidden in the "historical and cultural witness of the biblical writers. They did not err in what they proclaimed, but this does not mean that they were faultless in their recording of historical data or in their world view, which is now outdated."[116] Therefore, a view of error that "demands literal, exact, mathematical precision, something the Bible cannot provide," is rejected.[117] Such a view would place the case for Christianity on the unstable ground of scientific and historical research. Bloesch is not willing to abandon the doctrine of inerrancy, but he maintains that one must take Scripture's own understanding of this concept instead of imposing upon Scripture a view of inerrancy drawn from modern empirical philosophy and science. For example,

---

111. *The Future of Evangelical Christianity*, xxi.
112. *The Evangelical Renaissance*, 56.
113. See "Sword of the Spirit," *Reformed Review*, 66-67.
114. Ibid.
115. *Essentials*, 1:55.
116. Ibid., 1:65. He writes, 69, that the "kernel of the Gospel is always to a certain degree hidden in the husk of culturally conditioned concepts and imagery."
117. Ibid., 1:66.

> We must not infer from this [infallibility] that Scripture gives exact knowledge of mathematics or biology or any other science. Neither does it present a history of Israel or a biography of Jesus that accords with the standards of historical science. What we do have in Scripture is a faithful account of God's redemptive works, an incisive portrayal of the divine plan of salvation. What we receive is true but not exhaustive knowledge of divinity, for divinity remains enveloped in mystery even in the act of revelation.[118]

Even further, Bloesch contends that this type of infallibility extends to "theological and ethical ideas,"[119] that theological and ethical statements are historically and culturally bound. One would wish that such an enormously consequential statement such as this would have been explained further, but all that is added is that it is "only when their testimony [the biblical authors] is related to and refined by the self-revelation of Jesus Christ that it [Scripture] has the force of infallible authority." One could conclude, though perhaps erroneously, that Bloesch thinks biblical materials could contain a theological or ethical stance that would be in error. If so, this would be a decisive move away from Evangelical theology and even traditional orthodoxy. This author's reading of Bloesch sees such a perspective in disharmony with Bloesch's entire corpus, so it is best simply to suspend judgment. According to Bloesch, what is infallible and inerrant is "the Word within the Words, the divine meaning given in and through the human testimony."[120] Therefore, Bloesch "gently deprecates the recent precisionism involving inerrancy as missing the point of the Bible's importance."[121]

Bloesch is ambiguous in his own reflections on this subject, for he also writes:

> It is now said in many circles that the teaching or doctrine of the Bible is without error rather than everything reported in the Bible. The message of the Bible is said to be infallible, not the text itself; this message, moreover, is available to man only by the Holy Spirit. The new evangelicals are adamant in their contention, however, that the revealed Word of God, Jesus Christ, must not be set against the written Word, that the latter is the original and definitive witness to Jesus Christ.[122]

Again, he states:

---

118. "Sword of the Spirit," *Reformed Review,* 66.
119. *Essentials,* 1:68.
120. Ibid., 2:273.
121. This is Mark A. Noll's observation from the foreword to Bloesch's *The Future of Evangelical Christianity,* xi.
122. *The Evangelical Renaissance,* 34.

It is commonplace today to try and draw a wedge between the historical expression of the faith given in Scripture and the object of faith, which is Jesus Christ. Yet we must recognize that we cannot have the divine content apart from the cultural and historical form in which this content comes to us. We must be frank enough to acknowledge a certain degree of historical and cultural contingency in the biblical witness to God in Christ; at the same time, we must insist that there is also an unchanging truth.[123]

While accepting the use of historical criticism and refusing to "posit an absolute equation between the letter of the Bible and divine revelation," Bloesch affirms the "unity of the biblical words with the self-revelation of Jesus Christ to whom these words are directed by the inspiration of the Spirit."[124] As one might expect from this understanding of the nature of biblical inspiration, Bloesch does not feel that the term "evangelical" should be "equated with a particular position on biblical inerrancy."[125] This should be particularly apparent since some hold to biblical inerrancy yet deny virtually every other evangelical doctrine. He does state that "it is not misguided or presumptuous for evangelicals who stand on the primacy and authority of Scripture and salvation by grace through faith in Christ to contend that they represent true Christianity."[126]

Christological Hermeneutic. In line with Karl Barth's great emphasis, Bloesch embraces a christological hermeneutic by which to explore and interpret Scripture.[127] What we experience in divine revelation is not God in His primary objectivity but "God in His secondary objectivity, i.e., in His self-manifestation in Christ."[128] The self-revelation of God in Jesus Christ functions as the absolute norm, whereas the "Bible, the proclamation of the church, and the life of faith implanted in man by the Spirit" are the secondary norms.[129] Put another way, "Jesus Christ and

---

123. *The Future of Evangelical Christianity*, 118. The point is not that these statements are wrong, but they seem to retract what he has stated in regard to the problematic nature of biblical inerrancy and the nature of how it does not contain error.

124. *Essentials*, 1:xi.

125. Ibid., 1:3. Bloesch has given a great deal of attention to defining what is meant by the term "evangelical," such as his article "Toward the Recovery of Our Evangelical Heritage," *Reformed Review*, vol. 39, no. 3 (Spring 1986), 192-198.

126. Donald G. Bloesch, "To Reconcile the Biblically Oriented," *The Christian Century* (July 16-23, 1970), 733.

127. Karl Barth, *Church Dogmatics*, published in thirteen part-volumes (Edinburgh: T & T Clark, 1936-1969), originally published in German under the title *Die Kirkliche Dogmatik* by Evangelischer Verlag A.G., Zollikon-Zurich. Bloesch cites Barth as one of his "principal theological mentors"; see "Karl Barth: Appreciation and Reservations," *How Karl Barth Changed My Mind*, ed. Donald K. McKim (Grand Rapids: Eerdmans, 1986), 126. Bloesch has written on Barth's doctrine of salvation in *Jesus Is Victor! Karl Barth's Doctrine of Salvation* (Nashville: Abingdon, 1976).

128. *Ground of Certainty*, 71.

129. *Ground of Certainty*, 74.

the message about him constitute the material norm of our faith just as the Bible is the formal norm."[130]

Therefore Scripture is interpreted in light of God's fullest revelation in Jesus Christ.[131] "Complete dependence on Christ instead of reason," writes Bloesch, "signifies not blind faith, but rather blind sight. In faith we know our Guide, and we know that He is reliable."[132]

The christological significance of the text is decisive. "This approach," writes Bloesch, "seeks to supplement the historical-critical method by theological exegesis in which the innermost intentions of the author are related to the center and culmination of sacred history mirrored in the Bible, namely, the advent of Jesus Christ."[133] Methodologically, Bloesch's hermeneutic proceeds as follows:

> With the theology of the Reformation and Protestant orthodoxy, I hold that we should begin by ascertaining the literal sense of the text—what was in the mind of the author—and we can do this only by seeing the passage in question in its immediate context. But then we should press on to discern its christological significance—how it relates to the message of the cross of Christ.[134]

This is how Bloesch responds to individuals such as Gadamer who espouse the new hermeneutic and the fusion of horizons. Rather than a fusion by "poetic divination into the language of the text" or a "mystical identification with the preconceptual experience of the author of the text," Bloesch argues for a "breaking in of the Word of God from the Beyond into our limited horizons and the remolding of them, in some cases even the overthrowing of them."[135]

Bloesch's Criteria of Truth

A brief comment needs to be made regarding Bloesch's criteria of truth. In an analysis of the theological encounter with philosophy, Bloesch writes that "it is our thesis that theology has been strongest and most vital when it has clearly recognized the differences between itself and secular philosophy." "When it has sought to establish common ground with philosophy for apologetic purposes, it has forfeited its integrity and become

---

130. *Essentials*, 1:62.

131. Bloesch, "A Christological Hermeneutic: Crisis and Conflict in Hermeneutics," *The Use of the Bible in Theology: Evangelical Options*, ed. by Robert K. Johnston (Atlanta: John Knox, 1985), 78-102. This hermeneutical approach is in conscious distinction to the hermeneutics of Protestant scholastic orthodoxy, historicism, and existentialism.

132. *Theological Notebook, Vol. I*, 5.

133. "A Christological Hermeneutic," *Uses of the Bible in Theology*, 81.

134. Ibid., 82.

135. Ibid., 84.

just another philosophy of religion."[136] Thus Bloesch's discussion of the various criteria of truth are "reasons which faith itself gives, namely, the witness of the Scriptures, the resurrection of Christ and the assurance of salvation."[137] Bloesch's discussion of the criteria of truth does not extend the analysis and explication he has already provided regarding the concept of truth operative in his system of thought, and therefore can be safely left unexamined beyond this level to avoid redundancy.

Critique of Bloesch's Concept of Truth

Donald G. Bloesch has offered a concise understanding of the concept of truth which has been constructed from a lifelong pursuit of theological reflection and thoughtful interaction with diverse viewpoints. His writing is clear; his tone, ecumenical; and his theology represents a growing number of individuals embracing historic, mainstream Evangelical affinities.

Yet Evangelical reactions to Bloesch's system of thought, particularly his concept of truth in relation to the subject of inerrancy, have been rather mixed. Bloesch himself notes that some persons would not even acknowledge him as an Evangelical in the traditional sense because he accepts the historical criticism of Scriptures and refuses to maintain an absolute equation between the letter of the Bible and divine revelation.[138]

The first Evangelical concern is Bloesch's apparent embrace of a "basically Barthian theological orientation."[139] David Dockery notes that Bloesch gives us a view of Scripture "with a Neo-orthodox flavor" with results very similar to G. C. Berkouwer "in stressing the function of Scripture."[140] R. P. Lightner dismisses Bloesch as someone who reveals "left-wing elements of contemporary evangelicalism" largely on the basis of such "neo-orthodox leanings."[141]

---

136. *Ground of Certainty*, 26.

137. Ibid., 194. In another place, Bloesch writes that the "criterion and standard for truth is none other than Holy Scripture"; see "To Reconcile the Biblically Oriented," *The Christian Century*, 734.

138. *Essentials*, 1:xi. R. P. Lightner seizes upon this quote in his review of Bloesch's first volume of *Essentials* to intimate that indeed Bloesch is not an Evangelical, see "Review of *Essentials of Evangelical Theology, Vol. 1,*" *Bibliotheca Sacra*, vol. 136, no. 542 (April-June 1979), 181.

139. Anthony A. Hoekema, "Review of *Essentials of Evangelical Theology, Vol. 1,*" *Calvin Theological Journal*, Vol. 14, No. 1 (April, 1979), 86. This is echoed in many reviews of Bloesch's systematic effort, such as in John Godsey's review of *Essentials of Evangelical Theology, Vol. 1* in *The Christian Century*, vol. XCV, no. 32 (October 11, 1978), 961.

140. David S. Dockery, "Review of *Essentials of Evangelical Theology, Vol. 1 and 2,*" *Grace Theological Journal*, vol. 2, no. 1 (Spring 1981), 153.

141. Lightener, "Review," *Bibliotheca Sacra*, 181.

A second Evangelical concern is that at points "our author takes back with his left hand what he has given with his right,"[142] especially regarding biblical inerrancy. Bloesch is unwilling to agree that "an unbiased investigation will disclose that the Bible does not err,"[143] but then he goes on to say that "only an investigation made by faith and to faith will disclose that the Scriptures are indeed the infallible and inerrant Word."[144] Dockery finds that such "paradoxical statements characterize his [Bloesch's] discussion in many areas."[145] H. D. McDonald adds that the juxtaposition of these two statements might "suggest that, while reason may apprehend that there are errors, faith can declare that this is not so. This would seem to advocate a dangerous sort of fideism and be an extraordinary example of 'blind faith.'"[146] Even non-Evangelical reviewers have noted that Bloesch's understanding of inerrancy will not please Evangelicals.[147] Lightner goes so far as to call Bloesch's view of inerrancy "questionable," concluding that what Bloesch presents is a "weak and watered-down form of what is essential in evangelical theology."[148] Clark Pinnock even suggests that Bloesch's use of the term is simply to retain the attention of his conservative readers.[149]

A third Evangelical concern is Bloesch's distrust of logic. Nash asserts that if Bloesch's rejection of the belief that "man's logic and knowledge are identical with God's"[150] means to say that "Christianity is irrational in the sense that it violates the law of noncontradiction, his view leads to absurdity."[151] Nash feels that Bloesch is representative of a group of

---

142. Ralph W. Vunderlink, "Review of *The Ground of Certainty,*" *Calvin Theological Journal,* vol. 8, no. 1 (April 1973), 87. Or as Edmund D. Cohen writes, Bloesch keeps "one foot on the gas, and the other on the brake," *The Mind of the Bible-Believer* (Buffalo, N.Y.: Prometheus, 1986), 51.

143. *Essentials,* 1:68.

144. Ibid., 1:68.

145. Dockery, "Review of *Essentials,*" *Grace Theological Journal,* 153.

146. H. D. McDonald, "Review of *Essentials of Evangelical Theology, Vol. 1,*" *Journal of the Evangelical Theological Society,* vol. 22, no. 3 (September 1979), 280.

147. David Foxgrover, "Review of *Essentials of Evangelical Theology, Vol. 2,*" *The Christian Century,* vol. XCVI, no. 6 (February 21, 1979), 192.

148. R. P. Lightner, "Review of *Essentials of Evangelical Theology, Vol. 2,*" *Bibliotheca Sacra,* vol. 137, no. 547 (July-September 1980), 279.

149. Clark Pinnock, "Review of *Essentials of Evangelical Theology, Vol. 1 and 2, Theology Today,* vol. 36, no. 2 (July 1979), 268.

150. *Essentials,* 1:75.

151. Ronald H. Nash, *The Word of God and the Mind of Man: The Crisis of Revealed Truth in Contemporary Theology* (Grand Rapids: Zondervan, 1982), 96. Nash writes that "If God possesses knowledge and humans possess something entirely different, then whatever is attained, it cannot be knowledge." This concern is shared by Donald A. Carson, "Unity and Diversity in the New Testament: The Possibility of Systematic Theology," *Scripture and Truth,* ed. D. A. Carson and John D. Woodbridge (Grand Rapids: Academie, 1973), 375, n. 127. In another place Carson assigns Bloesch to the emerging "left-wing of Evangelicals"; see "Recent Developments in the Doctrine of Scripture," *Hermeneutics, Authority, and Canon,* ed. D. A. Carson and John D. Woodbridge (Grand Rapids: Academie, 1986), 363, n. 6.

Evangelicals who reject the Logos doctrine and have no real confidence in God's ability to communicate propositional truth to the human mind, and as a result, give an "extremely fuzzy treatment of the relation between revelation and the Bible."[152] Nash perceives Bloesch as stating that only salvational passages in Scripture are revealed and, therefore, true. For Nash, this is a confusion between two different senses of truth, leading Bloesch to assert, even if indirectly, that God does not reveal truth in a nonsalvational sense. Thus Bloesch's basic error is to confuse the difference between truth and the apprehension of truth.[153]

Summary

According to Donald Bloesch, the truth was embodied in Christ's flesh. From this fundamental assertion the nature of theological truth is posited as that which corresponds to the self-revelation of God in Christ. Far from a correspondence of ideas, Bloesch maintains that truth is a comprehensive alignment of thought and deed with the God-Man. Thus his understanding of truth and error is far different than scientific facticity or even rational, logical coherency. Rather, it is faithfulness to the Word (Jesus Christ) within the Word (Scripture). Bloesch summarizes his own position well when he writes:

> Truth in the Bible means conformity to the will and purpose of God. Truth in today's empirical, scientific milieu means an exact correspondence between one's ideas or perceptions and the phenomena of nature and history. Error in the Bible means a deviation from the will and purpose of God, unfaithfulness to the dictates of his law. Error in the empirical mind-set of a technological culture means inaccuracy or inconsistency in what is reported as objectively occurring in nature or history. Technical precision is the measure of truth in empiricism. Fidelity to God's Word is the biblical criterion for truth. . . . The difference between the rational-empirical and the biblical understanding of truth is the difference between transparency to Eternity and literal facticity.[154]

Those outside of Evangelicalism raise several broad questions after studying Bloesch's concept of truth. The first is the issue of how an individual reaches the biblical Word in a contextual bipolarity that will include understanding the Word itself as well as grasping the existential situation over which the Word stands in judgment.[155] Here is the prob-

---

152. Nash, *Word of God and Mind of Man*, 122.
153. Ibid., 124-131. Carl F. H. Henry voiced a similar concern in *God, Revelation, and Authority, Vol. III: God Who Speaks and Shows* (Waco: Word, 1979), 475-476, and in *God, Revelation, and Authority, Vol. IV: God Who Speaks and Shows* (Waco: Word, 1979), 282.
154. Bloesch, *The Future of Evangelical Christianity*, 120.
155. This point is carefully articulated by P. Joseph Cahill's review of Bloesch's *The Ground of Certainty* in *The Catholic Biblical Quarterly*, vol. 34 (1972), 203.

lem of religious meaning as developed by the historico-critical method
and the new hermeneutics.

A second question is Bloesch's tendency toward fideism.[156] First Bloesch makes an absolute separation of theology and philosophy of religion.
Then he attacks the philosophy of religion. Is this fair, especially since it is
launched from the non-philosophical vantage point of revelation. Some
think this will lead to the collapse of philosophy of religion into philosophy, or at least a radical inversion of the usual meaning of philosophy of
religion.[157] Bloesch's attack on metaphysics on the basis that the "all-
encompassing perspective is the possession of God only"[158] is also critiqued on the grounds that if this is truly the case, then Bloesch cannot
claim the authority he does for his evangelical theology.[159]

A third broad question posed to Bloesch's system of thought is the
christological basis of knowledge that his program suggests. How are
the different criteria of faith grounded ultimately in the Person and work
of Christ?[160]

A fourth concern is whether Bloesch's system of thought actually
addresses what Rice calls the "central problem facing theology today,
namely, the challenge of modernity to the meaning and truth of Christian faith."[161] Put another way,

> while the problems outlined by Bloesch in this work [*Essentials of Evan-
> gelical Theology, Vol. 1 and 2*] are of vital importance to Evangelicals,
> they are not necessarily the most significant ones facing Christendom
> today. Of far more urgency, for example, is that noted by Nineham: the
> problem of cultural change. For hanging on this are the questions of the
> Bible as knowledge, as an authority to be appropriated today.[162]

---

156. Cahill comments that Bloesch's effort at explaining the more fideistic approach
involves so much rationalism that he wonders if Bloesch is doing anything more than
"reviewing the Kierkegaardian option with a bit of rationalism that perhaps Kierkegaard
himself would have found objectionable"; see "Review of *Ground of Certainty*," *The Catholic Biblical Quarterly*, 203. A similar concern is voiced by Vunderlink in his review of *The
Ground of Certainty*, where he writes that Bloesch is "unable to rid himself of philosophical influences," *Calvin Theological Journal*, 88.

157. Jerry Robbins, "Review of *The Ground of Certainty*," *Journal of the American
Academy of Religion*, vol. 40, no. 4 (December 1972), 580.

158. *Ground of Certainty*, 11.

159. Ibid.

160. A question posed by Robert T. Walker in his review of *The Ground of Certainty*
in the *Scottish Journal of Theology*, vol. 25 (1972), 237.

161. Richard Rice in his joint review of Bloesch's *Essentials of Evangelical Theology,
Vol. 1 and 2* and Carl F. H. Henry's *God, Revelation, and Authority, Vols. 1-4* in *Religious
Studies Review*, vol. 7, no. 2 (April 1981), 114. Rice feels that Bloesch addresses this problem, but laments that he attempts to resolve it with a "rationalistic view of revelation and a
deductivist approach to religious truth which even his evangelical colleagues find questionable." Rice finds the answer in a theology which would be "substantively conservative
and methodologically liberal."

162. Rodney L. Petersen, "Review of *Essentials of Evangelical Theology, Vol. 1 and 2*,"
The Princeton Seminary Bulletin, vol. 2, no. 3 (New Series 1979), 290.

Finally, there is the view of truth as that which "represents a cumulative expression of human religious experience and insight," often posited against the Evangelical idea that the Bible contains "the divinely authorized formulation of truth."[163]

---

163. A very broad yet basic distinction that is brought to bear upon Bloesch by Richard Rice, see "Review of *Essentials of Evangelical Theology, Vol. 1 and 2* and *God, Revelation, and Authority, Vols. 1-4* in *Religious Studies Review*, 108.

Chapter Nine

SUMMARY
OF THE CONCEPT
OF TRUTH IN
CONTEMPORARY AMERICAN
EVANGELICAL THEOLOGY

"Nature has instilled in our minds an insatiable desire to see truth."[1] A study of truth is particularly invigorating for Christian minds since the study of truth is mandatory for theology. Tillich reminded us that "since theology claims to be true, it must discuss the meaning of the term 'truth,' the nature of revealed truth, and its relation to other forms of truth."[2]

This study of the concept of truth in the theology of contemporary American Evangelical theology, examined through the works of Cornelius Van Til, Francis A. Schaeffer, Carl F. H. Henry, Millard J. Erickson, and Donald G. Bloesch, has demonstrated certain marks which can be put forth as characteristic of that concept. These marks, relevant to any conceptualization regarding the nature of truth, fall into three major catego-

---

1. Cicero, *Disputations*, I, 19.
2. Paul Tillich, *Systematic Theology* (Chicago: University of Chicago, 1967), 100.

ries: philosophy, theological method, and epistemology. One might think that only the first of these three categories is germane to the focus of this study, and to a point, this conclusion is warranted. The difficulty with such a conclusion, however, is that Evangelical theology makes a mistake shared with many others when approaching the concept of truth, namely that of confusing "what is truth" with "what is true." The first question, which is the focus of this study, is an ontological question. The second question, though necessarily engaged throughout this work in order to discover the various answers of those surveyed to the ontological question, is clearly an epistemological question. This important distinction is seldom made by those who approach a study of the concept of truth, and the individuals surveyed in this study are no exception. Further, theological method and understandings of special revelation are inextricably intertwined with the Evangelical concept of truth.

The philosophical category involves an underlying philosophical assumption of the correspondence theory of truth with an allegiance to the law of non-contradiction. The theological method of Evangelical theology is largely presuppositional in orientation. Finally, there is an embrace of the epistemological priority of special revelation as found in the Bible, which is construed as having a propositional element in its form and being inerrant in its nature. Together these form the basis of the concept of truth in contemporary American Evangelical theology as evidenced by the leading theologians who have been surveyed in this work.

Philosophy of the Evangelical Concept of Truth

The correspondence theory of truth underlies the concept of truth in contemporary American Evangelical theology. This correspondence is understood to be between humanity's understanding and God's revealed knowledge. Bloesch writes that when Christian theologians speak of correspondence, they "have in mind the correspondence of our thinking and the meaning of the Gospel."[3] This correspondence is not that which is exhaustive, but that which is faithful. The knowledge found in the Bible faithfully corresponds with God's knowledge, for it is God's self-revelation. Thus truth can be said to be objective and absolute, for it rests with God apart from subjective appropriation.

Herein lies an area of disagreement between those surveyed, for Van Til asserts that the only knowledge we can have within this correspondence is analogical, while Henry argues for a univocal element within this knowledge. Van Til bases his contention upon the distinction between Creator and created, thus eliminating humanity's potential for univocal knowledge of God. Henry argues for direct but not exhaustive

---

3. See Donald Bloesch, *The Ground of Certainty: Toward an Evangelical Theology of Revelation* (Grand Rapids: Eerdmans, 1971), 129.

correspondence between our knowledge and God's knowledge. Erickson attempts a synthesis between analogical language and univocal language. All, however, would contend for a correspondence that allows the knowledge found in the Bible to correspond faithfully to God's knowledge, thus giving humanity an epistemic base on which to stand that embodies God's truth.

For Van Til and Henry, this adherence to correspondence is less epistemological than it is ontological, but the ultimate correspondence of all truth to God's truth is accepted without question. As a result, Van Til and Henry would be seen by most to embrace a coherence view of truth. It is more accurate to say that they do not embrace an evidentialist approach to apologetics, and therefore they feel that tying truth to what can be empirically demonstrated is specious. They would not, however, deny the ontological necessity of ultimate correspondence between our understanding of what is truth and God's truth. Even epistemologically, therefore, the correspondence theory of truth underlies the coherence understandings embraced by Henry and Van Til.

The rationalistic criterion which determines the truthfulness of various assertions is the Aristotelian law of non-contradiction. Evangelicals find this rooted not in Aristotle's philosophical system but in "reality." The law of non-contradiction is essentially this: if something is true, its opposite is false.[4] Thus the idea of coherence is also important to Evangelical thought, for all truth is God's truth.[5] Yet while systems of thought are valued as to their coherence, truth is understood to be that which corresponds to reality, which rests in God's knowledge.

This contention raises an obvious and crucial question, namely, what is "reality"? Such a question is beyond the scope of this study. Evangelical thought would generally respond that "God is reality." The crucial move would then be to explicate the relationship between God's reality and human reality.

Donald Bloesch's theological formulations should not be included in this summation, for he represents a view that is somewhat out of line with mainstream Evangelical theology. While Bloesch acknowledges the validity of the correspondence theory of truth, he is often interpreted as one who rejects the law of non-contradiction. A qualifying remark should also be made in reference to Cornelius Van Til, who saw the law of non-contradiction as neither necessary nor sufficient. Yet this could easily be misunderstood, for it is not the actual principle of non-contradiction that Van Til repudiates, but its use by those who wish to dilute

---

4. As Schaeffer notes, the "basic antithesis is that God objectively exists in contrast (in antithesis) to His not existing"; see *The God Who Is There* in *The Complete Works of Francis A. Schaeffer*, vol. 1 (Westchester, Ill.: Crossway, 1982), 8.

5. Evangelical understandings of the unitary nature of truth can be evidenced by efforts to bring in areas such as the arts into the conversation, see Frank E. Gaebelein and D. Bruce Lockerbie, *The Christian, The Arts, and Truth* (Portland: Multnomah, 1985), 79-97.

the Creator-created distinction and elevate reason as that which provides the meeting point between human knowledge and the mind of God. Van Til is unclear in what appears to be the simultaneous rejection and use of the law of non-contradiction. How Van Til's appropriation of the principle of non-contradiction coalesces with his disavowal of extra-biblical principles also remains unclear.

In light of these philosophical understandings, the Evangelicals surveyed would not fall into the classical category of "rationalists," meaning those who embrace the idea that one can autonomously begin with reason and observation and come to ultimate answers regarding reality. What can be ascribed to Evangelical theology is "rationality," that which upholds the validity of thought and reason. This reason is applied to God's self-revelation, which is essential to Evangelical understandings and ultimate answers to questions regarding ontology, axiology, and epistemology. Evangelical theologians wish to move beyond mere statistical probability to the ground of certainty available in the living God.

Methodology of the Evangelical Concept of Truth

The methodology of the Evangelical concept of truth is largely presuppositional in nature, meaning that certain affirmations are presupposed independent of empirical verification. From these presuppositions reasoning and reflection begin. Presuppositionalism is the mandatory establishment of a particular worldview or conceptual framework which is then used to interpret all of reality. Although this has been the predominant methodological strain in the systems of thought surveyed in this work, it should not be construed as that which is characteristic of all Evangelical thought, for the divide within Evangelicalism between presuppositionalists and evidentialists is pervasive.[6]

Cornelius Van Til and Carl F. H. Henry are clearly the most vociferous regarding presuppositionalism. Van Til's presuppositional methodology can best be understood in terms of "self-authenticating biblical claims" with all knowledge understood in terms of "analogy." Francis Schaeffer and Millard Erickson attempt to blend presuppositionalism and evidentialism, suggesting that one begins with presuppositions but then validates those presuppositions through evidence.[7]

---

6. Evangelical works in favor of an evidentialist perspective include R. C. Sproul, John Gerstner, and Arthur Lindsley, *Classical Apologetics: A Rational Defense of the Christian Faith and a Critique of Presuppositional Apologetics* (Grand Rapids: Academie, 1984), and John Warwick Montgomery, *Faith Founded on Fact: Essays in Evidential Apologetics* (Nashville: Thomas Nelson, 1978), whose introductory essay is a harsh polemic against Carl F. H. Henry's presuppositionalist methodology in *God, Revelation and Authority* (Waco: Word, 1976).

7. In an earlier chapter, I suggested that Schaeffer is best termed an evidentialist in regard to apologetics as opposed to being a Van Tillian presuppositionalist. This designation is in light of his comparison to Van Til's rejection of external validation of the Christian faith. In broad categories of theological method, however, Schaeffer would remain in the presuppositionalist camp. When pressed on this issue, Schaeffer denied falling into either category, perhaps as a result of his own inconsistency on this point.

Van Til's insistence on presuppositionalism is found within his view of the total depravity of humanity, a depravity which includes both thought and reason. Such a perspective mandates the presupposition of the truth of Scripture over and against the knowledge of humanity to avoid surrendering the sovereignty of God. For Van Til, the term "presupposition" is more than an epistemological or methodological axiom. It is rather an ontological referent. Henry's insistence on presuppositionalism is a reaction against aligning the truth of theology with what can be empirically verified, for that would omit the meaning and significance which divine revelation gives to factual events.

In spite of differing reasons for holding to a methodology of presuppositionalism, however, all surveyed in this study begin their theological construction presupposing a God "who is there who has not been silent."[8] As a result, the truthfulness of the Scriptures are accepted on the basis of the Scripture's own witness. Opinions differ, however, about the use of empirical verification once that presupposition is made. Van Til would allow for little if any, while Erickson would allow for much validation from external data. Henry asserts that in viewing this presuppositionalism, one should not assume that it is merely philosophical presuppositionalism, but rather that it is anchored in God's self-revelation.[9]

Epistemology of the Evangelical Concept of Truth

The epistemological question is simply "How do we know?" The Evangelical answers: "through God's self-revelation in the Bible." Most Evangelicals would give epistemological primacy to the self-revelation of God in Jesus Christ while asserting that our knowledge of Jesus Christ and subsequent interpretation of His life and ministry is found through the testimony of the primary witnesses recorded in Scripture.[10] This recorded testimony is inspired by God, not through mechanical dictation, but through the movement of the Holy Spirit upon the biblical authors to record what God intended.

Strictly speaking, this is not an epistemological answer, but rather a "source" or "basis" answer. Evangelicals insist we know through the appropriation of God's knowledge as revealed in Scripture. Other sources of knowledge, such as experience, are not denied; but the ultimate epistemic base is God, and thus His self-revelation is paramount.

---

8. This phrase is borrowed from Schaeffer's *He Is There and He Is Not Silent* in *The Complete Works of Francis A. Schaeffer*, vol. 1 (Westchester, Ill.: Crossway, 1982).

9. Henry, *God, Revelation and Authority*, 1:219.

10. Of those Evangelical theologians surveyed, Donald Bloesch has given the most conscious attention to the epistemological primacy of Jesus Christ, with Erickson giving the most emphasis to the epistemological primacy of God.

Scripture is understood to contain a propositional element in regard to form. Henry writes that the Bible is "rational communication conveyed in intelligible ideas and meaningful words, that is, in conceptual-verbal form."[11] Erickson contends that "truth is a quality of propositions."[12] Not every Evangelical should be caricatured, however, as holding to the idea that all of Scripture can be reduced to that which is strictly propositional in nature.

Evangelicals would also embrace Aristotle's concern that the "least deviation from the truth is multiplied later a thousandfold."[13] The Bible's inerrancy is posited as both ontologically and epistemologically necessary. Inerrancy is ontologically necessary as a result of God's nature[14] and epistemologically necessary in light of the perceived propositional nature of much of God's special revelation in Scripture.[15] By inerrancy, Evangelicals intend to say that God's Word provides knowledge regarding faith and morality that is without error. Further, Evangelicals would assert that biblical teaching regarding morality transcends time and context; thus the idea of "absolutes" regarding truth are conveyed. This stands opposed to the idea that every individual must decide personally what is right or wrong according to one's own perspective and situation. The Evangelical perspective holds that when the Bible speaks to issues outside of faith and morality, such as history or science, it speaks authoritatively and without error. This historical and scientific inerrancy is only asserted, however, in regard to those passages where the context intimates that the biblical author intended to speak to a historical or scientific issue in a factual manner. Thus the Evangelical concept of inerrancy involves the entire biblical narrative. Yet as Carl Henry's use of the "Chicago Statement" on biblical inerrancy demonstrates, not to mention Millard Erickson's definition of biblical inerrancy, this is not a wooden inerrancy that is removed from contemporary hermeneutical insights.

The degree and type of knowledge given by Scripture, however, is far from uniform in the writers surveyed. Van Til seems to conclude that if some proposition is not actually revealed in the Bible, then it is unknowable by human beings. This would intimate that all fields of knowledge, in order to be authentic, must find their epistemic base in

---

11. Henry, *God, Revelation and Authority*, 1:12.

12. Millard Erickson, *Christian Theology* (Grand Rapids: Baker, 1983, 1984, 1985), 56.

13. Aristotle, "On the Heavens," *The Oxford Translation of Aristotle*, ed. and trans. W.D. Ross (Oxford: Oxford University, 1928), 271b9.

14. The reasoning generally proceeds along the line that if a perfect God who has revealed Himself, then no error could be contained as part of that self-revelation. Or as J. I. Packer has written, "to assert biblical inerrancy . . . is just to confess faith in (i) the divine origin of the Bible and (ii) the truthfulness and trustworthiness of God"; see *Fundamentalism and the Word of God: Some Evangelical Principles* (Grand Rapids: Eerdmans, 1958), 96.

15. Such conclusions naturally flow from the correspondence theory of truth and the law of non-contradiction.

Scripture. Donald Bloesch, on the other hand, feels that the knowledge contained in Scripture is limited largely to the salvific mission of Jesus Christ. Schaeffer, Henry, and Erickson would contend that the truth Scripture intends to convey is tied to authorial intent and to that degree is comprehensive.

Evangelical Shift

This study reveals something of a transition within the concept of truth operative in American Evangelical theology, a transition that has been explored sociologically by James Davison Hunter and is best explored theologically through the various discussions surrounding the topic of biblical inerrancy.[16] Hunter has discovered that among a new generation of Evangelicals, the theory of biblical inerrancy has softened to the degree that some believe that the biblical writer may have intended the facticity of a statement which is in reality mistaken or contradictory. Hunter also found a growing neo-orthodoxy which advocates a subjectivist approach to biblical interpretation.

One of the more celebrated cases of this transition in Evangelical theology is Clark Pinnock. As an Evangelical who had argued passionately for biblical inerrancy based largely on a correspondence understanding of truth in previous publications,[17] Pinnock chose to depart from this epistemic base while continuing to hold to the Bible's trustworthiness and authority.[18] Pinnock concluded that those who hold to inerrancy are "elevating reason over Scripture at that point."[19] His own description of his evolution is one that goes beyond Modernism and Fundamentalism to a form of postmodern orthodoxy.[20] Koivisto's conclusion is that Pinnock's concept of truth changed from that of correspondence to that of pragmatism.[21] Erickson and Bloesch seem to have sympathies with Pinnock, particularly Bloesch, as they, too, have left the strict rationalism of Evangelical theology which had been characterized by such persons as Carl Henry, Ronald Nash, Kenneth Kantzer, and Gordon Clark.

---

16. See James Davison Hunter, *Evangelicalism: The Coming Generation* (Chicago and London: University of Chicago, 1987).

17. For example, see *A Defense of Biblical Infallibility* (Phillipsburg: Presbyterian and Reformed, 1967) and *Biblical Revelation, the Foundation of Christian Theology* (Chicago: Moody, 1971).

18. The work which clearly revealed Clark Pinnock's shift was *The Scripture Principle* (San Francisco: Harper and Row, 1984).

19. *The Scripture Principle*, 58.

20. See Pinnock's *Tracking the Maze: Finding Our Way through Modern Theology from an Evangelical Perspective* (San Francisco: Harper and Row, 1990).

21. See Rex A. Koivisto, "Clark Pinnock and Inerrancy: A Change in Truth Theory?," *Journal of the Evangelical Theological Society*, vol. 24, no. 2 (June 1981), 139-152. What is not addressed by Koivisto, yet decisive at this point, is the understanding that the pragmatic view does not address the concept of truth so much as the question of whether something is true.

The window for this transition has been through the various understandings of biblical inerrancy and the nature of special revelation.[22] The definition of inerrancy as held by Erickson, Bloesch, and Pinnock has become more nuanced and less tied to a correspondence theory of truth. These nuances can even be used to challenge the term's definitional efficacy.[23] What seems at issue is a growing awareness of the phenomenological status of Scripture as well as the personal element neo-orthodoxy stresses in relation to the Word of God. Evangelical reactions to the theology of Karl Barth are an excellent example of this shift. At first there was a vigorous, negative reaction among Evangelicals toward Barth's personal, subjective understanding of the Word of God in relation to personal response. This was most clearly manifested in Cornelius Van Til, Francis A. Schaeffer, and Carl F. H. Henry.[24] It was feared that neo-orthodoxy could lead to the meaning of a biblical narrative varying so widely from person to person that a radical subjectivism would be inevitable. Yet in contemporary American Evangelical theology we find Millard Erickson evidencing a growing respect for neo-orthodox insights, with Bloesch suggesting wholehearted acceptance on many decisive points.[25] One might therefore conclude with Johnston that "'Where is it written?'—as an appeal to Biblical authority—seems at present to be an inadequate basis for providing theological unity" for Evangelicals.[26] No debate occurs among Evangelicals that God is truth, and that in God's Word truth is revealed to us. The nature of that truth is at issue. A growing number of Evangelicals are making several pivotal modifications of earlier views: first, that Scripture is a narrative and needs to be interpreted in light of that narrative's intent and form; second, that the Word of God is primarily that which points to a Person,

---

22. See Richard Quebedeaux, *The Young Evangelicals: The Story of the Emergence of a New Generation of Evangelicals* (San Francisco: Harper and Row, 1974), 37-41, 73-81.

23. For example, Bloesch contends for an understanding of inerrancy that does "not imply factual accuracy"; see *The Evangelical Renaissance* (Grand Rapids: Eerdmans, 1973), 56. This applies even in the realm of "theological and ethical ideas"; see *Essentials of Evangelical Theology, Volume 1: God, Authority, and Salvation* (San Francisco: Harper and Row, 1978), 68. Individuals who have attempted to maintain a sense of coherence with the many definitional nuances include David S. Dockery, who posits nine different categories in relation to adherents of biblical inerrancy in "Variations on Inerrancy," *SBC Today* (May 1986), 10-11.

24. On Evangelical interpretations and reactions to Barth, see Gregory C. Bolich, *Karl Barth and Evangelicalism* (Downers Grove: InterVarsity, 1980), and Richard Albert Mohler, Jr., "Evangelical Theology and Karl Barth: Representative Models of Response" (Ph.D. dissertation, the Southern Baptist Theological Seminary, 1989).

25. Hunter notes the irony that neo-orthodoxy, a theological movement that has essentially "played itself out," is enjoying its resurgence within Evangelicalism, initially its most ardent foe, see *Evangelicalism: The Coming Generation*, 27. Hunter also reports that nearly 40 percent of all Evangelical theologians have now abandoned the belief in the inerrancy of Scripture, see 31.

26. Robert K. Johnston, *Evangelicals at an Impasse: Biblical Authority in Practice* (Atlanta: John Knox Press, 1979), 7.

and only secondarily to the primary witness to that Person as recorded in Scripture; third, that reason is limited and not all-encompassing; and fourth, that truth is not to be understood strictly in terms of correspondence, but that dynamic response, obedience, and effectiveness in regard to intent are just as decisive in one's conceptualization of truth.

Perhaps terming this an Evangelical "shift" is misleading, for what seems to be taking place is not so much a "shift" as a loss of consensus. There has never been a "golden age" of Evangelical thought where theological unanimity reigned supreme, for Evangelicalism has always been something of a mosaic (both theologically and sociologically); However, now there is a loss of consensus on those few issues that did bind Evangelicals together theologically. If the individual at Dallas Theological Seminary who stated that Evangelicalism rested upon the twin pillars of dispensationalism and biblical inerrancy was correct, then Evangelicalism is facing a difficult future, for those twin pillars are far from erect.[27]

---

27. Randall Balmer, *Mine Eyes Have Seen the Glory: A Journey into the Evangelical Subculture in America* (New York and Oxford: Oxford University Press, 1989), 31-32.

Chapter Ten

NON-EVANGELICAL
REACTIONS TO THE
EVANGELICAL
CONCEPT OF TRUTH

The three marks of the Evangelical concept of truth will provide the framework for a critique of the concept's tenability in terms of the wider theological conversation among non-Evangelicals. An evaluation of the strength or weakness of these critiques of Evangelical theology will be offered in the following section.

Philosophical Critique

The first critique of the philosophy of the Evangelical concept of truth is that which disavows the correspondence theory of truth. While many Evangelicals are divided over an epistemology based on coherence understandings versus correspondence understandings, few deny the ultimate ontological correspondence of all truth to God's truth. The non-Evangelical world, not as compelled to posit an ultimate referent such as God, is less eager to embrace such an understanding.

The scope of this study will not allow a comprehensive listing or evaluation of the many challenges to the correspondence theory of truth, so only a few of the more recent studies will be mentioned. Brian Ellis has examined the correspondence theory of truth and has posited five reasons for its rejection: (1) the failure of the various programs of analysis; (2) the variety of kinds of truth; (3) the lack of adequate truth bearers for a semantic theory; (4) if beliefs or other psychological states are the bearers of truth, then they are also the relata of logical relationships, and the subject matter of logic is psychological; and (5) the lack of epistemic value in correspondence relationships.[1] Donald Davidson finds that most critics reject the correspondence theory of truth on the grounds that there "is nothing interesting or instructive to which true sentences might correspond."[2] In other words, one needs to locate the fact or part of reality to which a true sentence corresponds. The argument is that

> one can locate individual objects, if the sentence happens to name or describe them, but even such location makes sense relative only to a frame of reference, and so presumably the frame of reference must be included in whatever it is to which a true sentence corresponds. Following out this line of thought . . . if true sentences correspond to anything at all, it must be the universe as a whole; thus, all true sentences correspond to the same thing.[3]

Davidson himself has difficulty with the correspondence theory of truth on the grounds that "such theories fail to provide entities to which truth vehicles (whether we take these to be statements, sentences or utterances) can be said to correspond."[4]

Another challenge comes from philosophical postmodernism, often called "deconstructive" or "eliminative" postmodernism. This perspective

---

1. On this, see Brian Ellis, *Truth and Objectivity* (Oxford: Basil Blackwell, 1990), 113-190. Another survey of arguments against the correspondence theory of truth can be found in W. D. Robinson's "Reason, Truth and Theology," *Modern Theology*, vol. 2, no. 2 (January 1986), 87-105.

2. Donald Davidson, "The Structure and Content of Truth," *The Journal of Philosophy*, vol. 87, no. 6 (June 1990), 303. This article was first presented as three lectures on "The Concept of Truth" given at Columbia University in November 1989. This argument was first presented by C. I. Lewis in *An Analysis of Knowledge and Valuation* (LaSalle, Ill.: Open Court, 1946), 50-55.

3. See Davidson, "The Structure and Content of Truth," *The Journal of Philosophy*, 303.

4. Davidson, "The Structure and Content of Truth," *The Journal of Philosophy*, 304. See also Ralph C. S. Walker, "Coherence, Correspondence, and Anti-Realism," in *The Coherence Theory of Truth: Realism, Anti-Realism, Idealism* (London: Routledge, 1989), 20-40, who shares a similar concern with the correspondence theory, but finds the essential problem in the incoherency of the idea of independently existing facts and the contention that an intelligible account can be given for the correspondence relation. Yet Davidson returns to the correspondence theory and defends a version of it in his essay "True to the Facts" in *Inquiries into Truth and Interpretation* (Oxford: Clarendon, 1984/1991), 37-54.

overcomes the modern world view through an anti-world view. David Ray Griffin writes that this movement "deconstructs or eliminates the ingredients necessary for a worldview, such as God, self, purpose, meaning, a real world, and truth as correspondence."[5]

A second critique of Evangelical philosophy concerns the rationalistic criterion of the law of non-contradiction. From a practical standpoint, it is maintained that the law of non-contradiction is not conducive to the process of theological construction. In other words, holding to the idea that God cannot be both personal and impersonal is far from supportive of the statement that the personal God who created the universe is the triune God of the Christian faith. Further, not every opposite is a contradictory. Therefore, the desire to show that the correspondence of the Christian faith with reality is true through the law of non-contradiction is deficient, for it can only show coherence, existential plausibility, and meaningfulness.

A third critique of Evangelical philosophy is the concern that theologians within Evangelicalism have not adequately explained the dynamics between the use of reason and the noetic consequences of the fall. Are such disciplines as mathematics prone to error in the same way that unregenerate thinking apart from biblical revelation is prone to error? This raises the question of Evangelical theology's comprehensive use of reason and logic.[6] Even certain Evangelicals, such as Arthur Holmes,

---

5. David Ray Griffin, "Introduction to SUNY Series in Constructive Postmodern Thought," *Varieties of Postmodern Theology* (New York: State University of New York, 1989), xii. Griffin notes that for the deconstructionist, "talk about truth as correspondence of interpretation to reality makes no sense"; see "Postmodern Theology and A/Theology: A Response to Mark Taylor," 34.

On deconstructionism, see Thomas J. J. Altizer, et al., *Deconstruction and Theology* (New York: Crossroad, 1982); Mark Taylor, *Deconstructing Theology*, American Academy of Religion Studies in Religion, No. 28 (New York: Crossroad and Scholars Press, 1982); and Charles E. Winquist, *Epiphanies of Darkness: Deconstruction in Theology* (Philadelphia: Fortress Press, 1986). The most important writer for deconstructionism is Jacques Derrida. An introduction to Derrida's writings would include the following: *Dissemination*, trans. Barbara Johnson (Chicago: University of Chicago, 1981); *Glas* (Paris: Editions Galilee, 1974); *Of Grammatology*, trans. G. C. Spivak (Baltimore: Johns Hopkins University, 1976); *Speech and Phenomena and Other Essays on Husserl's Theory of Signs*, trans. David Allison (Evanston: Northwestern University, 1973); and *Writing and Difference*, trans. Alan Bass (Chicago: University of Chicago, 1978).

6. An interesting conversation is taking place in contemporary physics that is beyond the scope of this study to explore but concerns the nature of scientific truth. The quantum theory in physics has encouraged many physicists to posit that objective reality is nonexistent, therefore discussions about truth are not meaningful to explore. Rather theories are explored as to their "usefulness." On this, see Paul Davies, *God and the New Physics* (New York: Simon and Schuster, 1983); Stephen W. Hawking, *A Brief History of Time: From the Big Bang to Black Holes* (New York: Bantam, 1988); and Roger Penrose, *The Emperor's New Mind: Concerning Computers, Minds, and the Laws of Physics* (Oxford: Oxford University, 1989). A recent work which will prove helpful in such discussions is Ian Barbour's *Religion in an Age of Science: The Gifford Lectures, 1989-1991, Volume One* (San Francisco: Harper and Row, 1990), particularly 95-124.

argue for the distinction between reason serving as a capacity for under-standing and reason as a capacity for proving universally true proposi-tions.[7] The underlying concern would seem to be the appearance that Evangelicals have elevated logic above God and personal encounter. Liberation theologians put forth another dimension to this. They posit that "there is no truth outside or beyond the historical events in which men are involved as agents. There is, therefore, no knowledge except in action itself, in the process of transforming the world through participa-tion in history."[8] Hegelian thinkers would further question whether truth is objective and absolute, arguing instead for an ongoing formula of the-sis, antithesis, and synthesis, which in turn becomes a thesis, continuing as an ongoing dialectic. Comprehensive defenses of philosophical rela-tivism also challenge Evangelical understandings of truth's objectivity and transcendence.[9]

Another related concern is that antithesis as the sole insight into the nature of truth fails to take into account the changing nature of language and thought, and leaves little room for ambiguity, paradox, or relativism. Therefore, a system of thought such as Carl F. H. Henry's is perceived as one that limits God to the bounds of reason through an insistence on univocal language. It is also charged that Enlightenment rationalism is being used indiscriminately and out of context as a framework for truth.

Perhaps the broadest question of all put to Evangelical sensibilities is whether truth is rational in an exclusively deductive sense. Thomas F. Torrance gives the impression of one who claims to find a difference between God's logic and human logic, concluding that human logic cannot be related to a transcendent God.[10] This view is somewhat espoused by two individuals surveyed in this study. Donald Bloesch contends that human logic and knowledge are not to be identified with God's. Cornelius Van Til contends that human knowledge and God's knowledge never coincide.

Methodological Critique

Presuppositionalism is perhaps most often challenged on the grounds that it is circular in its reasoning and by its very nature fideistic. Geisler critiques fideism as a method and test for truth as follows: (1) confusion between epistemology and ontology; (2) failure to distinguish between

---

7. Arthur F. Holmes, *All Truth Is God's Truth* (Grand Rapids: Eerdmans, 1977), 47.

8. See Jose Miguez Bonino, *Doing Theology in a Revolutionary Situation* (Philadel-phia: Fortress, 1975), 88.

9. For example, see Joseph Margolis' *The Truth About Relativism* (Oxford: Basil Blackwell, 1991). A more popular presentation of relativism with a "New Age" reinterpre-tation of history can be found in Richard Tarnas, *The Passion of the Western Mind* (New York: Harmony, 1991), 435.

10. See *Theological Science* (London: Oxford University, 1969).

belief "in" and belief "that" there is a God; (3) neglect to differentiate between the basis of belief in God and the support or warrant for that belief; (4) neglect and sometimes negation of the need for the propositional in its zeal to stress the personal; (5) failure to understand the implications of the difference between the unavoidability of and the justifiability of presuppositions; and (6) fideism faces the dilemma of whether it is making a truth claim or it is not.[11] The essence of the problem is that presuppositions are in and of themselves either true or false. Simply to proceed on the basis of one's own presuppositions without a rational defense gives the impression that faith is irrational. As John Hick has observed, "the majority of recent philosophical critics of religion have in mind a definition of faith as the believing of propositions upon insufficient evidences."[12] To be sure, the Evangelical theologians surveyed in this work would argue that their presuppositions are proven, not merely selected, but critics argue that their "proof" is indirect at best. For example, Cornelius Van Til's indirect proof is that the existence of God is necessary for the "uniformity of nature and for the coherence of all things in the world;" for Van Til, this is "absolutely certain proof."[13]

Epistemological Critique

The epistemology of the Evangelical concept of truth has received the most severe criticism. Critics do not so much deny special revelation as they question the idea which Evangelical theology puts forth as to the character of that special revelation. Critics ask whether the Bible contains truth which is inerrant in nature and propositional in form. In other words, the question is first raised regarding the assumption of the Bible's truthfulness in terms of propositions,[14] and then second, that those propositional truths are given in a rational form that addresses all of reality inerrantly. Theologians who oppose the propositional nature of God's truth include many of the leading thinkers of contemporary Christendom.[15] "God does not give us information by communication,"

---

11. Norman Geisler, *Christian Apologetics* (Grand Rapids: Baker, 1976), 61-64; in his exposition of major fideistic views, Geisler surveys Pascal, Kierkegaard, Barth, and Van Til, the latter of which he categorizes as one who embraces "revelational fideism."

12. John Hick, *Philosophy of Religion*, 4th ed. (Englewood Cliffs: Prentice Hall, 1990), 58.

13. See Cornelius Van Til, *Defense of the Faith*, 3rd ed. (Philipsburg, N.J.: Presbyterian and Reformed Publishing Co., 1967), 103.

14. On this, see L. Harold DeWolf, *The Case for Theology in Liberal Perspective* (Philadelphia: Westminster Press, n.d.) 46-59.

15. A summation of the many critiques lodged against a propositional understanding of revelation can be found succinctly stated by Avery Dulles in *Models of Revelation* (New York: Image, 1985), 48-52. Noteworthy theologians who would embrace a non-cognitive or non-propositional view of revelation would include H. Richard Niebuhr, *The Meaning of Revelation* (New York: Macmillan, 1962); Rudolf Bultmann, *Theology of the New Testament* (New York: Scribner, 1955); and Paul Tillich, *Systematic Theology* (Chicago: University of Chicago Press, 1951, 1957, 1963).

writes John Baillie, rather "He gives us Himself in communion."[16] Stated
another way, instead of information about Himself that is revealed, it is
God Himself who is disclosed.

George Lindbeck denies that sentences are even to be identified with
propositions in regard to doctrine.[17] Lindbeck sees three fundamental
approaches for theology: the propositional, the expressive-experiential,
and his own "cultural-linguistic." Lindbeck proposes a truth-theory that
combines the correspondence, coherence, and pragmatic theories of
truth by likening religion to a single gigantic proposition. He separates
ontology from methodological concerns, thereby making biblical doctrines second-order truth claims, affirming nothing about the extra-linguistic or extra-human reality. Concern can also be expressed that a
propositional understanding of God's special revelation becomes static
and lifeless, something which belongs to the past and is unable to
address adequately the contemporary situation.

Another group rejects propositional understandings of God's revelation because of God's transcendence.[18] In this understanding, God is so
radically "other" that the human mind is incapable of comprehending
the divine mind. This understanding is also put forth in terms of the perceived distinction between personal revelation and propositional revelation. If personal, then revelation becomes an event in which God
discloses Himself.[19] The existentialist perspective would argue that truth
belongs "to the concreteness of existence," something more "concrete
than the truth of propositions."[20] Phenomenologists would contend that
"truth refers to being, rather than to knowledge."[21] This contention also
forms the basis for the phenomenologist's rejection of a correspondence
understanding of truth, for truth is that which is "experienced" (Husserl)
or "manifested" (Heidegger). Many phenomenologists would also maintain a historicism that posits truth as a product of an epoch's or society's
convictional system. As David Tracy states, "Truth is here understood,
on the side of the object, as the power of disclosure and concealment in

16. John Baillie, *The Idea of Revelation in Recent Thought* (New York: Columbia University, 1956), 29.

17. George A. Lindbeck, *The Nature of Doctrine: Religion and Theology in a Postliberal Age* (Philadelphia: Westminster, 1984), 67-69.

18. Though he desires to hold on to something of a propositional element, Richard J.
Beauchesne maintains that transcendence itself accounts for the inadequacy of proposi-
tions; see "Truth, Mystery, and Expression: Theological Perspectives Revisited," *Journal of
Ecumenical Studies*, vol. 25, no. 4 (Fall 1988), 555-572.

19. Emil Brunner held to this view, maintaining that revelation is an "event"; see *Revelation and Reason* (Philadelphia: Westminster, 1946).

20. John Macquarrie, *Existentialism: An Introduction, Guide, and Assessment* (New
York: Penguin, 1972), 137. In a similar vein, Heidegger would seem to contend that truth is
something which "happens"; see "On the Essence of Truth," *Basic Writings*, ed. David Farrell Krell (San Francisco: Harper and Row, 1977), 117-141.

21. Louis Dupre, "Truth in Religion and Truth of Religion" in *Phenomenology of the
Truth Proper to Religion*, ed. Daniel Gurriere (Albany: State University of New York, 1990), 19.

the object itself; and that disclosure is related to truth as an experience of recognition on the side of the subject."[22]

Critiques of Evangelical epistemology seldom avoid the subject of biblical inerrancy, and usually include the following concerns: first, there is no inerrant copy of the inerrant original. Second, the extant copies which we do have in our possession contain "error." Third, positing the objective truth of Scripture as God's self-revelation does not address the question of subjective appropriation, thus making inerrancy irrelevant. Fourth, the Bible does not teach its own inerrancy. Fifth, the idea of biblical inerrancy is a philosophical category artificially imposed upon the biblical materials that is alien to the Bible's nature and intent. Sixth, biblical inerrancy demands either an infallible hermeneutic or a literal hermeneutic, both of which are problematic. Seventh, inerrancy flows from the faulty understanding of revelation as text as opposed to original witness to revelation.[23]

Another area of concern for many who come into contact with the epistemology of the Evangelical concept of truth is the perception that Evangelical theology maintains that biblical Christianity is the only rational interpretation of the universe in which we live. In other words, it is not uncommon, indeed perhaps characteristic, of Evangelical theology to assume that the truth of the Bible, God's truth, is given in propositional form. Moreover, many Evangelicals would assert that the Bible's truthfulness goes beyond faith and ethics and enters the realms of science and history. A fundamental question is whether this is indeed the case and whether there are fields of knowledge to which the Bible does not speak.

---

22. David Tracy, *Plurality and Ambiguity: Hermeneutics, Religion, Hope* (San Francisco: Harper and Row, 1987), 28. Tracy maintains that truth is that which manifests itself, or put another way, it is "manifestation," 29.

23. Some of the more recent publications which have argued against biblical inerrancy have been generated by the controversy within the Southern Baptist Convention, which has found itself embroiled in division over this very subject. Such works include, but are not limited to, the following: David S. Dockery and Philip D. Wise, "Biblical Inerrancy: Pro or Con?," *The Theological Educator*, no. 37 (Spring 1988), 15-44; Roy L. Honeycutt, Jr., *Biblical Authority: A Treasured Heritage* (Louisville: Review and Expositor, n.d.); Gordon James, *Inerrancy and the Southern Baptist Convention* (Dallas: Southern Baptist Heritage Press, 1986); Robison James, ed., *The Unfettered Word: Southern Baptists Confront the Authority-Inerrancy Questions* (Waco: Word, 1987); *The Proceedings of the Conference on Biblical Inerrancy, 1987* (Nashville: Broadman, 1987); Clayton Sullivan, *Toward a Mature Faith: Does Biblical Inerrancy Make Sense?* (Decatur: SBC Today, 1990). Beyond the recent writings generated by the controversy of the Southern Baptist Convention, one of the most persistent critics of biblical inerrancy has been James Barr, evidenced by such works as *Beyond Fundamentalism* (Philadelphia: Westminster, 1984); *Fundamentalism* (London: SCM, 1977); *Holy Scripture: Canon, Authority, Criticism* (Philadelphia: Westminster, 1983); and *The Scope and Authority of the Bible* (London: SCM, 1980). Barr's engagement has elicited many responses, the most focused being Paul Ronald Wells' *James Barr and the Bible: Critique of a New Liberalism* (Phillipsburg, N.J.: Presbyterian and Reformed, 1980).

What of the realms of science, mathematics, and psychology?[24] If biblical Christianity as a rational interpretation of the universe does not address these areas, from where does the truth of these other areas come? Perhaps this question could be stated more briefly in the following statement that many would embrace: not all truth is about God.

Finally, if the Bible is posited as the source of true knowledge about God, then the enormous hermeneutical question comes to the vanguard of all concerns.[25] Henry understands reason to be the over-arching hermeneutic for accessing the truth of the biblical materials. Many would see this as too closely joining the idea of special revelation with that of Enlightenment rationalism. Even further, recent hermeneutical insights contend that the interpreter stands in a stream of tradition which predisposes one's interpretive abilities. This, at least, is the suggestion of Hans Georg Gadamer, who understands the hermeneutical problem to be that of achieving an agreement with someone else about the shared world.[26] This communication takes the form of a dialogue that results in what Gadamer calls a "fusion of horizons." Tradition affects our reading of any text; thus we bring "legitimate prejudices" to bear upon our interpretation. David Tracy states, "No interpreter enters into the attempt to understand any text or any historical event without prejudgments formed by the history of the effects of her or his culture."[27] This would argue forcefully against approaching the Bible as any type of objective source of knowledge. John D. Caputo states that "what we today call hermeneutics, the theories of interpretation that have emerged in the wake of Heidegger's *Being and Time*, are to no small degree a relentless critique of objectivistic conceptions of truth, in particular, of historical objectivism."[28]

---

24. An excellent introduction to various Evangelical "standpoints" in terms of various fields of scholarship can be found in Mark A. Noll's *Between Faith and Criticism: Evangelicals, Scholarship, and the Bible in America* (San Francisco: Harper and Row, 1986), 143-161.

25. Excellent introductions to contemporary hermeneutical questions being raised can be found in Josef Bleicher, *Contemporary Hermeneutics: Hermeneutics as Method, Philosophy and Critique* (London: Routledge and Kegan Paul, 1980); Kurt Mueller-Vollmer, ed., *The Hermeneutics Reader: Texts of the German Tradition from the Enlightenment to the Present* (New York: Continuum, 1989); Richard E. Palmer, *Hermeneutics: Interpretation Theory in Schleiermacher, Dilthey, Heidegger, and Gadamer* (Evanston: Northwestern University, 1969); John B. Thompson, *Critical Hermeneutics: A Study in the Thought of Paul Ricoeur and Jurgen Habermas* (Cambridge: Cambridge University, 1981).

26. Hans Georg Gadamer, *Truth and Method* (New York: Crossroad, 1990). See also Gadamer's *Philosophical Hermeneutics*, ed. and trans. David E. Linge (Berkeley: University of California, 1976).

27. Robert M. Grant with David Tracy, *A Short History of the Interpretation of the Bible*, 2nd ed., revised and enlarged (Philadelphia: Fortress, 1984), 156.

28. See "Radical Hermeneutics and Religious Truth: The Case of Sheehan and Schillebeeckx" in *Phenomenology of the Truth Proper to Religion*, 146.

Chapter Eleven

DEFENSE OF THE EVANGELICAL CONCEPT OF TRUTH

Having discussed the three marks of the Evangelical concept of truth, and the critiques against them, it seems appropriate to assess the validity of those critiques. To engage thoroughly all of the criticisms mentioned in the preceding section, however, would be beyond the scope and ability of this chapter. Therefore, this section will address some of the fundamental themes of the critiques to determine their validity in relation to Evangelical theology and its concept of truth.

Response to the Philosophical Critique

Josiah Royce, an American philosopher who taught at Harvard University, once quipped that a liar is someone who willfully misplaces his ontological predicates. In other words, to lie is to say "is" when you think "is not."[1] To deny this fundamental understanding is to challenge the basic assumptions regarding communication and human perception.

---

1. As cited by Mortimer Adler, *Aristotle for Everybody* (New York: Macmillan, 1978), 152.

Edward J. Carnell has written that the "man on the street knows that
truth is a correspondence between a thing and that which signifies it."[2]
Adler adds that all of the great thinkers agree that truth "depends on the
conformity to reality."[3] Bertrand Russell concurs, stating that the correspondence theory of truth has "on the whole been commonest among
philosophers."[4]

Accordingly, the arguments against the usefulness of the correspondence theory of truth are not ontological in nature, but epistemological
and hermeneutical. For example, Brian Ellis, a critic of the correspondence theory of truth, states that "the correspondence theory of truth
may be right about what truth *is*. That is, it may provide us with what
Huw Price would call a correct *analysis* of truth."[5] Yet the Evangelical
insistence on correspondence is primarily ontological. When it is epistemological, it is claimed in relation to the revelation of God, as a solution
to many of the philosophical dilemmas posed by the existence of a referent. As Arthur Holmes has written, since "an ultimate referent for truth
exists in God's perfect knowledge, and in which God transcends the
creation he knows to perfection, some kind of correspondence theory
seems . . . appropriate."[6] Norman Geisler adds the following philosophical arguments in favor of a correspondence understanding of truth: (1)
lies are impossible without it; (2) ideas of truth or falsity are impossible
without it; (3) factual communication would break down without a correspondence view of truth; and (4) even other theories of truth, such as
the pragmatic or intentionality view, depend on the correspondence
theory of truth for their articulation and defense.[7]

The most substantive defense of a correspondence understanding of
truth in recent years is found in the work of Alfred Tarski. His arguments
are complicated. His defense and articulation of a correspondence understanding of truth turn largely to a semantic understanding of the correspondence theory. Sentences become the bearers of truth to the degree

---

2. Edward John Carnell, *The Case for Orthodox Theology* (Philadelphia: Westminster, 1959), 87.

3. Mortimer J. Adler, "Truth," *The Great Ideas: A Syntopicon of Great Books of the West-ern World, Volume II*, ed. Mortimer J. Adler, (Chicago: Encyclopedia Britannica, 1952), 916.

4. See "Truth and Falsehood," *The Problems of Philosophy* (Oxford: Oxford University, 1959), 121.

5. Brian Ellis, *Truth and Objectivity* (Oxford: Basil Blackwell, 1990), 159.

6. Arthur F. Holmes, "Truth," *New Dictionary of Theology*, ed. Sinclair B. Ferguson, David F. Wright, and J. I. Packer (Downers Grove: InterVarsity, 1988), 695.

7. Norman L. Geisler, "The Concept of Truth in the Inerrancy Debate," *Bibliotheca Sacra*, vol. 137, no. 548 (October-December 1980), 335-336.

that they represent or designate reality or the actual state of affairs.[8] For Tarski, the sentence "'snow is white' is true if, and only if, snow is white."[9]

To dismiss this category of truth would be counter-productive to any engaged in theological reflection. As David Edwards has written, "We want to know . . . what actually took place, who really said what, who wrote what . . . for that is the scientific method and the light of science is one of the weapons which humanity has against the darkness of ignorance and error."[10] When one reads the biblical materials, it becomes clear that the truth it posits is not simply an existential truth, but a historical truth. Bible readers desire this truth—both existential and historical. Thus, some idea of correspondence is in order.[11] Geoffrey Wainwright has added that both the "consensual and the pragmatic theories of truth require, from the Christian viewpoint, an underpinning in a correspondence theory that is finally grounded in the relation between Creator and creation."[12]

An understanding of truth ultimately resting in correspondence to reality also seems to be the most faithful to the biblical materials in terms of the word "truth" and its many uses throughout the text, though distinct ideas of truth as personal and ontological are present.[13] The familiar distinction between the biblical concept of truth as faithfulness (the Hebrew word 'emeth) contrasted with the Greek notion of truth as philosophic category has been discounted in recent years. Several notions of truth are apparent with the fundamental understanding of truth as that which is "real" or "authentic."[14] Further, John S. Feinberg is

---

8. For an introduction to Tarski's theories, see the following: "The Semantic Conception of Truth," Semantics and the Philosophy of Language, ed. Leonard Linsky (Chicago: University of Illinois Press, 1952); Logic, Semantics and Meta-Mathematics (Oxford: Oxford University Press, 1956). See also Hartry Field's "Tarski's Theory of Truth," Journal of Philosophy, vol. 69 (July 1972).

9. Tarski, "Semantic Conception of Truth," 15. It should be noted that Tarski himself did not apply these understandings to metaphysical or "revealed" truth.

10. David L. Edwards and John R. W. Stott, Evangelical Essentials: A Liberal—Evangelical Dialogue (Downers Grove: InterVarsity, 1988), 42.

11. Edwards, Stott, Evangelical Essentials, 43.

12. Geoffrey Wainwright, "Ecumenical Dimensions of Lindbeck's 'Nature of Doctrine,'" Modern Theology, vol. 4, no. 2 (January 1988), 125.

13. The two most detailed studies on the concept of truth as presented in the biblical materials are by Rudolf Bultmann, "alethia, alethes, alethinos, aletheuo," in Theological Dictionary of the New Testament, Volume I, ed. Gerhard Kittel, tran. by Geoffrey W. Bromiley (Grand Rapids: Eerdmans, 1964), 232-251, and Anthony C. Thiselton, "Truth," in New International Dictionary of New Testament Theology, Vol. 3, ed. Colin Brown (Grand Rapids: Zondervan/Regency Reference Library, 1978, 1986), 874-902. See also O. A. Piper, "Truth," in The Interpreter's Dictionary of the Bible, Vol. 4, ed. George A. Buttrick (Nashville: Abingdon, 1962), 713-717, and Roger Nicole's essay, "The Biblical Concept of Truth," in Scripture and Truth, ed. D. A. Carson and John D. Woodbridge (Grand Rapids: Zondervan/Academie, 1983), 287-298.

14. On this, see "Truth," Baker Encyclopedia of the Bible, Vol. 2, ed. by Walter A. Elwell (Grand Rapids: Baker, 1988), 2108, as well as Thiselton, "Truth," New International Dictionary of New Testament Theology, Vol. 3, 232-251.

correct in pointing out that even if one should be persuaded that the biblical concept of truth is purely that of "faithfulness," it is inappropriate to move from that understanding (the usage of a term) to the actual concept of truth assumed by the biblical writers.[15] Thus individuals who draw a firm line between discursive truth and biblical truth portray a truncated or even misguided understanding of the biblical concept of truth.[16]

So as Clark has observed, it is fairest to maintain that all of the biblical usages are derivative from the basic meaning of "the actual fact" or "the truth of an assertion,"[17] which dictates some understanding of correspondence. Some idea of correspondence seems to be inescapable—especially for the theologian—for theology seeks to offer statements which correspond with the truth of God.

The Law of Non-contradiction. The question of the validity or non-validity of the law of non-contradiction is perhaps best engaged by a simple but penetrating question: If one disavows the law of non-contradiction, what are the results? Aristotle's response to this question is that the law of non-contradiction has an ontological basis in reality, therefore its denial leads to absurdity.[18] Nash agrees, stating that "the law of non-contradiction is a necessary principle of thought because it is first a necessary principle of being."[19] In other words, to refute the law of non-contradiction involves using the law of non-contradiction. Daniel Taylor notes, "Those who disparage reason, ironically, often use reason to do so."[20]

---

15. On this, see "Truth, Meaning and Inerrancy in Contemporary Evangelical Thought," *Journal of the Evangelical Theological Society*, vol. 26, vo. 1 (March 1983), 17-30.

16. Such as Albert Outler in "Discursive Truth and Evangelical Truth," *Colleges and Commitments*, ed. Lloyd J. Averill and William W. Jellema (Philadelphia: Westminster, 1971), 102-106.

17. Gordon H. Clark, "Truth," *Evangelical Dictionary of Theology*, ed. by Walter A. Elwell (Grand Rapids: Baker, 1984), 1114.

18. Aristotle, "Metaphysics," translated by W. D. Ross, *Great Books of the Western World*, vol. 8 (Chicago: Encyclopedia Britannica, 1952), 499-626. Note also the careful defense of the law of non-contradiction in Gordon Clark's *Thales to Dewey: A History of Philosophy* (Boston: Houghton Mifflin, 1957), 96-107.

19. Ronald Nash, *Word of God and Mind of Man* (Grand Rapids: Zondervan, 1982), 104. An interesting essay in relation to this discussion was penned by William F. Lawhead, "Descartes Through the Looking-Glass: Is It Possible to Believe What Is Contradictory?," *Religious Studies*, vol. 21 (1985), 169-179, which answers the question in the title negatively.

20. Daniel Taylor, *The Myth of Certainty: The Reflective Christian and the Risk of Commitment* (Waco: Word/Jarrell, 1986), 69. Geisler and Brooks use a similar argument in making a case against the idea that logic does not apply to God or to any of the mysteries of the Christian faith, see *Come, Let Us Reason: An Introduction to Logical Thinking* (Grand Rapids: Baker, 1990), 15-17. In all fairness, the question is not, however, the utter disparagement of reason so much as whether one should apotheisize one form of reason. Here Evangelicals must wrestle with whether or not the law of non-contradiction is applicable to all epistemology, including paradox.

The critiques regarding the nature and limits of reason are well taken and need to be weighed seriously by Evangelical thinkers.[21] It is problematic to confuse reason as a test for truth with reason as a source of truth, which is the error of rationalism.[22] An overarching hermeneutic, overly rationalistic in nature, obscures the mysterious, the transcendent, the paradoxical, and often the aesthetic. God or His revelation is suprarational as opposed to non-rational. In other words, God is larger than our reason. Along with Hodge, it is agreed that

> reason is necessarily presupposed in revelation. Revelation is the communication of truth to the mind. But the communication of truth supposed the capacity to receive it. Revelations cannot be made to brutes or to idiots. Truths, to be received as objects of faith, must be intellectually apprehended.[23]

The frequent mistake is to move from the validity of reason to an overly high view of the capacity of reason as an overarching hermeneutical device for embracing and engaging God and His revelation. Many Evangelicals have come to an understanding of these concerns. The rejection of irrationalistic theologies and philosophies as well as the rejection of a rationalistic alternative based on autonomous human reason is reflected admirably in the recent "Evangelical Affirmations" put forth by the National Association of Evangelicals and Trinity Evangelical Divinity School.[24]

---

21. That Evangelicals are wrestling with these and other questions can be evidenced by the formation of the Society of Christian Philosophers in 1978, the product of a group of Roman Catholic and Evangelical philosophers. On this and the ongoing relationship between Evangelicalism and philosophy, see Richard J. Mouw, "Evangelicalism and Philosophy," *Theology Today*, vol. XLIV, no. 3 (October 1987), 329-337. See also the thoughtful essay by Paul Helm, "The Role of Logic in Biblical Interpretation," *Hermeneutics, Inerrancy, and the Bible*, ed. Earl D. Radmacher and Robert D. Preus (Grand Rapids: Academie/Zondervan, 1984), 841-858, with responses from Mark Hanna and John Gerstner, 861-878. Also to be noted is the collection edited by Hendrik Hart, Johan van der Hoeven, and Nicholas Wolterstorff, *Rationality in the Calvinian Tradition* (Lanham, MD: University Press of America, 1983).

22. As noted by E. J. Carnell in *Christian Commitment: An Apologetic* (Grand Rapids: Baker, 1957), 72.

23. See his *Systematic Theology, Vol. I* (Grand Rapids: Eerdmans, reprinted 1989), 49. Hodge rightly adds, 50, however, that it is important "to bear in mind the difference between knowing and understanding, or comprehending . . . men know unspeakably more than they understand."   Thus paradox and mystery are from the finite perspective and are not to be transferred to that which is part of God's nature. On this, see Arthur Holmes, *Christianity and Philosophy* (Chicago: InterVarsity Press, 1960), 16-17.

24. Kenneth S. Kantzer and Carl F. H. Henry, eds., *Evangelical Affirmations* (Grand Rapids: Academie/Zondervan, 1990). In May, 1989, over 650 registrants representing a broad range of denominations and theological viewpoints within Evangelicalism gathered for four days. This meeting resulted in a set of "Evangelical Affirmations" which intend to be a confession of what it means to be an Evangelical. In regard to recent discussion regarding reason and religion, see the defense of rational realism by Michael C. Banner, *The Justification of Science and the Rationality of Religious Belief* (Oxford: Clarendon, 1990).

Is truth rational? Certainly truth is rational, However, truth is not confined to rationality. The necessary contention is that human language and thought cannot exhaustively contain the truth of God. Those who are uncomfortable with acknowledging a paradox in theology are making the mistake that to acknowledge mystery is to embrace the non-rational for God. Yet the use of reason and logic should not be disparaged. We must conclude with Aristotle that logic is a part of reality, and not an artificial construct forced upon theological reflection.

Sin and Reason. The Evangelical concept of truth, faces perhaps its most difficult problem in defining the degree to which sin has affected the human ability to reason. Carl Henry asserts that reason is the means by which the truth of divine revelation is recognized.[25] The dilemma with such a statement is that Evangelicals strongly assert the doctrine of total depravity. A common Evangelical response is that different functions are affected in different ways, thus allowing a distinction between the effect of sin on human mental activity and its effect on subject matter.[26] Yet the belief that human beings are affected by the fall in every area but that of their reasoning capacity does not have a solid and clear biblical base.

It is also asserted that the law of non-contradiction is an eternal principle, and therefore unaffected by human depravity. However, it is not the law of non-contradiction itself which is the concern when discussing the noetic consequences of the fall, but rather the use of this law for the appropriation of knowledge. Evangelical theology often confuses the ontological necessity of the law of non-contradiction with the epistemological appropriation of the law of non-contradiction in human reasoning. In other words, simply saying that the law of non-contradiction as an eternal principle is unaffected by sin (an ontological claim) does not necessitate that humans are therefore capable of objective and reliable knowledge through the proper use of the laws of valid reasoning (an epistemological claim). If sin affects the ability to reason effectively, then it makes no difference if the law itself remains ontologically free from the consequences of sin, for it is human appropriation which is at issue.[27]

---

25. Carl F. H. Henry, *God, Revelation, and Authority, Vol. I: God Who Speaks and Shows* (Waco: Word, 1976), 215. It should be noted that such a perspective is indebted to Thomas Aquinas.

26. See, for example, Nash, *Word of God and Mind of Man*, 108-109.

27. Arthur Holmes responds as adequately as any honest Evangelical can to this concern by asserting that "careful exegesis and theology leave no doubt about the essentials of Biblical doctrine and morality. In all essentials of faith and practice, we have more than sufficient assurance of the content of the original manuscripts and can be confident in the conclusions we draw from them"; see *All Truth Is God's Truth* (Grand Rapids: Eerdmans, 1977), 8-79.

Response to the Methodological Critique

Much within the methodology of presuppositionalism is vulnerable to critique. Even Cornelius Van Til acknowledged that his "indirect proof" was incapable of satisfying humanity's sense of reason.[28] There is great difficulty in maintaining that an argument by presupposition is "objectively valid" even if it is "subjectively unacceptable" to the unregenerate mind. Schaeffer, Henry, and Erickson strengthen their cases by positing that the embrace of the law of non-contradiction protects their methods from charges of fideism.

One might ask, is not all reasoning in some sense circular? Further, is there not always an ultimate starting point in the reasoning and observation process which must be embraced without empirical proof, such as the acceptance of the reliability of the very sense apparatus we use to acknowledge and accumulate the empirical data?[29] I believe that these are sound questions which can be answered affirmatively.[30] As Cunningham notes, "No philosophy—empirical, rational, or any other—can conclusively prove the validity of its own first principles within the structures of its own methodology."[31] If one could proceed from absolute neutrality to truth, then non-circular argument would be a possibility; but since that is impossible, circular reasoning is inevitable. This is not to intimate that only a coherence theory of truth is possible, for it is to be maintained that presuppositions are in and of themselves either true or false. The many detractors of presuppositionalism, both inside and outside of Evangelicalism, seem to focus on presuppositionalism's inability to provide certainty.[32] Presuppositionalism does not give epistemological certainty as much as it is a part of methodological necessity. Presuppositionless thinking is an oxymoron. The problem with Evangelical usage of presuppositional methodologies is that such usage often seems arrested at the apologetic stage. Richard Mouw states that while

---

28. Cornelius Van Til, "My Credo," *Jerusalem and Athens*, 8.

29. The radical skepticism which denies the reality of that which our senses maintain, is seldom given a hearing in contemporary philosophy. As Freud has argued, "If it were really a matter of indifference what we believed then we might just as well build our bridges of cardboard as of stone, or inject a tenth of a gramme of morphia into a patient instead of a hundredth, or take tear-gas as a narcotic instead of ether. But the intellectual anarchists themselves would strongly repudiate such a practical application of their theory," as quoted in "Truth," *The Great Ideas: A Syntopicon of Great Books of the Western World, Volume II*, 915.

30. Huston Smith concurs, arguing that objectivity and neutrality in the sense of presuppositionless thinking is impossible, see "Objectivity and Commitment," *Colleges and Commitments*, ed. by Lloyd J. Averill and William W. Jellema (Philadelphia: The Westminster Press, 1971), 34-59.

31. Richard B. Cunningham, "A Case for Christian Philosophy," *Review and Expositor,* vol. 82, no. 4 (Fall 1985), 500.

32. For example, Hanna seems to reject presuppositionalism on these grounds, see *Crucial Questions in Apologetics* (Grand Rapids: Baker, 1981), 101.

Evangelicals made much of the fact that presuppositions are decisive in the shaping of one's world view and thus scholarly programs, "they did not do much to demonstrate that fact by actually pursuing scholarly programs."[33]

Response to the Epistemological Critique

The personal dimension and dynamic of revelation are areas that receive the vanguard of concerns. There is little doubt that revelation contains a personal dimension.[34] Ronald Nash is correct in pointing to the misconception that Evangelicals believe that all revelation is propositional or that a personal element is not acknowledged in divine revelation.[35] Nash also lists the following confusions regarding the idea of propositional revelation: (1) it should not be confused with the separate doctrine of verbal inspiration; (2) the advocate of propositional revelation does not hold that God's written revelation must assume a particular literary form; (3) while all Scripture is inspired, not all Scripture declares truth in sentences that are to be interpreted literally; (4) a propositional view does not minimize revelation in the sense of event; and (5) it does not involve a reduction of God's revelation to something static.

Revelation and Propositions. Carl Henry is often caricatured as an example of the viewpoint that reduces all of revelation to propositions. Henry argues for the place of propositional truth, not the reduction of all truth to propositional form. Reviewers of Henry's writings who claim that Henry is a "hyper-rationalist" who construes all truth in propositional form have either failed to read him carefully or have failed to read him comprehensively.[36] Perhaps what needs to be addressed by such detractors is what they mean by propositional and nonpropositional truth. If nonpropositional is understood as noncognitive, then yes, Henry discounts any understanding of truth as noncognitive. However, this is far different than the common understanding of propositional truth.

Richard J. Coleman has noted that one of Evangelicalism's strengths has been the balance it has kept between personal and propositional revelation.[37] In light of existentialism's claim to the contrary, Helmut

---

33. Mouw, "Evangelicalism and Philosophy," *Theology Today*, 333.

34. See John V. Dahms, "The Nature of Truth," *Journal of the Evangelical Theological Society*, vol. 28, no. 4 (December 1985), 455-465.

35. Nash, *Word of God and Mind of Man*, 43-54.

36. Such as Alan Padgett in "A Critique of Carl Henry's Summa," *TSF Bulletin*, vol. 9, no. 3 (January-February, 1986), 28-29.

37. Richard J. Coleman, *Issues of Theological Conflict: Evangelicals and Liberals* (Grand Rapids: Eerdmans, 1972), 48. As Bernard Ramm has noted, the personal and the propositional are inseparable, for "revelation is event and interpretation, encounter and truth, a Person and knowledge"; see *Special Revelation and the Word of God* (Grand Rapids: Eerdmans, 1961), 160.

Thielicke critiques Kierkegaard's existentialism on the grounds that the objective sphere of knowledge is "screened off" from the existential perception of truth. In other words, Kierkegaard and those of like sensibilities have no means by which to detect the significance of factual knowledge. This occurs as a result of making the content secondary to the fact of existential truth.[38]

If an over-emphasis on the propositional element has been evident in Evangelical thought, it can be largely accounted for as a reaction to the devaluation of the propositional within neo-orthodoxy. Evangelicals proclaim that some revelation is propositional and thus conveys cognitive information about God. This does not assert, as Nash reminds us, that all revelation must be cognitive or reducible to human language.[39] "Evangelicals make it clear that they believe revelation can be both personal and cognitive."[40] The human logos can know the logos of God. In other words, a relationship exists between the human mind and the divine mind that is sufficient to ground the communication of truth from God to humanity.[41]

Inherent within this view is the embrace of a univocal understanding of language. God knows all truth, and unless we share that which God knows, our ideas are fundamentally in error.

This univocal understanding should not be interpreted as arguing for an exhaustive correspondence between the mind of humanity and the mind of God. It should be observed that an analogical understanding of language should not preclude these same conclusions. The position entails the belief that "some revelatory acts have a cognitive or informational character and that this revealed truth is deposited in the various literary forms found in the Bible."[42] Those who reject this propositional element in revelation, Nash asserts, do so because they "confuse the proclamation or delivery of truth with the reception of truth."[43]

C. Stephen Evans discusses the propositional element in special revelation in the context of the philosophical discussion regarding miracles or "special acts" of God. He makes the following points in favor of the propositional view: first, theology is greatly assisted if the propositional view is indeed correct, and therefore, it should be given a careful hearing; second, since speaking itself is a kind of action, and if God is capa-

---

38. Helmut Thielicke, *Modern Faith and Thought*, trans. Geoffrey Bromiley (Grand Rapids: Eerdmans, 1990), see 490-545, especially 514-519.

39. Nash writes that it "asserts only that some revelation is cognitive and has been expressed in human language," *Word of God and Mind of Man*, 45.

40. Ibid., 46. Nash writes that "the more person A knows about person B, the better A can know B in a personal way." In other words, increased cognitive knowledge enhances personal knowledge in regard to relationship.

41. Ibid., 14.

42. Ibid., 54.

43. Ibid., 53.

ble of any special actions at all, then there is no reason for thinking that speaking to or through human beings would not be in His repertoire of actions;[44] finally, the many arguments against the propositional view presuppose false dichotomies, such as that between God revealing Himself and God revealing propositions.[45] Evans adds that none of these arguments propose that God has revealed Himself propositionally, only that if God reveals Himself at all, one could expect the revelation to consist of the kind of thing the propositional view supposes. Harold Netland agrees, adding that propositional statements are the minimal vehicle for truth.[46]

These arguments are compelling for the Evangelical embrace of a propositional element present in the nature of Scripture. What must be added to this, however, is an acknowledgment of the limitations of language. Language should be put forth as a reliable and sufficient vehicle for the communication of information about reality. This should be clearly distanced, however, from the assertion that language exhausts what it attempts to convey, especially in the area of metaphysics.[47]

Biblical Inerrancy. Although what it intends to convey in regard to Scripture's truthfulness and trustworthiness is laudable and important, the term "inerrant" is not a particularly good one because of the following reasons: first, it is not taken from the biblical materials, as are the terms "inspiration" and "authoritative;" second, it conveys a mathematically precise, contemporary understanding of "fact" that is not always fair to the nature and context of the biblical narrative. Nonetheless, the term is now a part of theological dialogue, and therefore should not be fought but rather carefully defined.[48] It must also be asserted that what is decisive for Evangelical theology is not the inerrancy of Scripture, but the authority of Scripture.[49] This is not to say that inerrancy does not

---

44. Further, this address must have content, for one cannot simply speak—there must be something said.

45. C. Stephen Evans, *Philosophy of Religion: Thinking About Faith* (Downers Grove: InterVarsity Press, 1985), 97-107.

46. See his *Dissonant Voices: Religious Pluralism and the Question of Truth* (Grand Rapids: Eerdmans, 1991), particularly chapter 4.

47. This understanding is absent from Lindbeck's treatment of the "propositional" approach in *The Nature of Doctrine*. If it had been present, his dismissal of the propositional understanding would have lost much of its basis. What Evangelical propositionalists maintain is that there is ontological faithfulness, not ontological exhaustiveness.

48. On the Bible's inerrancy, see the author's article titled "Inspiration and Authority" in *The New American Introduction to the Bible* (Nashville: Broadman, 1991).

49. A perspective increasingly challenged on many fronts in many ways, such as Schubert Ogden, "Sources of Religious Authority in Liberal Protestantism," *Journal of the American Academy of Religion*, vol. 44, no. 3 (September 1976), 403-416, who finds authority primarily in religious experience and the so-called "Jesus-kerygma" of the Synoptic tradition that is revealed through historical reconstruction (it is the latter of these two that forms Ogden's understanding of "canon").

speak to the authority question, but rather that inerrancy is secondary to the authority question.

Evangelicals have written extensively about inerrancy and have defended the doctrine with great ability and care.[50] Of the many critiques aimed at inerrancy, Evangelicals need to take seriously the ongoing confusion between metaphysics and epistemology. This was mentioned above under the "philosophical critique" of the law of non-contradiction as an ontological principle and the epistemological appropriation of that principle through human reason. In regard to biblical inerrancy, epistemological objectivity is often proposed as necessary for metaphysical objectivity. The difficulty with such a view is that universals are not necessarily equated with absolutes. While this is a valid insight that is often an accurate critique of Evangelical formulations, it is more of a critique of a bad argument for inerrancy rather than a substantive weakening of the idea that biblical inerrancy intends to convey. Such argument does not necessarily challenge the appropriateness of holding to that which biblical inerrancy desires to put forward concerning biblical authority.

Evangelical responses to the many arguments lodged against biblical inerrancy include the following: (1) The problem of the lack of an errant original is countered by stating that we do not have an errant original which can be produced to validate the alternative view. F. F. Bruce, an Evangelical who was a noted New Testament scholar, has added that the Bible now in our possession is extraordinarily reliable.[51] (2) While some Evangelicals have made herculean attempts at forced harmonization in light of an allegiance to biblical inerrancy,[52] most Evangelicals have addressed the textual difficulties with honesty, attempting to answer them from a scholarly viewpoint.[53] An example of Evangelical efforts honestly to address the textual concerns of non-inerrantists can be found in such carefully constructed proposals as "The Chicago State-

---

50. A good introduction to Evangelical interactions with opposing views can be found in *Challenges to Inerrancy: A Theological Response*, ed. by Gordon R. Lewis and Bruce Demarest (Chicago: Moody, 1984), and in Harvie M. Conn, ed., *Inerrancy and Hermeneutic: A Tradition, A Challenge, A Debate* (Grand Rapids: Baker, 1988). One of the best summaries of opposing philosophical frameworks in view of the biblical materials is Royce Gordon Gruenler's *Meaning and Understanding: The Philosophical Framework for Biblical Interpretation*, vol. 2 of the Foundations of Contemporary Interpretation series (Grand Rapids: Zondervan, 1991).

51. See *The New Testament Documents*, 6th ed. (Grand Rapids: Eerdmans, 1984).

52. Though not meant to dismiss summarily or to discredit either work, one does find this tendency in Gleason Archer's *Encyclopedia of Biblical Difficulties* (Grand Rapids: Zondervan, 1982) and in Harold Lindsell's *The Battle for the Bible* (Grand Rapids: Zondervan, 1976).

53. See the discussions found in Mark A. Noll's *Between Faith and Criticism: Evangelicals, Scholarship, and the Bible in America* (San Francisco: Harper and Row, 1986), 122-141, 154-161.

ment on Biblical Inerrancy."[54] It could be proposed that the many qualifications in the "Chicago Statement," especially Article XIII, make the
term "inerrancy" vacuous. In fairness, such an evaluation should take
into account the definitional specificity such a term as "inerrancy" would
necessarily demand for meaningful theological dialogue. It is to be
noted that such rules of interpretation have accompanied Evangelicalism's understanding of biblical inerrancy long before the "Chicago Statement."[55] (3) In regard to inerrancy being critiqued for joining revelation
and text, Evangelicals insist that the "event" of revelation cannot be separated from its biblical interpretation for the contemporary exegete. To
separate the two in regard to truthfulness would lead to epistemological
nihilism. (4) The critique that inerrancy demands an infallible hermeneutic is not held by any Evangelical scholar of whom this writer is aware.
What is maintained by Evangelicals is that once a biblical teaching has
been correctly identified, trust may be placed in that teaching without
regard for falsity.

Accepting the Bible as a source of knowledge means also that it is
not seen as an exhaustive source of knowledge. All fields of knowledge
do not find their foundation within its pages. As Frank E. Gaebelein has
written, "there are areas of truth not fully explicated in Scripture and . . .
these, too, are part of God's truth."[56] Wherever truth is found, it is
related to God. The theological importance of this is that to posit something outside of God, such as truth, is to posit that which is other or
greater than God. Such a presupposition is untenable to any sense of
orthodox Christian faith. As Machen has written, "all truth, ultimately, is
one."[57]

---

54. See "The Chicago Statement on Biblical Inerrancy," in Lewis A. Drummond, *The Word of the Cross* (Nashville: Broadman, 1992), 338-350 or *Evangelicals and Inerrancy*, ed. Ronald Youngblood (Nashville: Thomas Nelson, 1984), 238-239.

55. Evidenced by such careful treatments as Bernard Ramm's "The Problem of Inerrancy and Secular Science in Relation to Hermeneutics" in *Protestant Biblical Interpretation: A Textbook of Hermeneutics for Conservative Protestants* (Boston: W.A. Wilde, 1956),
182-195.

56. Frank E. Gaebelein, *The Pattern of God's Truth: A Basic Contribution to Christian
Educational Philosophy* (Chicago: Moody Press, 1968), 21. Gaebelein adds that to fail to
adhere to this understanding inevitably leads to a misleading distinction between the
sacred and the secular. On this, see also Arthur Holmes, *All Truth Is God's Truth*, 8-9.

57. J. Gresham Machen, *The Virgin Birth of Christ* (Grand Rapids: Baker, 1930;
reprinted 1985), 219.

Hermeneutics. Evangelicals have reflected broadly and written exten-sively on hermeneutics.[58] Yet perhaps the best response to hermeneuti-cal concerns often voiced against Evangelical epistemology comes from one who is not identified with Evangelicalism; E. D. Hirsch, a winsome and compelling thinker, who effectively argues for the possibility of understanding between text and reader to occur in such a way as to allow for more than radical subjectivity in interpretation through autho-rial intent.[59] Hirsch maintains that to banish authorial intent from inter-pretive understandings is to relegate interpretation to a radical, personal subjectivity. Authorial intent as the primary hermeneutical key for understanding the biblical text was affirmed by the recent "Evangelical Affirmations" of the National Association of Evangelicals.[60] This is made possible, says Hirsch, through the limitation of linguistic possibilities.

This is decisive for Evangelical understandings. Individual horizons brought to the text should have their horizon molded and shaped by the biblical narrative. Such a view shares some affinities with the narrative theologians who contend that hermeneutical approaches should reflect

---

58. Evangelical interactions with hermeneutical theory include, but are not limited to, the following: Raymond Bailey, ed., *Hermeneutics for Preaching* (Nashville: Broadman, 1993), D. A. Carson and John D. Woodbridge, eds., *Hermeneutics, Authority, and Canon* (Grand Rapids: Zondervan/Academie, 1986); Peter Cotterell and Max Turner, *Linguistics and Biblical Interpretation* (Downers Grove: InterVarsity, 1989); Donald K. McKim, ed., *A Guide to Contemporary Hermeneutics: Major Trends in Biblical Interpretation* (Grand Rap-ids: Eerdmans, 1986); Bernard Ramm, et al., *Hermeneutics* (Grand Rapids: Baker, 1971); Moises Silva, *Has The Church Misread the Bible? The History of Interpretation in the Light of Current Issues*, Foundations of Contemporary Interpretation, vol. 1 (Grand Rapids: Zonder-van/Academie, 1987); and Anthony C. Thiselton, *The Two Horizons: New Testament Hermeneutics and Philosophical Description with Special Reference to Heidegger, Bult-mann, Gadamer, and Wittgenstein* (Grand Rapids: Eerdmans, 1980). See also "The Chi-cago Statement on Biblical Hermeneutics," in *Hermeneutics, Inerrancy and the Bible*, ed. Earl D. Radmacher, Lewis A. Drummond, *The Word of the Cross* (Nashville: Broadman Press, 1992) or Robert D. Preus (Grand Rapids: Zondervan, 1984), 881-887. See also the survey of Evangelical hermeneutics offered by Gabriel Fackre in "Evangelical Hermeneu-tics: Commonality and Diversity," *Interpretation*, vol. 43, no. 2 (April 1989), 117-129.

59. E. D. Hirsch, *The Validity of Interpretation* (New Haven: Yale University, 1967); see also *The Aims of Interpretation* (Chicago: University of Chicago, 1976). An interesting study outside the bounds of this exploration but relevant to discussions regarding the pos-sibility of objectivity is the critique of contemporary epistemological relativism put forth by Harvey Siegel, who maintains in *Relativism Refuted* (Dordrecht, Holland: D. Reidel Pub-lishing, 1987) that relativism as a philosophical option cannot be coherently maintained.

60.   See *Evangelical Affirmations*, 33. See also the essay by Elliot E. Johnson, "Author's Intention and Biblical Interpretation" in *Hermeneutics, Inerrancy and the Bible*, 409-429, with responses from Earl D. Radmacher and Walter C. Kaiser, Jr., 433-447. See also the series of four articles by Gordon Fee titled "Issues in Evangelical Hermeneutics" in *Crux*, beginning with vol. 26, no. 2 (June 1990), 21-26, where Fee continues the Evangeli-cal emphasis on authorial intention as central to hermeneutics.

the character of the biblical narrative.[61] What cannot be affirmed with some in the camp of narrative theology is that the truth question can be "bracketed off," acknowledging the authorial intent as the literal sense but refusing to designate historical reference to the "plain sense" of the biblical story. This is highly problematic, for the kind of story we find in many of the biblical narratives demands that certain facts be true in the sense of faithful correspondence with historical reality. As John Macquarrie has asked, "Just how irrelevant can the factual content of the gospel become without its ceasing to be a gospel?"[62] Tracy adds that "hermeneutically . . . I am bound to struggle critically with the fact that its claim to truth is part of its meaning. To understand the religious classic at all, I cannot ultimately avoid its provocations to my present notions of what constitutes truth."[63]

An emphasis on objective interpretation through authorial intent should not, however, diminish the subjective element one brings to the text.[64] Wittgenstein illustrates this dimension with the following picture:[65]

Is this a duck or a rabbit? Approached from the left one sees the bill of a duck. Approached from the right, we see a rabbit with outstretched ears. The picture did not change—it is what it is—but it can be interpreted in either fashion with integrity. Even though the picture allows for some subjective interpretation, it does not allow for infinite interpretations. Perhaps either a rabbit or a duck, it is clearly not a portrait of Sir Winston Churchill or a technical drawing of the engine of a Stealth Bomber. Therefore, while admitting the subjective element, one should not subscribe to hermeneutical nihilism. Arthur Holmes, for example, maintains that one should hold metaphysical objectivity and epistemological subjectivity together but should not make the mistake of assum-

---

61. On this, see Hans Frei, *The Eclipse of Biblical Narrative: A Study in Eighteenth and Nineteenth Century Hermeneutics* (New Haven: Yale University, 1974); Michael Goldberg, *Theology and Narrative* (Nashville: Abingdon, 1981); Garrett Green, ed., *Scriptural Authority and Narrative Interpretation* (Philadelphia: Fortress, 1987); Stanley Hauerwas and L. Gregory Jones, eds., *Why Narrative? Readings in Narrative Theology* (Grand Rapids: Eerdmans, 1989); Richard John Neuhaus, ed., *Biblical Interpretation in Crisis: The Ratzinger Conference on Bible and Church* (Grand Rapids: Eerdmans, 1989); George W. Stroup, *The Promise of Narrative Theology* (Atlanta: John Knox, 1981); and Terrence W. Tilley, *Story Theology* (Wilmington, DE: Michael Glazier, 1985).

62. See John Macquarrie, *The Scope of Demythologizing* (London: SCM, 1960), 20.

63. David Tracy, *Plurality and Ambiguity: Hermeneutics, Religion, Hope* (San Francisco: Harper and Row, 1987), 98.

64. A point that is made by David S. Dockery in "Toward a Balanced Hermeneutic in Baptist Life," *Search* (Spring 1989), 47-51.

65. Ludwig Wittgenstein, *Philosophical Investigations*, trans. G. E. M. Anscombe (Oxford: Basil Blackwell, 1968), 194.

ing rampant subjectivity. Objective controls—historical, contextual, and linguistic—still operate on interpretation. Such controls also include public evidence and logical arguments.[66] What Evangelicals suggest: (1) objectivity of enquiry must be held as an ideal; (2) any attitude which dispenses with the need for objective truth is meaninglessness; and (3) the disparagement of objectivity involves considerable inconsistencies.[67] As Paul Ricoeur has maintained, we must move beyond the hermeneutical impasse and let the text bridge the gulf between reader and author. Ricoeur would maintain that the triadic relationship of sign, interpretant, and object can be used to explicate the possibility of objective interpretation. The text therefore interprets the reader, allowing a second naivete to take place when approaching the biblical materials. Ricoeur also argues for a surplus of meaning that transcends authorial intent, acknowledging the role of the stream of tradition in the act of interpretation.[68] Yet Ricoeur states that to say that a discourse is true it is to say that the language relates to the world.[69] What is at hand in regard to truth and interpretation is the dialectic between language and the ontological condition of being in the world. Ricoeur also argues for a logic or probability over and against a logic of verification in regard to validation. This use of Ricoeur should not be interpreted as a wholesale acceptance of his system of thought, but rather an attempt to gain from some of his many insights into the dynamics of interpretation.[70]

In such conclusions, however, it is important to maintain the distinction Hirsch makes between the meaning of a text and the significance of a text. The meaning of a text is that which is represented by a text. "Significance, on the other hand, names a relationship between that meaning and a person, or a conception, or a situation, or indeed anything imaginable."[71] It is only the meaning which remains unchanged, in other words, that which the author meant by his or her use of a particu-

---

66. See Arthur Holmes, *Contours of a World View* (Grand Rapids: Eerdmans, 1983), 145-152.

67. On these contentions, see Paul Helm, ed., *Objective Knowledge: A Christian Perspective* (Leicester, England: InterVarsity, 1987).

68. Representative works by Ricoeur regarding philosophical hermeneutics include, but are not limited to, the following: *Essays in Biblical Interpretation*, ed. Lewis Mudge (Philadelphia: Fortress, 1980); *Hermeneutics and the Human Sciences*, ed. and trans. John B. Thompson (Cambridge: Cambridge University, 1981); *Interpretation Theory: Discourse and the Surplus of Meaning* (Fort Worth: Texas Christian University, 1976); *The Symbolism of Evil*, trans. Emerson Buchanan (Boston: Beacon, 1967).

69. Ricoeur, *Interpretation Theory*, 20. Ricoeur adds that "the decisive fact here is that language has a reference only when it is used."

70. For a sustained and balanced engagement of Ricoeur's thought from an Evangelical perspective, see Kevin J. Vanhoozer's *Biblical Narrative in the Philosophy of Paul Ricoeur* (Cambridge: Cambridge University Press, 1990). Vanhoozer has great respect for Ricoeur but finds that Ricoeur has not done justice to the Gospel's literal truth in terms of its historical reference.

71. Hirsch, *Validity in Interpretation*, 8.

lar sign sequence. Meaning is found in what the signs represent. Therefore, validity in interpretation is the correspondence between an
interpretation and a meaning which is represented by a text. Hirsch
states that authorial meaning can never be known with certainty, but
this is distinct from the conclusion that the author's intended meaning is
inaccessible and therefore a useless object of interpretation. Hirsch
argues for the separation of knowledge from certainty. It is the former,
not the latter, that makes authorial meaning useful for interpretive exploration. Hirsch maintains that one can find the intended meaning of a
text—not everything within an author's mind at the time of writing—on
the basis of the text's words and sentences. Therefore, what is at hand is
the verbal meaning which an author intended, determined by many factors, such as the criterion of legitimacy, the correspondence of linguistic
components in the text, generic appropriateness, and coherence.[72]
There is a normative, objective meaning, but numerous significances.

---

72.   *Validity in interpretation*, Appendix I: "Objective Interpretation," 209-244.

Chapter Twelve

PROPOSALS FOR THE EVANGELICAL CONCEPT OF TRUTH

At the beginning of this study it was suggested that Evangelical theology has three choices: (1) maintain previous conceptualizations of truth as correspondence, theological method as presuppositional, and an epistemology which is grounded in special revelation that is propositional in form and inerrant in nature; (2) abandon that view completely for another conceptualization; (3) strive for a synthesis between its traditional understandings and views which take into account the dynamics of the pragmatic view of truth, the non-propositional perspective toward revelation, and the hermeneutical insight of individual personal horizon.

The choice made from among these three options will have a decisive impact on Evangelical theology. The correspondence theory of truth lies behind the theory of inerrancy as the model for understanding the relationship between inspiration and Scripture. This theory of inerrancy gives Evangelical theology much of its distinctiveness.

This study has engaged many of the critiques lodged against the Evangelical concept of truth and has found all of the concerns understandable but insufficient for dismissal of the central tenets Evangelical theologians have put forth for theological dialogue. Therefore, of the three "choices" suggested for Evangelical theology, it would seem that the choice of "synthesis" is in order. This synthesis would not involve compromise, but rather a deeper reflection and a new, integrated theological construction. Many of the authors surveyed in this study have made noteworthy attempts at just such an integration. This study leads to certain proposals that would perhaps assist Evangelical theology as it engages the issues of the modern world and interacts with other disciplines and world views. These proposals can be summarized in the following two understandings: first, an unashamed positing of revelation as the prime referent for the correspondence theory of truth; and second, embracing the polymorphous character of truth in regard to biblical narrative.

Revelation and Correspondence

One of the principal critiques against the correspondence theory of truth is that of the referent, necessary to give credence to any such theory. If I claim that a statement "It is raining" corresponds to reality, then validation (that is, referent) is achieved by determining if it is indeed raining. The dilemma of the correspondence theory of truth for spiritual statements is just this sort of validation. For example, if I make the statement that "God exists," one cannot walk out his or her front door and determine if God does or does not exist in a way that is empirically verifiable. This is the basis for the claim of logical positivists that all language about God is non-sensical and meaningless.[1]

This puts those who espouse Evangelical theology into something of a quandary, for they want to hold to the most simple and basic truth concepts, namely correspondence, yet join with all of philosophy in recognizing the difficulty of proposing a referent for its validation. Evangelicals are unwilling to accept the logical positivist idea that religious language is meaningless, yet they also wish to shy away from sheer fideism.

Assistance with this dilemma is found in the inescapability of presuppositions in any kind of formulation—whether it be scientific, sociological, or theological. Presuppositions are held by any and all involved in the enterprise of reflection and formulation. Alvin Plantinga and others of the renewed "reformed epistemology" perspective state that religious presuppositions which cannot be verified by empirical evidence are just

---

1. The classic presentation of logical positivism can be found in A. J. Ayer, *Language, Truth, and Logic*, 2nd. rev. ed. (New York: Dover, 1946).

as rational and coherent as any other assumption from which reasoning begins.[2]

These suggestions lead us to assert revelation as the outside referent from God which can be used to determine the correspondence of a religious statement with objective truth, in spite of the objections of the empiricist. For the Christian, the Creator-created epistemic chasm has been bridged through special revelation. As Harry Blamires has written, the conception of truth to the Christian mind is one that is "supernaturally grounded."[3] To be sure, the biblical statements are not truth as God is Truth in His own Person, but they find their truth in reference to God.[4] Os Guinness maintains that if God speaks "in self-disclosure that is both encounter and proposition, then because he is the infinite reference point, such revelation allows the possibility of 'true' knowledge that can be accepted by man even if he does not have exhaustive knowledge."[5] The possibility of such a perspective does not seem to be recognized as a possibility by those who reject the idea of correspondence in regard to truth and theological construction.[6]

The great philosophical dilemma regarding truth is answered in Christianity with the omniscient God breaking through in self-revelation. Scripture is true because of Who has revealed it (God) and what it has revealed (God's knowledge). As Stanley Obitts has stated, it is a sound move to go from "the fact of a statement in the Bible having its source in

2. A balanced introduction to this "reformed epistemology" can be found in a chapter added to the fourth edition of John Hick's *Philosophy of Religion* (Englewood Cliffs, N.J.: Prentice-Hall, 1990), 68-81, titled "Evidentialism, Foundationalism, and Rational Belief." See also William Wainwright's chapter, "Anti-evidentialism," in *Philosophy of Religion* (Belmont, Ca.: Wadsworth Publishing Co., 1988), 131-165, especially 153-159. Note also James A. Keller, "Accepting the Authority of the Bible: Is It Rationally Justified," *Faith and Philosophy*, vol. 6, no. 4 (October 1989), 378-397, who argues that the contemporary Christian is justified in using the views expressed in the Bible as normative for his beliefs and practices on the basis of understanding how the biblical author's faith was expressed and then using that understanding as a guide for the construction of a set of beliefs.

3. Harry Blamires, *The Christian Mind: How Should a Christian Think?* (Ann Arbor: Servant Books, 1963), 106.

4. A similar point is made by Thomas F. Torrance in *Reality and Evangelical Theology* (Philadelphia: The Westminster Press, 1982). Torrance adds, 130, that this prevents "the fallacious tendency to pass from the truth of being to the truth of signification and then to the truth of composition, which has the effect of substituting syntactic validity for semantic truth." Torrance thus maintains, 131, that statements are correctly interpreted when they are understood in their compulsory reference to the things signified, and "when those things signified are understood for what they are and for what in accordance with their natures they must be."

5. Os Guinness, *The Dust of Death: A Critique of the Counter Culture* (Downers Grove: InterVarsity Press, 1973), 336.

6. An example of which is Gordon D. Kaufman's epilogue to *An Essay on Theological Method*, AAR Studies in Religion 11, rev. ed. (Missoula, Mont.: Scholars Press/American Academy of Religion, 1975, 1979), 75-76. Much of Kaufman's concern with truth as correspondence would be alleviated with the acceptance of the possibility that God can (and has) "broken" into our existential situation with a word of truth that corresponds to Himself in supplement to our conceptions.

God to the fact of its truth."[7] Therefore, truth is that which corresponds with God's knowledge, a knowledge which has been revealed most fully in Jesus Christ, and then through the Scriptures, which present the primary witness to Jesus Christ. The knowledge found in Scripture corresponds with God's knowledge, for it is God's self-revelation. As one might guess, this turns many of the questions raised in this study over to the realm of hermeneutics, which leads us to a second proposal, namely the polymorphous character of biblical truth.[8]

Polymorphous Character of Biblical Truth

A central concern in many of the critiques against Evangelical conceptualizations of truth is that the idea of truth as special revelation that is propositional in form and inerrant in nature in a strict, factual sense does not correspond with the phenomenon of Scripture. The Bible contains diverse narratives with a variety of intents for the conveyance of knowledge.

Thiselton discusses the polymorphous character of biblical truth, contending that no single concept of truth exists in relation to the biblical materials, but rather the understanding of truth varies according to context.[9] When approaching a document such as the Bible, the concept of truth must vary in relation to the "language game" at hand.[10] Thiselton writes:

> Sometimes what is at issue is correspondence between statements and facts. Truth *is* this, in this context. At other times what is at issue is correspondence between word and deed. In other contexts what truth *is* depends on the nature of revealed doctrine; while in others, what truth *is* depends on holding together several different strands of a multiform

7. See Stanley Obitts, "A Philosophical Analysis of Certain Assumptions of the Doctrine of the Inerrancy of the Bible," *Journal of the Evangelical Theological Society*, vol. 26, no. 2 (June 1983), 136.

8. Growing numbers of Evangelicals are coming to an awareness that hermeneutics are central, evidenced by J. I. Packer's article, "The Centrality of Hermeneutics Today," in *Scripture and Truth*, ed. by D. A. Carson and John D. Woodbridge (Grand Rapids: Zondervan, 1983), 325-356. Gerhard Ebeling makes an interesting point in maintaining that "for theology the hermeneutic problem is . . . today becoming the place of meeting with philosophy," see *Word and Faith* (London: SCM, 1963), 317.

9. Anthony C. Thiselton, *The Two Horizons: New Testament Hermeneutics and Philosophical Description* (Grand Rapids: Eerdmans, 1984), 408-415.

10. The term "language game" is borrowed by Thiselton from Wittgenstein. Thiselton contends the concept has great similarity with Heidegger's understanding of "world" and even Gadamer's notion of the interpreter's horizons; see *Two Horizons*, 33. For Wittgenstein's views, see his *Philosophical Investigations* (Oxford: Basil Blackwell, 1968), where he maintains that truth is found in the way it functions within a given language or area of language; thus, it must be judged according to the purposes and functions of that language.

concept. The question "What is truth?" cannot be asked outside of a given language game.[11]

John Macquarrie also posits a polymorphous concept of truth, adding that this does not mean "that any statement whatever could claim to be true and then have this claim supported by some highly esoteric concept of truth."[12] Macquarrie's qualification is to be noted, for to maintain the polymorphous character of truth as it is conceptually used in the biblical materials is distinct from asserting the ontological nature of truth as polymorphous, thus giving rise to radical subjectivism. Macquarrie makes an incorrect assessment of the nature of theological truth as existential rather than verbal. To be fair to the biblical materials, one must at least maintain that both the existential and the verbal are present in the intent of the text.

What is suggested is that one must interact with a particular biblical text in light of the nature of the truth it is intending to convey. Placher, putting it in terms of story, states that "the kind of claims you make depends on the particular story you use and the way you use it."[13] This truth might be poetic in nature; it might be propositional or didactic in nature; it may be discussing truth in terms of personal response, and so on. It is all truth and to be seen in ultimate terms of correspondence, but the hermeneutical mandate demands an acknowledgment of the polymorphous character of truth in regard to manifestation.[14] However, Placher errs in concluding that the truth question regarding such issues as historicity can be bracketed off as inconsequential to the reading of the narrative.

Placher's definition of "historical," however, might alter this concern. As used by Evangelicals, the term "history" usually refers to faithful correspondence with reality, meaning that if one were present, one would find the events as described by the biblical narrative to be authentic to what actually transpired in space and time. Alternative views of history, however, challenge this perspective. What needs to be maintained, according to this author's perspective, is that one affords to Scripture the degree of truthfulness, historical or otherwise, to the degree the author of that biblical narrative intended.

Kevin J. Vanhoozer, in "The Semantics of Biblical Literature," draws together several of the points posited by Evangelical theology regarding

---

11. Thiselton, *Two Horizons*, 414-415.

12. John Macquarrie, *Principles of Christian Theology*, 2nd ed. (New York: Charles Scribner's Sons, 1977), 146.

13. William C. Placher, *Unapologetic Theology: A Christian Voice in a Pluralistic Conversation* (Louisville: Westminster/John Knox, 1989), 130.

14. This is in line with Article XIII of "The Chicago Statement on Biblical Inerrancy," which reads "we deny that it is proper to evaluate Scripture according to standards of truth and error that are alien to its usage or purpose"; see Ronald Youngblood, ed., *Evangelicals and Inerrancy* (Nashville: Thomas Nelson, 1984), 230-239.

truth along with several important insights suggested by those outside of Evangelicalism.[15] Vanhoozer begins by defining propositional revelation as that which discloses truth in a cognitive manner or that which is put forth for consideration. In regard to the biblical materials, a proposition is that which "God has propounded for our consideration."[16] He then moves on to discuss the nature of those propositions, categorizing them as either "ordinary" or "philosophical." Propositions in the philosophical sense are those which are assertive or declarative. Propositions in the ordinary sense are those which are verbal statements regarding that which is being "said" in the text. Only a small portion of the Bible can be said to be propositional in the philosophical sense; the vast majority is in the ordinary sense. Vanhoozer is correct in pointing out that one of the primary charges leveled at Evangelicals by critics such as Barr and Kelsey is that "what is said" is collapsed into "what is asserted." Further, Barr objects primarily to the understanding of propositions in the ordinary sense as any kind of "proof-text," and Kelsey objects to propositions in the philosophical sense that are extracted from the text.

Vanhoozer contends "that diverse literary forms and truth are by no means incompatible."[17] Scripture's literary forms should determine the hermeneutical approach. As a result, differing narratives should not be read in the same way. This has much to say to the Evangelical concept of truth in terms of the relationship between biblical inerrancy and epistemology, for Vanhoozer insists that the literary form of the text should be allowed to determine the form of inerrancy that is maintained for the text. Vanhoozer maintains that "inerrancy must be construed broadly enough to encompass the truth expressed in Scripture's poetry, romances, proverbs, parables—as well as histories."[18] In this sense "inerrancy" becomes a subset of "infallibility." Vanhoozer writes:

15. Kevin J. Vanhoozer, "The Semantics of Biblical Literature," in *Hermeneutics, Authority, and Canon*, ed. D. A. Carson and John D. Woodbridge (Grand Rapids: Academie/Zondervan, 1984), 53-104. See also Vanhoozer's *Biblical Narrative in the Philosophy of Paul Ricoeur* (Cambridge: Cambridge University Press, 1990), particularly the chapter titled "A Literal Gospel?," 148-189.

16. Vanhoozer, "The Semantics of Biblical Literature," 92. Vanhoozer adds, 93, that the personal/propositional dichotomy is a false one, for "God personally confronts us by means of the scriptural propositions that He propounds in various ways for our consideration.

17. Ibid., 68. This point is also made, in the context of an overview of the philosophical discussion of form and matter, in William L. Hendricks "The Difference Between Substance (Matter) and Form in Relationship to Biblical Inerrancy," *The Proceedings of the Conference on Biblical Inerrancy, 1987* (Nashville: Broadman, 1987), 481-489.

18. Ibid., 79. Vanhoozer is correct to point out that such a view does not do violence to the hermeneutical concept of authorial intent, but rather complements it, for Hirsch stated that the verbal meaning of a text is tied to its genre. Indeed, it is the "controlling idea of the whole," determining what a text "is." On this, see Vanhoozer, "The Semantics of Biblical Literature," 80, and E. D. Hirsch, Jr., *Validity in Interpretation* (New Haven: Yale University, 1967), 79. Vanhoozer also mentions Ricoeur's insistence that the literary forms are in and of themselves theologically significant, for "not just any theology may be attached to the story form"; see Ricoeur's "Toward a Hermeneutic of the Idea of Revelation," in *Essays on Biblical Interpretation* (Philadelphia: Fortress, 1980), 75.

> On those occasions when Scripture does affirm something, the affirmation is true. Thus, we may continue to hold to inerrancy while at the same time acknowledging that Scripture does many other things besides assert. Logically, however, infallibility is prior to inerrancy. God's Word invariably accomplishes its purpose (infallibility); and when this purpose is assertion, the proposition of the speech act is true (inerrancy).[19]

Rather than leading to a radically subjective view of truth, this "literary" approach simply allows the text to determine the nature of truth which is being proposed. Vanhoozer contends that the diversity of literary forms does not imply that Scripture contains competing kinds of truth, but rather various kinds of "fact," such as historical fact, metaphysical fact, moral fact, and so on. Thus the correspondence theory of truth remains intact and viable in that a sentence or text is true "if things are as it says they are, but as Aristotle observed, 'Being may be said in many ways.'"[20] The correspondence theory must be expanded to include "this secondary sense in which nonassertive illocutions may be said to be true."[21] Vanhoozer contends that "the nature of the correspondence to reality (and thus the nature of truth) of an utterance is determined by its illocutionary aspect and literary form."[22] Thus, scientific statements involve one type of correspondence to reality; poetic statements, another type of correspondence to reality; and so on. It is imperative to understand that in one form or another all speech acts, even those which are not "assertive," correspond to reality. It is hoped that this would also preserve the absolute nature of truth as opposed to the ideas put forth by process thought regarding truth. It is also hoped that such a perspective would point toward the direction to be taken to exploring the coherence, correspondence, and relevance of the various theories regarding differing fields of truth, though such an exploration is beyond the scope of this study.

To summarize, an understanding of the polymorphous character of truth in regard to various narrative forms would allow for the foundation of the correspondence theory of truth along with the employment of various other conceptualizations of truth to be exercised both hermeneutically and epistemologically as the narrative demands. In other words, one holds ontologically to the concept of truth as correspondence, but epistemologically and hermeneutically one must embrace various understandings of truth in relation to authorial intent and mean-

---

19. Vanhoozer, "The Semantics of Biblical Literature," 95. A similar point is made by John S. Feinberg in his essay "Truth: Relationship of Theories of Truth to Hermeneutics," *Hermeneutics, Inerrancy, and the Bible*, ed. Earl D. Radmacher and Robert D. Preus (Grand Rapids: Zondervan, 1984), when he states, 6, that since "only declarative sentences (statements) can be true or false, the scope of the inerrancy debate must be significantly limited, if one defines inerrancy in terms of truth."

20. Vanhoozer, "The Semantics of Biblical Literature," 85. Vanhoozer's quote by Aristotle is from *Metaphysics*, 4.2.

21. "The Semantics of Biblical Literature," 101.

22. Ibid.

ing as found in the form of the particular narrative in question. There is ultimate unity in the concept of truth, but practical diversity, thus allowing for ontology and epistemology to be separated methodologically but unified metaphysically in God's knowledge.

Wolfhart Pannenberg contends that this unity is possible only as a historical process and can be known only from the end of this process. For this reason Pannenberg maintains that the unity of truth is constituted only by the proleptic revelation of God in Jesus Christ.[23] Thiselton finds much to be gained from this perspective, writing that "Pannenberg has pointed the way forward to recovering a sense of the unity and comprehensiveness of truth in theology."[24]

Pannenberg acknowledges that the truth of theological discourse is always presupposed.[25] He discounts Habermas' embrace of a consensus view of truth, seeing its value only as a criterion of truth, and that only if it arises free from any coercion. Only conventionality could then be said to have been established, but not necessarily universal truth.[26] Pannenberg contends for the correspondence theory of truth as the epistemological nature of the truth, but sees coherence in interpretation as the central criterion of truth. "If the unity of the content of scripture is not accepted," writes Pannenberg, "the clarity of its meaning is of little use."[27] Pannenberg does not wish to divide the nature of truth from its criterion, or even to divide the question of the truth of Christian doctrine (apologetics) from the content of Christian doctrine (dogmatics). Instead, Pannenberg contends for the "truth of Christian doctrine as the theme of systematic theology."[28] Though they are not his terms, it would seem that Pannenberg hopes to demonstrate the union of the great divide between presuppositional approaches and evidentialist approaches in regard to the construction and explication of Christian theology. Further, he wishes to point the way to a union of coherence and correspondence understandings of truth, seeing an ultimate coherence between the correspondence of judgment and fact. Truth, understood in this way, unavoidably becomes ontological. As a result, God alone can be the ontological locus of the unity of truth.[29]

---

23. See Wolfhart Pannenberg, "What Is Truth," *Basic Questions in Theology, Volume II*, trans. George H. Kehm (Philadelphia: Westminster, 1971), 1-27.

24. Anthony C. Thiselton, "Truth," *The New International Dictionary of New Testament Theology, Vol. 3* (Grand Rapids: Regency Reference Library/Zondervan, 1986), 900.

25. For his most recent reflections on the nature and criterion of truth, see Wolfhart Pannenberg, *Systematic Theology*, vol. 1, trans. Geoffrey W. Bromiley (Grand Rapids: Eerdmans, 1991).

26. On this, see Beckermann's critique of Habermas, "Die realistischen Voraussetzungen der Konsenstheorie von J. Habermas," *Zeitschrift für Allgemeine Wissenschaftstheorie 3* (1972), 63-80.

27. Pannenberg, *Systematic Theology*, vol. 1, 31.

28. Hence the title for the first section of *Systematic Theology*, vol. 1, 1-61.

29. Pannenberg, *Systematic Theology*, vol. 1, 53.

CONCLUSION

Jeffrey Stout writes that theology "seems to have lost its voice, its ability to command attention as a distinctive contributor to the conversation of high culture."[1] The reason for this loss may well be the diminution of the concept of truth in Christian Thought. The prevalent view today "tends to place philosophical opinions and religious belief on the side of taste rather than on the side of truth."[2] Robert J. Palma agrees, noting that the "retreat from truth and truth claims and the rise of phenomenalism have become increasingly manifest in the disciplines of theology and religious studies."[3] Yet as J. I. Packer reminds us, "only truth can be authoritative,"[4] David Tracy states that "theology . . . must always struggle in every age to constitute itself anew as a normative and self-constituting discipline concerned with that elusive reality 'truth.'"[5]

---

1. Jeffrey Stout, "The Voice of Theology in Contemporary Culture," *Religion and America: Spirituality in a Secular Age*, ed. by Mary Douglas and Steven M. Tipton (Boston: Beacon Press/American Academy of Arts and Sciences, 1982, 1983), 249.

2. Mortimer J. Adler, *Six Great Ideas* (New York: Macmillan, 1981), 61. Adler adds to this statement that this "has not always been the regnant view, nor is it necessarily the correct one."

3. Robert J. Palma, "The Rehabilitation of Truth in Theology," *Scottish Journal of Theology*, vol. 28 (Edinburgh: Scottish Academic Press, 1975), 204.

4. J. I. Packer, *Fundamentalism: and the Word of God: Some Evangelical Principles* (Grand Rapids: Eerdmans, 1958), 20. Perhaps even more to the point, Packer writes, 116, that "truth is fundamental to trust."

5. David Tracy, *The Analogical Imagination: Christian Theology and the Culture of Pluralism* (New York: Crossroad, 1986), 20. As the title of Tracy's work intimates, he argues, 86, n. 34, for an analogical meaning of truth.

The Evangelical insistence on the existence of revealed truth from God that human mind can apprehend can make a decisive contribution to the current malaise of theological reflection and pronouncement. The assumption of the truthfulness of God's Word as revealed in Scripture is not irrational; it is a coherent proposal put forth as an alternative world view which confronts the prevailing culture and philosophy with its truth and claims. Truth is not subjective in the sense that what is "true for you is true for you, and what is true for me is true for me." Truth is objectively that which corresponds to the living God who has made His truth known to us through His Son and through the primary witness to the Son in Scripture.

As Christians seek to give witness to their faith, the correspondence, coherence, and pragmatic theories of truth can become mutually complementary. As John Jefferson Davis notes, the believer "finds the claims of Christ verified in personal experience, in the unfolding of a comprehensive and coherent view of reality, and in the correspondence of the biblical data to the facts of history."[6] Davis rightly adds, however, that in the last analysis "the believer's certitude rests on the inner testimony of the Holy Spirit to the Word of God.[7]

It should be noted that any theory of truth is far from the last word on the subject of truth, for Christian theology should ultimately posit God as Truth. This Truth does not correspond with anything outside of God's self. Thus ultimate truth is not an idea or a correspondence, but is personal, and ultimately resides as an attribute of the very nature of God.

---

6. John Jefferson Davis, *Theology Primer* (Grand Rapids: Baker, 1981), 61.
7. Ibid.

BIBLIOGRAPHY

A. American Evangelicalism

Books

Alan, J. D. *The Evangelicals: An Illustrated History.* Grand Rapids: Baker, 1989.

Ayling, Stanley. *John Wesley.* London: Collins, 1979.

Balmer, Randall. *Mine Eyes Have Seen The Glory: A Journey into the Evangelical Subculture in America.* New York/Oxford: Oxford University, 1989.

Barker, William S. and Robert W. Godfrey, eds. *Theonomy: A Reformed Critique.* Grand Rapids: Academie/Zondervan, 1990.

Bratt, J. D. *Dutch Calvinism in Modern America.* Grand Rapids: Eerdmans, 1984.

Bushman, Richard L., ed. *The Great Awakening: Documents on the Revival of Religion, 1740-1745.* Chapel Hill: University of North Carolina Press, 1969.

Carpenter, Joel A., ed. *Fundamentalism in American Religion, 1880-1950.* 45-Volume Facsimile Series. New York: Garland.

_____ and Wilbert R. Shenk, eds. *Earthen Vessels: American Evangelicals and Foreign Missions, 1880-1980.* Grand Rapids: Eerdmans, 1990.

Cohen, Norman J. *The Fundamentalist Phenomenon.* Grand Rapids: Eerdmans, 1990.

Cole, Stewart. *The History of Fundamentalism.* Hamden, Conn.: Archon, 1963.

Dallimore, Arnold A. *George Whitefield: The Life and Times of the Great Evangelist of the Eighteenth Century Revival,* 1 vols., Amer. ed. Westchester, Ill.: Cornerstone, 1980.

Dayton, Donald W. *Discovering an Evangelical Heritage.* New York: Harper and Row, 1976.

_____. *Theological Roots of Pentecostalism.* Grand Rapids: Zondervan, 1988.

_____ and Robert K. Johnston, eds. *The Variety of American Evangelicalism.* Downers Grove: InterVarsity, 1991.

De Klerk, P. and R. R. De Ridder, eds. *Perspectives on the Christian Reformed Church.* Grand Rapids: Baker, 1983.

Dobson, Ed. *In Search of Unity.* Nashville: Thomas Nelson, 1985.

Douglas, Mary and Steven M. Tipton, eds. *Religion and America: Spirituality in a Secular Age.* Boston: Beacon, 1982.

Drakeford, John W, ed. *John Wesley.* Nashville: Broadman, 1979.

Edwards, Jonathan. *The Works of Jonathan Edwards,* vol. 4, New Haven: Yale University, 1957.

Ellingsen, Mark. *The Evangelical Movement: Growth, Impact, Controversy, Dialog.* Minneapolis: Augsburg, 1988.

Erdman, Charles, ed. *The Fundamentals,* 12 vols. Los Angeles, Ca.: The Bible Institute of Los Angeles, 1917.

Flake, Carol. *Redemptorama: Culture, Politics, and the New Evangelicalism.* New York: Penguin, 1984.

Frank, Douglas. *Less Than Conquerors: How Evangelicals Entered the Twentieth Century.* Grand Rapids: Eerdmans, 1986.

Fraser, David A., ed. *Evangelicalism: Surviving Its Success/The Evangelical Round Table, vol. 2.* Princeton: Princeton University/Eastern College and the Eastern Baptist Theological Seminary, 1987.

Furniss, Norman F. *The Fundamentalist Controversy, 1918-1931.* New Haven: Yale University, 1954.

Gaebelein, Frank E. *Christianity Today.* New York: Pyramid, 1968.

Gaustad, Edwin W. *The Great Awakening in New England.* New York: Harper and Row, 1957.

Guinness, Os. *The Gravedigger File: Papers on the Subversion of the Modern Church.* Downers Grove: InterVarsity, 1983.

Harrell, David Edwin, Jr. *Varieties of Southern Evangelicalism.* Macon: Mercer University, 1981.

Hatch, Nathan O. and Mark Noll, eds. *The Bible in America.* Oxford: Oxford University, 1982.

_____. *The Democratization of American Christianity.* New Haven: Yale University, 1989.

Heimert, Alan. *Religion and the American Mind.* Cambridge, Mass.: Harvard University, 1966.

Hoffecker, W. A. *Piety and the Princeton Theologians.* Philipsburg, N.J.: Presbyterian and Reformed and Grand Rapids: Baker, 1981.

Hoover, Stewart M. *Mass Media Religion: The Social Sources of the Electronic Church.* Newbury Park: Sage Publications, 1988.

Horton, Michael Scott. *Made in America: The Shaping of Modern American Evangelicalism.* Grand Rapids: Baker, 1991.

House, H. Wayne and Thomas Ice. *Dominion Theology: Blessing or Curse? An Analysis of Christian Reconstructionism.* Portland: Multnomah, 1988.

Hubbard, David Alan. *What We Evangelicals Believe: Expositions of Christian Doctrine Based on "The Statement of Faith" of Fuller Theological Seminary,* Pasadena, Ca.: Fuller Theological Seminary, 1979.

Hunter, James Davison. *American Evangelicalism: Conservative Religion and the Quandary of Modernity.* New Brunswick, N.J.: Rutgers University, 1983.

_____. *Evangelicalism: The Coming Generation.* Chicago: University of Chicago, 1987.

Hutcheson, Jr., Richard G. *Mainline Churches and the Evangelicals: A Challenging Crisis?* Atlanta: John Knox, 1981.

Johnston, Robert K. *Evangelicals at an Impasse.* Atlanta: John Knox, 1979.

Kantzer, Kenneth and Carl F. H. Henry, eds. *Evangelical Affirmations.* Grand Rapids: Academie/Zondervan, 1990.

Kik, J. Marcellus. *Ecumenism and the Evangelical.* Philadelphia: The Presbyterian and Reformed Pub. Co., 1958.

Kromminga, John H. *The Christian Reformed Church: A Study in Orthodoxy.* Grand Rapids: Baker, 1949.

LaHaye, Tim. *The Battle for the Mind.* Old Tappan, N.J.: Fleming H. Revell, 1980.

Leonard, Bill J., editor. *Early American Christianity.* Nashville: Broadman, 1983.

Lindsey, Hal. *The Late Great Planet Earth.* Grand Rapids: Zondervan, 1971.

Lotz, David W. ed. with Donald W. Shriver, Jr. and John F. Wilson. *Altered Landscapes: Christianity in America, 1935-1985.* Grand Rapids: Eerdmans, 1989.

Lovelace, Richard F. *Dynamics of Spiritual Life: An Evangelical Theology of Renewal.* Downers Grove: InterVarsity, 1979.

Machen, J. Gresham. *Christianity and Liberalism.* Grand Rapids: Eerdmans, 1923.

George M. Marsden, ed. *Evangelicalism and Modern America.* Grand Rapids: Eerdmans, 1984.

_____. *The Evangelical Mind and the New School Presbyterian Experience: A Case Study of Thought and Theology in Nineteenth Century America.* New Haven: Yale University, 1970.

_____. *Fundamentalism and American Culture: The Shaping of Twentieth-Century Evangelicalism, 1980-1925.* Oxford: Oxford University Press, 1980.

_____. *Reforming Fundamentalism: Fuller Seminary and the New Evangelicalism.* Grand Rapids: Eerdmans, 1987.

_____. *Understanding Fundamentalism and Evangelicalism.* Grand Rapids: Eerdmans, 1991.

Marshall, Peter and David Manuel. *From Sea to Shining Sea.* Old Tappan, NJ: Fleming H. Revell, 1986.

_____. *The Light and the Glory.* Old Tappan, NJ: Fleming H. Revell, 1977.

Martin, William. *A Prophet With Honor: The Billy Graham Story.* New York: William Morrow, 1991.

Marty, Martin E. *Modern American Religion, Volume 1: The Irony of It All, 1983-1919.* Chicago: University of Chicago, 1986.

_____. *A Nation of Behavers.* Chicago: University of Chicago, 1976.

McLoughlin, William C. *Revivals, Awakenings, and Reform.* Chicago and London: University of Chicago, 1978.

_____, ed. *The American Evangelicals, 1800-1900: An Anthology.* Gloucester, Mass.: Peter Smith, 1976.

Miller, Perry and Alan Heimert, eds. *The Great Awakening: Documents Illustrating the Crisis and its Consequences.* Indianapolis: Bobbs-Merrill, 1967.

_____. *Jonathan Edwards.* New York: William Sloane, 1949.

Murch, James DeForest. *Cooperation Without Compromise: A History of the National Association of Evangelicals.* Grand Rapids: Eerdmans, 1956.

Nash, Ronald H. *Evangelicals in America: Who They Are, What They Believe.* Nashville: Abingdon, 1987.

_____. *Christian Faith and Historical Understanding.* Grand Rapids: Zondervan, 1984.

_____, ed. *Evangelical Renewal in the Mainline Churches.* Westchester, IL: Crossway, 1987.

_____. *The New Evangelicalism.* Grand Rapids: Zondervan, 1963.

Neuhas, Richard John and Michael Cromartie, eds. *Piety and Politics: Evangelicals and Fundamentalists Confront the World.* Washington: Ethics and Public Policy Center/University Press of America, Inc., 1987.

Noll, Mark A., ed. *The Princeton Theology, 1812-1921.* Grand Rapids: Baker, 1983.

Oden, Thomas C. and Leiscester R. Longden, eds. *The Wesleyan Theological Heritage: Essays of Albert C. Outler.* Grand Rapids: Zondervan, 1991.

Outler, A. C., ed. *John Wesley.* New York: Oxford University, 1964.

Pollock, John. *Billy Graham: The Authorized Biography.* New York: McGraw Hill, 1966.

Quebedeaux, Richard. *The Young Evangelicals.* New York: Harper and Row, 1974.

Ramm, Bernard L. *After Fundamentalism.* San Francisco: Harper and Row, 1983.

_____. *The Evangelical Heritage.* Waco: Word, 1973.

Reagan, Ronald, C. Everett Koop, and Malcolm Muggeridge. *Abortion and the Conscience of the Nation.* Nashville: Thomas Nelson, 1984.

Russell, C. Allyn. *Voices of American Fundamentalism.* Philadelphia: Westminster, 1976.

Sandeen, E. L. *Voices of American Fundamentalism.* Philadelphia: Westminster, 1976.

Schultze, Quentin J., ed. *American Evangelicals and the Mass Media.* Grand Rapids: Academie/Zondervan, 1990.

_____. *Televangelism and American Culture.* Grand Rapids: Baker, 1991.

Smith, Harold B., ed. *Pentecostals from the Inside Out.* Wheaton: Victor/Christianity Today, 1990.

Stoeffler, F. Ernest. *Continental Pietism and Early American Christianity.* Grand Rapids: Eerdmans, 1976.

_____. *German Pietism During the Eighteenth Century.* Leiden: E. J. Brill, 1973.

_____. *The Rise of Evangelical Pietism.* Leiden: E. J. Brill, 1965.

Stout, Harry S. *The Divine Dramatist: George Whitefield and the Rise of Modern Evangeli-calism.* Grand Rapids: Eerdmans, 1991.

Stonehouse, Ned B. *J. Gresham Machen: A Biographical Memoir.* Carlisle, PA: The Banner of Truth Trust, 1987.

Sweet, Leonard I., ed. *The Evangelical Tradition in America.* Macon: Mercer University, 1984.

_____. *Revivalism in America.* Gloucester, MA: Peter Smith, 1965.

Torrey, R. A., et al. *The Fundamentals: The Famous Sourcebook of Foundational Biblical Truths.* Grand Rapids: Kregel, 1990.

Webber, Robert E. and Donald G. Bloesch, eds. *The Orthodox Evangelicals: Who They Are and What They Are Saying.* Nashville: Thomas Nelson, 1978.

Wells, David F. and John D. Woodbridge, eds. *The Evangelicals: What They Believe, Who They Are, Where They Are Changing.* Nashville: Abingdon, 1975.

_____. *Dutch Reformed Theology.* Grand Rapids: Baker, 1989.

_____. *Reformed Theology in America.* Grand Rapids: Eerdmans, 1985.

Wells, William W. *Welcome to the Family: An Introduction to Evangelical Christianity.* Downers Grove: InterVarsity, 1979.

White, Jerry. *The Church and The Parachurch: An Uneasy Marriage.* Portland: Mult-nomah, 1983.

Williams, George Hunston and Angel M. Mergal, eds. *Spiritual and Anabaptist Writers: Documents Illustrative of the Radical Reformation.* The Library of Christian Classics. Philadelphia: Westminster, 1957.

Wills, Garry. *Under God: Religion and American Politics.* New York: Simon and Schuster, 1990.

Wuthnow, Robert. *The Struggle for America's Soul: Evangelicals, Liberals and Secularism.* Grand Rapids: Eerdmans, 1989.

Articles

Becker, U. "Gospel, Evangelize, Evangelist." In *The New International Dictionary of New Testament Theology,* vol. 2. ed. Colin Brown, Grand Rapids: Regency Reference Library, 1976 and 1986.

Boer, Harry R. "Evangelical Theologians," *The Reformed Journal,* 35, no. 4 (April 1985): 2-3.

Cameron, Nigel M., ed., "The Challenge of Evangelical Theology: Essays in Approach and Method," *Scottish Bulletin of Evangelical Theology,* 5 (Spring 1987): v-viii, 1-153.

Carpenter, Joel A. "Fundamentalist Institutions and the Rise of Evangelical Protestantism, 1929-1942," *Church History* 49 (March 1980): 62-75.

Daly, Peter J. "Keeping the Faith in High-Tech America: Does Communion Over Cable TV Still Count?," *The Washington Post National Weekly Edition* (September 12-18, 1988): 21-22.

Dayton, Donald W. "An Interview with Donald W. Dayton," *Faith and Thought* 1 (Spring 1983): 25.

Finger, Thomas. "Evangelical Theology: Where Do We Begin?," *TSF Bulletin,* 8, no. 2 (November-December 1984): 10-14.

Friedrich, Gerhard. "Euangelizomai, euangelion, proeuangelizomai, euangelistes." In *Theological Dictionary of the New Testament.* vol. II. ed. Gerhard Kittel. Grand Rapids: Eerdmans, 1964, 707-737.

"Fundamental Conflict on the Right," *Washington Post National Weekly Edition* (January 14, 1985): 6.

Gaebelein, A. C. "The Present Day Apostasy," *The Coming and Kingdom of Christ: A Stenographic Report of the Prophetic Bible Conference Held at the Moody Bible Institute of Chicago, Feb. 24-27, 1914. Chicago: 1914.*

"God and Politics," *Newsweek* (September 17, 1984): 28.

Grounds, Vernon. "American Evangelicalism: Quo Vadis?" *TSF Bulletin*, vol. 10, no. 5 (May-June 1987): 7-10.

Hardman, Keith. "God's Wonderful Working: The First Great Awakening," *Christian History*, vol. VIII, no. 3, Issue 23, 12-23.

Jacobsen, Douglas. "Re-Visioning Evangelical Theology," *The Reformed Journal*, vol. 35, no. 10 (October 1985), 18-22.

Laws, Curtis Lee. "Convention Side Lights," *The Watchman-Examiner* (July 1, 1920).

Lawson, Kim A. "A Fourth 'R'?," *Christianity Today* (December 9, 1988:53

Leonard, Bill J. "The Origin and Character of Fundamentalism," *Review and Expositor*, LXXIX, 1 (Winter 1982).

McLoughlin, William G. "Pietism and the American Character," *American Quarterly* 17 (Summer 1965): 163-186.

Miller, E. L., "A Barometer of Evangelical Theology," *The Iliff Review*, 44 (Spring 1987): 49-56.

Noll, Mark A. "Common Sense Traditions and American Evangelical Thought," *American Quarterly*, 37, no. 2 (Summer 1985): 216-238.

_____. "The Princeton Theology." In *The Princeton Theology*. David F. Wells ed., Grand Rapids: Baker, 1989.

Rabinove, Samuel. "Williamsburg Charter Fuels Debate," *The Christian Century* (November 9, 1988): 1007-1008.

Schmiechen, Peter M. "The Challenge of Conservative Theology," *The Christian Century*, 97, (April 9, 1980): 402-406.

Shelley, Bruce L. "Evangelicalism." In *Dictionary of Christainity in America*. ed. Daniel G. Reid, Robert D. Linder, Bruce L. Shelley, Harry S. Stout. Downers Grove: InterVarsity, 1990.

Smith, Harold B., ed. "CT at Thirty: Looking Back at the Faces of American Evangelicalism," *Christianity Today*, 30, no. 15 (October 17, 1986): 19-28.

Smith, Maurice. "Parachurch Movements," *Missions USA* (October- December, 1984): 145-149.

Smith, Timothy L. "The Evangelical Kaleidoscope and the Call to Christian Unity," *Christian Scholar's Review* 15/2 (1986): 125-140.

Steinfels, Peter. "Radio Psychologist is 'Rising Star' of Religious Right," *The Courier-Journal* (Sunday, June 17, 1990), editorial section: 1, 4.

Sweet, Leonard I. "Millennialism in America: Recent Studies," *Theological Studies* 40 (September 1979): 510-531.

Wilson, Ron. "Parachurch: Becoming Part of the Body," *Christianity Today*, 24 (September 19, 1980): 18.

Woodward, Kenneth L. with John Barnes and Laurie Lisle. "Born Again: The Year of the Evangelicals," *Newsweek* (October 25, 1976): 68-78.

Youngren, J. Alan. "Parachurch Proliferations: The Frontier Spirit Caught in Traffic," *Christianity Today*, 25 (November 6, 1981): 6.

B. The Concept Of Truth

Books

Ackerman, Robert J. *Belief and Knowledge.* Garden City: Doubleday, 1972.

Adler, Mortimer. *Aristotle for Everybody: Difficult Thought Made Easy.* New York: Macmillan, 1978.

_____ and William Gorman. *The Great Ideas: A Syntopicon of Great Books in the Western World*, vol. 2. Chicago: Encyclopedia Britannica, 1952.

_____. *Six Great Ideas.* New York: Macmillan, 1981.

_____. *Ten Philosophical Mistakes: Basic Errors in Modern Thought—How They Came About, Their Consequences, and How to Avoid Them.* New York: Macmillan, 1985.

_____. *Truth in Religion: The Plurality of Religions and the Unity of Truth.* New York: Macmillan, 1990.

Altizer, Thomas J. J., et al. *Deconstruction and Theology.* New York: Crossroad, 1982.

Aristotle, "Metaphysica: (trans. W. D. Ross), "Categoriae" and "Deinterpretatione" (trans. E. M. Edghill). *The Great Books of the Western World*, vol. 8. ed. Robert Maynard Hutchins. Chicago :Encyclopedia Britannica, 1952.

_____. "On the Heavens," *The Oxford Translation of Aristotle.* ed. and trans. W. D. Ross. Oxford: Oxford University, 1928.

Armstrong, D. M. *Belief, Truth and Knowledge.* Cambridge: Cambridge University, 1973.

Ayer, A. J. *The Problem of Knowledge.* London: Macmillan, 1956.

Banner, Michael C. *The Justification of Science and the Rationality of Religious Belief.* Oxford: Clarendon, 1990.

Barbour, Ian. *Religion in an Age of Science: The Gifford Lectures, 1989-1991. Volume One.* San Francisco: Harper and Row, 1990.

Berkouwer, G. C. and A. S. van der Woude, eds. *Wat is Wahreit.* Kampen: Kok, 1973.

Bleicher, Josef. *Contemporary Hermeneutics: Hermeneutics as Method, Philosophy and Critique.* London: Routledge and Kegan Paul, 1980.

Bloom, Harold, et al. *Deconstructionism and Criticism.* New York: Seabury, 1979.

Brown, Colin, *Philosophy and the Christian Faith/* Downers Grove: InterVarsity, 1968.

_____. *Christianity and Western Thought, Vol. 1: A History of Philosophers, Ideas and Movements.* Downers Grove: InterVarsity, 1990.

Brunner, Emil. *Revelation and Reason.* Philadelphia: Westminster, 1946.

_____. *Wahrheit als Begegnung.* Berlin: Im Furche-Verlag, 1938.

Bush, L. Russ. *A Handbook for Christian Philosophy.* Grand Rapids: Zondervan, 1991.

Cragg, Gerald R. *The Church and the Age of Reason, 1648-1789.* New York: Penguin, 1970.

Darcy, Jonathan. *An Introduction to Contemporary Epistemology.* Oxford: Basil Blackwell, 1985.

Davidson, Donald. *Inquiries into Truth and Interpretation.* Oxford: Clarendon Press, 1991.

Derrida, Jacques. *Dissemination.* Barbara Johnson, trans. Chicago: University of Chicago, 1981.

_____. *Glas.* Paris: Editions Galilee, 1974.

_____. *Grammatology.* trans. G. C. Spivak. Baltimore: Johns Hopkins University, 1976.

_____. *Speech and Phenomena and Other Essays on Husserl's Theory of Signs.* Trans. David Allison. Evanston: Northwestern University, 1973.

_____. *Writing and Difference.* trans. Alan Bass. Chicago: University of Chicago, 1978.

Devitt, Michael. *Realism and Truth.* Oxford: Basil Blackwell, 1984.

Dreyfuss, Herbert L. and Paul Rainbow. *Michael Foucault: Beyond Structuralism and Hermeneutics*, 2nd ed. Chicago: University of Chicago, 1982.

Durant, Will. *The Story of Philosophy: The Lives and Opinions of the Greater Philosophers*. New York: Simon and Schuster, 1961.

Ebeling, Gerhard. *Word and Faith*. London: SCM, 1963.

Edwards, Paul, ed. *The Encyclopedia of Philosophy* (8 volumes). New York: Macmillan and Free Press, 1967.

Ellis, Brian. *Truth and Objectivity*. Oxford: Basil Blackwell, 1990.

Ferre, Frederick. *Language, Logic, and God*. New York: Harper and Row, 1961.

Fletcher, Joseph. *Situation Ethics: The New Morality*. Philadelphia: Westminster, MCMLXVI.

Frei, Hans W. *The Eclipse of Biblical Narrative: A Study in Eighteenth and Nineteenth Century Hermeneutics*. New Haven: Yale University, 1974.

Gadamer, Hans Georg (translation ed. Garrett Barden and John Cumming). *Truth and Method*. New York: Crossroad, 1986.

_____. *Philosophical Hermeneutics*. trans. and ed. David E. Linge. Berkeley: University of California, 1976.

GJertsen, Derek. *Science and Philosophy: Past and Present*. New York: Penguin, 1989.

Goldberg, Michael. *Theology and Narrative*. Nashville: Abingdon, 1981.

Green, Garrett, ed. *Scriptural Authority and Narrative Interpretation*. Philadelphia: Fortress, 1987.

Griffin, David Ray, William A. Beardslee, and Joe Holland. *Varieties of Postmodern Theology*. New York: State University of New York, 1989.

Guerriere, Daniel, ed. *Phenomenology of the Truth Proper to Religion*. New York: State University of New York, 1990.

Hauerwas, Stanley and L. Gregory Jones, eds. *Why Narrative? Readings in Narrative Theology*. Grand Rapids: Eerdmans, 1989.

Hegel, G. W. F. *Faith and Knowledge*. trans. Walter Cert and H. S. Harris. Albany: State University of New York, 1977.

_____. *The Logic of Hegel*. 2nd ed. trans. William Wallace. London: Oxford University, 1873.

_____. *The Philosophy of History*. J. Sibree, trans. Great Books of the Western World, vol. 46. ed. Robert Maynard Hutchins. Chicago: Encyclopaedia Britannica, 1952.

_____. *The Philosophy of Right*. trans. T. M. Knox. Great Books of the Western World, vol. 46. ed. Robert Maynard Hutchins. Chicago: Encyclopaedia Britannica, 1952.

Helm, Paul. *The Varieties of Belief*. New York: Humanities Press, 1973.

Hick, John. *Philosophy of Religion*, 4th ed. Englewood Cliffs: Prentice-Hall, 1990.

Hirsch, E. D., Jr. *The Aims of Interpretation*. Chicago: University of Chicago, 1976.

_____. *Validity in Interpretation*. New Haven: Yale University, 1967.

Hodges, Wilfrid. *Logic: An Introduction to Elementary Logic*. New York: Penguin, 1977.

Kaufman, Gordon. *An Essay on Theological Method*, rev. ed. Missoula, Mont.: Scholars Press/American Adademy of Religion, 1975, 1979.

_____. *Relativism, Knowledge and Faith*. Chicago: University of Chicago, 1960.

Kaufman, Walter. *Critique of Religion and Philosophy*. New York: Harper and Brothers, 1958.

Kee, Howard Clark. *Knowing the Truth*. Minneapolis: Fortress, 1989.

Keegan, Terrence J. *Interpreting the Bible: A Popular Introduction to Biblical Hermeneutics*. New York: Paulist, 1985.

Kuhn, Thomas. *The Structure of Scientific Revolutions*, 2nd ed. Chicago: University of Chicago, 1970.

James, William. *Pragmatism*. New York: Longman's, Green and Co., 1907.

Lewis, C. I. *An Analysis of Knowledge and Valuation*. LaSalle, Ill.: Open Court, 1946. ·

Macquarrie, John. *Existentialism: An Introduction, Guide, and Assessment.* New York: Penguin, 1972.

_____. *Principles of Christian Theology,* 2nd ed. New York: Charles Scribner's Sons, 1977.

_____. *The Scope of Demythologizing.* London: SCM, 1960.

Margolis, Joseph. *The Truth About Relativism.* Oxford: Basil Blackwell, 1991.

McKim, Donald, ed. *A Guide to Contemporary Hermeneutics: Major Trends in Biblical Interpretation.* Grand Rapids: Eerdmans, 1986.

Mitchell, Basil. *The Justification of Religious Belief.* London: Macmillan, 1973.

_____. *Philosophy of Religion.* Oxford: Oxford University, 1971.

Muller, Eberhard, ed. *Der Gott der Wahrheit.* Berlin: Furche, 1936.

Neuhaus, Richard John, ed. *The Ratzinger Conference on Bible and Church.* Grand Rapids: Eerdmans, 1989.

Newell, R. W. *Objectivity, Empiricism and Truth.* London: Routledge and Kegan Paul, 1986.

Pannenberg, Wolfhart. *Basic Questions in Theology, Vol. II* trans. George H. Kehm. Philadelphia: Fortress, 1975.

_____. *Systematic Theology, Volume 1.* Grand Rapids: Eerdmans, 1991.

Placher, William C. *Unapologetic Theology: A Christian Voice in a Pluralistic Conversation.* Louisville: Westminster/John Knox, 1989.

Plantinga, Alvin and Nicholas Wolterstorff, eds. *Faith and Rationality.* Notre Dame: University of Notre Dame, 1983.

Pollock, John L. *Contemporary Theories of Knowledge.* New Jersey: Rowan and Littlefield, 1986.

Prado, C. J. *The Limits of Pragmatism.* Atlantic Highlands, N.J.: Humanities Press International, 1987.

Reese, W. L. *Dictionary of Philosophy and Religion: Eastern and Western Thought.* New Jersey: Humanities, 1980.

Reiss, Timothy J. *The Uncertainty of Analysis: Problems in Truth, Meaning and Culture.* Ithaca: Cornell University, 1988.

Ricoeur, Paul. *Essays in Biblical Interpretation.* Philadelphia: Fortress, 1980.

_____. *Interpretation Theory: Discourse and the Surplus of Meaning.* Fort Worth: Texas Christian University, 1976.

_____. *Hermeneutics and the Human Sciences.* ed. and trans. John B. Thompson. Cambridge: Cambridge University, 1981.

Russell, Bertrand. *An Inquiry into Meaning and Truth.* New York: W. W. Norton, 1940.

_____. *The Problems of Philosophy.* London: Oxford University, 1959.

Sartre, Jean-Paul. *Existentialism and Human Emotions.* New York: Philosophical Library, 1957.

Siegel, Harvey. *Relativism Refuted.* Dordrecht: D. Reidel Publishing, 1987.

Spanos, William. *Toward a Post-Modern Literary Hermeneutics.* Bloomington: Indiana University, 1980.

Stroup, George. *The Promise of Narrative Theology.* Atlanta: John Knox 1981.

Swinburne, Richard. *Faith and Reason.* Oxford: Clarendon, 1981.

Tarnas, Richard. *The Passion of the Western Mind: Understanding the Ideas that Have Shaped Our World View.* New York: Harmony, 1991.

Tarski, Alfred. *Logic, Semantics and Meta-Mathematics.* Oxford: Oxford University, 1956.

Taylor, Mark. *Deconstructing Theology.* American Academy of Religion Studies in Religion, no. 28. New York: Crossroad and Scholars, 1982.

Thielicke, Helmut. *Modern Faith and Thought.* Geoffrey Bromiley, trans. Grand Rapids: Eerdmans, 1990.

Thompson, John B. *Critical Hermeneutics: A Study in Thought of Paul Ricoeur and Jurgen Habermas.* Cambridge: Cambridge University, 1981.

Tilley, Terrence. *Story Theology.* Wilmington, Del.: Michael Glazier, 1985.

Tillich, Paul. *Systematic Theology,* Three Volumes in One. Chicago: University of Chicago, 1967.

Torrance, Thomas F. *Theological Science.* London: Oxford University, 1969.

Tracy, David. *The Analogical Imagination: Christian Theology and the Culture of Pluralism.* New York: Crossroad, 1986.

_____. *Plurality and Ambiguity: Hermeneutics, Religion and Hope.* San Francisco: Harper and Row, 1987.

Trueblood, David Elton. *Philosophy of Religion.* New York: Harper and Brothers, 1957.

Vanhoozer, Kevin J. *Biblical Narrative in the Philosophy of Paul Ricoeur.* Cambridge: Cambridge University, 1990.

Virkler, Henry A. *Hermeneutics: Principles and Processes of Biblical Interpretation.* Grand Rapids: Baker, 1981.

Wainwright, William. *Philosophy of Religion.* Belmont, Ca.: Wadsworth Pub. Co., 1988.

Walker, C. S. *The Coherence Theory of Truth.* London: Routledge, 1989.

Warner, Rex, *The Greek Philosophers.* New York: Mentor, 1986.

White, Morton, ed. *The Age of Analysis: 20th Century Philosophers.* New York: Meridian, 1983.

Winquist, Charles E. *Epiphanies of Darkness: Deconstruction in Theology.* Philadelphia: Fortress, 1986.

Wittgenstein, Ludwig. *Philosophical Investigations.* G. E. M. Anscombe. Oxford: Basil Blackwell, 1968.

Wuthnow, Robert. *The Struggle for America's Soul: Evangelicals, Liberals and Secularism.* Grand Rapids: Eerdmans, 1989.

Articles

Beauchesne, Richard J. "Truth, Mystery, and Expression: Theological Perspectives Revisited," *Journal of Ecumenical Studies,* 25 (Fall 1988): 555-572.

Blocher, Henri. "The Biblical Concept of Truth," *Themelios,* 4, no. 2 (1967): 8-20.

Bradley, Francis Herbert. "On Truth and Coherence." In *Essay on Truth and Reality.* Oxford: Clarendon, 1914, 202-218.

Buckley, Michael J. "Transcendence, Truth, and Faith: The Ascending Experience of God in all Human Inquiry," *Theological Studies,* 39 (December 1978): 633-655.

Bultmann, Rudolf. "Alethia, alethes, alethinos, aletheno." In *Theological Dictionary of the New Testament,* I. ed, Gerhard Kittel, trans. Geoffrey W. Bromiley. Grand Rapids: Eerdmans, 1964, 232-251.

Burke, Ronald. "Orthodox Modernist with a Modern View of Truth," *The Journal of Religion,* 57 (April 1977): 124-143.

Burnaby, John. "Truth," *Theology,* 81 (November 1978): 438-440.

Cauthen, Kenneth. "Biblical Truths and Rational Knowledge," *Review and Expositor,* 53 (October 1956): 467-476.

Cunningham, Richard B. "A Case for Christian Philosophy," *Review and Expositor,* LXXII, no. 4 (Fall 1985).

Davidson, Donald. "The Structure and Content of Truth," *The Journal of Philosophy,* LXXXVII, no. 6 (June 1990).

Davis, H. Francis. "Faith and Truth," *Scottish Journal of Theology,* 9 (December 1956): 359-373.

Fields, Hartry. "Tarski's Theory of Truth," *Journal of Philosophy,* 69 (July 1972).

Hebblethwaite, Brian L. "Religious Truth and Dialogue," *The Scottish Journal of Religious Studies*, 5, no. 1 (Spring 1984): 3-17.

Heidegger, Martin. "On the Essence of Truth." In *Basic Writings*. ed. David Farrell. San Francisco: Harper and Row, 1977, 117-141.

Keller, James A. "Accepting the Authority of the Bible: Is it Rationally Justified," *Faith and Philosophy*, 6, no. 4 (October 1989): 378-397.

Lawhead, William F. "Descartes Through the Looking Glass: Is it Possible to Believe What Is Contradictory?," *Religious Studies*, 21 (June 1985): 169-179.

Muck, Terry. "Truth's Intrepid Ambassador," *Christianity Today*, 34, no. 17 (November 17, 1990): 34.

Ogden, Schubert M. "Sources of Religious Authority in Liberal Protestantism: for Van A. Harvey on his 50th Birthday," *Journal of the American Academy of Religion*, 44 (September 1976): 403-416.

Palma, Robert J. "Rehabilitation of Truth in Theology," *Scottish Journal of Theology*, 28, no. 3 (1975): 201-226.

Peters, Ted. "Truth in History: Gadamer's Hermeneutics and Pannenberg's Apologetic Method," *The Journal of Religion*, 55 (January 1975): 36-56.

Peper, O. A. "Truth." In *Interpreter's Dictionary of the Bible*, vol. 4. ed. George A. Buttrick. Nashville: Abingdon, 1962.

Plantinga, Alvin. "Advice to Christian Philosophers," *Faith and Philosophy*, 2, no. 3 (July 1984): 253-271.

Quell, Gottfried, Gerhard Kittel, and Rudolf Bultmann. "Alethia." In *Theological Dictionary of the New Testament*, vol. 1, ed. Gerhard Kittel. Grand Rapids: Eerdmans, 1964, 233-251.

Reese, W. L. "Truth." In *Dictionary of Philosophy and Religion: Eastern and Western Thought*. New Jersey: Humanities, 1980, 588-590.

Robbins, J. Wesley. "Christian World View Philosophy and Pragmatism." *Journal of the American Academy of Religion*, 56, (Fall 1988): 529-543.

Schrader, David A. "Faith and Fallibilism," *International Journal for Philosophy of Religion*, 22, no. 1-2 (1987): 55-67.

Shaw, D. W. D. "Criteria of Theological Truth," *Reformed World*, 33 (June 1975): 250-255.

Sturch, Richard L. "Historical Relativism," *Churchman: Journal of Anglican Theology*, 91 (July 1977): 221-228.

Tarski, Aflred. "The Semantic Conception of Truth." In *Semantics and the Philosophy of Language*. Chicago: University of Illinois Press, 1962.

Thiselton, Anthony C. "Truth," *The New International Dictionary of New Testament Theology*, III (Exeter: The Paternoster Press, 1978): 874-902.

Thorson, Walter R. "The Concept of Truth in the Natural Sciences," *Themelios*, 5, no. 2 (1968): 27-39.

Tillich, Paul. "The Two Types of Philosophy of Religion," *Union Seminary Quarterly Review*, I (May 1946): 3-13.

_____. "What is Truth," *Canadian Journal of Theology*, 1 (July 1955): 117-122.

Wainwright, Geoffrey. "Ecumenical Dimensions of Lindbeck's 'Nature of Doctrine,'" *Modern Theology*, 4, no. 2 (January 1988).

C. The Concept of Truth in American Evangelicalism

Books

Archer, Gleason L. *Encyclopedia of Bible Difficulties*. Grand Rapids: Zondervan, 1982.

Berkouwer, G. C. *Holy Scripture: Studies in Dogmatics*. Grand Rapids: Eerdmans, 1975.

Blamires, Harry. *The Christian Mind*. New York: Seabury, 1963.

_____. *A Defense of Dogmatism*. London: SPCK, 1965.

Boer, Harry R. *Above the Battle: The Bible and Its Critics*. Grand Rapids: Eerdmans, 1977.

Boice, James M., ed. *The Foundations of Biblical Authority*. Grand Rapids: Zondervan, 1977.

Bolich, Gregory C. *Karl Barth and Evangelicalism*. Downers Grove: InterVarsity, 1980.

Bush, L. Russ and Tom J. Nettles. *Baptists and the Bible*. Chicago: Moody, 1980.

Carnell, Edward John. *The Case for Biblical Christianity*, ed. Ronald H. Nash. Grand Rapids: Eerdmans, 1969.

_____. *The Case for Orthodox Theology*. Philadelphia: Westminster, 1959.

_____. *Christian Commitment*. New York: Macmillan, 1957.

_____. *An Introduction to Christian Apologetics*. Grand Rapids: Eerdmans, 1950.

_____. *A Philosophy of the Christian Religion*. Grand Rapids: Eerdmans, 1952.

Carson, D. A. and John D. Woodbridge, eds. *Hermeneutics, Authority and Canon*. Grand Rapids: Academie, 1986.

_____. *Scripture and Truth*. Grand Rapids: Academie, 1983.

Clark, Gordon H. *A Christian Philosophy of Education*. Grand Rapids: Eerdmans, 1946.

_____. *A Christian View of Men and Things*. Grand Rapids: Eerdmans, 1952.

_____. *Karl Barth's Theological Method*. Nutley: Presbyterian and Reformed, 1963.

_____. *The Philosophy of Science and Belief in God*. Nutley: Craig, 1972.

_____. *Religion, Reason and Revelation*. Nutley: Presbyterian and Reformed, 1961.

_____. *Thales to Dewey*. Boston: Houghton Mifflin Co., 1957.

Clark, Kelly James. *Return to Reason*. Grand Rapids: Eerdmans, 1990.

Coleman, Richard J. *Issues of Theological Conflict*, rev. ed. Grand Rapids: Eerdmans, 1979.

Colson, Charles. *Against the Night: Living in the New Dark Ages*. Ann Arbor: Servant Publications, 1989.

Cotterell, Peter and Max Turner. *Linguistics and Biblical Interpretation*. Downers Grove: InterVarsity, 1989.

Davis, Stephen T. *The Debate About the Bible: Inerrancy Versus Infallibility*. Philadelphia: Westminster, 1977.

Dockery, David S. *The Doctrine of the Bible*. Nashville: Convention Press, 1991.

Dooyeweerd, Herman. *In the Twilight of Western Thought*. Nutley, N.J.: Craig, 1975.

Elwell, Walter A. *Evangelical Dictionary of Theology*. Grand Rapids: Baker, 1984.

Evans, C. Stephen. *Philosophy of Religion: Thinking About Faith*. Downers Grove: InterVarsity, 1982.

Gaebelein, Frank E. *The Pattern of God's Truth*. Chicago: Moody, 1968.

_____ and D. Bruce Lockerbie. *The Christian, the Arts, and Truth*. Portland: Multnomah, 1985.

Garrett, Duane A. and Richard Melick, Jr. *Authority and Interpretation: A Baptist Perspective*. Grand Rapids: Baker, 1987.

Garrett, James Leo. *Systematic Theology: Biblical, Historical, and Evangelical*, vol. 1. Grand Rapids: Eerdmans, 1990.

Geisler, Norman L., ed. *Biblical Errancy: An Analysis of Its Philosophical Roots*. Grand Rapids: Zondervan, 1978.

_____. *Christian Apologetics*. Grand Rapids: Baker, 1976.

_____. and Ronald M. Brooks. *Come Let Us Reason: An Introduction to Logical Thinking.* Grand Rapids: Baker, 1990.

_____. *Decide for Yourself: How History Views the Bible.* Grand Rapids: Zondervan, 1982.

_____. *Inerrancy.* Grand Rapids: Academie, 1980.

_____ and P. D. Feinberg. *An Introduction to Philosophy.* Grand Rapids: Baker, 1980.

_____. *Philosophy of Religion.* Grand Rapids: Zondervan, 1974.

Gruenler, Royce Gordon. *Meaning and Understanding: The Philosophical Framework for Biblical Interpretation.* Grand Rapids: Zondervan, 1991.

Guinness, Os. *The Dust of Death.* Downers Grove: InterVarsity, 1973.

Hart, Hendrik, Johan van der Hoeven, and Nicholas Wolterstorff. *Rationality in the Calvinian Tradition.* Lanham, MD: University Press of America, 1983.

Helm, Paul, ed. *Objective Knowledge: A Christian Perspective.* Leicester: InterVarsity, 1987.

Hodge, Charles. *Systematic Theology,* 3 vols. Grand Rapids: Eerdmans, reprinted September 1989.

Holmes, Arthur F. *All Truth is God's Truth.* Grand Rapids: Eerdmans, 1977.

_____. *Christianity and Philosophy.* Chicago: InterVarsity Press, 1960.

_____. *Contours of a World View.* Grand Rapids: Eerdmans, 1983.

_____. *Faith Seeks Understanding.* Grand Rapids: Eerdmans, 1971.

_____. , ed. *The Making of a Christian Mind: A Christian World View and the Academic Enterprise.* Downers Grove: InterVarsity, 1984.

Johnston, Robert K., ed. *The Use of the Bible in Theology: Evangelical Options.* Atlanta; John Knox, 1985.

Lewis, Gordon R. and Bruce Demarest, eds. *Challenges to Inerrancy: A Theological Response.* Chicago: Moody, 1984.

Lewis, Gordon R. *Testing Christianity's Truth Claims: Approaches to Christian Apologetics.* Chicago: Moody, 1976.

Lindsell, Harold. *The Battle for the Bible.* Grand Rapids: Zondervan, 1976.

_____. *The Bible in the Balance.* Grand Rapids: Zondervan, 1979.

Longman, Tremper III. *Literary Approaches to Biblical Interpretation.* Grand Rapids: Academie/Zondervan, 1987.

Machen, J. Gresham. *Christianity and Liberalism.* Grand Rapids: Eerdmans, 1946.

_____. *The Virgin Birth of Christ.* Grand Rapids: Baker, 1930.

Montgomery, John Warwick. *Faith Founded on Fact: Essays in Evidential Apologetics.* Nashville: Thomas Nelson, 1978.

_____, ed. *Evidence for Faith: Deciding the God Question.* Dallas: Probe, 1991.

Nash, Ronald H. *Faith and Reason: Searching for a Rational Faith.* Grand Rapids: Academie/Zondervan, 1988.

_____, ed. *Philosophy of Gordon Clark: A Festschrift.* Philadelphia: Presbyterian and Reformed, 1968.

_____. *The Word of God and the Mind of Man: The Crisis of Revealed Truth in Contemporary Theology.* Grand Rapids: Zondervan, 1982.

Nelson, Rudolph. *The Making and Unmaking of an Evangelical Mind: The Case of Edward Carnell.* Cambridge: Cambridge University, 1988.

Netland, Harold A. *Dissonant Voices: Religious Pluralism and the Question of Truth.* Grand Rapids: Eerdmans, 1991.

Newbigin, Lesslie. *Truth to Tell: The Gospel as Public Truth.* Grand Rapids: Eerdmans, 1991.

Nicole, Roger R. and J. Ramsey Michaels, eds. *Challenges to Inerrancy: A Theological Response.* Chicago: Moody, 1984.

Noll, Mark A. *Between Faith and Criticism: Evangelicals, Scholarship, and the Bible in America*. San Francisco: Harper and Row, 1986.

Oden, Thomas C. *After Modernity . . .What? Agenda for Theology*. Grand Rapids: Academie/Zondervan, 1990.

Packer, James I. *"Fundamentalism" and the Word of God*. Grand Rapids: Eerdmans, 1958.

Pinnock, Clark. *Biblical Revelation, the Foundation of Christian Theology*. Chicago: Moody, 1971.

——————. *A Defense of Biblical Infallibility*. Philadelphia: Presbyterian and Reformed, 1967.

——————. *The Scripture Principle*. San Francisco: Harper and Row, 1984.

——————. *Tracking the Maze: Finding Our Way through Modern Theology from an Evangelical Perspective*. San Francisco: Harper and Row, 1990.

Radmacher, Earl D. and Robert D. Preus, eds. *Hermeneutics, Inerrancy and the Bible*. Grand Rapids: Zondervan, 1984.

Ramm, Bernard. *Protestant Biblical Interpretation*. Boston: W. A.Wilde, 1956.

——————. *Special Revelation and the Word of God*. Grand Rapids: Eerdmans, 1961.

——————. *Varieties of Christian Apologetics*. Grand Rapids: Baker, 1962.

Rogers, Jack B. and Donald R. McKim. *The Authority and Interpretation of the Bible: An Historical Approach*. San Francisco: Harper and Row, 1979.

——————, ed. Biblical Authority. Waco: Word, 1977.

Silva, Moises. *Has the Church Misread the Bible?* Grand Rapids: Academie, 1987.

——————. *God, Language and Scripture: Reading the Bible in the Light of General Linguistics*. Grand Rapids: Zondervan, 1990.

Southern Baptist Convention. Broadman Press. *The Proceedings of the Conference on Biblical Inerrancy*. Nashville: Broadman, 1987.

Sproul, R. C., J. Gerstner, and A. Lindsley. *Classical Apologetics*. Grand Rapids: Zondervan, 1984.

Taylor, Daniel. *The Myth of Certainty*. Waco: Word, 1986.

Thiselton, Anthony C. *The Two Horizons: New Testament Hermeneutics and Philosophical Description*. Grand Rapids: Eerdmans, 1984.

Thorsen, Donald A. D. *The Wesleyan Quadrilateral: Scripture, Tradition, Reason and Experience as a Model of Evangelical Theology*. Grand Rapids: Zondervan, 1990.

Torrance, Thomas Forsyth. *Reality and Evangelical Theology*. Philadelphia: Westminster, 1982.

Torrey, R. A., et al., eds., *The Fundamentals*. Los Angeles: The Bible Institute of Los Angeles, 1917.

Trueblood, D. Elton. *Philosophy of Religion*. Grand Rapids: Baker, 1957.

Warfield, Benjamin B. *The Inspiration and Authority of the Bible*. Phillipsburg, N.J.: Presbyterian and Reformed, 1948.

Wells, David F. *Princeton Theology*. Grand Rapids: Baker, 1989.

Wells, Paul Ronald. *James Barr and the Bible: Critique of a New Liberalism*. Philipsburg, NJ: Presbyterian and Reformed, 1980.

Wolfe, David L. *Epistemology: The Justification of Belief*. Downers Grove: InterVarsity, 1982.

Wuthnow, Robert. *The Struggle for America's Soul: Evangelicals, Liberals, and Secularism*. Grand Rapids: Eerdmans, 1989.

Youngblood, Ronald, ed. *Evangelicals and Inerrancy*. Nashville: Thomas Nelson, 1984.

Articles

Brow, Robert. "Evangelical Megashift," *Christianity Today* (February 19, 1990): 12-17.

Cameron, Nigel M. "The Logic of Infallibility: An Evangelical Doctrine at Issue," *The Scottish Bulletin of Evangelical Theology*, 1 (1983): 39-43.

Carnell, E. J. "The Case for Orthodox Theology," *Christianity Today*, 3 (April 27, 1959): 12-13.

Clark, Gordon H. "The Bible as Truth," *Bibliotheca Sacra* 114 (April 1957): 157-170.

_____. "Can Moral Education Be Grounded on Naturalism?" 21-23.

_____. "Faith and Reason," *Christianity Today*, 1 (February 18, 1957 and March 4, 1957): 8-10, 11-12.

_____. "Incarnation: Fact or Theory?" *Christianity Today*, 1 (December 10, 1956): 3-5.

_____. "Is Christianity Unique?" *Christianity Today*, 4 (December 21, 1959): 24-25.

_____. "Limits and Use of Science. In *Horizons of Science*, ed. Carl F. H. Henry. San Francisco: Harper and Row, 1978, 258-276.

_____. "Resurrection," *Christianity Today*, 1 (April 15, 1957): 17-19.

Dahms, John V. "The Nature of Truth," *Journal of the Evanglical Theological Society*, 28, no. 4 (December 1985): 455-465.

Dockery, David S. "Toward a Balanced Hermeneutic in Baptist Life," *Search* (Spring 1989): 47-51.

_____. "Variations on Inerrancy," *SBC Today* (May 1986): 10-11.

_____ and Philip D. Wise. "Biblical Inerrancy: Pro or Con?," *The Theological Educator*, no. 37 (Spring 1988): 15-44.

Fackre, Gabriel. "Evangelical Hermeneutics: Commonality and Diversity," *Interpretation*, 43 (April 1989): 117-129.

Feinberg, John S. "Rationality, Objectivity, and Doing Theology," *Trinity Journal*, 10 NS, no. 2 (Fall 1989): 161-184.

_____. "Truth: Relationship of Theories of Truth to Hermeneutics," In *Hermeneutics, Authority and Canon.* ed. Donald A. Carson and John D. Woodbridge. Grand Rapids: Academie/Zondervan, 1986.

_____. "Truth, Meaning and Inerrancy in Contemporary Evangelical Thought," *Journal of the Evangelical Theological Society*, 26, no. 1 (March 1983): 17-30.

Garrett, Duane A. and Richard R. Melick, Jr. In *Authority and Interpretation.* Grand Rapids: Baker, 1987.

Geisler, Norman L. "The Concept of Truth in the Inerrancy Debate," *Bibliotheca Sacra*, 137, no. 548 (October-December 1980): 327-339.

Grenz, Stanley J. "Reason and Hope," *The Reformed Journal*, 38 (July 1988): 4-6.

Hagner, Donald A. "What is Distinctive About Evangelical Scholarship?," *TSF Bulletin*, 7, no. 3 (January-February 1984): 5-7.

Hendricks, William L. "The Difference Between Substance (Matter) and Form in Relationship to Biblical Inerrancy. In *The Proceedings of the Conference on Biblical Inerrancy.* Nashville: Broadman, 1987.

Holmes, Arthur F. "Christianity and Naturalism," *Christianity Today*, 3 (June 8, 1959): 10-11.

_____. "Language, Logic, and Faith." In *Jerusalem and Athens*, ed. E. Geehan (Philadelphia: Presbyterian and Reformed, 1971); 428-444.

_____. "On Gadamer, Bork, and Moses," *The Reformed Journal*, 37 (October 1987): 2-3.

_____. "Ordinary Language Analysis and Theological Method," *Bulletin of Evangelical Theological Society*, 11 (Summer 1968): 131-138.

Jacobsen, Douglas. "From Truth to Authority to Responsibility: The Shifting Focus of Evangelical Hermeneutics, 1915-1986 (Part I)," *TSF Bulletin*, 10 (March-April 1987): 8-15.

Kovisto, Rex A. "Clark Pinnock and Inerrancy: A Change in Truth Theory," *Journal of the Evangelical Theological Society*, 24 (June 1981): 139-151.

Lundin, Roger. "Deconstructive Therapy," *The Reformed Journal*, 36, issue 1 (January 1986): 15-20.

Macky, Peter W. "The Role of Metaphor in Christian Thought and Experience as Understood by Gordon Clark and C. S. Lewis," *Journal of the Evangelical Theological Society*, 24 (September 1981): 239-250.

Mouw, Richard J. "Evangelicalism and Philosophy," *Theology Today*, XLIV, no. 3 (October 1987): 329-337.

Nash, Ronald H. "Truth by Any Other Name," *Christianity Today*, 22 (October 7, 1977): 17-23.

Nelson, Rudolph L. "Fundamentalism at Harvard: The Case of Edward John Carnell," *Quarterly Review*, 2 (Summer 1982): 79-98.

Netland, Harold. "Exclusivism, Tolerance and Truth," *Evangelical Review of Theology*, 12 (July 1988): 240-260.

Nicole, Roger. "The Inspiration and Authority of Scripture: J. D. G. Dunn versus B. B. Warfield," *Churchman: Journal of Anglican Theology*, 97, no. 3 (1983): 198-215.

Obitts, Stanley. "A Philosophical Analysis of Certain Assumptions of the Doctrine of the Inerrancy of the Bible," *Journal of the Evangelical Theological Society*, 26, no. 2 (June 1983): 129-136.

Osborne, Grant R. "The Evangelical and Redaction Criticism: Critique and Methodology," *Journal of the Evangelical Theology Society*, 22 (December 1979): 305-322.

Owens, Virginia Stem. "Seeing Christianity in Red and Green As Well As Black and White: Propositional Truth is Not the Whole Truth," *Christianity Today*, 27, no. 13 (September 2, 1983): 38-40.

Plantinga, Alvin. "Philosophy from a Christian Perspective," *Faith and Philosophy*, 4 (October 1987): 365-505.

Price, Robert M. "Inerrant the Wind: The Troubled House of North American Evangelicals," *The Evangelical Quarterly*, 55 (July 1983): 129-144.

Ramm, Bernard. "Evangelicals and the Enlightenment: Beyond Liberalism and Fundamentalism," *TSF Bulletin*, 6, no. 3 (January-February 1983): 2-5.

Reid, Stephen B. "An Evangelical Approach to Scripture," *TSF Bulletin*, 8, no. 4 (March-April 1985): 2-5.

Salier, William S. "Reformed Apologetics Revisited," *Evangelical Journal*, 2, no. 1 (Spring 1984): 16-26.

Stackhouse, John G., Jr. "Who Follows in His Train: Edward John Carnell as a Model for Evangelical Theology," *Crux*, 21, no. 2 (June 1985): 19-27.

Trembath, Kern R. "Evangelicalism and Biblical Inspiration," *Evangelical Review of Theology*, 12 (January 1988): 29-40.

Turner, David L. "Evangelicals, Redaction Criticism, and the Current Inerrancy Crisis," *Grace Theological Journal*, 4, no. 2 (Fall 1983): 263-299.

Vanhoozer, Kevin J. "The Semantics of Biblical Literature." In *Hermeneutics, Authority and Canon*. ed. Donald A. Carson and John D. Woodbridge. Grand Rapids: Academie/ Zondervan, 1986, 53-104.

Whitehead, Priscilla Felisky and Tom McAlpine. "Evangelical/LiberalTheology - A False Dichotomy: Report on the Harvard/Gordon-Conwell Dialogue," *TSF Bulletin*, 5, no. 4 (March-April 1982): 8-11.

Woodbridge, John D. "Recent Interpretations of Biblical Authority, Part 4: Is Biblical Inerrancy a Fundamentalist Doctrine?," *Bibliotheca Sacra*, 142 (October-December 1985): 292-305.

_____. "Biblical Authority: Towards an Evaluation of the Rogers and McKim Proposal," *Trinity Journal*, 1 (Fall 1980): 165-236.

D. Critiques of American Evangelicalism and American Evangelical Theology

Books

Achtemeier, Paul. *The Inspiration of Scripture: Problems and Proposals.* Philadelphia: Westminster, 1980.

Averill, Lloyd J. and William W. Jellema. *Colleges and Commitments.* Philadelphia: Westminster, 1971.

Baillie, John. *The Idea of Revelation in Recent Thought.* New York: Columbia University, 1956.

Barr, James. *Beyond Fundamentalism.* Philadelphia: Westminster, 1984.

_____. *Fundamentalism.* London: SCM, 1977.

_____. *Holy Scripture.* Philadelphia: Westminster, 1983.

Bauckham, Richard and Benjamin Drewery. *Scripture, Tradition and Reason.* Edinburgh: T & T Clark, 1988.

Bloesch, Donald G. *The Future of Evangelical Christianity: A Call for Unity and Diversity.* Colorado Springs: Helmers and Howard, 1988.

Coleman, Richard. *Issues of Theological Warfare: Evangelicals and Liberals.* Grand Rapids: Eerdmans, 1972.

Dayton, Donald. *Discovering an Evangelical Heritage.* New York: Harper and Row, 1976.

DeWolf, L. Harold. *The Case for Theology in Liberal Perspective.* Philadelphia: Westminster, 1959.

Drewery, Benjamin. *Scripture, Tradition and Reason.* Edinburgh: T & T Clark, 1988.

Dulles, Avery. *Models of Revelation.* New York: Image Books, 1985.

Edwards, David L. and John R. W. Stott. *Evangelical Essentials: A Liberal-Evangelical Dialogue.* Downers Grove: InterVarsity, 1988.

Ferm, Deane William. *Contemporary American Theologies: A Critical Survey.* Minneapolis: Seabury, 1981.

Frank, Douglas W. *Less Than Conquerors: How Evangelicals Entered the Twentieth Century.* Grand Rapids: Eerdmans, 1986.

Garrett, James Leo, Jr., E. Glenn Hinson, and James E. Tull. *Are Southern Baptists "Evangelicals"?* Macon: Mercer University, 1983.

Henry, Carl F. H. *Evangelicals in Search of Identity.* Waco: Word, 1976.

_____. *The Uneasy Conscience of Modern Fundamentalism.* Grand Rapids: Eerdmans, 1947.

Hodgson, Peter C. and Robert H. King. *Christian Theology: An Introduction to Its Traditions and Tasks.* Philadelphia: Fortress, 1985, esp. chapters 1 and 4.

Hutcheson, Richard G., Jr. *Mainline Churches and the Evangelicals: A Challenging Crisis?* Atlanta: Knox, 1981.

Hutchison, William R., ed. *American Protestant Thought: The Liberal Era.* New York: Harper and Row, 1968.

James, Robison B., ed. *The Unfettered Word: Southern Baptists Confront the Authority-Inerrancy Question.* Waco: Word, 1987.

Kelsey, David H. *The Uses of Scripture in Recent Theology.* London: SCM, 1975.

Lewis, Gordon R. and Bruce Demarest, eds. *Challenges to Inerrancy: A Theological Response.* Chicago: Moody, 1984.

Lindbeck, George A. *The Nature of Doctrine: Religion and Theology in a Postliberal Age.* Philadelphia: Westminster, 1984.

Macquarrie, John. *Twentieth-Century Religious Thought: The Frontiers of Philosophy and Theology, 1900-1960.* London: SCM, 1963, esp. ch. 5.

Miller, Ed. L. "A Barometer of Evangelical Theology," *The Iliff Review*, vol. 44 (Spring 1987), 49-56.

Marsden, George, ed. *Evangelicalism and Modern America*. Grand Rapids: Eerdmans, 1984.

Marty, Martin. *A Nation of Behavers*. Chicago: University of Chicago Press, 1976, esp. ch. 4.

Morris, Thomas V. *Francis Schaeffer's Apologetics: A Critique*. Chicago: Moody, 1976.

Nelson, Rudolph. *The Making and Unmaking of an Evangelical Mind: The Case of Edward Carnell*. Cambridge: Cambridge University, 1988.

Niebuhr, Richard. *The Meaning of Revelation*. New York: MacMillan, 1962.

Pinnock, Clark H. and Delwin Brown. *Theological Crossfire: An Evangelical/Liberal Dialogue*. Grand Rapids: Zondervan, 1990.

Quebedeaux, Richard. *The Worldly Evangelicals*. New York: Harper and Row, 1974.

Southern Baptist Convention. Broadman Press. *The Proceedings of the Conference on Biblical Inerrancy*. Nashville: Broadman, 1987.

Torrance, Thomas Forsyth. *Reality and Evangelical Theology*. Philadelphia: Westminster, 1982.

Trembath, Kern Robert. *Evangelical Theories of Biblical Interpretation*. New York: Oxford, 1987.

Wells, David F. and John D. Woodbrige, eds. *The Evangelicals: What They Believe, Who They Are, Where They Are Changing*. Nashville: Abingdon, 1975.

Wuthnow, Robert. *The Struggle for America's Soul: Evangelicals, Liberals, and Secularism*. Grand Rapids: Eerdmans, 1989.

Articles

Ashcraft, Morris. "The Strengths and Weaknesses of Fundamentalism. "In *The Proceedings of the Conference on Biblical Inerrancy*. Nashville: Broadman, 1987: 531-541.

Averill, Lloyd J. "Can Evangelicalism Survive in the Context of Free Inquiry?," *The Christian Century*, 92 (October 22, 1975): 924-928.

Baker, Tony. "Evangelical Approaches to Theological Dialogue," *Churchman: Journal of Anglican Theology*, 102, no. 1 (March 1988): 44-53.

Basinger, Randall. "Evangelicals and Process Theism: Seeking a Middle Ground," *Christian Scholar's Review*, 15, no. 2 (1986): 157-167.

Brow, Robert. "Evangelical Megashift," *Christianity Today* (February 15, 1990): 25-36.

Brown, Harold O. J. "Kierkegaard's Leap or Schaeffer's Skip?" *Christianity Today*, 28 (December 14, 1984): 82.

Cameron, Nigel M. ed. "The Challenge of Evangelical Theology: Essays in Approach and Method," *Scottish Bulletin of Evangelical Theology*, 5 (Spring 1987): v-viii, 1-153.

Clark, Gordon H. "A Semi-defense of Francis Schaeffer," *Christian Scholar's Review*, 11 (1982): 148-149.

Cunningham, Stuart. "Towards a Critique of Francis Schaeffer's Thought," *Interchange*, 24 (1979): 205-221.

Fackre, Gabriel. "Carl F. H. Henry." In *A Handbook of Christian Theologians* (enlarged edition), ed. Martin E. Marty and Dean G. Peerman. Nashville: Abingdon, 1984, 583-607.

_____. "Evangelical Hermeneutics: Commonality and Diversity," *Interpretation: A Journal of Bible and Theology*, vol. 43 (April 1989), 117-129.

Fosdick, Harry Emerson. "Shall the Fundamentalists Win?" In *The Annals of America*, vol. 14. Chicago: Encyclopedia Britannica, 1976, 325-330.

Geehan, E. R. "The 'Presuppositional' Apologetic of Francis Schaeffer," *Themelios*, 8, no. 1 (1972): 10-18.

Grenz, Stanley J. "Wolfhart Pannenberg's Quest for Ultimate Truth," *The Christian Century* (September 24-21, 1988): 795-798.

Han, Chul-Ha. "An Asian Critique of Western Theology," *Evangelical Review of Theology*, 7, no. 1 (April 1983): 34-47.

Harper, Kenneth C. "Edward John Carnell: An Evaluation of His Apologetics," *Journal of the Evangelical Theological Society*, 20 (June 1977): 133-145.

_____. "Francis A. Schaeffer: An Evaluation," *Bibliotheca Sacra*, 133 (April 1976): 130-142.

Hearn, Arnold W. "Fundamentalist Renascence," *The Christian Century* (April 30, 1958): 527-530.

Henry, Carl F. H. "Evangelical Profits and Losses," *The Christian Century*, 95 (January 25, 1978): 69-70.

Hill, Kent R. "Francis Schaeffer (1912-1984): An Evaluation of His Life and Thought." In *Faith and Imagination: Essays on Evangelicals and Literature*, ed. Noel Riley Finch and Richard W. Etulain. Albuquerque: Far West Books, 1985, pp. 137-171.

Holmer, Paul L. "Contemporary Evangelical Faith: An Assessment and Critique. In *The Evangelicals: What They Believe, Who They Are, Where They Are Changing*, ed. David F. Wells and John D. Woodbrige. Nashville: Abingdon, 1975, 68-95.

Jacobsen, Douglas. "Re-visioning Evangelical Theology," *The Reformed Journal*, 35, no. 10 (October 1985): 18-22.

Leonard, Bill J. "The Origin and Character of Fundamentalism," *Review and Expositor*, LXXIX, no. 1 (Winter, 1982).

Marty, Martin E. "The Years of the Evangelicals," *The Christian Century*, 106, no. 5 (February 15, 1989): 171-174.

Nicole, Roger. "The Inspiration and Authority of Scripture: J. D. G. Dunn versus B. B. Warfield," *Churchman: Journal of Anglican Theology*, 97, no. 3 (1983): 198-215.

Outler, Albert C. "Discursive Truth and Evangelical Truth." In *Colleges and Commitments*, ed. L. Averill. Philadelphia: Westminster, 1971, 101-106.

Pipkin, H. Wayne. "The Neo-Evangelical Alternative: (Re)Discovering a Social Gospel," *Mid-Stream: An Ecumenical Journal*, 22 (July-October 1983): 386-400.

Price, Robert M. "Neo-Evangelicals and Scripture: A Forgotten Period of Ferment," *Christian Scholar's Review*, 15, no. 4 (1986): 315-330.

Ramm, Bernard. "Evangelicals and the Enlightenment: Beyond Liberalism and Fundamentalism," *TSF Bulletin*, 6, no. 3 (January-February 1983): 2-5.

Roddy, Sherman. "Fundamentalists and Ecumenicity," *The Christian Century* (April 20, 1958): 1100-1110.

Root, Michael. "Truth, Relativism, and Postliberal Theology," *Dialog*, 25, no. 3 (Summer 1986): 175-180.

Schmiechen, Peter M. "The Challenge of Conservative Theology," *The Christian Century*, 97 (April 9, 1980): 402-406.

Sheppard, Gerald T. "Biblical Hermeneutics: The Academy Language of Evangelical Identity," *Union Seminary Quarterly Review*, 32 (Winter 1977): 81-94.

Trembath, Kern R. "Evangelical Subjectivism: Edward John Carnell and the Logic of God," *The Evangelical Quarterly*, 60 (October 1988): 317-342.

Wood, Ralph C. "Christ on Parnassus: P. T. Forsyth Among the Liberals," *Literature and Theology*, 2 (March 1988): 83-95.

Yoder, John Howard. "A Critique of North American Evangelical Ethics," *Transformation*, 2, no. 1 (January-March 1985): 28-31.

E. Cornelius Van Til

Books

Dennison, William D. *Paul's Two-Age Construction and Apologetics*. New York: University Press of America, 1985.

Frame, J. *Van Til the Theologian*. Phillipsburg, NJ: Pilgrim, 1976.

Geehan, E. *Jerusalem and Athens: Critical Discussion on the Theology and Apologetics of Cornelius Van Til*. Philadelphia: Presbyterian and Reformed, 1971.

Halsey, Jim. *For Such a Time As This: An Introduction to the Reformed Apologetic of Cornelius Van Til*. Philipsburg, NJ: Presbyterian and Reformed, 1976.

Lewis, Gordon R. *Testing Christianity's Truth Claims: Approaches to Christian Apologetics*. Chicago: Moody, 1976.

North, Gary, ed. *Foundations of Christian Scholarship: Essays in the Van Til Perspective*. Ross House, 1976.

Notaro, T. *Van Til and the Use of Evidence*. Philipsburg, NJ: Craig, 1980.

Ramm, Bernard. *Types of Apologetic Systems*. Wheaton: Van Kampen Press, 1953.

Reymond, Robert L. *The Justification of Knowledge: An Introductory Study in Christian Apologetic Methodology*. Philipsburg, NJ: Presbyterian and Reformed, 1976.

Rushdoony, Rousas J. *By What Standard? An Analysis of the Philosophy of Cornelius Van Til*. Philipsburg, NJ: Presbyterian and Reformed, 1960.

_____. *The Institutes of Biblical Law*. Philipsburg, NJ: Presbyterian and Reformed, 1973.

_____. *Van Til*. Philipsburg, NJ: Presbyterian and Reformed, 1960.

VanderStelt, J. C. *Philocophy and Scripture: A Study in Old Princeton and Westminster Theology*. Marlton, NJ: Mack, 1978.

Van Til, Cornelius. *Christian Apologetics*, Syllabus from Westminster Theological Seminary. Philipsburg, NJ: Presbyterian and Reformed, copyright 1976.

_____. *A Christian Theory of Knowledge*. Philadelphia: Presbyterian and Reformed, 1975.

_____. *Christian Theistic Evidences*. Philadelphia: Westminster Theological Seminary, 1961.

_____. *A Christian Theory of Knowledge*. Nutley, NJ: Presbyterian and Reformed, copyright den Dulk Christian Foundation. 1974.

_____. *Common Grace and the Gospel*. Philadelphia: Presbyterian and Reformed, 1972.

_____. *The Defense of the Faith*. Philadelphia: Presbyterian and Reformed, 1955.

_____. *The Doctrine of Scripture*. Ripon: Den Dulk, 1967.

_____. *The Infallible Word: A Symposium*, 3rd rev. ed. Philipsburg, NJ: Presbyterian and Reformed, 1946.

_____. *An Introduction to Systematic Theology*. Philadelphia: Presbyterian and Reformed, 1974.

_____. *A Survey of Christian Epistemology*. Nutley, N.J.: Presbyterian and Reformed, 1977.

_____. *Why I Believe in God*. Philadelphia: Presbyterian and Reformed, n.d.

Vickers, D. *Cornelius Van Til and the Theologian's Theological Stance*. Wilmington, DE, 1976.

White, W. *Van Til, Defender of the Faith*. Nashville, 1979.

Articles

Bahnsen, G. L. "Inductivism, Inerrancy, and Presuppositionalism," *Journal of the Evangelical Theological Society* 20 (1977): 292-295.

Clowney, Edmund P. "Preaching the Word of the Lord: Cornelius Van Til," *The Westminster Theological Journal*, 46, no. 2 (Fall 1984): 233-253.

Frame, John M. "Van Til and the Ligonier Apologetic," *The Westminster Theological Journal*, 47, no. 2 (Fall 1985): 279-299.

Grier, James M., Jr. "The Apologetical Value of the Self-Witness of Scripture," *Grace Theological Journal* (1980): 71-76.

Halsey, Jim. "Preliminary Critique of Van Til: the Theologian," *The Westminster Theological Journal*, 39 (Fall 1976): 120-136.

Knudsen, Robert D. "The Transcendental Perspective of Westminster's Apologetic," *The Westminster Theological Journal*, 48, no. 2 (Fall 1986): 223-239.

Kucharsky, David E. "At the Beginning, God: An Interview with Cornelius Van Til," *Christianity Today* (December 30, 1977): 415.

Nash, Ronald H. "Review of Van Til's *A Christian Theory of Knowledge,*" *Christianity Today* (January 16, 1970): 349.

Noll, Mark A. "The Founding of Princeton Seminary," *Westminster Theological Journal* 42 (Fall 1979): 72-110.

Oliphint, Scott. "The Consistency of Van Til's Methodology," *Westminster Theological Journal*, 52, no. 1 (Spring 1990).

_____. "Jerusalem and Athens Revisited," *The Westminster Theological Journal*, 49 (Spring 1987): 65-90.

Salier, William S. "Reformed Apologetics Revisited," *Evangelical Journal*, 2, no. 1 (Spring 1984): 16-26.

Spencer, Stephen R. "Fideism and Presuppositionalism," *Grace Theological Journal*, 8 (Spring 1987): 89-99.

Turner, David L. "Cornelius Van Til and Romans 1:18-21: A Study in the Epistemology of Presuppositional Apologetics," *Grace Theological Journal*, 2, no. 1 (Spring 1981): 45-58.

Van Til, Cornelius. "At the Beginning, God: An Interview," *Christianity Today*, 22 (December 30, 1977): 414-418.

_____. "Has Karl Barth Become Orthodox?," *The Westminster Theological Journal*, 16 (May 1954): 135-181.

_____. "Nature and Scripture." In *The Infallible Word: A Symposium*. Nutley: Presbyterian and Reformed, 1967.

_____. "What of the New Birth?," *Christianity Today*, 3 (June 8, 1959): 5-7.

Whitcomb, John C. "Contemporary Apologetics and the Christian Faith, Part I: Human Limitations in Apologetics," *Bibliotheca Sacra* (April-June 1977): 99-107.

F. Francis A. Schaeffer

Books

Catherwood, Christopher. *Five Evangelical Leaders*. Wheaton: Harold Shaw, 1985.

Dennis, Lane T. *Francis Schaeffer: Portraits of the Man and His Work*. Westchester: Crossway, 1986.

_____. *Letters of Francis A. Schaeffer*. Westchester: Crossway, 1985.

Jackson, Jeremy C. *Study Guide for How Should We Then Live?* Old Tappan, N.J.: Fleming H. Revell, 1976.

Morris, Thomas V. *Francis Schaeffer's Apologetics: A Critique*. Chicago: Moody, 1976.

Parkhurst, L. G. *Francis Schaeffer: The Man and His Message*. Wheaton: Tyndale, 1985.

Ruegsegger, Ronald W., ed. *Reflections on Francis Schaeffer*. Grand Rapids: Academie Books, 1986.

Schaeffer, Edith. *L'Abri*. Wheaton: Tyndale, 1969.

_____. *The Tapestry*. Waco: Word, 1981.

_____. *What Is a Family?* Old Tappan, N.J.: Fleming H. Revell, 1975.

Schaeffer, Francis A. *The Complete Works of Francis A Schaeffer, Vol. 1: A Christian View of Philosophy and Culture*. Westchester: Crossway, 1982.

_____. *The Complete Works of Francis A Schaeffer, Vol. 2: A Christian View of the Bible As Truth*. Westchester: Crossway, 1982.

_____. *The Complete Works of Francis A Schaeffer, Vol. 3: A Christian View of Spirituality*. Westchester: Crossway, 1982.

_____. *The Complete Works of Francis A Schaeffer, Vol. 4: A Christian View of The Church*. Westchester: Crossway, 1982.

_____. *The Complete Works of Francis A Schaeffer, Vol. 5: A Christian View of The West*. Westchester: Crossway, 1982.

_____. *The Francis A. Schaeffer Trilogy: The Three Essential Books in One Volume*. Westchester, IL: Crossway, 1990.

_____. *The Great Evangelical Disaster*. Westchester, IL: Crossway, 1984.

Schaeffer, Franky. *Addicted to Mediocrity*. Westchester, IL: Crossway, 1981.

_____. *Bad News for Modern Man*. Westchester, IL: Crossway, 1984.

_____. *A Time for Anger*. Westchester, IL: Crossway, 1982.

Articles

Blomberg, D. G. "Apologetic Education: Francis Schaeffer and L'Abri," *Journal of Christian Education*, 54 (December 1975): 5-20.

Board, Stephen. "An Evangelical Thinker Who Left His Mark: Francis A. Schaeffer IV: 1912-1984," *Christianity Today*, 28 (June 15, 1984): 60-61.

_____. "The Rise of Francis Schaeffer," *Eternity*, 28 (June 1977): 40-42.

Brown, Harold O. J. "Kierkegaard's Leap or Schaeffer's Skip?" *Christianity Today*, 28 (December 14, 1984): 82.

Clark, Gordon H. "A Semi-defense of Francis Schaeffer," *Christian Scholar's Review*, 11 (1982): 148-149.

Cunningham, Stuart. "Towards a Critique of Francis Schaeffer's Thought," *Interchange*, 24 (1979): 205-221.

Davis, Stephen T. "How Should We Then Live? A Review," *The Evangelical Quarterly* 50 (April-June 1978): 109-112.

Forbes, W. Merwin. "Review Article: A Christian Manifesto," *Grace Theological Journal* 4.2 (1983): 303-309.

Franz, Harold J. "The God Who Is There," *Westminster Theological Journal*, XXXII (November 1969-May 1970): 116.

Geehan, E. R. "The 'Presuppositional' Apologetic of Francis Schaeffer," *Themelios*, 8, no. 1 (1972): 10-18.

Giacumakis, George, Jr., and Gerald C. Tiffin. "Francis Schaeffer's New Intellectual Enterprise: Some Friendly Criticisms," *Fides et Historia* IX:2 (Spring 1977): 52-58.

Gill, David W. "Jacques Ellul and Francis Schaeffer: Two Views of Western Civilization," *Fides et Historia*, 13, no. 2 (Spring-Summer 1981): 23-37.

Harper, Kenneth C. "Francis A. Schaeffer: An Evaluation," *Bibliotheca Sacra*, 133 (April 1976): 130-142.

Hendricks, Wm. L. "He Is There and He Is Not Silent," *Southwestern Journal of Theology*, XV:1 (Fall 1972): 139.

Hill, Kent R. "Francis Schaeffer (1912-1984): An Evaluation of His Life and Thought." In *Faith and Imagination: Essays on Evangelicals and Literature*, ed. Noel Riley Finch and Richard W. Etulain. Albuquerque: Far West Books, 1985: 137-171.

Holmes, Arthur. "The God Who Is There," *HIS Magazine* 29 (February 1969): 26.

Hurley, J. "Notes on the Philosophy and Writings of Francis and Edith Schaeffer: A Bibliographic Essay," *Christian Librarian*, 20 (July 1977): 15-16.

Marsden, George. "Francis A. Schaeffer," *Reformed Journal*, 34 (June 1984): 2-3.

Pierard, Richard V. "The Unmasking of Francis Schaeffer: An Evangelical Tragedy," *The Wittenberg Door* 78 (April-May 1984): 27-31.

Pinnock, Clark. "Breakthrough for Evangelicals," *Christianity Today* 13 (January 3, 1969): 24.

Reid, W. Stanford. "How Should We Then Live: Review Article," *Westminster Theological Journal* XL (Fall 1977-Spring 1978): 380.

Rogers, Jack. "Francis Schaeffer: The Promise and the Problem (two parts)," *Reformed Journal*, 27 (May, June 1977): 12-15, 15-19.

Ruegsegger, Ron W. "Francis Schaeffer on Philosophy," *Christian Scholar's Review*, 10 (1981): 238-254.

──────────. "A Reply to Gordon Clark," *Christian Scholar's Review*, 11 (1982): 150-152.

Schaeffer, Edith. "God is Giving Me New Opportunities," *Decision* (July-August 1985): 23-24.

Schaeffer, Francis A. "Are Christians Headed for Disaster?" *Moody Monthly*, vol 84 (July-August 1984): 18-20.

──────────. "Christianity and Culture," *Themelios*, 2 (1962): 5-16.

──────────. "Irrationality of Modern Thought," *Christianity Today*, 15 (December 4, 1970): 10-14.

──────────. "A Review of a Review," *The Bible Today* 42 (October 1948): 7-9.

──────────. "Schaeffer on Scripture," *Christianity Today*, 19 (August 29, 1975): 29.

──────────. "Tragic Loss of Our Era," *Christianity Today*, 5 (May 22, 1961): 3-5.

──────────. "Why and How I Write My Books," *Eternity*, 24 (March 1973): 64f.

Stadler, G. Thomas. "Renaissance Humanism: Francis Schaeffer Versus Some Contemporary Scholars," *Fides et Historia*, 21 (June 1989): 4-20.

Thomas, Cal. "Crusader for Truth," *Fundamentalist Journal*, 3, no. 7 (July-August 1984): 47-49.

Wells, Ronald A. "Whatever Happened to Francis Schaeffer?," *Reformed Journal*, 33 (May 1983): 10-13.

Woodward, Kenneth L. "Guru of Fundamentalism," *Newsweek* (November 1, 1982: 88.

Yancey, Philip. "Francis Schaeffer: A Prophet for Our Times?," *Christianity Today*, 23 (March 23, 1979): 14-18.

──────────. "Schaeffer on Schaeffer" (two parts), *Christianity Today*, 23 (March 23, 1979), 19-21 and (April 9, 1979): 21-26.

G. Carl F. H. Henry

Books

Henry, Carl F. H., ed. *Basic Christian Doctrines*. Grand Rapids: Baker, 1962.

_____, ed. *The Biblical Expositor*, 3 vols. Philadelphia: A. J. Holman, 1960.

_____. *Carl Henry at His Best*. Portland: Multnomah, 1990.

_____. *Christian Countermoves in a Decadent Culture*. Portland: Multnomah, 1986.

_____. *Christian Faith and Modern Theology*. New York: Channel, 1964.

_____. *The Christian Mindset in a Secular Society*. Portland: Multnomah, 1984.

_____. *Christian Personal Ethics*. Grand Rapids: Eerdmans, 1957.

_____. *Confessions of a Theologian: An Autobiography*. Waco: Word, 1986.

_____. *Contemporary Evangelical Thought*. New York: Harper and Bros., 1957.

_____. *Conversations with Carl Henry: Christianity for Today*. Lewiston, NY: Edwin Mellen, 1986.

_____. *The Drift of Western Thought*. Grand Rapids: Eerdmans, 1951.

_____. *Evangelical Responsibility in Contemporary Theology*. Grand Rapids: Eerdmans, 1957.

_____. *Evangelicals at the Brink of Crisis: Significance of the World Congress on Evangelism*. Waco: Word, 1967.

_____. *Evangelicals in Search of Identity*. Waco: Word, 1976.

_____. *Fifty Years of Protestant Theology*. Boston: W. A. Wilde, 1950.

_____. *Frontiers in Modern Theology: A Critique of Current Theological Trends*. Chicago: Moody, 1966.

_____. *Fundamentals of the Faith*. Grand Rapids: Zondervan, 1970.

_____. *Giving a Reason for Our Hope*. Boston: W. A. Wilde, 1949.

_____. *Glimpses of a Sacred Land* (1953).

_____. *God, Revelation and Authority, Vol. I: God Who Speaks and Shows* (preliminary considerations). Waco: Word, 1976.

_____. *God, Revelation and Authority, Vol. II: God Who Speaks and Shows* (fifteen theses, part one). Waco: Word, 1976.

_____. *God, Revelation and Authority, Vol. III: God Who Speaks and Shows* (fifteen theses, part two). Waco: Word, 1979.

_____. *God, Revelation and Authority, Vol. IV: God Who Speaks and Shows* (fifteen theses, part three). Waco: Word, 1979.

_____. *God, Revelation and Authority, Vol. V: God Who Stands and Stays* (part one). Waco: Word, 1982.

_____. *God, Revelation and Authority, Vol. VI: God Who Stands and Stays* (part two). Waco: Word, 1983.

_____. *The God Who Shows Himself*. Waco: Word, 1966.

_____, ed. *Horizons of Science: Christian Scholars Speak Out*. San Francisco: Harper and Row, 1978.

_____. *Jesus of Nazareth: Saviour and Lord*. Grand Rapids: Eerdmans, 1966.

_____. *Notes on the Doctrine of God*. Boston: Wilde, 1948.

_____. *Personal Idealism and Strong's Theology*. Wheaton: Van Kampen, 1951.

_____. *The Protestant Dilemma*. Grand Rapids: Eerdmans, 1949.

_____. *Remaking the Modern Mind*, 2nd ed. Grand Rapids: Eerdmans, 1948.

_____. *Revelation and the Bible*. Grand Rapids: Eerdmans, 1958.

_____. *Toward a Recovery of Christian Belief*. Westchester: Crossway, 1990.

_____. *Twilight of a Great Civilization*. Westchester, IL: Crossway Books, 1988.

_____. *The Uneasy Conscience of Modern Fundamentalism*. Grand Rapids: Eerdmans, 1947.

Patterson, Bob. *Carl F. H. Henry*. Waco: Word, 1983.

Articles

Fackre, Gabriel, "Carl F. H. Henry." In *A Handbook of Christian Theologians* (enlarged edition), ed. Martin E. Marty and Dean G. Peerman. Nashville: Abingdon, 1984, 583-607.

Henry, CArl F. H. "American Evangelicals in a Turning Time," *Theologians in Transition*, ed. James M. Wall. New York: Crossroad, 1981: 41-49.

_____. "The Authority and Inspiration of the Bible." In *The Expositor's Bible Commentary*, 1. ed. Frank E. Gaebelein. Grand Rapids: Regency Reference Library, 1979.

_____. "Biblical Authority and the Social Crisis." In *Authority and Interpretation*. ed. Duane A. Garrett and Richard R. Melick, Jr. Grand Rapids: Baker, 1987.

_____. "The Concerns and Considerations of Carl F. H. Henry," *Christianity Today*, 25 (March 13, 1981): 18-23.

_____. "The Cultural Relativizing of Revelation," *Trinity Journal* 1 NS (1980): 153-164.

_____. "Doing Your Own Thing," *Theology Today*, 32 (January 1976): 403-410.

_____. "Evangelical Profits and Losses," *The Christian Century*, 95 (January 25, 1978): 69-70.

_____. "Firm on the Fundamentals," *Christianity Today*, 32 (November 15, 1988): 19.

_____. "Interview by J. Wallis and W. Michaelson," *Sojourners*, 2 (February 13, 1976): 6-9.

_____. "An Interview with Carl F. H. Henry," *TSF Bulletin*, 10 (March-April 1987): 16-19.

_____. "Justification by Ignorance: A Neo-Protestant Motif?," *Christianity Today* (January 2, 1979): 10-15.

_____. "Liberation Theology and the Scriptures." In *Liberation Theology*. ed. Ronald H. Nash. Grand Rapids: Baker, 1988.

_____. "Narrative Theology: An Evangelical Appraisal," *Trinity Journal*, no. 8 (Spring 1987): 3-19.

_____. "The Priority of Divine Revelation," *Journal of the Evangelical Theological Society*, 27 (March 1984): 77-92.

_____. "The Reality and Identity of God," *Christianity Today*, 13 no. 12 (March 14, 1969): 3-6.

_____. "The Reality and Identity of God," *Christianity Today*, 13, no. 13 (March 28, 1969): 12-16.

_____. "Theology and Biblical Authority," *Journal of the Evangelical Theological Society* 19 (1976): 315-323.

_____. "Where Will Evangelicals Cast Their Lot?," *This World* 18 (1987): 3-11.

Mohler, R. Albert, Jr. "Carl F. H. Henry." In *Baptist Theologians*. ed. Timothy George and David S. Dockery. Nashville: Broadman, 1990.

Padgett, Alan. "A Critique of Carl Henry's Summa," *TSF Bulletin*, 9, no. 3 (January-February 1986): 28-29.

H. Millard Erickson

Books

Erickson, Millard. *Christian Theology*. Grand Rapids: Baker, 1986.

_____. *Concise Dictionary of Christian Theology*. Grand Rapids: Baker, 1986.

_____. *Contemporary Options in Eschatology*. Grand Rapids: Baker, 1977.

_____. *The New Evangelical Theology*. London: Marshall, Morgan and Scott, 1969.

_____. *The Living God: Readings in Christian Theology*. Grand Rapids: Baker, 1973.

_____. *Man's Need and God's Gift: Readings in Christian Theology*. Grand Rapids: Baker, 1976.

_____. *The New Life: Readings in Christian Theology*. Grand Rapids: Baker, 1979.

_____. *Relativism in Contemporary Christian Ethics*. Grand Rapids: Baker, 1974.

_____. *Responsive Faith*. Arlington Heights: Harvest Publications, 1987.

_____. *Salvation: God's Amazing Plan*. Wheaton: Victor, 1978.

_____. *The Word Became Flesh: A Contemporary Incarnational Theology*. Grand Rapids: Baker, 1991.

Articles

Bush, L. Russ. "Review of *Christian Theology*," *Southwestern Journal of Theology*, XXVII, no. 2 (Spring 1985): 62-63.

Chaney, Charles L. "Review of *Christian Theology*," *Review and Expositor*, LXXXIII, no. 1 (Winter 1986): 134-135.

_____. "Review of *Christian Theology*," *Review and Expositor*, LXXXIV, no. 3 (Summer 1987). 541-542.

Culpepper, Robert H. "Review of *Christian Theology*," *Faith and Mission*, III, no. 1 (Fall 1985): 96-97.

Demarest, Bruce. "Review of *Christian Theology*," *Journal of the Evangelical Theological Society*, 29 (1986): 236-237.

Dockery, David. "Millard J. Erickson: Baptist and Evangelical Theologian," *Journal of the Evangelical Theological Society*, 32, no. 4 (December 1989): 519-532.

_____. "Millard Erickson." In *Baptist Theologians*. ed. Timothy George and David S. Dockery. Nashville: Broadman, 1990, 640-659.

_____. "Review of *Christian Theology*," *Grace Theological Journal*, 5, no. 2 (Fall 1984): 302-303.

_____. "Review of *Christian Theology*," *Grace Theological Journal*, 7, no. 1 (Spring 1986): 140-142.

_____. "Review of *Christian Theology*," *Grace Theological Journal*, 8, no. 2 (Fall 1987): 295-296.

Erickson, Millard. "Apologetics Today: Its Task and Shape," *Bethel Seminary Journal*, XVIII, no. 1 (Autumn 1969): 1-13.

_____. "The Basis of Our Hope," *The Standard*, 61, no. 17 (September 20, 1971): 20-21.

_____. "The Bible, Science and Creation - How to Interpret the Evidence," *The Standard*, 58, no. 15 (July 15, 1968): 23-24.

_____. "Biblical Inerrancy: The Last Twenty-Five Years," *Journal of the Evangelical Theological Society*, 25, no. 4 (December 1982): 387-394.

_____. "The Foundation Does Not Move," *The Standard*, 61, no. 13 (June 28, 1971): 15-18.

_____. "How Do You Deal With Doubt?" *The Standard*, 77, no. 7 (July 1987): 21-23.

_____. "A New Look at Various Aspects of Inspiration," *Bethel Seminary Journal*, XV, no. 1 (Autumn, 1966): 16-26.

_____. "Immanence, Transcendence, and the Doctrine of Scripture." In *The Living and Active Word of God*, ed. Morris Inch and Ronald Youngblood. Winona Lake: Eisenbrauns, 1983, 193-205.

_____. "Narrative Theology: Translation or Transformation?" In *Festschrift: A Tribute to Dr. William Hordern*, ed. Walter Freitag. Saskatoon: University of Saskatchewan Press, 1985, 29-39.

_____. "Pannenberg's Use of History as a Solution to the Religious Language Problem," *Journal of the Evangelical Theological Society*, 17, no. 2 (Spring 1974): 99-105.

_____. "The Potential of Apologetics: (two parts), *Christianity Today*, XIV, no. 21 (July 17, 1970), 6-8; vol. XIV, no. 22 (July 31, 1970): 13-15.

_____. "Presuppositions of Non-Evangelical Hermeneutics." In *Hermeneutics, Inerrancy and the Bible*, ed. Earl Radmacher and Robert D. Preus. Grand Rapids: Zondervan, 1985: 591-612.

_____. "Principles, Permanence, and Future Divine Judgment: A Case Study in Theological Method," *Journal of the Evangelical Theological Society*, 28, no. 3 (September 1985): 317-325.

_____. "Problem Areas Related to Biblical Inerrancy," In *The Proceedings of the Conference on Biblical Inerrancy 1987* (Nashville: Broadman, 1987), 175-189.

Grenz, Stanley J. "Review of *Christian Theology*," *Christian Scholar's Review*, XIV, no. 1 (1984): 86-87.

_____. "Review of *Christian Theology*," *Christian Scholar's Review*, XVI, no. 1 (1986): 93-96.

Howe, F. R. "Review of *Christian Theology*," *Bibliotheca Sacra*, 143, no. 569 (January-March 1986): 75-76.

Jones, Peter Rhea. "Response to Millard J. Erickson." In *Proceedings of the Conference on Biblical Inerrancy*. Nashville: Broadman, 1987.

Keylock, Leslie R. "Evangelical Leaders You Should Know: Meet Millard J. Erickson," *Moody Monthly* (June 1987): 71-73.

Landegent, David. "Review of *Christian Theology*," *Reformed Review*, 39, no. 2 (Winter 1986): 121.

_____. "Review of *Christian Theology*," *Reformed Review*, 40, no. 1 (Autumn 1986): 67-68.

Lewis, Gordon R. "A Response to Presuppositions of Non-Evangelical Hermeneutics." In *Hermeneutics, Inerrancy and the Bible*. ed. Earl Radmacher and Robert D. Preus. Grand Rapids: Zondervan, 1985.

Melick, Richard R. "Response to Millard J. Erickson." In *Proceedings of the Conference on Biblical Inerrancy*. Nashville: Broadman, 1987.

Pinnock, Clark H. "Erickson's Three-Volume Magnum Opus," *TSF Bulletin*, 9, no. 3 (January-February 1986): 29-30.

Vunderlink, Ralph W. "Review of *Christian Theology*," *Calvin Theological Journal*, 20, no. 2 (November 1985): 291-295.

_____. "Review of *Christian Theology*," *Calvin Theological Journal*, 22, no. 1 (April 1987): 139-144.

Wells, David. "A Capable, Usable Text," *Eternity*, 38, no. 2 (February 1987): 41.

White, James Emery. "Review of *Concise Dictionary*," *Criswell Theological Review*, 3, no. 1 (Fall 1988).

Young, W. C. "Review of *New Evangelical Theology*," *Foundations*, no. 12 (1969): 95-96.

I. Donald Bloesch

Books

Bloesch, Donald G. *The Battle for the Trinity: The Debate Over Inclusive God-Language.* Ann Arbor: Vine Books, 1985.

_____. *Centers of Christian Renewal.* Philadelphia: United Church, 1964.

_____. *The Christian Life and Salvation.* Grand Rapids: Eerdmans, 1967.

_____. *The Christian Witness in a Secular Age.* Minneapolis: Augsburg, 1968.

_____. *The Crisis of Piety.* Grand Rapids: Eerdmans, 1968.

_____. *Crumbling Foundations: Death and Rebirth in an Age of Upheaval.* Grand Rapids: Academie/Zondervan, 1984.

_____. *Essentials of Evangelical Theology, Vol. I: God, Salvation and Authority.* San Francisco: Harper and Row, 1978.

_____. *Essentials of Evangelical Theology, Vol. II: Life, Ministry and Hope.* San Francisco: Harper and Row, 1979.

_____. *The Evangelical Renaissance.* Grand Rapids: Eerdmans, 1973.

_____. *Faith and Its Counterfeits.* Downers Grove: InterVarsity, 1981.

_____. *Freedom for Obedience: Evangelical Ethics for Contemporary Times.* San Francisco: Harper and Row, 1987.

_____. *The Future of Evangelical Christianity: A Call for Unity and Diversity.* Colorado Springs: Helmers and Howard, 1988.

_____. *The Ground of Certainty: Toward an Evangelical Theology of Revelation.* Grand Rapids: Eerdmans, 1971.

_____. *The Invaded Church.* Waco: Word, 1975.

_____. *Is the Bible Sexist? Beyond Feminism and Patriarchalism.* Westchester: Crossway, 1982.

_____. *Jesus is Victor! Karl Barth's Doctrine of Salvation.* Nashville: Abingdon, 1976.

_____. *Light a Fire.* St. Louis: Eden, 1975.

_____ and Robert E. Webber, eds. *The Orthodox Evangelicals: Who They Are and What They Are Saying.* Nashville: Thomas Nelson, 1978.

_____. *The Reform of the Church.* Grand Rapids: Eerdmans, 1970.

_____. *The Struggle of Prayer.* San Francisco: Harper and Row, 1980.

_____. *Theological Notebook: Volume I, 1960-1964.* Colorado Springs: Helmers and Howard, 1989.

_____. *Wellsprings of Renewal: Promise in Christian Communal Life.* Grand Rapids: Eerdmans, 1974.

Articles

Bloesch, Donald G. "A Christological Hermeneutic: Crisis and Conflict in Hermeneutics." In *The Use of the Bible in Theology: Evangelical Options,* ed. Robert K. Johnston. Atlanta: John Knox, 1985, 78-102.

_____. "Crisis in Biblical Authority," *Theology Today,* 35 (January 1979): 455-462.

_____. "Karl Barth: Appreciation and Reservations." In *How Karl Barth Changed My Mind,* ed. Donald D. McKim. Grand Rapids: Eerdmans, 1986, 126-130.

_____. "The Sword of the Spirit: The Meaning of Inspiration," *Reformed Review,* 33 (Winter 1980): 65-72.

_____. "To Reconcile the Biblically Oriented," *The Christian Century,* 97 (July 16-23, 1980): 733-735.

_____. "Toward the Recovery of Our Evangelical Heritage," *Reformed Review,* 39, no. 3 (Spring 1986): 192-198.

Cahill, P. Joseph. "Review of *Ground of Certainty,*" *The Catholic Biblical Quarterly,* XXXIV, no. 34 (1972): 203.

Dockery, David S. "Review of *Essentials,*" *Grace Theological Journal,* 2, no. 1 (Spring 1981): 153.

Foxgrover, David. "Review of *Essentials,*" *The Christian Century,* XCVI, no. 6 (February 21, 1979): 192.

Godsey, John. "Review of *Essentials,*" *The Christian Century,* XCV, no. 32 (October 11, 1978): 961.

Hoekema, Anthony A. "Review of *Essentials,*" *Calvin Theological Journal,* 14, no. 1 (April 1979): 86.

Keylock, Leslie R. "Evangelical Leaders You Should Know: Meet Donald G. Bloesch," *Moody Monthly* (March 1988).

Lightner, R. P. "Review of *Essentials,*" *Bibliotheca Sacra,* 136, no. 542 (April-June 1979): 181.

_____. "Review of *Essentials,*" *Bibliotheca Sacra,* 137, no. 547 (July-September 1980): 279.

McDonald, H. D. "Review of *Essentials,*" *Journal of the Evangelical Theological Society,* 22, no. 3 (September 1979): 280.

Noll, Mark A. "Surprising Optimism of Donald Bloesch," *Center Journal,* 3, no. 3 (Summer 1984): 95-104.

Petersen, "Review of *Essentials,*" *The Princeton Seminary Bulletin,* II, no. 3 (New Series 1979): 290.

Pinnock, Clark. "Review of *Essentials,*" *Theology Today,* XXXVI, no. 2 (July 1979): 268.

Robbins, Jerry. "Review of *Ground of Certainty,*" *Journal of the American Academy of Religion,* XL, no. 4 (December 1972): 88.

Vunderlink, Ralph W. "Review of *The Ground of Certainty,*" *Calvin Theological Journal,* 8, no. 1 (April 1973): 87.

Walker, Robert T. "Review of *Ground of Certainty,*" *Scottish Journal of Theology,* 25 (1972): 237.

J. Background and Miscellaneous Sources

Books

Abraham, William. *The Coming Great Revival.* San Francisco: Harper and Row, 1984.

Ahlstrom, Sydney E. *A Religious History of the American People.* New Haven and London: Yale University, 1972.

Aquinas, Thomas. *The Summa Theologica of St. Thomas Aquinas.* vol. 14 Trans. Fathers of the English Dominican Province. London: Burns, Oates, and Washbourne, 1934.

Bainton, Roland H. *The Reformation of the Sixteenth Century.* Boston: Beacon, 1952 and 1985.

Barna, George. *What Americans Believe.* Ventura: Regal, 1991.

Barraclough, Geoffrey. *The Christian World.* New York: Harry N. Abrams, 1981.

Barth, Karl. *Church Dogmatics,* ed. G. W. Bromiley and T. F. Torrance. Edinburgh: T & T Clark, 1936-1969.

Bellah, Robert, Richard Madsen, William M. Sullivan, Ann Swidler, and Steven M. Tipton. *Habits of the Heart.* Berkeley: University of California, 1985.

Berger, Peter and Neuhaus, Richard, eds. *Against the World, For the World.* New York: Seabury, 1976.

_____. *The Heretical Imperative.* Garden City: Doubleday, 1979.

_____. *A Rumor of Angels: Modern Society and the Rediscovery of the Supernatural.* New York: Anchor/Doubleday, 1969.

_____. *The Sacred Canopy: Elements of a Sociological Theory of Religion.* Garden City: Anchor, 1969.

_____. and Thomas Luckmann. *The Social Construction of Reality: A Treatise in the Sociology of Knowledge.* New York: Anchor, 1967.

Berkhof, Hendrikus. *Christian Faith: An Introduction to the Study of the Faith.* Grand Rapids: Eerdmans, 1986.

_____. *Two Hundred Years of Theology: Report of a Personal Journey.* Grand Rapids: Eerdmans, 1989.

Berkouwer, G. C. *Holy Scripture.* Grand Rapids: Eerdmans, 1975.

_____. *Studies in Dogmatics: Theology* 13 vols. Grand Rapids: Eerdmans, 1952, 1076.

Berkhof, Louis. *The History of Christian Doctrines.* Edinburgh: Banner of Truth Trust, 1969.

_____. *Introduction to Systematic Theology.* Grand Rapids: Baker, 1979.

_____. *Systematic Theology.* Grand Rapids: Eerdmans, 1941.

Berlin, Isaiah, ed. *The Age of Enlightenment.* New York: Meridian, 1984.

Bleicher, Josef. *Contemporary Hermeneutics: Hermeneutics as Method, Philosophy and Critique.* London: Routledge and Kegan Paul, 1980.

Bloom, Allan. *The Closing of the American Mind.* New York: Simon and Schuster, 1987.

Boethius. *The Consolation of Philosophy.* trans. with an Introduction by V. E. Watts. New York: Penguin, 1969.

Boice, James Montgomery. *Foundations of the Christian Faith.* Downers Grove: InterVarsity, 1986.

Bollier, John A. *The Literature of Theology: A Guide for Students and Pastors.* Philadelphia: Westminster, 1979.

Bonino, Joes Miguez. *Doing Theology in a Revolutionary Situation.* Philadelphia: Fortress, 1975.

Boorstin, Daniel J. *The Discoverers.* New York: Random House, 1983.

_____. *The Americans: The Colonial Experience.* New York: Vintage, 1958.

Brightman, Edgar. *The Finding of God.* New York: Abingdon, 1931.

_____. *Person and Reality: An Introduction to Metaphysics*. Boston: Boston University Press, 1958.

_____. *Personalism in Theology*. Boston: Boston University, 1943.

_____. *Personality and Religion*. New York: Abindgon, 1943.

_____. *Philosophy of Religion*. New York: Prentice-Hall, 1940.

_____. *The Problem of God*. New York: Abingdon, 1930.

Bruce, F. F. *The New Testament Documents*, 6th ed. Grand Rapids: Eerdmans, 1984.

Bultmann, Rudolph. *Theology of the New Testament*. New York: Scribner, 1955.

Buswell, J. O. *A Christian View of Being and Knowing*. Grand Rapids: Zondervan, 1960.

Calvin, John. *Institutes of the Christian Religion*. ed. John T. McNeill. trans. Ford Lewis Battles. The Library of Christian Classics, vol. 21. Philadelphia: Westminster, 1960.

Campbell, Joseph. *The Power of Myth* ed. Bill Moyers and Betty Sue Flowers. New York: Doubleday, 1988.

Chadwick, Owen. *The Reformation*. New York: Penguin, 1972.

Chandler, Russell. *Understanding the New Age*. Dallas: Word, 1988.

Cherry, Conrad, ed. *God's New Israel: Religious Interpretations of American Destiny*. Englewood, NJ: Prentice-Hall, 1971.

Cole, Stewart G. *The History of Fundamentalism*. New York: Richard R. Smith, Inc., 1931.

Conn, Harry. *Four Trojan Horses of Humanism*. Milford, MI: Mott Media, 1982.

Copleston, Frederick. *A History of Philosophy* (9 vols. in 3 books). New York: Image, 1985.

Cuddihy, John Murray. *No Offense: Civil Religion and Protestant Taste*. New York: Seabury, 1978.

Culpepper, R. Alan and Jacquelyn. *Manual of Procedure, Form, and Style*. R. Alan and Jacquelyn Culpepper, 1985.

Darwin, Charles. *The Descent of Man and Selection in Relation to Sex*, vol. 49, The Great Books of the Western World. ed. Robert Maynard Hutchins. Chicago: Encyclopaedia Britannica, 1952.

_____. *The Origin of Species by Means of Natural Selection*, Vol. 49, The Great Books of the Western World. ed. Robert Maynard Hutchins. Chicago: Encyclopaedia Britannica, 1952.

Davies, Paul. *God and the New Physics*. New York: Simon and Schuster, 1983.

Davis, John Jefferson. *Theology Primer: Resources for the Theological Student*. Grand Rapids: Baker, 1981.

Dennison, C. G., ed. *The Orthodox Presbyterian Church, 1936-1986*. Philadelphia: Committee for the Historian of the Orthodox Presbyterian Church, 1986.

_____ and R. C. Gamble, eds. *Pressing Toward the Mark: Essays Commemorating Fifty Years of the Orthodox Presbyterian Church*. Philadelphia: Orthodox Presbyterian Church, 1986.

Dooyeweerd, Herman. *A New Critique of Theoretical Thought, 4-Vols*. Amsterdam: J. H. Paris and Presbyterian and Reformed, 1953-1958.

Dulles, Avery. *Models of Revelation*. New York: Image, 1985.

Duncan, Homer. *Secular Humanism: The Most Dangerous Religion in America*. Lubbock, TX: Missionary Crusader, 1980.

Durant, Will. *The Reformation*. New York: Simon and Schuster, 1957.

Elwell, Walter A., ed. *Evangelical Dictionary of Theology*. Grand Rapids: Baker, 1986.

Ferguson, Sinclair B., David F. Wright, and J. I. Packers, eds. *New Dictionary of Theology*. Downers Grove: InterVarsity Press, 1988.

Fischer, David Hackett. *Albion's Seed: Four British Folkways in America*. Oxford: Oxford University, 1989.

Flannery, Austin, ed. *Vatican Council II: The Conciliar and Postconciliar Documents*, 1981 edition. Grand Rapids: Eerdmans, 1975.

_____. *Vatican II: More Postconciliar Documents*. Grand Rapids: Eerdmans, 1982.

Fremantle, Anne, ed. *The Age of Belief.* New York: Meridian, 1982.

Furniss, Norman F. *The Fundamentalist Controversy, 1918-1931.* Hamden: Archon, 1963.

Gadamer, Hans Georg. *Philosophical Hermeneutics.* trans. David Linge. Berkeley: University of California, 1977.

Gaustad, Edwin Scott. *A Religious History of America.* new rev. ed. San Francisco: Harper and Row, 1990.

George, Timothy. *Theology of the Reformers.* Nashville: Broadman, 1988.

Gerstner, John H. *Reasons for Faith.* Grand Rapids: Baker, 1967.

Gilkey, Langdon. *Naming the Whirlwind: The Renewal of God-Language.* Indianapolis: Bobbs-Merril, Co., 1969.

_____. *Through the Tempest: Theological Voyages in a Pluralistic Culture.* selected and edited by Jeff B. Pool. Minneapolis: Fortress, 1991.

Gonzalez, Justo L. *A History of Christian Thought, Vol. III: From the Protestant Reformation to the Twentieth Century.* rev. ed. Nashville: Abingdon, 1987.

Gorman, G. E. and Lyn Gorman. *Theological and Religious Reference Materials: General Resources and Biblical Studies.* Westport, Connecticut: Greenwood, 1984.

Graham, Franklyn and Jeanette Lockerbie. *Bob Pierce: This One Thing I Do.* Waco: Word, 1983.

Grant, Robert M. with David Tracy. *A Short History of the Interpretation of the Bible*, 2nd ed. Philadelphia: Fortress, 1985.

Green, Michael. *I Believe in the Holy Spirit.* Grand Rapids: Eerdmans, 1975.

Groothius, Douglas R. *Unmasking the New Age.* Downers Grove: InterVarsity, 1986.

Halbrooks, C. Thomas. *Pietism.* Nashville: Broadman, 1981.

Hampshire, Stuart, ed. *The Age of Reason.* New York: Meridian, 1956.

Hampson, Norman. *The Enlightenment.* New York: Penguin, 1968.

Hannah, M. M. *Crucial Questions in Apologetics.* Grand Rapids: Baker, 1981.

Hardison, O. B., Jr. *Disappearing Through the Skylight: Culture and Technology in the Twentieth Century.* New York: Viking, 1989.

Harnack, Adolf. *What is Christianity?* Gloucester: Peter Smith, 1957.

Harrison, Everett F., ed. *Baker's Dictionary of Theology.* Grand Rapids: Baker, 1960.

Harvey, Van. *A Handbook of Theological Terms.* New York: Collier, 1964.

Hatch, Nathan O. and Harry S. Stout, eds. *Jonathan Edwards and the American Experience.* Oxford: Oxford University, 1988.

_____ and Mark A. Noll, eds. *The Bible in America: Essays in Cultural History.* Oxford: Oxford University, 1982.

_____. *The Democratization of American Christianity.* New Haven: Yale, 1989.

Hawking, Stephen. *A Brief History of Time: From the Big Bang to Black Holes.* New York: Bantam, 1988.

Hendricks, William L. *A Theology for Aging.* Nashville: Broadman, 1986.

_____. *A Theology for Children.* Nashville: Broadman, 1980.

Heppe, Heinrich. *Reformed Dogmatics.* rev. and ed. Ernst Bizer. trans. G. T. Thomson. Grand Rapids: Baker, 1950.

Hirsch, E. D., Jr. *Cultural Literacy: What Every American Needs to Know* (Updated and Expanded). New York: Vintage, 1988.

Hitchcock, James. *What is Secular Humanism? Why Humanism Became Secular and How It Is Changing Our World.* Ann Arbor, MI: Servant Books, 1982.

Hodge, Charles. *Systematic Theology.* New York: Scribner, 1871.

Hodgson, Peter C. and Robert H. King. *Christian Theology: An Introduction to Its Traditions and Tasks.* Philadelphia: Fortress, 1985.

Hoover, Stewart M. *Mass Media Religion: The Social Sources of the Electronic Church.* Newbury Park: Sage Publications, 1988.

House, H. Wayne and Thomas Ice. *Dominion Theology: Blessing or Curse? An Analysis of Christian Reconstructionism.* Portland: Multnomah, 1988.

Johnson, Paul. *Intellectuals.* New York: Harper and Row, 1988.

Kant, Immanuel. *Critique of Pure Reason.* trans. Norman Kemp Smith. New York: St. Martin's, 1965.

_____. *Critique of Practical Reason* and *The Critique of Judgment.* The Great Books of the Western World, vol. 42. ed. Robert Maynard Hutchins. Chicago: Encyclopedia Britannica, 1952.

_____. *Religion Within the Limits of Reason Alone.* trans. with an Introduction and Notes by Theodore M. Greene and Hoyt M. Hudson. New York: Harper and Row, 1960.

Kaufman, Gordon D. *An Essay on Theological Method* (A.A.R. Studies in Religion no. 11, ed. Conrad C. Cherry). Missoula: Scholars Press, 1975.

Keegan, Terence. *Interpreting the Bible: A Popular Introduction to Biblical Hermeneutics.* New York: Paulist, 1985.

Kelley, Dean M. *Why Conservative Churches Are Growing.* New York: Harper and Row, 1972.

Kelley, J. N. D. *Early Christian Doctrines,* Revised Edition. San Francisco: Harper and Row, 1978.

Kepple, Robert J. *Reference Works for Theological Research: An Annotated Selective Bibliographical Guide,* 2nd ed. Lanham: University Press of America, 1981.

Kirk, Russell. *The Wise Men Know What Wicked Things Are Written on the Sky.* Washington: Regnery Gateway, 1987.

Kliever, Lonnie D. *The Shattered Spectrum: A Survey of Contemporary Theology.* Atlanta: John Knox Press, 1981.

Kurtz, Paul, ed. *The Humanifest Manifesto I and II.* New York: Prometheus Books, 1973.

Langford, Thomas A. *Practical Divinity: Theology in the Wesleyan Tradition.* Nashville: Abingdon, 1983.

Lindbeck, George A. *The Nature of Doctrine: Religion and Theology in a Postliberal Age.* Philadelphia: Westminster, 1984.

Luther, Martin. *Luther's Works.* ed. Jaroslav Pelikan and Helmut Lehmann. American edition. 56 vols. St. Louis and Philadelphia: Concordia and Fortress, 1955.

Lundin, Roger, Anthony C. Thiselton, and Clarence Walhout. *The Responsibility of Hermeneutics.* Grand Rapids: Eerdmans/Paternoster, 1985.

Macquarrie, John. *Principles of Christian Theology,* 2nd ed. New York: Charles Scribner's Sons, 1977.

Manschreck, Clyde L. *A History of Christianity in the World,* 2nd ed. Englewood Cliffs, NJ: Prentice-Hall, 1985.

Marshall, I. Howard. *Biblical Inspiration.* Grand Rapids: Eerdmans, 1982.

Martin, David. *A General Theory of Secularization.* Oxford: Blackwell, 1978.

Marty, Martin E. *Pilgrims in Their Own Land: 500 Years of Religion in America.* New York: Penguin, 1984.

May, Henry. *The Enlightenment in America.* New York: Oxford University 1976.

McBrien, Richard P. *Catholicism,* Study Edition. San Francisco: Harper and Row, 1981.

McGrath, Alister E. *Reformation Thought: An Introduction.* New York: Basil Blackwell, Inc., 1988.

Mead, Sidney E. *The Lively Experiment: The Shaping of Christianity in America.* New York: Harper and Row, 1963.

Mills, Watson E., ed. *Speaking in Tongues: A Guide to Research on Glossolalia.* Grand Rapids: Eerdmans, 1986.

Mueller, David L. *Karl Barth.* Makers of the Modern Theological Mind Series. ed. Bob E. Patterson. Waco: Word, 1972.

Naisbitt, John and Patricia Aburdene. *Megatrends 2000: Ten New Directions for the 1990's.* New York: William Morrow, 1990.

Nash, Ronald H. *Christian Faith and Historical Understanding.* Grand Rapids: Zondervan/ Probe, 1984.

Neuhaus, Richard John. *The Naked Public Square: Religion and Democracy in America.* Grand Rapids: Eerdmans, 1984.

Niebuhr, H. Richard. *Christ and Culture.* New York: Harper, 1951.

Noll, Mark A., Nathan O. Hatch, and George M. Marsden. *The Search for Christian America.* Westchester, IL: Crossway, 1983.

Osborne, Grant R. *The Hermeneutical Spiral: A Comprehensive Introduction to Biblical Interpretation.* Downers Grove: InterVarsity, 1991.

Packer, J. I. *Beyond the Battle for the Bible.* Westchester: Cornerstone, 1980.

Palmer, Richard E. *Hermeneutics: Interpretation Theory in Schleiermacher, Dilthey, Heidegger, and Gadamer.* Evanston: Northwestern University, 1969.

Patterson, James and Peter Kim. *The Day America Told the Truth.* New York: Prentice-Hall, 1991.

Pelikan, Jaroslav. *The Christian Tradition,* 5 vols. Chicago: University of Chicago, 1971-1989.

_____. *Development of Christian Doctrine.* New Haven: Yale, 1969.

Penrose, Roger. *The Emperor's New Mind: Concerning Computers, Minds, and the Laws of Physics.* Oxford: Oxford University, 1989.

Pinnock, Clark. *Tracking the Maze: Finding Our Way through Modern Theology from an Evangelical Perspective.* San Francisco: Harper and Row, 1990.

Placher, William C. *Unapologetic Theology: A Christian Voice in a Pluralistic Conversation.* Louisville: Westminster/John Knox Press, 1989.

Plantinga, Alvin and Nicholas Wolterstorff. *Faith and Rationality: Reason and Belief in God.* Notre Dame: University of Notre Dame, 1983.

Rahner, Karl. *Foundations of Christian Faith.* New York: Crossroad, 1986.

Reid, Daniel G., Robert D. Linder, Bruce L. Shelley, and Harry S. Stout, eds. *Dictionary of Christianity in America.* Downers Grove: InterVarsity, 1990.

Richardson, Alan and John Bowden, eds. *The Westminster Dictionary of Christian Theology.* Philadelphia: Westminster, 1983.

Ricoeur, Paul. *The Symbolism of Evil.* trans. E. Buchanan. Boston: Beacon, 1967.

Ringenberg, William C. *The Christian College: A History of Protestant Higher Education in America.* Grand Rapids: Eerdmans and Christian University, 1984.

Roof, Wade Clark and William McKinney. *American Mainline Religion: Its Changing Shape and Future.* New Brunswick/London: Rutgers University, 1987.

Russell, C. Allyn. *Voices of American Fundamentalism.* Philadelphia: Westminster, 1976.

Rust, Eric C. *Religion, Revelation and Reason.* Macon: Mercer University, 1981.

Ruthven, Malise. *The Divine Supermarket: Shopping for God in America.* New York: William Morrow, 1989.

Sandeen, Ernest. *The Roots of Fundamentalism: British and American Millenarianism 1800-1930.* Chicago: University of Chicago, 1970.

Sayers, Dorothy L. *The Whimsical Christian.* New York: Macmillan/Collier, 1987.

Schaff, Philip. *The Creeds of Christendom with a History and Critical Notes.* Grand Rapids: Baker, 1977.

Schleiermacher, Friedrich. *The Christian Faith.* trans. H. R. Mackintosh and J. S. Stewart. Edinburgh: T & T Clark, 1928.

Soulen, Richard N. *Handbook of Biblical Criticism,* 2nd ed. Atlanta: John Knox Press, 1981.

Southern, R. W. *The Middle Ages.* New York: Penguin, 1970.

Spener, Jacob. *Pia Desideria*. ed. and trans. Theodore G. Toppert. Philadelphia: Fortress, 1964.

Spengler, Oswald. *The Decline of the West* (2 Vols.). Authorized Translation with Notes by Charles Francis Atkinson. New York: Alfred A. Knopf, 1926 and 1928.

Stoeffler, F. Ernest. *Continental Pietism and Early American Christianity*. Grand Rapids: Eerdmans, 1976.

_____. *German Pietism During the Eighteenth Century*. Leiden: E. J. Brill, 1973.

Strunk, William Jr. and E. B. White. *The Elements of Style*, 3rd ed. New York: MacMillan, Inc., 1979.

Thompson, John B. *Critical Hermeneutics: A Study in the Thought of Paul Ricoeur and Jurgen Habermas*. Cambridge: Cambridge University, 1981.

Thompson, Norma H., ed. *Religious Pluralism and Religious Education*. Birmingham, Alabama: Religious Education Press, 1988.

Tillich, Paul. *Systematic Theology*. Chicago: University of Chicago, 1951-1963.

Tracy, David. *The Analogical Imagination*. New York: Crossroad, 1986.

_____. *Blessed Rage for Order*. Minneapolis: Seabury, 1975.

_____. *Plurality and Ambiguity*. San Francisco: Harper and Row, 1987.

Unger, Irwin. *These United States*. Boston: Little, Brown and Co., 1978.

Walbank, T. Walter. *Civilization Past and Present*. Glenview: Scott, Foresman and Company, 1981.

Walker, Williston, Richard A. Norris, David W. Lotz, and Robert T. Handy. *A History of the Christian Church*, 4th ed. New York: Charles Scribner's Sons, 1985.

Warfield, B. B. *The Inspiration and Authority of the Bible*. Philadelphia: Presbyterian and Reformed Publishing Co., 1948.

Webber, Robert Eugene. *Secular Humanism: Threat and Challenge*. Grand Rapids: Zondervan, 1982.

Wendel, Francois. *Calvin: Origins and Development of His Religious Thought*. Philip Mairet, trans. Durham, NC: Labyrinth, 1963.

Williams, G. H. *The Radical Reformation*. Philadelphia: Westminster, 1962.

Wilson, Bryan R. *Religion in Secular Society*. London: C. A. Watts, 1966